French Cuisine

French Cuisine
The Gourmet's Companion

Jeffrey A. Sadowski

JOHN WILEY & SONS, INC.

New York   Chichester   Weinheim   Brisbane   Singapore   Toronto

Copyright © 1997 by Jeffrey A. Sadowski
Published by John Wiley & Sons, Inc.

Library of Congress Cataloging-in-Publication Data:

Sadowski, Jeffrey A.
    French cuisine : the gourmet's companion / Jeffrey A. Sadowski.
        p.   cm.
    Includes bibliographical references.
    ISBN 0-471-14908-X (Paper : alk. paper)
    1. Food—Dictionaries. 2. Cookery, French—Dictionaries.
    3. Food—Dictionaries—French. 4. French language—Dictionaries—
    English   5. English language—Dictionaries—French 6. Cookery,
    French—Dictionaries—French.   I. Title.
    TX349.S23   1997
    641.5944'03—dc20   96-15469

Printed in the United States of America

10 9 8 7 6 5 4 3 2 1

"A land of wheat and barley, and vines, and fig trees, and pomegranates; a land of olive oil and honey; a land wherein thou shalt eat bread without scarceness, thou shalt not lack anything in it."

Deuteronomy 8:8–9

Preface

This book is intended as a convenient reference tool for those possessing an advanced knowledge of food and cooking—chefs, culinary students and instructors, and serious amateur cooks. Cooking terms such as *reduce, stock, deglaze, finish, garnish,* and *au gratin* are commonly used throughout the book, particularly in Part 1. To the professional and dedicated amateur, these are part of the everyday language used in the kitchen.

French Cuisine: The Gourmet's Companion will also, however, be a handy "companion" for restaurant goers negotiating their way through French menus at home and abroad. Referring to the alphabetical list of dishes in Part 1 will allow them to ascertain how a dish is prepared and what ingredients it contains.

The book consists of two sections. Part 1 is an alphabetized list of dishes categorized under the appropriate course. Part 2 consists of French culinary terms, French provinces and cities, regional specialties, ingredients, wines and liquors, and cooking methods. In some cases, listings in Part 1 are referenced to Part 2—usually because a dish is a specialty particular to one region of France. The definitions and "recipes" are short and to the point. This is not a typical cookbook and is not meant to be one. Rather, it is a quick reference that allows the chef to comprehend a term and prepare a dish by knowing the components.

Jeffrey A. Sadowski

Acknowledgments

My warmest and deepest thanks to the people that have made this book possible: Laurie Sadowski, Mary Ansaldo, Claire Thompson, Maria Colletti, Jean Sadowski, Joseph Sadowski, Robin Riesseman, Bob and Phil Ansaldo, Libby Sadowski, Karen Ansaldo, Steve Siska, George Perry. I would like to especially thank Rob Ansaldo, without whose help I'd have abandoned this project long ago.

Contents

PART I — French Dishes, by Course — 1

Hors d'Œuvres — Appetizers — 3

Potages — Soups — 9

Œufs — Eggs — 14

Poisson — Fish — 19

Volaille — Poultry — 27

Viande — Meat — 31

Abats de Boucherie — Variety Meats — 39

Gibier — Game — 40

Légumes — Vegetables — 43

Salade — Salad — 48

Desserts — Desserts — 48

PART II — French Food and Beverage Vocabulary — 51

French Pronunciation Key — 53

Part I

French Dishes, by Course

HORS D'ŒUVRES — APPETIZERS

Allumettes Puff pastry strips; the base for several appetizers.

— *aux anchois* Puff pastry strips spread with anchovy purée.

— *à la norvégienne* Puff pastry strips spread with creamed hard-cooked eggs and garnished with anchovy fillets.

Anchois, filets d' Anchovy fillets; typically marinated in oil and spices.

Anchois roulés Pitted olives wrapped with anchovy fillets; stuffed with anchovy butter.

Anges à cheval See Part II.

Anguille fumée Smoked eel.

Anguille marinée au vinaigre Eel cooked in stock and vinegar.

Artichauts à la croque-au-sel Salted, uncooked baby artichokes.

Assiette anglaise An assorted cold meat platter; pickled tongue, sliced ham, roast beef, and so on.

Attereaux Hot appetizers served on skewers; dipped in beaten eggs or sauce and coated with bread crumbs; deep-fried.

— *à la niçoise* Skewers of tuna chunks, olives, and mushrooms; dipped in *sauce Villeroi* (which has been seasoned with tomato and tarragon); breaded and deep-fried.

— *d'huîtres* Oyster and mushroom skewers dipped in *sauce Villeroi* and deep-fried.

Baraquilles See Part II.

Barquettes Small boat-shaped pastry shells containing various fillings; for hot and cold appetizers.

— *à l'américaine* (Hot) Filled with diced lobster bound with *sauce à l'américaine;* topped with lobster mousse and baked.

— *aux anchois* (Hot) Filled with anchovy purée mixed with chopped sautéed onions and mushrooms; topped with bread crumbs and baked.

— *Aurora* (Cold) Filled with diced, cooked root vegetables, diced green beans, capers, and hard-cooked eggs; bound with mayonnaise sauce mixed with tomato purée.

— *Bagration* (Cold) Filled with chicken purée; topped with sliced chicken breast and truffles; coated with aspic.

— *Beauharnais* (Cold) Filled with chopped chicken meat and truffles bound with mayonnaise sauce seasoned with tarragon; coated with aspic.

— *à la bouquetière* (Hot) Filled with a *salpicon* of diced, cooked vegetables bound with béchamel sauce; garnished with asparagus tips.

— *à la cancalaise* (Cold) Filled with fish mousse and garnished with cooked oysters.

— *à l'indienne* (Cold) Filled with rice bound with chicken and ham purée; seasoned with curry and garnished with hard-cooked eggs.

— *Marivaux* (Cold) Filled with a *salpicon* of shrimp and mushrooms bound with mayonnaise sauce; garnished with hard-cooked eggs.

— *aux marrons* (Hot) Filled with chestnut purée; topped with Parmesan cheese and baked.

— *Mirabeau* (Cold) Filled with chopped hard-cooked eggs and anchovy fillets; bound with softened butter.

— *Norma* (Cold) Filled with tuna salad and garnished with caviar.

— *à la normande* (Cold) Filled with sole and truffle mousse;

Barquettes à la normande (cont.) topped with *sauce chaud-froid* and garnished with truffles and crayfish tails.

Beignets Fritters; foods dipped or mixed in batter and fried.

— **d'artichauts** Blanched, marinated artichokes dipped in batter and fried.

— **bernois** Chopped ham bound with béchamel sauce and Gruyère cheese; dipped in batter and fried.

— **à la florentine** Small balls of chopped spinach combined with béchamel sauce and Parmesan cheese; rolled in flour and fried.

— **au fromage** *Chou* paste combined with Parmesan cheese; deep-fried.

— **aux harengs** Marinated herring coated with fish purée; dipped in batter and fried.

— **de légumes** Various blanched vegetables dipped in batter and fried.

— **Lucullus** Pâté de foie gras sandwiched between thin rounds of truffle; dipped in batter and fried.

— **de riz** Small rice balls mixed with Parmesan cheese; dipped in batter and fried.

— **soufflés** *Chou* paste mixed with various ingredients; deep-fried.

— **soufflés à la hongroise** *Chou* paste mixed with diced sautéed onions and seasoned with paprika; fried.

Betterave à la crème Julienne of beetroot served in mustard cream sauce.

Bigarreaux confits Cherries marinated in vinegar; seasoned with salt and tarragon.

Bouchées Small puff pastry cases filled with various mixtures; served hot.

— **à la bénédictine** Filled with salt cod purée and sliced truffles.

— **à la bouquetière** Filled with diced cooked vegetables; bound with béchamel sauce.

— **à la Clamart** Filled with green pea purée.

— **à la Crécy** Filled with purée of carrots.

— **à la dieppoise** Filled with a *salpicon* of shrimp and mussels; bound with *sauce vin blanc*.

— **à la financière** Filled with cockscombs and kidneys, mushrooms, and truffles; bound with *sauce financière*.

— **à la julienne** Filled with matchstick vegetables; bound with béchamel sauce.

— **à la périgourdine** Filled with a *salpicon* of foie gras and truffles; bound with demi-glace sauce.

— **à la reine** Filled with *salpicon* of chicken breast, mushrooms, and truffles; bound with béchamel sauce.

— **à la Saint-Hubert** Filled with a purée of game.

Brochettes Small raw food tidbits cooked on a skewer.

Canapés Small rounds or squares of toasted bread; a base for various hot and cold appetizers.

— **à la danoise** Spread with horseradish-butter and topped with smoked salmon and herring; garnished with caviar.

— **à la livonienne** Spread with horseradish and topped with marinated herring and apple relish.

— **au jambon** Topped with chopped ham mixed with demi-glace sauce; garnished with parsley.

— **Victoria** Topped with a *salpicon* of lobster, mushrooms, and truffles; bound with béchamel sauce mixed with shrimp butter; sprinkled with crumbs and baked.

Carolines Tiny hot and cold éclairs

filled with various savory mixtures.

— *Joinville* Filled with chopped shrimp mixed with béchamel sauce.

Cassolettes Small ovenproof containers used to hold various mixtures; often topped with pastry or duchess potatoes, which serves as a lid.

— *ambassadrice* Filled with chicken livers; topped with duchess potatoes.

— *bouquetière* Filled with vegetable macédoine bound with cream; topped with duchess potatoes.

— *marquis* Filled with a *salpicon* of crayfish tails, mushrooms, and truffles; bound with *sauce Nantua*; topped with puff pastry.

— *régence* Filled with chopped chicken meat and truffles; bound with *sauce velouté*; topped with duchess potatoes.

— *Sagan* Filled with chopped truffles and mushrooms bound with *sauce velouté*; sprinkled with Parmesan cheese and browned in the oven; garnished with sliced calf's brain.

— *à la vénitienne* Filled with macaroni mixed with Parmesan cheese and cream; sprinkled with crumbs and browned in the oven.

Caviar Sturgeon roe.

— *à l'andalouse* Caviar combined with chopped hard-cooked eggs and bread crumbs; stuffed into a hollowed-out onion and baked; served with toast squares and anchovy butter.

— *au blini* Caviar stuffed inside a thin pancake and rolled; served with sour cream.

Cèpes marinés Blanched mushrooms marinated in oil, vinegar, and spices.

Cerneaux See Part II.

Champignons à la diable Sautéed mushrooms seasoned with salt, lemon juice, and cayenne pepper.

— *farcis* Mushroom caps stuffed with various fillings; served hot.

Choux Small pastry shells made from *chou* paste; filled with various fillings.

— *au fromage* Filled with Gruyère cheese.

— *à la Nantua* Filled with a purée of crayfish tails.

— *à la royale* Filled with creamed truffles.

— *à la strasbourgeoise* Filled with a *salpicon* of foie gras and truffles; bound with demi-glace sauce.

Concombres à la grecque Cucumber chunks poached in seasoned liquid; chilled and served over ice.

Coquilles Scallop shells; the name for appetizers served in scallop shells.

— *de crevettes* Filled with chopped shrimp bound with béchamel sauce; sprinkled with Parmesan cheese and baked.

— *d'huîtres à la diable* Filled with oysters coated with béchamel sauce and seasoned with cayenne pepper; sprinkled with crumbs and baked.

— *de volaille princesse* Filled with chicken breast meat; bound with *sauce allemande* and garnished with sliced truffles and asparagus tips.

Cornets d'York Thinly sliced York ham rolled in a cone and filled with various flavored butters.

Cornichons Gherkins; usually served as a garnish or part of an assorted cold platter.

Crêpes fourrées gratinées Stuffed (rolled) baked pancakes filled with a variety of preparations, e.g., duxelles, chicken liver, foie gras, mousses, *salpicons*, and so on.

Cromesquis Various *salpicons* dipped in batter or wrapped in crêpes (or pig's caul) and deep-fried; similar to croquettes.

— *à la bonne-femme* Minced beef bound with *sauce lyonnaise*; dipped in batter and deep-fried.

— *à la Carmélite* Puréed salt cod mixed with garlic and cream; wrapped in a small crêpe and dipped in batter before deep-frying.

Croquets Macaroni croquettes bound with béchamel sauce and Parmesan cheese; breaded and fried; served with tomato sauce.

Croquettes *Salpicons* or purées dipped in egg and coated with bread crumbs; deep-fried.

— *d'amourettes* Poached marrow and mushrooms chopped and bound with *sauce allemande*.

— *cressonnières* Duchess potatoes seasoned with watercress.

— *Montrouge* Chopped mushrooms and ham bound with egg yolks.

— *de pommes de terre à la niçoise* Duchess potato mixture combined with pimentoes, tomatoes, garlic and tarragon.

— *printanières* Chopped blanched spring vegetables; bound with preferred sauce.

— *de riz à la piémontaise* Risotto mixed with Parmesan cheese and white truffles.

Croustade A shell made from pastry, duchess potatoes, rice, or semolina used to contain various preparations; served hot.

— *à l'alsacienne* A duchess potato case filled with sautéed sauerkraut and garnished with slices of Strasbourg sausage.

— *à la forestière* Duchess potato case filled with creamed morels.

— *à la napolitaine* Pastry case filled with pasta tossed with tomato sauce and Parmesan cheese.

— *vert-pré* Duchess potato case filled with diced French beans, peas, and asparagus tips.

— *Vichy* Rice case filled with glazed carrots.

Croûtes Round or square pieces of toasted bread hollowed out and filled with various hot mixtures.

— *Brillat-Savarin* Filled with chopped hard-cooked eggs, chopped mushrooms, and truffles; garnished with anchovy fillets.

— *Du Barry* Filled with cooked cauliflower coated with *sauce Mornay*; sprinkled with Parmesan cheese.

— *à la paysanne* Filled with chopped sautéed vegetables; seasoned with Parmesan cheese.

Crudités Raw julienne-cut vegetables; served with a variety of spreads and dips.

Dartois Strips of puff pastry spread with appropriate filling and topped with another strip of pastry; similar to *allumettes*; served hot.

— *Laguipière* Filled with veal sweetbreads, chopped truffles, and chopped vegetables; bound with *sauce velouté*.

— *Lucullus* Filled with chopped truffles and foie gras mixed with demi-glace sauce.

Éperlans marinés Fried marinated smelts.

Foie gras Goose or duck liver; prepared in numerous ways.

— *en gelée* Poached foie gras coated with aspic which has been flavored with Port.

—, *médaillons de* Goose liver purée piped on small toast rounds and sprinkled with chopped truffles.

—, *mousse de* Puréed foie gras

combined with a mixture of *sauce velouté*, aspic, and unsweetened whipped cream; used as a filling for various appetizers.

— *à la nordique, mousse de* Foie gras mousse piped into a hollowed out fried bread round; garnished with truffles and coated with aspic.

Fondants Very small croquettes. See *Croquettes*, this section.

— *Argenteuil* Purée of asparagus mixed with béchamel sauce.

— *Crécy* Purée of carrots mixed with béchamel sauce.

Fondue au fromage Gruyère cheese melted in white wine and cream; served in a crock with bread cubes (for dipping).

Fritots Small pieces of meat, vegetables, or fish dipped in batter and deep-fried.

— *d'huîtres* Marinated oysters dipped in batter and fried.

— *de légumes* Fresh vegetables coated with batter and fried.

Fruits de mer, cocktail de Assorted shellfish poached in seasoned stock and served cold over ice with lemon wedges and various cold sauces.

Grenouilles à la grecque Frogs' legs poached in seasoned stock with lemon juice; served cold with lemon.

Harengs Herring.

— *salés, filets de* Salted herring served with various cold sauces and accompaniments.

— *fumés à la russe* Smoked herring marinated in *sauce vinaigrette* to which sour cream has been added.

Huîtres Oysters.

— *en brochette* Poached oysters wrapped in bacon and skewered; dipped in egg and bread crumbs and deep-fried.

—, *cocktail d'* Poached chilled oysters served in a glass with cocktail sauce and lemon wedges.

— *frites* Oysters dipped in egg and bread crumbs and deep-fried; served with lemon wedge and tartare sauce.

— *au naturel* Raw oysters served on the half-shell over ice; accompanied with lemon wedges, horseradish, and red pepper sauce.

Langue écarlate, fumée Smoked pickled tongue.

Mazagrans Duchess potato shells filled with various preparations and sealed with potato mixture; baked.

Melon cantaloup Fresh ripe cantaloupe cut in wedges and served over ice.

Moules à la ravigote Poached mussels marinated in *sauce vinaigrette*; garnished with hard-cooked eggs and gherkins.

Œufs farcis Halved hard-cooked eggs stuffed with the yolks creamed with mayonnaise sauce.

Œufs mignons Egg-shaped cases made from breaded, deep-fried duchess potatoes; hollowed out and stuffed with various fillings.

— *Beauharnais* Filled with purée of chicken breast; seasoned with tarragon.

— *à la nivernaise* Filled with a *salpicon* of carrots and onions.

Oie fumée Sliced smoked goose breast.

Olives farcies Pitted olives filled with anchovy butter.

Pannequets Small pancakes spread with appropriate filling and rolled.

— *à la brunoise* Filled with chopped sautéed vegetables mixed with béchamel sauce.

— *à la ligurienne* Filled with anchovies, chopped hard-cooked eggs, and tomato *concassée*.

Pâté Various forcemeats cooked and presented in numerous ways.

— *de faisan* Pheasant pâté baked in crust; served cold.

— *de saumon* A pastry-lined terrine filled with fish forcemeat and salmon pieces; baked and served hot.

Petits pâtés Mini pâtés wrapped in pastry.

Petits soufflés Mini soufflés prepared in small receptacles.

Pied de mouton à la vinaigrette Boned sheeps' trotters poached and marinated in olive oil, vinegar, and seasonings; served cold.

Poireaux à la grecque Strips of fresh leeks blanched and marinated in olive oil, lemon juice, and spices.

Poireaux à la russe Blanched marinated leeks stuffed with caviar and chopped hard-cooked eggs; served with horseradish sauce.

Pomponnettes Small round turnovers stuffed with various mixtures.

Quiche lorraine Small *tartelette* shells filled with egg custard; combined with chopped bacon and Gruyère cheese; baked.

Rissoles Small deep-fried turnovers containing various fillings.

— *à la bohémienne* Chopped foie gras and truffles mixed with demi-glace sauce and wrapped in brioche; deep-fried.

— *Cédrillon* Brioche turnovers filled with chopped chicken breast, truffles, and foie gras.

— *Pompadour* Smoked tongue, truffles, and mushrooms wrapped in brioche and fried.

Saumon fumé à la moscovite Rolled smoked salmon strips stuffed with caviar.

Subrics Small pan-fried patties made of various *salpicons*.

— *de foie gras* Made of goose liver bound with cream.

— *de semoule* Small fried semolina patties.

Talmouses Small pastries filled with various preparations featuring cheese.

— *à l'ancienne* Cheese soufflé mixture wrapped inside puff pastry and baked. Sprinkled with Gruyère cheese.

— *Bagration* Puff pastry tartlets filled with *chou* paste mixed with Gruyère cheese.

— *de Saint-Denis* A puff pastry turnover filled with a cream cheese-egg mixture.

Tartelettes Small open shortdough pastries filled with various forcemeats, *salpicons*, ragoûts, and so forth.

— *Béatrix* Filled with a *salpicon* of shrimp and oysters bound with *sauce normande*.

— *à la japonaise* Filled with chinese artichokes cooked in cream.

— *Printania* Filled with creamed morels and garnished with asparagus tips.

Terrine The collective name for pâtés or similar preparations cooked and/or served in a terrine.

— *de caneton* A caul-lined terrine filled with duck forcemeat and slices of marinated duck breast; served cold.

— *maison* Forcemeat mixture mixed with chunks of chicken livers, pork, pistachios, and mushrooms; baked in a bacon-lined terrine and served cold.

Timbales The collective name for appetizers prepared in a timbale, which is usually lined with pastry, forcemeat, or duchess potato.

— *Beauvilliers* Brioche-lined timbale filled with chopped chicken breast and truffles mixed with *sauce allemande*.

— *à la Rossini* Timbale lined with chicken forcemeat and filled with foie gras and truffles; garnished with sliced truffles.

Tomates Tomatoes.

— *à la génoise* Sliced tomatoes marinated in *sauce vinaigrette* with sweet peppers and anchovies; served with sliced cooked potatoes.

— *à la vinaigrette* Skinned and seeded tomatoes cut in strips and marinated in *sauce vinaigrette*.

Truites marinées Small trout cooked in white wine, fish fumet, and spices; cooled in the cooking liquid and served with lemon wedges.

POTAGES — SOUPS

Aïgo à la ménagère See Part II.
Aïgo bouïdo See Part II.
Aïgo San d'Iou See Part II.
Aïgo saou See Part II.
Bijane See Part II.
Bouillabaisse See Part II.
— *corse* See Part II.
— *de Morue* See Part II.
Bouilleture d'anguilles See Part II.
Bouillinada See Part II.
Bourride See Part II.
Braou-Bouffat See Part II.
Bréjaude See Part II.
Consommé A strong, crystal clear broth garnished with various ingredients.

— *Adèle* Chicken consommé garnished with peas, carrots, and chicken dumplings.

— *à l'africaine* Beef consommé seasoned with curry and garnished with rice, chopped artichokes, and *chou* dumplings.

— *à l'alsacienne* Chicken consommé garnished with braised sauerkraut and sliced Strasbourg sausage.

— *à l'andalouse* Chicken consommé flavored with tomato and garnished with tiny dumplings, diced ham, and rice.

— *à la basquaise* Chicken consommé garnished with red pepper strips, rice, and diced tomatoes.

— *Béhague* Chicken consommé garnished with poached eggs.

— *Belle-Hélène* Chicken consommé garnished with strips of *royale*.

— *Berchoux* Game consommé garnished with chestnut purée, strips of quail meat, and diced mushrooms and truffles.

— *à la bretonne* Beef consommé garnished with leeks, mushrooms, and celery.

— *Brillat-Savarin* Chicken consommé thickened with tapioca and garnished with julienne of chicken breast, strips of *royale*, and braised lettuce.

— *brunoise* Consommé garnished with finely diced vegetables.

— *à la cancalaise* Fish consommé thickened with tapioca and garnished with poached oysters, pike quenelles, and chopped chervil.

— *cardinal* Fish consommé garnished with lobster quenelles.

— *carême* Chicken consommé garnished with root vegetables, braised lettuce, and asparagus tips.

— *Célestine* Chicken consommé thickened with tapioca and garnished with strips of truffle *royale*.

— *chasseur* Game consommé garnished with chopped mushrooms and game quenelles.

— *à la Colbert* Consommé garnished with chopped vegetables and small poached eggs; seasoned with port.

— *à la Crécy* Chicken consommé thickened with tapioca and garnished with carrot *royale*.

— *Dalayrac* Slightly thickened chicken consommé garnished with strips of chicken breast, chopped mushrooms, and truffles.

— *aux diablotins* Chicken consommé garnished with Parmesan croutons.

— *diplomate* Chicken consommé garnished with slices of chicken forcemeat and strips of truffle.

— *duchesse* Chicken consommé garnished with sago, braised lettuce, and diced *royale*.

— *Duse* Chicken consommé garnished with diced tomatoes, chicken quenelles, small tortellini, and pasta.

— *fermière* Beef consommé garnished with diced carrots, turnips, potatoes, and parsnips.

— *à la flamande* Consommé garnished with Brussels sprouts *royale*, green peas, and chopped chervil.

— *Florence* Chicken consommé garnished with vermicelli and truffle strips.

— *germinal* Beef consommé seasoned with tarragon and garnished with chopped green vegetables.

— *Grimaldi* Chicken consommé garnished with diced *royale*, julienne of celery, and tomato purée.

— *à la hollandaise* Beef consommé garnished with veal quenelles and poached marrow; sprinkled with chervil.

— *à l'impériale* Chicken consommé garnished with chicken quenelles, cockscombs and kidneys, and green peas.

— *à l'infante* Chicken consommé garnished with profiteroles filled with foie gras.

— *à l'italienne* Chicken consommé garnished with three different *royales*—chicken, tomato, and spinach—representing the colors of the Italian flag.

— *julienne* Consommé garnished with a julienne of vegetables.

— *Lorette* Chicken consommé garnished with strips of truffle; asparagus tips, and chopped chervil; *Lorette* potatoes served separately.

— *Macdonald* Beef consommé garnished with calf's-brain *royale*, tiny raviolis, and diced cucumbers.

— *à la madrilène* Chicken consommé garnished with tomatoes *concassée* and seasoned with cayenne pepper; served cold.

— *marquis* Chicken consommé garnished with poached marrow and chicken dumplings flavored with hazelnuts.

— *Mercédès* Chicken consommé flavored with sherry and garnished with cockscomb and red pepper.

— *mignon* Fish consommé garnished with shrimp quenelles and chopped truffle.

— *Mikado* Chicken consommé flavored with tomato and garnished with diced tomatoes and chicken.

— *mimosa* See Part II, *Mimosa, consommé*.

— *Mogador* See Part II, *Mogador, consommé*.

— *à la napolitaine* Beef consommé garnished with tomatoes, macaroni, and Parmesan cheese.

— *Nesselrode* Game consommé garnished with small profiteroles filled with chestnut and onion purée; diced mushrooms.

— *Nimrod* Game consommé flavored with port and garnished with truffled game quenelles.

— *à la nivernaise* Beef consommé garnished with diced root vegetables and strips of *royale*.

— *à l'Orléans* Chicken consommé garnished with three different quenelles; spinach, tomato, and chicken.

— *au pain* Chicken consommé garnished with Parmesan croutons.

— *parfait* Thickened chicken consommé garnished with diced *royale*.

— *à la parisienne* Chicken consommé garnished with potatoes and leeks.

— *Pépita* Chicken consommé flavored with tomato and garnished with tomato *royale* and red pepper.

— *à la piémontaise* Chicken consommé seasoned with tomato and saffron and garnished with white Piedmont truffles, rice, and chopped ham.

— *à la polonaise* Chicken consommé garnished with slices of crêpes filled with chicken forcemeat.

— *princesse* Chicken consommé garnished with chicken quenelles and asparagus tips.

— *printanier* Consommé garnished with diced spring vegetables.

— *Rachel* Chicken consommé garnished with sliced artichoke bottoms, fried croutons, and poached marrow.

— *à la Reine-Jeanne* Chicken consommé garnished with chicken quenelles and profiteroles filled with chicken forcemeat.

— *riche* Chicken consommé garnished with chicken quenelles and truffles.

— *Rothschild* See Part II, *Rothschild, consommé*.

— *à la royale* Consommé garnished with *royale*.

— *Saint-Germain* See Part II, *Saint-Germain, consommé*.

— *à la Saint-Hubert* Game consommé garnished with game *royale* and sliced mushrooms.

— *Sans-Gêne* See Part II, *Sans-Gêne, consommé*.

— *à la semoule* Consommé garnished with cooked semolina and Parmesan cheese.

— *à la strasbourgeoise* Beef consommé garnished with juniper berries, braised red cabbage, and sliced Strasbourg sausage; served with grated horseradish.

— *Talleyrand* See Part II, *Talleyrand, consommé*.

— *à la Tosca* Chicken consommé thickened with tapioca and garnished with profiteroles filled with chicken forcemeat; seasoned with turtle herbs; see *Herbe à Tortue* (Part II).

— *à la valenciennes* Chicken consommé garnished with chicken quenelles, braised lettuce, and chopped chervil.

— *à la vénetienne* Beef consommé seasoned with thyme, tarragon, and chervil; garnished with rice and gnocchi.

— *aux vermicelles* Consommé garnished with vermicelli.

— *Villeroi* Chicken consommé garnished with slices of chicken and tomato quenelles.

Cousinat See Part II.

Cousinette See Part II.

Faubonne See Part II.

Freneuse Turnips and potatoes cooked in stock and enriched with cream.

Hochepot See Part II.

Oulade See Part II.

Potage A rich soup often puréed and enriched with egg yolks and/or cream.

— *ambassadeurs* Purée of green pea soup garnished with rice and lettuce strips; enriched with butter and cream.

— *andalou* Purée of tomatoes and rice; garnished with onions, rice, tomato, and red pepper.

— *bonne-femme* Potato and leek soup thickened with butter and cream.

— *camélia* Purée of green pea soup; garnished with sliced leeks, julienne of chicken, and tapioca.

— *crème Agnès Sorel* Chicken soup combined with purée of mushrooms and garnished with strips of chicken, tongue, and mushrooms; thickened with cream.

— *crème algérien* Purée of sweet potato garnished with roasted hazelnuts; enriched with cream.

— *crème Argenteuil* Purée of asparagus thickened with cream and garnished with asparagus tips.

— *crème à l'aurore* Cream of chicken soup flavored with tomato juice; garnished with chopped tomato and julienne of chicken.

— *crème Beaucaire* Barley soup thickened with cream; garnished with julienne of chicken, chopped celery, and green onions.

— *crème Bercy* Turnip and potato soup thickened with cream and garnished with croutons; enriched with butter.

— *crème breton* Purée of navy beans seasoned with onions and leeks; thickened with cream.

— *crème cardinal* Fish *velouté* combined with purée of lobster; garnished with lobster *royale* shaped into crosses.

— *crème Choisy* Velouté enriched with cream; garnished with braised lettuce, chervil, and croutons.

— *crème duchesse* Chicken soup thickened with cream and garnished with truffles, asparagus tips, and julienne of chicken.

— *crème à la flamande* Purée of potato garnished with Brussels sprouts; enriched with cream.

— *crème à la gastronome* Cream of chicken soup garnished with truffles, chestnuts, cockscombs, and mushrooms.

— *crème à la gauloise* Purée of celery thickened with cream; garnished with chestnuts, chopped tomatoes, and croutons.

— *crème grand-duc* Cream of partridge soup garnished with mushrooms and quenelles.

— *crème à l'hôtelière* Cream of potato and green beans; garnished with lentils and croutons.

— *crème maintenon* Cream of chicken soup garnished with julienne of carrots, turnips, and potatoes.

— *crème à la maréchale* Purée of chicken thickened with cream; garnished with chopped truffles, chicken, and asparagus tips.

— *crème Navarin* Cream of green pea garnished with crayfish tails and peas.

— *crème à la princesse* Chicken and asparagus purée thickened with cream and garnished with asparagus tips and diced chicken.

— *crème régence* See Part II, *Régence, potage crème.*

— *crème à la soissonaise* Navy bean purée enriched with cream and garnished with croutons.

— *crème vigneron* Cream of pumpkin and red beans; garnished with leeks and croutons.

— *Fontanges* Cream of green pea garnished with braised sorrel and chervil.

— *Longchamps* Same as *potage Fontanges* with the addition of vermicelli.

— *Marigny* Cream of green pea garnished with French beans, peas, sorrel, and chervil.

— *paysan* Purée of spring vegetables; garnished with croutons.

— *portugais* Tomato purée garnished with rice.

— *purée Beaulieu* Purée of vegetables mixed with consommé; garnished with diced vegetables.

— *purée Condé* Purée of red beans flavored with red wine; garnished with croutons.

— *purée Crécy au riz* Purée of carrots garnished with rice; enriched with cream.

— *purée Darblay* Potato purée garnished with julienne of root vegetables.

— *purée Du Barry* Purée of cauliflower garnished with cauliflower and enriched with cream.

— *purée Lamballe* Purée of green pea combined with tapioca; enriched with butter.

— *purée de marrons* Chestnut purée enriched with game stock and garnished with croutons.

— *purée Médicis* Purée of carrots and green peas enriched with butter and cream.

— *purée Parmentier* Potato purée garnished with sautéed leeks and croutons.

— *purée Royan* Purée of cauliflower and tapioca; enriched with butter.

— *purée Saint-Germain* Green pea purée enriched with cream; garnished with green peas and croutons.

— *purée Valois* Pheasant purée garnished with green peas and quenelles.

— *Saint-Cloud* Green pea and lettuce purée enriched with butter and cream; garnished with braised lettuce and croutons.

— *Saint-Germain* See Part II, *Saint-Germain, Potage.*

— *Sarah Bernhardt* See Part II, *Sarah Bernhardt, Potage.*

— *à la sicilienne* Cream of tomato soup garnished with tapioca.

— *à la tyrolienne* Green pea purée thickened with cream and garnished with braised sorrel, diced cucumbers, and croutons.

— *velours* Carrot purée garnished with tapioca.

— *velouté à l'Ardennes* Pheasant *velouté* garnished with red beans, croutons, and julienne of pheasant; flavored with port.

— *velouté Bagration* Veal *velouté* enriched with cream; garnished with macaroni and Parmesan cheese.

— *velouté Bonvalet* *Velouté* mixed with root vegetable purée and garnished with green beans and carrot *royale.*

— *velouté Carmen* Chicken *velouté* enriched with cream and garnished with rice, julienne of chicken, tomatoes, and red pepper.

— *velouté Claremont* Chicken *velouté* flavored with champagne; garnished with julienne of chicken, asparagus tips, and chicken dumplings.

— *velouté diplomate* Chicken *velouté* garnished with rice, truffles, tapioca, and chicken dumplings.

— *velouté Excelsior* *Velouté* garnished with pearl barley and asparagus tips; enriched with cream.

— *velouté germinal* Chicken *velouté* seasoned with tarragon and garnished with asparagus tips and chervil.

— *velouté à l'indienne* Chicken *velouté* seasoned with curry and enriched with coconut milk; garnished with rice.

— *velouté à la lyonnaise* Chicken *velouté* garnished with chestnut *royale*.

— *velouté Montreuil* Chicken *velouté* garnished with chicken dumplings, spinach, and chopped tomatoes.

— *velouté Nelusko* Chicken *velouté* garnished with chicken quenelles and toasted hazelnuts; enriched with egg yolks.

— *velouté Soubise* Onion purée combined with *velouté*; garnished with croutons.

— *velouté Xavier* Cream of rice soup combined with chicken *velouté*; garnished with *royale*.

Pot-au-feu See Part II.

— *à l'albigeoise* See Part II.

Santé Potage purée Parmentier with the addition of braised sorrel and chervil; enriched with cream and served with croutons.

Sobronade See Part II.

Soupe A hearty chunky soup usually served with bread.

— *du berger* See Part II.

— *dauphinoise* Root vegetables cooked in stock and garnished with beet greens and vermicelli.

— *à l'eau de Boudin* See Part II.

— *au farci* See Part II.

— *fermière* Chicken stock garnished with chopped fresh vegetables and croutons.

— *flamande* Soup stock garnished with diced potatoes and Brussels sprouts.

— *maraîchère* Potato and leek soup garnished with vermicelli

and braised greens.

— *Nevers* Soup stock garnished with sautéed carrots and Brussels sprouts; chervil and vemicelli.

— *normande* Consommé garnished with white beans, carrots, potatoes, and leeks; enriched with butter.

— *à l'oignon* See Part II, *Oignon, Soupe à l'*.

— *à l'oignon gratinée* Caramelized onions simmered in beef stock; garnished with croutons and Gruyère cheese; browned under the broiler.

— *paysanne* White stock garnished with diced fresh vegetables and white navy beans.

— *au pistou* See Part II, *Pistou, Soupe au*.

— *villageoise* Consommé garnished with sautéed leeks, braised cabbage, and vermicelli.

ŒUFS — EGGS

Œufs Eggs.

— *à l'agenaise* Eggs baked in a dish on a bed of chopped onions that have been sautéed in goose fat; garnished with fried eggplant.

— *Aladin* Describes various egg preparations garnished with saffron-risotto and sautéed peppers and onions; topped with tomato sauce.

— *à l'ancienne* Various egg dishes utilizing sauerkraut and ham.

— *Apicius* Describes various egg preparations served on a bed of cooked mushrooms and garnished with crayfish tails, truffles, and *sauce normande*.

— *Argenteuil* Describes various egg preparations served with asparagus or asparagus purée.

— *à l'auvergnate* Describes various egg preparations served on braised cabbage and garnished with slices of grilled sausage.

— **Bercy** Baked eggs garnished with tomatoes and grilled sausage; served with tomato sauce.

— **Bernis** Describes various egg preparations served over chicken purée in a pastry shell and topped with suprême sauce.

— **Brillat-Savarin** Various egg preparations using morels and asparagus tips.

— *brouillés* Scrambled eggs.

- *à l'américaine* 1) Scrambled eggs cooked with bits of bacon and garnished with bacon strips and sliced tomatoes. 2) Scrambled eggs garnished with diced lobster tail.

- *à l'arlésienne* Cooked with chopped tomatoes and eggplant.

- *à la batelière* Cooked with chopped parsley and garnished with purée of sole.

- *Chambord* Served on fried eggplant slices; topped with demi-glace sauce.

- *Clamart* Cooked with green pea purée; garnished with green peas.

- *à l'espagnole* Served on fried tomato slices; garnished with julienne of red pepper.

- *à la forestière* Garnished with sautéed morels and chopped bacon.

- *Héloise* Cooked with diced tongue and chicken; garnished with sliced mushrooms and served with tomato sauce.

- *à l'italienne* Served over a bed of risotto and garnished with chopped tomatoes; topped with tomato sauce.

- *à la mexicaine* Served with tomato sauce and julienne of sweet peppers.

- *à la nantaise* Served over croutons with fried sardines.

- *à la Nantua* Cooked with crayfish tails and truffles; garnished with truffle slices topped with *sauce Nantua*.

- *à la norvégienne* Served on croutons with fillet of anchovies.

- *panetière* Cooked with ham and mushrooms and served in hollowed out bread that has been toasted; topped with Parmesan cheese.

- *à la périgourdine* Cooked with foie gras and truffles and garnished with sliced truffles.

- *à la romaine* Cooked with anchovy fillets, chopped tomatoes, and spinach; sprinkled with Parmesan cheese and served with demi-glace sauce.

- *Rossini* Served in a pastry shell and garnished with foie gras and truffles; topped with *sauce Madeira*.

- *Saint-Hubert* Served with game purée and game-flavored demi-glace sauce.

- *à la suisse* Served in pastry shells; topped with Swiss cheese and browned.

— *carême* Various egg dishes featuring truffles and sometimes mushrooms and sweetbreads.

— *à la charcutière* Describes various egg preparations cooked or garnished with small sausage patties.

— *chasseur* Describes various egg preparations served with chicken livers and *sauce chasseur*.

— *à la Chivry* Describes various egg preparations served on croutons and garnished with asparagus tips; topped with *sauce Chivry*.

— *Choron* Describes various egg preparations served on croutons; garnished with green peas and

Œufs Choron (cont.)
topped with béarnaise sauce and *sauce Choron.*

— *en cocotte* Eggs baked or steamed in small oven-proof dishes *(cocottes).*

- *à la crème* Baked in cream.
- *à la bordelaise* Baked with poached marrow; topped with *sauce bordelaise.*
- *à la diplomate* Cooked with foie gras; served with tomato sauce.
- *au jus* Topped with beef juice.
- *à la périgourdine* Baked in co-cotte over sliced truffles; dressed with *sauce périgourdine.*
- *à la portugaise* Cooked on a bed of chopped tomatoes and shal-lots; with tomato sauce.
- *à la strasbourgeoise* Garnished with sliced truffled foie gras; topped with *sauce Madeira.*
- *à la tartare* Baked in cream over chopped raw beef.

— *Condé* Various egg dishes gar-nished with red bean purée.

— *à la coque* Soft-boiled eggs.

— *Daumont* Cooked in a large mushroom cap; garnished with crayfish tails bound with *sauce Nantua;* sliced truffles.

— *durs* Hard-cooked (boiled) eggs.

- *à l'aurore* Hard-cooked egg slices coated with *sauce aurore* and sprinkled with Parmesan cheese; baked au gratin and garnished with chopped hard-cooked yolks.
- *Belloy* Halved hard-cooked egg whites stuffed with creamed yolks (with *sauce Mornay*), lob-ster, and truffles; coated with *sauce Mornay* and baked au gra-tin.
- *Chimay* Stuffed with crushed yolks and duxelles.
- *Lucullus* Halved hard-cooked egg white stuffed with yolks

mixed with foie gras purée and covered with remaining egg white half; breaded and deep-fried.

- *à la Soubise* Sliced hard-cooked eggs over a bed of onion purée; topped with *sauce Soubise* and baked au gratin.

— *frits* Fried eggs.

- *à la bayonnaise* Served over fried croutons; garnished with Bayonne ham.
- *à la languedocienne* Served on a slice of fried eggplant; served with garlic-tomato sauce.
- *à la nivernaise* Served on fried croutons; garnished with pearl onions and small carrot balls.
- *à la romaine* Served on a bed of braised spinach and gar-nished with anchovy fillets.
- *Villeroi* Cold poached eggs dipped in *sauce Villeroi,* breaded, and deep-fried.

— *froids* Cold eggs.

- *aux asperges* Cold poached eggs coated with *sauce chaud-froid;* decorated with truffles and glazed with aspic; garnished with asparagus tips.
- *Chartres* Cold poached eggs garnished with tarragon leaves and glazed with aspic; served on a bed of chicken forcemeat.
- *à la niçoise* Cold poached eggs served in a pastry case over po-tato-tomato-green bean *salpi-con;* topped with mayonnaise sauce diluted with tomato juice.

— *en gelée* Eggs in jelly (aspic); decorated with truffles, foie gras, vegetables, and so on.

— *Halévy* Eggs baked in pastry shell over chicken mousse; topped with *sauce allemande* and tomato sauce.

— *Masséna* See Part II, *Masséna, œufs.*

— *en meurette* Eggs poached in red wine; served on croutons and garnished with onion slices.

— *Mirette* Poached yolks served in a tartlet shell over a *salpicon* of chicken breast and truffles; topped with suprême sauce.

— *miroir* See *Œufs sur le plat.*

— *mollets* Soft-cooked eggs.

- *à la dauphinoise* Soft-cooked eggs dipped in egg and bread crumbs and deep-fried; served with tomato sauce.

- *Clamart* Served in a pastry shell over green pea purée; topped with suprême sauce and garnished with truffles.

— *Monselet* Served over sautéed artichokes; topped with suprême sauce and garnished with sliced truffles.

— *Mornay* Describes various egg preparations coated with *sauce Mornay* and grated cheese; baked au gratin.

— *moulés* Eggs baked in special molds; turned out and served on croutons or similar base.

- *à la Chartres* Served on croutons and topped with a tarragon-flavored demi-glace sauce; garnished with tarragon leaves.

- *Orsay* Served on croutons and topped with *sauce Château-briand.*

— *opéra* Various egg dishes garnished with chicken livers bound with demi-glace sauce; sautéed asparagus tips.

— *de Pâques* Easter eggs; decorated hard-cooked eggs (in shell).

— *sur le plat* Fried eggs sunny-side up; also called *œufs au plat* and *œufs miroir.*

- *à la bayonnaise* Fried eggs sunny-side up served with Bayonne ham and sautéed cèpes.

— *pochés* Poached eggs.

- *à l'africaine* Served on croutons and garnished with sliced bacon, chopped tomatoes, and rice.

- *à l'alsacienne* Served on braised sauerkraut and garnished with sliced ham or sausage.

- *à la boulangère* Served on fried croutons and garnished with sautéed mushrooms; coated with *sauce Mornay* and browned under the broiler.

- *béchamel* Served on croutons and coated with béchamel sauce.

- *Benedict* Served on sliced ham and croutons; coated with hollandaise sauce.

- *à la Célestine* Served on croutons and garnished with anchovy fillets and lobster chunks; topped with béchamel sauce.

- *Chantilly* Served over green pea purée in pastry case; coated with *sauce mousseline.*

- *Cédrillon* Served in baked potato cups and garnished with truffle slices; coated with *sauce Mornay* and baked au gratin.

- *Clermont* Served on croutons and garnished with chopped mushrooms; topped with tomato-curry sauce.

- *à la danoise* Served on croutons and garnished with smoked salmon.

- *à la finnoise* Served on croutons and garnished with green peppers and tomato sauce.

- *à la hollandaise* Served in pastry case and garnished with salmon purée; coated with hollandaise sauce.

- *Montrouge* Served on grilled mushroom caps; coated with mushroom-flavored suprême sauce.

- *à la napolitaine* Served over risotto; topped with tomato sauce and grated Parmesan cheese.
- *à la normande* Served in pastry case and garnished with poached oysters; coated with *sauce normande.*
- *à la polonaise* Served on a *salpicon* of mutton and mushrooms bound with demi-glace sauce; topped with *sauce poivrade.*
- *Sardou* Served on croutons and garnished with asparagus tips and truffles; coated with béchamel sauce mixed with artichoke purée.
- *Soubise* Served over onion purée in a pastry case; coated with *sauce Soubise.*
- *à la Suzette* Served in a baked potato cup and coated with *sauce Mornay;* baked au gratin and decorated with truffles.
- *Viroflay* Served over sautéed spinach in a pastry case; topped with suprême sauce.
— *poêlés à l'Antiboise* Eggs baked in small casseroles with Gruyère cheese; garnished with chopped parsley and roe.
— *Sans-Gêne* See Part II, *Sans-Gêne, œufs.*

Omelette Beaten eggs cooked in a frying pan until firm. Omelettes are usually filled or topped with assorted ingredients.
— *Agnès Sorel* Filled with chopped mushrooms, chicken purée, and sliced tongue.
— *archiduc* Filled with chicken livers glazed with *sauce Madeira;* garnished with truffles and drizzled with *sauce archiduc.*
— *à la Bercy* Seasoned with fines herbes and filled with sliced sausages; with tomato sauce.
— *à la bigourdane* Filled with truffles, foie gras, and *sauce Madeira.*

— *à la bouchère* Filled with poached marrow and meat glaze.
— *à la bretonne* Plain omelette seasoned with sautéed mushrooms, onions, and leeks.
— *Choisy* Stuffed with braised lettuce and suprême sauce.
— *à la diplomate* Filled with chopped truffles and artichoke hearts; with *sauce aux truffes.*
— *à la française* Omelette mixture combined with whipped cream and sautéed shallots.
— *à la gasconne* A flat omelette cooked with onions, ham, garlic, and parsley sautéed in goose fat.
— *à la hollandaise* Egg mixture combined with smoked salmon; coated with hollandaise sauce.
— *à la jardinière* A flat omelette cooked with diced sautéed vegetables.
— *à la limousine* Cooked with diced potatoes and ham.
— *à la lyonnaise* Cooked or filled with sautéed onions and parsley.
— *Maintenon* Filled with chopped chicken, mushrooms, and truffles; topped with *sauce soubise.*
— *à la marseillaise* Filled with salt cod purée and diced tomatoes; with *sauce Nantua.*
— *mexicaine* Eggs mixed with sweet peppers, diced mushrooms, and tomatoes and cooked flat; with tomato sauce.
— *nature* Plain omelette.
— *Newburg* Filled and garnished with diced lobster and *sauce Newburg.*
— *à la niçoise* Eggs mixed with tomatoes, parsley, and garlic; garnished with anchovy fillets.
— *à la normande* Filled with oysters and *sauce normande.*
— *plate* Flat omelette.
— *à la Reine* Filled with chicken purée; coated with suprême sauce.

— **Saint-Hubert** Filled with game purée and garnished with sautéed mushroom caps in demi-glace sauce.

— **à la savoyarde** A flat omelette cooked with sliced sautéed potatoes and Gruyère cheese.

— **Vichy** Stuffed with glazed carrots and parsley.

Pipérade A flat omelette made with a fondue of tomatoes, bell peppers, onions, and garlic.

Quiche Lorraine See Part II.

POISSON — FISH

Aiglefin See *Aigrefin*, this section.

Aigrefin Haddock; also aiglefin and églefin.

— **à l'ancienne** Poached and coated with *sauce aux câpres*.

— **aux fines herbes** Poached in white wine with fine herbs and aromatic vegetables.

— **à la flamande** Poached in white wine and garnished with mushroom caps and onions; coated with the reduced poaching liquid.

— **maître d'hôtel** Fried and served with maître d'hotel butter.

Alose Shad.

— **Bercy** Baked and coated with *sauce Bercy*.

— **farcie** 1) Stuffed with fish mousseline and baked; coated with *sauce Bercy*. 2) Stuffed with fish mousseline and braised in red wine; topped with the reduced braising liquid finished with butter.

— **frite** Dipped in egg and crumbs and deep-fried; served with tartare sauce.

— **à la hollandaise** Poached in court bouillon and coated with hollandaise sauce.

— **à la nantaise** Poached in white wine with mushrooms; garnished with crayfish, oysters, and truffles;

served with hollandaise sauce.

— **à la Soubise** Broiled and coated with *sauce Soubise*.

Anchois Anchovy.

— **à la basque** Dipped in egg and crumbs and deep-fried; garnished with chopped tomatoes and capers; coated with béarnaise sauce.

— **frits** Dipped in crumbs or batter and deep-fried; served with tartare sauce.

— **grillés** Brushed with oil and grilled; with *sauce remoulade*.

— **marinés** Fried and marinated in oil, vinegar, and spices.

Anguille Eel.

— **à l'anglaise** Poached and served with *sauce persil*.

— **à la bonne-femme** Poached in white wine and garnished with croutons and fried potatoes; coated with the reduced poaching liquid finished with butter.

— **à la bordelaise** Poached in seasoned white wine; topped with the reduced poaching liquid which has been combined with *sauce bordelaise* and finished with anchovy butter.

— **à la fermière** Poached in white wine with vegetables fondue; topped with the reduced poaching liquid enriched with heavy cream.

— **à l'italienne** Braised with white wine, tomato sauce, and mushrooms; seasoned with tarragon.

— **en matelote** Poached in red wine with *mirepoix* and bouquet garni; poaching liquid reduced and thickened with beurre manié; garnished with mushrooms, onions, and croutons.

— **à la provençale** Braised in white wine with chopped tomatoes, garlic, and onions.

— **au vert** Sautéed with green herbs and finished cooking in

Anguille au vert (cont.)
white wine; served in the poaching liquid which has been reduced and thickened with egg yolk.

Barbue Brill.

— **au beurre noir** Poached in court bouillon and topped with brown butter mixed with capers.

— **braisée** Braised in white wine, fish stock, and aromatic vegetables.

— **à la cancalaise** Braised (see *Barbue braisée*) and coated with *sauce normande*; garnished with poached oysters and shrimp.

— **à la dieppoise** Braised (see *Barbue braisée*) and garnished with mussels and shrimp; with *sauce vin blanc*.

— **au gratin** Coated with *sauce italienne* and dipped in bread crumbs; baked.

— **Mornay** Poached in stock; coated with *sauce Mornay* and Gruyère cheese; baked au gratin.

— **au vin blanc** Braised (see *Barbue braisée*) and coated with *sauce vin blanc*.

Bouillabaisse See Part II.

— **de morue** See Part II.

Brochet Pike.

— **au bleu** Plunged alive in salted water with vinegar; garnished with boiled potatoes and served with hollandaise sauce.

—, **farce de** Pike forcemeat; boned and skinned pike flesh ground with *panade,* egg whites, and minced beef suet; used as a stuffing in several preparations.

— **à la marinière** Poached in white wine and stock with mushrooms and onions; garnished with crayfish tails and croutons; coated with *sauce velouté*.

— **du meunier** Lightly floured and fried in butter; sprinkled with parsley, lemon, and *beurre noisette*.

— **persillé** Poached in stock and sprinkled with parsley, lemon, and *beurre noisette*.

—, **quenelles de** Minced seasoned pike flesh bound with *panade,* eggs, or cream; poached in seasoned stock.

Cabillaud Cod; also *Morue fraiche* (fresh cod).

— **à la boulangère** Sprinkled with crumbs and baked with sliced potatoes, garlic and onions; garnished with fresh parsley.

— **bouilli** Boiled in salted water; served with boiled potatoes and accompanied with various butters or fish-based sauces.

— **en coquille à la florentine** Baked in a scallop shell with spinach and mushrooms; coated with *sauce Mornay* and bread crumbs; baked au gratin.

— **Mornay** Poach in white wine and coated with *sauce Mornay* and Gruyère cheese; baked au gratin.

— **Newburg** Poached in white wine and fish stock; garnished with sliced lobster tails and topped with *sauce Newburg*.

Calmar Squid.

— **farci à la marseillaise** Braised squid stuffed with onions, garlic, tomatoes, and bread crumbs; served with the reduced braising liquid.

— **en matelote** Sautéed with onions, mushrooms, garlic, and tomatoes and simmered in white wine; served in the cooking liquid thickened with butter.

Carpe Carp.

— **à la bière** Braised in beer with onions, carrots, celery, and gingerbread crumbs; served with the strained sauce thickened with beurre manié.

— **au bleu** Poached live in salted water with vinegar; served with boiled potatoes, melted butter, and fresh grated horseradish.

— *Chambord* Whole skinned fish studded with truffles and stuffed with fish mousseline and roe; braised in red wine and fish stock and served on a bed of rice; garnished with fish quenelles, fried roe, truffles, and fluted mushrooms.

— *en matelote* Braised in red wine with mushroom caps and pearl onions; served in the braising liquid thickened with beurre manié; garnished with croutons.

Coquilles Saint-Jacques Scallops.

— *en brochette* Poached scallops dipped in egg and crumbs and skewered (alternating with bacon slices); broiled and served with *sauce Colbert.*

— *frites* Dipped in egg and bread crumbs and deep-fried; served with tartare sauce.

— *au gratin* Braised in white wine and mushroom essence and placed in scallop shell; coated with *sauce Mornay* and Gruyère cheese and browned under the broiler.

— *Mornay* Same as "au gratin."

— *à la parisienne* Braised in white wine with mushroom essence and placed in scallop shell; coated with *sauce vin blanc* and garnished with mushrooms and truffles; bordered with duchess potatoes and browned in the oven.

— *à la Provençale* Braised in white wine and garlic; served in scallop shell.

Cotriade See Part II.

Crabe Crab.

— *en bouillon* Boiled; served with a sauce composed of chopped tomatoes, garlic, onions, crab shells, and fish stock; strained and seasoned with saffron and pepper.

— *à la diable* Stuffed with crab meat bound with béchamel sauce and seasoned with onions, red pepper, mustard powder, and Worcestershire sauce; breaded and baked au gratin.

— *farci au gratin* Shell stuffed with cooked crab meat bound with *sauce Mornay*; topped with more sauce and Gruyère cheese and baked au gratin.

— *froid* Poached in court bouillon and chilled; accompanied with various cold sauces.

Crevettes Shrimp.

— *à la créole* Sautéed in butter and served on rice bed; coated with *sauce créole.*

— *au cari* Sautéed and tossed with *sauce au cari*; served on rice bed.

— *frites* Dipped in egg and crumbs and deep-fried; served with tartare sauce.

— *nature* Poached in salt water; served chilled with lemon and various cold sauces.

Écrevisses Crayfish.

— *à la bordelaise* Sautéed in butter; flamed with brandy and simmered in white wine; served in the poaching liquid thickened with egg yolks and butter.

— *en coquille cardinal* Served in scallop shell bordered with duchess potatoes; topped with *sauce cardinal* and garnished with truffles.

—, *Mousse d'* See Part II, *Mousse d'Écrevisses.*

— *à la nage* Poached in seasoned stock; served cold in stock.

— *à la Nantua* Poached in seasoned stock; served in *sauce Nantua.*

— *soufflées piémontaises* Crayfish purée, white truffles, egg yolks, and Gruyère cheese combined with béchamel sauce; lightened with beaten egg whites and baked in hot oven; served immediately.

Églefin See *Aigrefin*, this section.

Éperlans Smelts.

— *à l'anglaise* Dipped in egg and bread crumbs and fried in butter; served with various sauces.

— *Bercy* Braised in white wine, butter, shallots, and lemon; served with the reduced braising liquid.

— *grillés* Dredged in flour and butter and grilled; with lemon and tartare sauce.

— *mousseline* Purée of smelt bound with cream; lightened with whipped cream and poached in stock.

Escargots Snails. Escargots must be cleaned thoroughly, parcooked, and served piping hot.

— *à la bourguignonne* Snail shell filled with snail and *beurre d'escargot*; cooked in the oven and served piping hot.

— *à la chablaisienne* Baked in shell and served with white wine reduced with meat glaze and *beurre d'escargot*.

— *à la dijonnaise* Cooked in shell; served in sauce composed of white wine, shallots, marrow, truffles, and seasonings.

— *à la mode de l'abbaye* Shelled and sautéed in butter with garlic and chopped onions; simmered in cream and finished with egg yolks and butter.

— *Villebernier* Shelled; simmered in red wine, vinegar, shallots, and red pepper; served with the reduced cooking liquid thickened with butter.

Esturgeon Sturgeon.

— *à la brimont* Braised in white wine and butter with aromatic vegetables and potatoes; when nearly cooked it is coated with bread crumbs and browned.

Grenouilles, cuisses de Frogs' legs.

—, *à la béchamel* Poached in white wine and butter; served in béchamel sauce enriched with butter and cream.

—, *au gratin* Poached; coated with *sauce Mornay* and placed in scallop shell; sprinkled with Gruyère cheese and bread crumbs and baked au gratin.

—, *à la poulette* Poached in white wine with mushroom essence; coated with *sauce poulette*.

Harengs Herring.

— *bouillis* Boiled in salt water and vinegar and served with melted butter; accompanied with boiled potatoes.

— *à la diable* Coated with hot mustard and bread crumbs; baked. Served with *sauce ravigote*.

— *farcis* Stuffed with fish forcemeat and cooked *en papillote*.

— *frits* Dipped in egg or mustard and coated with bread crumbs; fried and served with various cold sauces.

— *grillés* Brushed with oil and grilled; served with mustard sauce.

— *marinés* Smoked herring marinated in oil with aromatic herbs and vegetables.

— *à la meunière* Dredged in seasoned flour and fried in butter; seasoned with fresh chopped parsley and lemon.

— *salés* Salted herring.

Homard Lobster.

— *à l'américaine* See Part II.

— *à la cardinal* Cooked diced lobster meat bound with *sauce cardinal* and replaced in lobster shell; topped with grated cheese and baked au gratin.

— *à la hongroise* Raw lobster meat sautéed in butter with onions and paprika; flamed with brandy and thickened with cream and egg yolks; served over toasted croutons.

— *à la nage* Boiled in court bouillon; served in hot stock with various sauces.

— *à la Newburg* Boiled lobster chunks sautéed in butter; flamed with brandy and sherry; thickened with cream and egg yolks and served on toasted croutons.

— *à la thermidor* Cooked diced meat seasoned with mustard and bound with *sauce Bercy* mixed with *sauce Mornay*; replaced in shell and sprinkled with grated cheese; baked au gratin.

Huîtres Oysters.

— *à l'américaine* 1) Poached and placed in half shells; sprinkled with buttered bread crumbs and browned in the oven. 2) Poached and placed in half shells; coated with *sauce à l'américaine* and browned in the oven.

—, *barquettes d', à la Nantua* Poached and placed in half shells; garnished with crayfish tails; coated with *sauce Nantua* and browned in the oven.

—, *beignets d'* Dipped in batter and deep-fried; served with lemon and various cold sauces.

— *en brochette à la Villeroi* Poached and skewered; dipped in *sauce Villeroi* and bread crumbs; deep-fried.

— *à la florentine* Poached; placed in half shells over cooked spinach and coated with *sauce Mornay* and grated cheese; baked au gratin and garnished with truffles.

— *frites* Poached; dipped in egg and crumbs and deep-fried; served with various cold sauces.

- *Colbert* Prepared as for *huîtres frites* and served with maître d'hotel butter.

— *à la Mornay* Poached; placed in the half shell and coated with *sauce Mornay* and grated cheese; baked au gratin.

— *à la Rothschild* See Part II, *Rothschild, huîtres à la.*

Maquereaux Mackerel.

— *au beurre noir* Fried in butter and sprinkled with grated Parmesan; drizzled with browned butter mixed with capers.

— *au court-bouillon* Poached in court bouillon and arranged on *serviette*; served with choice of sauce.

— *frits* Marinated in oil and seasonings; dredged in flour and deep-fried; served with tomato sauce.

— *grillés* Seasoned, brushed with oil, and grilled; served with melted butter, tartare sauce, or *sauce ravigote.*

— *au vin blanc* Poached in white wine and fish stock; coated with *sauce vin blanc.*

Marmite Dieppoise See Part II.

Matelote Fish stew.

— *à la canotière* A variety of fish stewed in white wine and brandy; garnished with mushroom caps, pearl onions, and crayfish tails; served in the cooking liquid thickened with beurre manié.

— *marinière* A variety of freshwater fish stewed in white wine with mushrooms, pearl onions, and crayfish tails; served in the cooking liquid combined with fish *velouté.*

— *à la normande* Assorted seafood braised in cider and Calvados; fish *velouté* added and enriched with cream; garnished with mushrooms and croutons.

Merlan Whiting.

— *à l'anglaise* Dipped in egg and bread crumbs and deep-fried.

— *à la bonne-femme* Braised in white wine with mushrooms and shallots; served in the reduced braising liquid blended with fish *velouté*.

— *à l'espagnole* Dipped in egg and bread crumbs and deep-fried; served with tomato sauce.

— *frit en lorgnette* Rolled fillets skewered and dipped in egg and bread crumbs; deep-fried.

— *au vin blanc* Poached in white wine and coated with *sauce vin blanc*.

Morue Cod.

— *fraiche* See *Cabillaud*, this section.

— *à la languedocienne* See Part II.

— *à la provençale* See Part II.

— *salée* Salt cod; also referred to simply as "morue."

— *salée à la créole* Poached and flaked; arranged in a baking dish with chopped tomatoes, garlic, onions, and lemon; sprinkled with *beurre noir*.

— *salée frite* Soaked in milk; dredged in seasoned flour and deep-fried; served with lemon.

— *salée à l'indienne* Poached and coated with *sauce au cari*.

— *salée à la provençale* Poached and flaked; arranged in a baking dish with olive oil, chopped tomatoes, garlic, onions, black olives, capers, and parsley.

Mouclade See Part II.

Moules Mussels.

— *à la bourguignonne* Boiled and tossed with *sauce bourguignonne*.

—, *brochette de* Shelled and skewered with bacon pieces and tomatoes; broiled.

— *à la crème* Poached in white wine and lemon; served in the reduced cooking liquid mixed with béchamel sauce and cream.

— *frites* Marinated in oil, lemon, and seasonings; dipped in batter and deep-fried.

— *à la marinière* See Part II, *Marinière, moules*.

— *à la poulette* Poached in seasoned white wine; arranged in baking dish and coated with the cooking liquid combined with *sauce poulette*; browned in the oven.

Perche Perch.

— *à la meunière* Lightly floured and fried in butter; sprinkled with parsley, lemon juice, and brown butter.

Raie Skate.

— *au beurre noir* See Part II.

— *Sauce aux câpres* Poached and coated with *sauce aux câpres*.

Revesset See Part II.

Rougets Red mullet.

— *à la bordelaise* Dredged in seasoned flour and fried in butter; coated with *sauce bordelaise*.

— *Danicheff* Poached in fish stock flavored with truffle essence; coated with the reduced poaching liquid thickened with butter.

— *à la niçoise* Brushed with oil and grilled; topped with sautéed tomatoes, black olives, and garlic; garnished with anchovy fillets.

— *en papillote* Seared in butter and wrapped in foil or parchment with mushrooms, shallots, lemon juice, and white wine; baked.

Sardines Sardines.

— *à l'antiboise* Dipped in egg and bread crumbs and deep-fried; served with chopped tomatoes sautéed with onions and garlic.

— *à la basquaise* Dipped in egg and bread crumbs and deep-fried; served with béarnaise sauce and capers.

— *aux épinards à la provençale* Dipped in egg and bread crumbs and deep-fried; served on a bed of braised spinach and coated with garlic butter.

— *frites* 1) Dipped in egg and bread crumbs and deep-fried. 2) Dredged in flour and deep-fried. 3) Dipped in batter and deep-fried; served with assorted sauces.

— *gratinées* Baked *en casserole* with sautéed eggplant and grated Parmesan cheese; covered with tomato sauce.

— *grillées* Brushed with oil and grilled; served with *sauce Bercy* or garlic butter.

Saumon Salmon.

— *braisé* Whole fish braised in fish fumet; served with various sauces and garnishes.

—, *coquilles de* Cooked and/or served in a scallop shell.

-, *aux crevettes* Poached salmon chunks and shrimp covered with *sauce Mornay* and baked.

-, *à la Victoria* Cut in chunks and placed in baking dish with mushrooms and truffles; coated with *sauce Nantua* and Parmesan cheese and baked.

—, *côtelettes de* Salmon cutlets.

-, *aux champignons à la crème* Dredged in flour and seared; baked with mushrooms and coated with fish *velouté* flavored with Madeira wine and enriched with cream and butter.

-, *à la Nantua* Poached and chilled; coated with *sauce chaud-froid* and decorated with crayfish tails, truffles, and crayfish quenelles.

-, *aux truffes* Braised with truffles; coated with the reduced poaching liquid mixed with demi-glace sauce; garnished with truffles.

— *en croûte à la cardinal* Fillet spread with fish mousse and

baked in puff pastry; served with *sauce cardinal.*

—, *darne de* Salmon steaks.

-, *bouillie* Cooked in fish fumet and served with *sauce beurre blanc.*

-, *grillée au beurre d'escargot* Brushed with oil and grilled; served with *beurre d'escargot.*

-, *pochée au vin blanc* Poached in fish fumet with white wine; coated with *sauce vin blanc* mixed with the reduced poaching liquid.

—, *escalopes de* Thin slices of salmon.

— *froid en mayonnaise* Raw marinated escalopes arranged on shredded lettuce and topped with mayonnaise sauce; garnished with anchovy fillets, capers, and black olives; served cold.

— *mariné* Raw marinated escalopes served with various cold sauces.

—, *pâté chaud de* Thin slices folded into pike forcemeat (see *Brochet, Farce de;* this section) and baked *en croûte.*

— *pôché froid* Poached in fish fumet and cooled in the liquid; served cold with choice of sauce and garnishes.

Sole Sole.

— *à l'amiral* Poached in white wine and fish fumet; garnished with crayfish tails, fried oysters, mussels *à la Villeroi,* and sliced truffles; coated with the reduced poaching liquid enriched with crayfish butter.

— *Bercy* Poached in white wine and fish stock; coated with the reduced poaching liquid enriched with generous amounts of butter; glazed under the broiler.

— *à la bretonne* Poached in stock and garnished with mushroom

Sole à la bretonne (cont.)
caps and *fleurons*; coated with
sauce bretonne.

— *cardinal* Fillets stuffed with fish
mousse and lobster meat and
poached in court bouillon; garnished with lobster coral and
sliced lobster meat; coated with
sauce cardinal.

— *dorée* Dredged in seasoned flour
and fried in butter; garnished with
lemon slices and chopped parsley.

—, *filets de* Sole Fillets.

-, *à l'armoricaine* Poached in
white wine; garnished with
sliced lobster meat and poached
oysters; coated with *sauce à
l'américaine.*

-, *aux champignons* Poached in
white wine and fish fumet and
garnished with mushroom
caps; coated with the reduced
poaching liquid thickened with
cream and butter.

-, *Chivry* Rolled and poached in
fish fumet; served with fried
croutons and coated with *sauce
Chivry.*

-, *Cubat* Poached in stock; coated
with duxelles and garnished
with sliced truffles; coated with
sauce Mornay and browned in
the oven.

-, *grillés* Brushed with oil and
grilled; served with lemon, parsley, and maître d'hôtel butter.

-, *Marguery* See Part II, *Marguery,
Filets de Sole.*

-, *Pompadour* See Part II, *Pompadour, Filets de Sole.*

-, *Sarah Bernhardt* See Part II,
Sarah Bernhardt, Filets de Sole.

— *frite* Dipped in egg and bread
crumbs and deep-fried; served
with tartare sauce or *sauce remoulade* and lemon wedges.

— *marinette* See Part II, *Marinette,
Sole.*

— *meunière* Lightly floured and
fried in butter; sprinkled with
chopped parsley, lemon juice, and
beurre noisette.

— *à la Nantua* Poached in stock
and garnished with crayfish tails
and sliced truffles; coated with
sauce Nantua.

— *à la niçoise* Brushed with oil and
grilled; topped with chopped tomatoes sautéed in oil with garlic,
black olives, and anchovy butter.

— *à la normande* Poached in stock
and garnished with shrimp, oysters, mussels, mushroom caps,
crayfish tails, and fried gudgeon
(see *Goujon,* Part II); coated with
sauce normande.

—, *paupiettes de* Rolled fillets, usually stuffed.

-, *à l'ancienne* Stuffed with fish
forcemeat mixed with duxelles;
dipped in egg and bread crumbs
and deep-fried; garnished with
shrimp, truffles, and mushrooms.

-, *Mont-Bry* Stuffed with whiting
forcemeat and poached; garnished with tomatoes and saffron rice; coated with the reduced poaching liquid thickened with cream.

— *à la Saint-Germain* Coated
with bread crumbs and fried in
butter; garnished with noisette
potatoes and coated with béarnaise sauce.

— *Véron* Brushed with butter and
dipped in bread crumbs; fried in
butter and coated with *sauce
Véron.*

— *Villeroi* Stuffed and rolled;
dipped in *sauce Villeroi* and bread
crumbs; deep-fried and served
with tomato sauce.

Thon Tuna.

— *en daube* Studded with anchovy fillets and braised in red

wine with tomatoes, garlic, and seasonings; coated with the reduced braising liquid.

— *grillé* Steak marinated in seasoned oil and grilled; served with anchovy butter.

— *à la provençale* Marinated in oil, garlic, onion, white wine, and stock; braised in the marinade and coated with the reduced liquid; garnished with capers and parsley.

Truite Trout.

— *aux amandes* See Part II.

— *au bleu* See Part II.

— *au court-bouillon* Poached in court bouillon with vinegar added; served with boiled potatoes and melted butter.

— *frite* Dipped in egg and bread crumbs and deep-fried; served with lemon wedges and tartare sauce.

— *meunière* Dredged in seasoned flour and fried in butter; sprinkled with chopped parsley, lemon juice, and *beurre noisette*.

— *saumonée* Salmon trout.

- *Beauharnais* Stuffed with whiting forcemeat and braised in white wine and fish stock; garnished with potatoes *parisienne* and artichoke bottoms filled with béarnaise sauce; drizzled with the reduced braising liquid.

- *Georges Sand* Poached in stock and white wine and garnished with sliced truffles, fish quenelles, and shrimp; coated with *sauce aux crevettes*.

Turbot Turbot.

— *bouilli* Cooked in court bouillon to which milk has been added; served with choice of sauces and garnishes.

— *Cambacérès* Braised in white wine and fish fumet seasoned with truffle essence; garnished

with fried mussels, mushroom caps, and crayfish tails; coated with the reduced braising liquid mixed with *sauce velouté*.

— *Dugléré* Poached in stock with tomatoes, onions, shallots, and parsley; topped with the reduced poaching liquid thickened with butter.

— *grillé* Brushed with butter and grilled; served with maître d'hotel butter.

— *Saint-Malo* Brushed with oil and grilled; served with noisette potatoes and *sauce Saint-Malo*.

— *au vin blanc* Braised in white wine and fish stock; coated with *sauce vin blanc*.

VOLAILLE — POULTRY

Canard Duck.

— *braisé* Browned in bacon fat and butter; simmered in white wine and chicken stock; with various garnishes.

- *à l'alsacienne* Garnished with braised sauerkraut and sliced Strasbourg sausage.

- *à la chipolata* Garnished with chestnuts, pearl onions, and *chipolata* sausages.

- *à l'orange* Braised in demi-glace sauce flavored with orange and lemon; coated with the strained sauce and garnished with orange sections.

— *rôti* Seasoned, trussed, and roasted in the oven or over a hot fire; with various garnishes.

— *sauvage* Wild duck.

- *à la bigarade* Prepared as for *caneton à la bigarade*.

- *braisé* Braised in stock with pork fat, juniper berries, peppercorns, and aromatic vegetables; served with *sauce aux champignons*.

- *à la chasseur* Seasoned and roasted; served with *sauce Chasseur*.
- *à l'orange* Prepared as for *canard braisé à l'orange*.
- *au Porto* Prepared as for *caneton rouennaise au Porto*.
- *à la presse* Prepared as for *caneton rouennaise à la presse*.

Caneton Duckling.

— *d'Albufera* Braised in butter and Madeira wine with ham and onions; garnished with sliced ham and fluted mushrooms and coated with the reduced braising liquid combined with *sauce financière*.

—, *ballotines de* Boned minced meat combined with pork fat, ground veal, egg yolks, panade, and chunks of foie gras, truffles, and duck breast; wrapped in duck skin in the shape of a ball and poached in stock; served with the reduced poaching liquid and appropriate garnish.

— *à la bigarade* Roasted breast coated with *sauce bigarade* and garnished with orange slices.

— *braisé* Prepared as for Canard Braisé.

— *nantais* A variety of duckling characterized by its small, plump, mildly flavored flesh.

- *aux navets* Braised in demi-glace sauce and garnished with glazed turnips and onions; coated with the thickened braising sauce.

— *à la rouennaise* A plump, succulent breed of duck slaughtered by smothering, thereby retaining its blood and imparting a much prized and unique flavor; always roasted rare.

- *aux cerises* Roasted with morello cherries; garnished with cherries and coated with pan juices deglazed with veal stock

and enriched with butter.

- *au chambertin* Garnished with mushroom caps and truffles; coated with the pan juices deglazed with *sauce chambertin*.
- *au champagne* Served with the pan juices deglazed with champagne and combined with demi-glace sauce.
- *au Porto* Coated with the pan juices deglazed with Port and demi-glace sauce made with duck stock.
- *à la presse* The breast of a whole roasted duck is removed (this presentation is often done tableside in front of the guests) and placed in a warm dish; the remaining carcass (save the legs) is then pressed in a special duck press to remove juices; the breasts are coated with the hot juices, which are flavored with cognac and thickened with butter.

Dinde Turkey.

Dindonneau Young turkey.

— *à l'Anglaise* Trussed and poached in chicken stock; garnished with sliced tongue and boiled vegetables.

— *braisée* Trussed; braised in chicken stock and drizzled with the reduced braising liquid; garnished appropriately.

— *à la catalane* Cut into sections and browned in butter; braised in demi-glace sauce with white wine and tomato *concassée*; served in the sauce and garnished with mushrooms, chestnuts, onions, and sausages.

— *à la chipolata* Braised as for *à la catalane*; serve in sauce and garnish with pearl onions, chestnuts, carrots, pork chunks, and *chipolata* sausages.

— *en daube à la bourgeoise* Young

hen browned in butter and braised in stock with baby carrots, onions, and pork fat; drizzled with the reduced braising liquid.

— *farcie aux marrons* Stuffed with sausage meat, chestnuts, and seasonings; roasted and drizzled with pan juices.

— *Michael, suprêmes de* Roasted breast; roasting pan deglazed with white wine, brandy, pineapple juice, and demi-glace sauce; sliced breast garnished with risotto, fried pineapple chunks (seasoned with curry powder), chopped tomatoes, and sweet potatoes.

— *rôtie* Trussed and seasoned, barded with bacon, and roasted; served with pan juices and appropriate garnish.

— *truffée* Small turkey stuffed with truffles for one or two days as to impart flavor; discard truffles; stuffed with foie gras, pork fat, and truffles; roasted and served with *sauce périgourdine* mixed with pan juices.

Oie Goose.

— *à l'alsacienne* Stuffed with sausage meat; trussed and browned in butter; roasted with braised sauerkraut and bacon.

— *à la bourguignonne* Browned in butter and bacon fat; cooked in demi-glace sauce mixed with red wine and the pan juices; served in sauce with mushrooms and onions.

— *braisée* Browned in butter and simmered in stock; served with pan juices and choice of garnish.

—, *civet d'* Goose meat and giblets stewed in red wine with cognac, stock, and the animal's blood; garnished with small onions, carrots, mushrooms, chopped tomatoes, and bacon.

—, *confit d'* Sections marinated in salt and cooked very slowly in goose fat; preserved in cooking fat.

— *en daube capitole* Stuffed with sausage meat, foie gras, and truffles; braised in stock and garnished with olives, mushrooms, and sliced sausage; served with the reduced braising liquid.

— *farcis, cous d'* Boned necks stuffed with sausage meat, foie gras, truffles, and chopped goose meat; cooked slowly in goose fat and stored in stoneware pot covered with fat; served hot or cold.

— *à la flamande* Braised; garnished with braised cabbage and root vegetables; drizzled with the reduced braising liquid.

— *aux marrons* Stuffed with sausage meat and chestnuts; served with the reduced braising liquid.

Oisen au raifort Braised gosling; served with *sauce raifort* and buttered noodles.

Coq French word for cock; however, the name may also simply refer to chicken.

— *au Vin* See Part II.

- *à la bourguignonne* Cut into sections and browned in butter; simmered in red Burgundy wine with chicken stock and brandy; garnished with mushrooms and onions.

Fricassée Chicken stew.

— *de poulet à l'ancienne* Cut into sections and browned in butter; stewed in *sauce velouté* with mushrooms, onions, and seasonings; finished with cream and egg yolks; served in sauce.

Poularde Chicken.

— *à l'aurore* Poached in chicken stock and coated with *sauce aurore* flavored with the reduced poaching liquid.

— *à la Chantilly* Stuffed with rice and foie gras and steamed; gar-

Poularde à la Chantilly (cont.)
nished with sliced truffles and foie gras; served with *sauce velouté* flavored with the reduced pan juices.

— *demi-deuil* Poached in stock and coated with suprême sauce; garnished with pastry cases filled with a *salpicon* of lamb's sweetbreads, mushrooms, and truffles.

— *à l'estragon* Poached in stock with fresh tarragon; garnished with tarragon leaves and served with the thickened, reduced poaching liquid.

— *à la Godard* Braised in white wine and chicken stock and garnished with truffled chicken quenelles, cockscombs and kidneys, mushroom caps, and truffles; coated with *sauce Godard*.

— *à la niçoise* Whole bird browned in oil and braised in white wine, tomato sauce, and garlic; garnished with black olives, potatoes, summer squash, and tomatoes.

— *à la périgourdine* Stuffed with truffles and foie gras and roasted; served with the pan juices deglazed with Madeira wine.

— *princesse* Poached in chicken stock; garnished with pastry cases filled with asparagus tips and truffles sautéed in butter; coated with *sauce allemande*.

Poule Hen.

— *au pot* Stuffed and poached in stock; several variations.

- *à la béarnaise* Stuffed with sausage meat, chopped Bayonne ham, chicken livers, and seasonings; poached in *petite marmite* stock with vegetables; also called *poulet à la ficelle*.

Poulet Chicken.

— *Belle-Hèléne* See Part II, *Belle-Hèléne, Poulet*.

— *farci à l'ariégeoise* Stuffed with

ham, chicken livers, and bread moistened with the bird's blood; poached in beef stock and garnished with boiled potatoes and stuffed cabbage; with tomato sauce.

— *à la ficelle* See *Poule au pot à la béarnaise*, this section.

— *grillé à la diable* Par-roasted; glazed with a mustard-cayenne pepper mixture and coated with bread crumbs; broiled and garnished with gherkins; served with *sauce diable*.

— *à la reine* Stuffed with chopped cooked chicken meat bound with *sauce velouté*; poached in chicken stock and garnished with pastry cases filled with chicken purée and truffles; served with *sauce allemande*.

— *rôti* Inside cavity brushed with seasoned butter; trussed and coated with the same butter; roasted, basting regularly; served with pan juices deglazed with chicken stock.

— *sauté* Chicken sautées are prepared with chicken sections or with boned chunks; typically, the garnishes are cooked in the same pan with the chicken at some point (depending on cooking time), and the sauce is an extention of the pan juices; served in the sauce.

- *Armagnac* Lightly sautéed with sliced truffles; deglazed with Armagnac and lemon juice and simmered in cream; finished with crayfish butter and served *en cocotte*.

- *à la biarrote* Sautéed in oil with garlic and deglazed with white wine; simmered in tomato sauce; garnished with sautéed cèpes, eggplant, potatoes, and onions.

- *à la bordelaise* Sautéed in butter with shallots, onions, and artichoke hearts; deglazed with chicken stock and served in sauce.
- *à la bretonne* Sautéed in butter with leeks, mushrooms, and onions; suprême sauce added and enriched with cream.
- *chasseur* Sautéed in butter with mushrooms and shallots and deglazed with white wine and brandy; simmered in demi-glace sauce flavored with tomato.
- *aux fines herbes* Sautéed in butter; deglazed with white wine and veal stock; demi-glace sauce added and enriched with butter mixed with parsley, chervil, tarragon, and chives.
- *aux morilles* Sautéed with morels and deglazed with brandy and beef stock; enriched with butter.
- *à la niçoise* Sautéed in oil with garlic and deglazed with white wine and tomato sauce; artichoke hearts, black olives, and boiled potatoes served separately; seasoned with tarragon.
- *à la Périgord* Sautéed with black truffles and tossed with *sauce périgourdine*.
- *à la provençale* Sautéed in oil with onions, tomatoes, and garlic; moistened with white wine and veal stock and garnished with black olives and anchovy fillets.
- *vallée d'Auge* Sautéed in butter and oil with sliced apples; deglazed with cider and thickened with cream.

Poussin A very small young chicken.
- *frit* Cut in sections; dredged in flour, dipped in egg and bread crumbs; fried.

- *à la viennoise* Sections dipped in egg and crumbs and pan-fried; garnish with fried parsley and lemon .

Suprêmes de volaille Boneless, skinless chicken breast to which the wing is (usually) attatched. *Suprêmes* are often stuffed by making an incision in the breast and filled with various ingredients.
- *carême* Stuffed with a *salpicon* of mushrooms, truffles, and cockscomb and pan-fried; garnished with croutons, chicken dumplings, and truffles; served with tomato-flavored demi-glace sauce.
- *Jean-Marie* Stuffed with giblets, salt pork, and bread crumbs; wrapped in cabbage leaves and poached in stock; garnished with fresh vegetables.
- *Montpensier* Dipped in egg and bread crumbs and pan-fried; garnished with asparagus tips and truffle slices; served with *beurre noisette*.
- *Verdi* Sautéed; served in a pastry case filled with macaroni and foie gras; garnished with truffles and served with *sauce Madeira*.

Volaille, poitrine de Chicken breast.
—, *au vinaigre* Browned in garlic-butter and poached in tomato sauce with chicken stock and vinegar; served in the reduced poaching liquid enriched with butter.

VIANDE — MEAT

BŒUF — BEEF

Aloyau Sirloin.
- *braisé* Larded and marinated; seared in butter and braised in stock.

— *à la bourgeoise* Seasoned and roasted; garnished with pearl onion and carrots sautéed with chopped bacon; with demi-glace sauce.

— *à la nivernaise* Braised (see *Aloyau braisé*) and garnished as for *Aloyau à la bourgeoise.*

Bifteck Beefsteak; from fillet.

— *à l'américaine* Minced raw filet of beef shaped in a pattie and garnished with raw egg yolks, chopped onions, and capers.

— *à cheval* Pan-fried in butter; garnished with fried egg and pan juices.

— *haché* Ground beef.

— *marchand de vin* Pan-fried in butter; served with *sauce Marchand de vin.*

— *à la tartare* See Part II, *Tartare, Bifteck à la.*

Bœuf Beef.

— *à la bourguignonne* See Part II. *Bourguignonne, Boeuf à la.*

— *bouilli* Boiled Beef; simmered in water with aromatic herbs and vegetables until tender.

- *à la hongroise* Diced boiled meat sautéed in butter with chopped onions and paprika; tossed with béchamel sauce.

- *à la provençale* Diced boiled beef sautéed in butter with onions and garlic; tossed in tomato sauce.

- *sauce raifort* Sliced boiled beef served with *sauce Raifort.*

— *au gros sel* Boiled beef served with boiled vegetables and served with coarse sea salt.

— *à la mode* See Part II, *Mode, Boeuf à la.*

— *salé* Brisket soaked in brine; simmered in water with cabbage and root vegetables.

Carbonnade See Part II.

Chateaubriand See Part II.

Contre-filet High quality cut from the sirloin; also called *faux filet.*

— *braisé à la bourgeoise* Larded and seasoned; braised with vegetables and calf's feet.

Entrecôte Rib steak.

— *à la béarnaise* Grilled; garnished with château potatoes and coated with béarnaise sauce.

— *à la bordelaise* Grilled; garnished with poached marrow and coated with *sauce bordelaise.*

— *châtelaine* Grilled; garnished with artichokes filled with onion purée, broiled chestnuts, and noisette potatoes; with *sauce Madeira.*

— *à la lyonnaise* Pan-fried with onions; deglazed with vinegar and white wine and combined with demi-glace sauce.

— *maître d'hôtel* Grilled; coated with *sauce vin rouge.*

— *à la marchand de vin* Grilled; accompanied with *beurre vin rouge.*

— *à la minute* Pounded thin and sautéed quickly in butter; topped with pan juices, lemon juice, and watercress.

— *à la niçoise* Sautéed in oil with chopped tomatoes, new potatoes, black olives, and garlic; deglazed with white wine and demi-glace sauce.

Faux Filet See *Contre-filet.*

Filet de Bœuf Tenderloin.

— *Du Barry* Grilled; garnished with cauliflower florets coated with *sauce Mornay* which have been browned under the broiler.

— *gouffé* Roasted; garnished with risotto, sliced truffles, mushroom caps, and veal quenelles; with *sauce Madeira.*

— *à la périgourdine* -Studded with slivered truffles and braised in *sauce Madeira*; garnished with sliced truffles, foie gras, and croutons.

— *Richelieu* Roasted; garnished with mushroom caps, château potatoes, and stuffed tomatoes; with demi-glace sauce.

— *Stroganoff* Julienne strips sautéed in butter with tomato sauce and simmered in *sauce espagnole*; enriched with sour cream and served in sauce.

— *à la toscane* Grilled and garnished with chopped tomatoes, Brussels sprouts, and fried croutons; with tomato-flavored demi-glace sauce.

Filet mignon See Part II.

Pièce de bœuf Top of the rump; also called *pointe de culotte*.

— *à la bourguignonne* Larded and marinated in brandy and spices; braised in red wine and stock and garnished with diced bacon, pearl onions, and mushroom caps.

— *à la mode* Braised in red wine with pearl onions, carrots, and calf's feet; coated with the reduced braising liquid and garnished with calf's feet and vegetables.

Pointe de culotte See *Pièce de bœuf*.

Tournedos Small thick tenderloin steaks.

— *Aïda* Pan-fried, topped with cooked shrimp, and coated with béchamel sauce; browned under the broiler and served with *sauce Madeira*.

— *Baltimore* Grilled and served on fried croutons and garnished with creamed corn, sliced tomato, and green pepper rings; with *sauce Châteaubriand*.

— *à la béarnaise* Grilled and coated with béarnaise sauce; served with château potatoes.

— *à la bordelaise* Grilled; topped with poached marrow and coated with *sauce bordelaise*.

— *Choron* Sautéed in butter and served on fried croutons; coated with *sauce Choron* and garnished with artichoke bottoms and asparagus tips.

— *Deslignac* Grilled; coated with *sauce Choron* and garnished with château potatoes.

— *Favorite* Grilled and topped with sliced foie gras, truffle, and asparagus tips.

— *Foyot* Grilled; coated with *sauce Foyot* and garnished with *pommes de terre pailles*.

— *Maréchale* Grilled; topped with sliced truffles and asparagus tips; sprinkled with *glace de viande*.

— *Marguery* See Part II. *Marguery, tournedos.*

— *Masséna* See Part II, *Masséna, tournedos.*

— *Mirabeau* Grilled; garnished with tarragon sprigs, black olives wrapped with anchovy fillets, and anchovy butter.

— *Orlov* See Part II. *Orlov, tornedos.*

— *à la périgourdine* Pan-fried; topped with sautéed truffle slices and coated with *sauce Madeira*.

— *Pompadour* See Part II, *Pompadour, tournedos.*

— *Rossini* Rossini, tournedos.

— *à la tourangelle* Grilled; served with flageolots and French beans coated with béchamel sauce.

— *Wellington* Sautéed and topped with duxelles and foie gras; wrapped in puff pastry and baked; with *sauce périgourdine*.

MOUTON ET AGNEAU — MUTTON AND LAMB

Carré d'agneau Loin of lamb.

— *à la Clamart* Browned in butter and braised with peas.

— *Parmentier* Slow roasted with potatoes; served with the pan

Carré d'agneau Parmentier (cont.) juices deglazed with white wine and veal stock.

— **La Varenne** Pounded flat and dipped in eggs and bread crumbs; pan-fried and served with creamed mushrooms and *beurre noisette*.

Côtelettes d'agneau Lamb chops.

— **Argenteuil** Breaded and pan-fried in butter; garnished with asparagus tips.

— *à la bressane* Sautéed in butter; garnished with a *salpicon* of truffles, chicken livers, and mushrooms bound with demi-glace sauce.

— **Du Barry** Grilled and garnished with cauliflower florets coated with *sauce Mornay* and browned in the oven.

— *à la française* Parcooked; spread with chicken forcemeat and baked; garnished with pastry cases filled with truffles and lambs sweetbreads.

— *à la mexicaine* Pan-fried in butter; garnished with banana fritters and served with the pan juices deglazed with vinegar and orange-flavored demi-glace sauce.

— *en papillotes* Partially braised; coated with slivers of ham and duxelles and drizzled with braising liquid; wrapped in greased parchment and baked.

— **Périnette** Dipped in egg and coated with bread crumbs mixed with diced ham; pan-fried in butter and garnished with roasted red peppers, tomato fondue, and fried zucchini.

— *à la royale* Sautéed in butter and served on a tartlet filled with purée of goose liver; garnished with soufflé potatoes and served with *sauce Madeira*.

— *à la sarladaise* Grilled; served

with *pommes de terre à la sarladaise*; with *sauce Périgueux*.

— **Soubise** Grilled and coated with *sauce Soubise*.

Épaule d'agneau Lamb shoulder; preparation includes boning, rolling, and tying; roasted or braised.

— *à l'anglaise* Braised and garnished with root vegetables; served with *sauce aux câpres*.

— *braisée aux haricots* Studded with garlic cloves and braised in white wine, chopped tomatoes, and stock; served with white beans and the strained braising liquid.

— *à la gasconne* Stuffed with chopped ham and seasoned bread crumbs; braised in pot-au-feu stock with potatoes and vegetables.

— *de mouton à la catalane* Mutton shoulder braised in white wine and stock with ham, aromatic vegetables, and lots of garlic.

— *à la sauce menthe* Seasoned and roasted; served with *sauce menthe*.

Gigot d'agneau Leg of lamb.

— *à l'anglaise* Prepared as for *Épaule d'agneau à l'anglaise*.

— *persillé* Roasted (see *Gigot d'agneau rôti*); coated with a mixture of garlic, parsley, and bread crumbs and returned to the oven to brown; served with lemon and watercress.

— *rôti* Studded with garlic cloves and brushed with seasoned oil; roasted with aromatic vegetables and served with the pan drippings deglazed with beef stock.

Gigot de mouton à la bretonne Roasted leg of mutton (see *Gigot d'agneau rôti*); garnished with white beans and served with the pan juiced deglazed with stock.

Navarin printanier Lamb stew; chunks dredged in flour and browned; stewed in thickened stock with potatoes and spring vegetables.

Noisettes d'agneau Small, round lamb steaks.

— *Armenonville* Grilled and perched on Anna potato nests; garnished with a *salpicon* of morels, truffles, and cockscombs and kidneys bound with béchamel sauce; coated with demi-glace sauce.

— *Cussy* Sautéed and served on croutons; garnished with cock's kidneys, artichoke bottoms, and duxelles; with *sauce Madeira*.

— *à la Favorite* Sautéed and served on sliced foie gras; garnished with asparagus tips and sliced truffle; with demi-glace sauce.

— *Melba* Sautéed and served on croutons; garnished with cherry tomatoes, which are filled with a *salpicon* of mushrooms, chicken, and truffles and browned in the oven; served with *sauce Madeira*.

— *Montpensier* Sautéed and garnished with asparagus tips and truffle slivers; served with *sauce Madeira*.

— *Rivoli* Grilled and served on Anna potato nests; with *sauce Madeira* flavored with truffles.

— *Soubise* Sautéed and served on croutons; served with artichoke bottoms filled with onion purée and browned under the broiler; with *sauce Madeira*.

Poitrine d'agneau Lamb breast.

— *à la diable* Dipped in mustard mixed with cayenne pepper and coated with bread crumbs; grilled and served with *sauce diable*.

— *à la vert-pré* Sautéed; served with seasoned butter and accompanied with *pommes de terre pailles* and watercress.

Poitrine de mouton farcie à l'ariè-geoise Breast of mutton stuffed with chopped ham and seasoned bread crumbs; braised in white wine, tomato sauce, and stock; garnished with boiled potatoes and braised cabbage; drizzled with pan juices.

Sauté d'agneau Lamb sauté; shoulder, neck, and breast chunks are typically used in sautéed lamb dishes.

— *aux aubergines* Sautéed with garlic and eggplant slices; coated with the pan juices deglazed with white wine, tomato purée, and demi-glace sauce.

— *aux champignons* Sautéed in butter with garlic and mushrooms; deglazed with white wine, tomato purée, and demi-glace sauce; served in sauce.

— *à la minute* Sautéed in butter with lemon and parsley; deglazed with white wine and simmered in demi-glace sauce; served in sauce.

PORC — PORK

Carré de Porc Pork loin.

— *à l'alsacienne* Seasoned and roasted until nearly done; sauerkraut added to the roasting pan and finished cooking; garnished with Strasbourg sausage, boiled potatoes, and sauerkraut; drizzled with pan juices.

— *à la limousine* Roasted and garnished with braised red cabbage and chestnuts; drizzled with pan juices.

— *à la provençale* Infused with fresh sage; seasoned with garlic and herbs and brushed with olive oil; roasted and sprinkled with pan juices.

Choucroute garnie Shoulder and loin browned in goose fat with onions and sauerkraut; braised in

Choucroute garnie (cont.)
white wine and stock; garnished with boiled potatoes, sauerkraut, and sausage; accompanied with mustard.

Côtes de porc Pork chops.

— *à l'ardennaise* Sautéed in butter with chopped onions and bacon; deglazed with white wine and simmered in demi-glace sauce flavored with juniper berries; served in sauce.

— *à l'auvergnate* Braised with sautéed cabbage and onions in cream; sprinkled with grated Parmesan and bread crumbs and browned.

— *à la bayonnaise* Rubbed with seasoned oil, garlic, vinegar; browned in pork fat with potatoes and cèpes and finished baked in the oven.

— *braisées à la moutarde* Browned in fat and arranged in casserole; covered with sautéed onions and braised in stock; coated with braising liquid thickened with cream and flavored with mustard and lemon.

— *charcutières* Dipped in melted butter and bread crumbs and grilled; braised in *sauce Charcutière*; served with mashed potatoes.

— *à la gasconne* Marinated as for *côtes de porc à la bayonnaise*; browned in goose fat and baked with garlic in a covered dish; when nearly cooked, white wine and stock are added along with pitted olives; returned to oven to complete cooking.

— *sauce Robert* Grilled over low heat; served with mashed potatoes and *sauce Robert*.

— *à la Vosgienne* Braised in demi-glace sauce with white wine and mirabelle plums; served with the strained braising liquid.

Filet mignon de porc à l'autrichienne Braised in veal stock and sour cream with onions, carrots, and turnips; garnished with the vegetables and boiled potatoes and coated with the reduced braising liquid.

Médaillons de porc aux oignons et fromage Sautéed in butter and arranged in a baking dish; coated with sautéed onions and Gruyère cheese and browned under the broiler.

Noisettes de porc aux pruneaux Dredged in seasoned flour and browned in butter; braised in white wine and stock with prunes; garnished with prunes and coated with the braising liquid thickened with cream.

Ragoût de porc Chunks of shoulder and breast meat dredged in flour and browned; stewed in thickened stock with potatoes, onions, mushrooms, and root vegetables.

Rôti de porc boulangère Seasoned loin roasted with aromatic vegetables and herbs; garnished with boiled potatoes and coated with the strained pan drippings, which has been deglazed with stock.

Rôti de porc à la bourguignonne Loin marinated in red wine with aromatic vegetables, herbs, and garlic; roasted and served with boiled potatoes and the reduced pan juices thickened with butter.

VEAU — VEAL

Blanquette de veau à l'ancienne Veal chunks stewed in *sauce velouté* with onions and mushrooms; served in the sauce, which has been thickened with egg yolks and cream.

Côtes de veau Veal chops.

— *à l'ardennaise* Coated with a

mixture of crushed juniper berries, basil, and black pepper and browned in butter; coated with fried bread crumbs and braised in red wine and chicken stock; served with the reduced braising liquid.

— *aux champignons sauvages* Dredged in seasoned flour and sautéed in butter with wild mushrooms; coated with the pan juices deglazed with white wine and brandy and thickened with cream.

— *Chapelle Saint-Martin* Braised with aromatic vegetables in chicken stock; coated with the strained braising liquid thickened with butter and garnished with the vegetables.

— *à la Dreux* Studded with slivers of truffles and tongue and sautéed in butter; garnished with veal quenelles, truffles, cockscomb and kidneys, and pitted olives; coated with *sauce Madeira* mixed with the pan juices.

— *à la paysanne* Browned in butter and placed in a baking dish; topped with sliced turnips, onions, potatoes, and leeks; baked; drizzled with thickened veal stock.

— *vert-pré* Grilled and garnished with *pommes de terre pailles* and watercress; drizzled with seasoned butter.

Épaule de veau Shoulder of veal; the meat is boned (stuffing is optional), rolled, and tied before roasting or braising.

— *à la bourgeoise* Braised with onions, carrots, and celery; garnished with the vegetables and served with the reduced braising liquid.

— *farcie* Stuffed with sausage meat, garlic, and seasoned bread crumbs; braised in stock; drizzled with the reduced braising liquid.

Escalopes de veau Thin slices taken from the filet; usually flattened before sautéeing.

— *à la badoise* Sautéed in butter and garnished with buttered noodles and spinach cooked in cream.

— *Casimir* Seasoned with paprika and sautéed in butter; garnished with sautéed artichoke bottoms, truffles, and julienne of carrots; coated with the pan juices thickened with cream and seasoned with paprika.

— *cordon bleu* Layered with sliced ham and Gruyère cheese, and rolled; dipped in egg and crumbs and fried in butter.

— *à la crème* Sautéed in butter with mushrooms; deglazed with port and thickened with cream; seasoned with a pinch of cayenne pepper.

— *à la hongroise* Dredged in flour seasoned with paprika and browned in butter; simmered in white wine and finished with sour cream; served with buttered noodles tossed with paprika butter.

— *à la savoyarde* Dredged in seasoned flour and and sautéed in butter; deglazed with white wine and thickened with cream.

Fricadelles de veau panées Ground veal combined with bread crumbs, cream, and seasonings; formed into patties and coated with bread crumbs; fried in butter and sprinkled with pan juices and chopped parsley.

Fricandeau de veau braisé Bottom round larded with bacon and browned in butter; braised in veal stock with onions, carrots, garlic, and tomatoes; served with the reduced braising liquid.

Longe de veau Veal loin; typically braised or roasted.
— *à l'alsacienne* Roasted; served with braised sauerkraut and sliced ham; drizzled with the pan juices deglazed with veal stock.
— *à la dauphine* Roasted and coated with *sauce Madeira*; served with dauphine potatoes.
— *à la piémontaise* Braised; served with risotto with white truffles and sprinkled with the reduced braising liquid.
— *à la Renaissance* Braised; garnished with fresh cooked vegetables and potatoes; drizzled with the reduced braising liquid.
— *à la Romanoff* Braised; garnished with duxelles and sautéed fennel; served with reduced braising liquid.
Médaillons de veau à la chablisienne Dredged in flour and sautéed in butter; deglazed with Chablis and chicken stock and thickened with butter; coated with sauce and garnished with chopped sautéed tomatoes.
Paupiettes de veau Thin slices stuffed and rolled; typically braised.
— *Belle-Hélène* Stuffed with veal forcemeat and braised; garnished with sliced truffles and asparagus tips; with demi-glace sauce.
— *braisées à blanc* Stuffed with pork forcemeat and braised in white stock; drizzled with the reduced braising liquid.
— *braisées à brun* Stuffed with pork forcemeat and braised in white wine; coated with the reduced braising liquid combined with demi-glace sauce.
Poitrine de veau Breast of veal.
— *à l'allemande* Stuffed with pork forcemeat and braised in white stock; served with horseradish sauce.

— *à l'alsacienne* Stuffed with bread stuffing and braised in white stock with sauerkraut; garnished with sauerkraut and drizzled with the reduced braising liquid.
Sauté de veau Prepared with chunks of shoulder, neck, or breast meat.
— *chasseur* Sautéed in butter and simmered in brown stock, white wine, and tomato purée.
— *à l'indienne* Sautéed with chopped onions; simmered in *sauce velouté*, which has been seasoned with curry; served with rice.
— *Marengo* Sautéed with chopped onion and garlic; deglazed with white wine and simmered in demi-glace sauce and tomato purée; garnished with mushrooms and onions.
— *à la printanière* Sautéed; deglazed with white wine and simmered in demi-glace sauce with fresh garden vegetables.
— *au vin rouge* Sautéed with onions and garlic; deglazed with red wine and simmered in white stock with mushrooms; finished with *beurre manié*.
Selle de veau Orlov See Part II, *Orlov, Selle de veau.*
Tendrons de veau "Gristle"; cut of veal extending from the end of the rib to the breastbone.
— *à l'allemande* Braised with mushrooms in *sauce allemande*; garnished with rice.
— *à la bourgeoise* Braised in white wine and veal stock with onions, carrots, and bacon; served with the vegetables and reduced braising liquid.
— *à la jardinière* Braised in stock; garnished with French beans, kidney beans, carrots, and turnips; drizzled with the reduced braising liquid.

— *à la nivernaise* Braised in stock with turnips; served with the turnips and reduced braising liquid.

— *à la Villeroi* Braised in white stock and cooled; dipped in sauce Villeroi and bread crumbs and deep-fried; served with tomato sauce.

ABATS DE BOUCHERIE — VARIETY MEATS

Cervelle Brains.

— *de veau au beurre noir* Parcooked, dredged in flour, and sautéed; sprinkled with browned butter flavored with vinegar and capers.

— *de veau à la bourguignonne* Simmered with mushrooms in *sauce bourguignonne*; served over fried croutons.

— *de veau poulette* Simmered with mushrooms in *sauce poulette*.

Foie de veau Calf's liver.

— *aux fines herbes* Sliced, dredged in flour, and sautéed in butter; served with *sauce aux fines herbes*.

— *meunière* Slices dredged in flour and sautéed in butter; drizzled with lightly browned butter seasoned with lemon and parsley.

— *aux oignons et câpres* Slices dredged in flour and sautéed in butter with onions, capers, and garlic; served with pan juices deglazed with vinegar and thickened with butter.

— *piqué* Larded with pork fat and marinated in seasoned oil and vinegar; roasted and garnished with stuffed tomatoes.

— *sauté* Thinly sliced; dredged in flour and sautéed in butter with shallots; deglazed with white wine and stock; simmered in sauce and served over buttered noodles.

Gras-double Tripe; see also *Tripes*.

— *à la lyonnaise* Sliced; sautéed in butter with onions; drizzled with vinegar and parsley.

— *à la voironnaise* Simmered with onions in *sauce espagnole* and white wine; served in sauce.

Langue Tongue.

— *de bœuf à la bourgeoise* Braised in white wine, stock, and tomato sauce with sliced carrots, pearl onions, and bacon slices; served together in sauce.

— *de veau à l'italienne* Braised in white wine, stock, and tomato sauce; garnished with green olives.

Ris de veau Veal sweetbreads.

— *au beurre noir* Par-boiled; dredged in flour and sautéed in butter; drizzled with browned butter.

— *Melba* Par-boiled; dredged in flour and sautéed in butter; served in pastry case filled with duxelles and garnished with truffle slices.

— *panés* Slices dipped in egg and crumbs; fried in butter and served with braised endive.

— *poêlés* Par-boiled slices dredged in flour and sautéed in butter; served with choice of sauce.

— *Rossini* Braised and sliced; served with foie gras, sliced truffles, and *sauce Madeira*.

Rognons Kidneys.

— *d'agneau sautés Turbigo* Sautéed in butter; garnished with chipolata sausages and poached mushrooms; served with demiglace sauce flavored with tomato.

— *en casserole* Sautéed in butter and removed from pan; deglazed with white wine and thickened with butter and mustard; kidneys returned to pan and served in sauce.

— *de veau grillés* Seasoned and pierced with a skewer in order to keep its shape; grilled over low heat, basting frequently; served with seasoned butter.

— *de veau à la Montpensier* Slices sautéed in butter; pan deglazed with Madeira wine and concentrated beef stock; thickened with butter and seasoned with lemon and parsley; garnished with asparagus tips and sliced truffles.

Tripes Tripe; see also *Gras-double*.

— *à la créole* Par-boiled; sautéed with onions, green peppers, tomatoes, and garlic; served with rice.

— *aux fines herbes* Par-boiled; sautéed in butter with onions, shallots, and fine herbs.

— *à la mode de Caen* Par-cooked; arranged in a casserole with chopped onions, carrots, calf's feet, and seasonings.

— *à la moutarde* Par-boiled; dipped in mustard, egg, and bread crumbs and deep-fried; served with tomato sauce.

GIBIER — GAME

Alouettes Larks. See also *Mauviettes*.

— *en croûte* Boned, stuffed with veal forcemeat, truffles and foie gras; par-roasted; placed in hollowed out bread loaf and finished cooking in the oven; served with the pan juices deglazed with Madeira wine.

—, *pâté d'* Boned and stuffed as for *alouettes en croûte*; placed in dough-lined pan surrounded with veal forcemeat and baked; served chilled.

— *de père Philippe* Browned in butter; wrapped in bacon and placed in hollowed out baked potato and covered with remaining potato half; wrapped in greased paper and baked.

Becasses Woodcock.

— *de carême* Roasted rare; breast removed and coated with French mustard; pan deglazed with brandy and game stock; served with strained sauce.

—, *salmis de* Par-roasted and cut into sections; finished cooking in *sauce salmis* with mushrooms and truffles; served in sauce over fried croutons.

— *sautées à l'Armagnac* Cut into sections and browned in butter; removed from pan and deglazed with Armagnac and demi-glace sauce flavored with game stock; seasoned with cayenne pepper and the chopped intestines; sauce poured over meat.

— *truffées rôties* Stuffed with chicken forcemeat and truffles; wrapped in greased paper and roasted; served on croutons and drizzled with pan juices deglazed with brandy.

Cailles Quails.

— *grillées* Brushed with seasoned oil and slow grilled.

— *en casserole* Pan-fried in butter; deglazed with brandy and game stock; served in casserole with reduced pan juices.

— *Lucullus* Sautéed in butter; served on fried croutons and garnished with slices of foie gras and truffles; drizzled with the pan juices deglazed with Madeira wine.

— *à la normande* Par-roasted; served over sliced apples; drizzled with Calvados and wrapped in pastry; served with roasting juices deglazed with Calvados and thickened with cream.

— *à la turque* Trussed, seasoned, and roasted; served over rice pilaf and drizzled with pan juices deglazed with game stock.

Canard sauvage Wild duck.

— **au Chambertin** Roasted medium-done; coated with *sauce Chambertin* and garnished with mushrooms and truffles.

— **rôti** Seasoned and roasted in hot oven until medium-rare done.

— **rôti à la bigarade** Roasted; coated with *sauce bigarade* and garnished with orange and lemon slices.

Chevreuil Roebuck.

—, **civet de** Cut in pieces (shoulder, neck, breast, and/or loin) and sautéed in butter with mushrooms, onions, and bacon; simmered in red wine and stock and thickened with hare's blood.

—, **côtelettes de** Roebuck cutlet.

- **Conti** Sautéed in oil; garnished with lentil purée and sliced tongue; coated with *sauce poivrade* combined with the pan juices.

- **aux Marrons** Sautéed in butter; placed on fried croutons and served with braised chestnuts and *sauce poivrade*.

—, **noisettes de** Small roebuck steaks.

- **Romanoff** Sautéed in butter; coated with *sauce poivrade* enriched with cream; garnished with duxelles and cucumbers stuffed with chicken forcemeat.

- **Valencia** Sautéed; served on croutons and coated with *sauce bigarade*; garnished with sliced oranges.

—, **selle de** Saddle of roebuck.

- **à l'allemande** Larded, marinated, and roasted; served with pan juices deglazed with stock and thickened with cream.

- **Beaujeu** Larded, marinated,

and roasted; garnished with braised chestnuts and artichokes filled with lentil purée; served with the pan juices combined with demi-glace sauce.

Faisan Pheasant.

— **à la bohémienne** Stuffed with foie gras and slivered truffles and roasted; served with the pan juices deglazed with brandy and combined with demi-glace sauce (made with game stock).

— **en casserole** Sautéed in butter; deglazed with brandy and game-flavored demi-glace sauce and served *en casserole*.

— **en cocotte** Prepare as for *faisan en casserole*; garnished with mushroom caps, pearl onions, and truffles.

— **en chartreuse** Sections sautéed and arranged in a mold lined with braised cabbage; alternate layers of cabbage and meat; turned out on platter and served with demi-glace sauce.

— **à la normande** Sautéed in butter; arranged in terrine with sautéed apples; drizzled with cream and finished cooking in the oven; served with the strained pan juices.

—, **suprême de** Breast of pheasant.

- **à la royale** Sautéed; coated with *sauce aux truffes* and garnished with pheasant quenelles and sliced truffles.

Lapin Rabbit.

— **sauté au paprika** Marinated sections browned in butter and stewed in white wine and stock with mushrooms and onions; thickened with cream and seasoned heavily with paprika.

— **sauté chasseur** Sautéed with mushrooms and bacon; coated with *sauce Chasseur*; served with boiled potatoes.

Lièvre Hare.

—, civet de See Part II; *Civet, lièvre de.*

— à la périgourdine See *Lièvre à la royale*, this section.

— à la royale Stuffed with the animals liver, heart and lungs along with foie gras, bread crumbs, truffles, and the animal's blood; braised in white wine and served with the reduced braising liquid flavored with game fumet.

— étoffé à la périgourdine Boned and stuffed with the animal's liver, kidneys, heart, and blood along with ground veal, foie gras, truffles, and cognac; poached in stock; served cold.

— farci en cabessal Stuffed with ground veal and pork, shallots, and lots of garlic; braised in red wine and served with the braising liquid reduced with the animal's blood, vinegar, and garlic.

Mauviettes Lark; see also *Alouettes.*

— à la bonne-femme Barded with bacon and roasted; served on croutons and drizzled with the pan juices deglazed with brandy.

— à la minute Butterflied (split and flattened) and sautéed; coated with the pan juices deglazed with brandy and demi-glace sauce.

— à la piémontaise Stuffed with game forcemeat and sautéed; served over polenta and drizzled with Parmesan and game fumet.

Orlotans à la Landaise See Part II.

Perdreau Partridge.

—, ballotine de Boned and stuffed with game forcemeat made with truffles and foie gras; rolled, tied, and braised in stock; served with the reduced braising liquid.

— à la catalane Seasoned and roasted; garnished with bitter oranges and drizzled with the pan juices combined with the juice of bitter oranges.

— en chartreuse Roasted and cut in sections; placed in a mold lined with braised cabbage; alternated layers of cabbage and meat; unmolded and served with demi-glace sauce made with game stock.

— aux choux Roasted and served with braised cabbage; drizzled with demi-glace sauce flavored with game fumet.

— aux pistaches Roasted and garnished with toasted pistachio nuts.

—, suprêmes de, Véron Sautéed; served on croutons and garnished with game purée and chestnut purée; coated with game-flavored demi-glace sauce.

Pigeonneaux Squabs.

— en crapaudine Half bird dipped in melted butter and bread crumbs and slow-grilled; with *sauce diable.*

— en papillote Half bird, breast-bone removed, browned in butter; topped with duxelles and chopped ham; wrapped in greased paper and baked.

— suprêmes de, aux truffes *Suprêmes* (boneless breast filets) dipped in butter and placed in an oven-proof dish over game forcemeat; baked and garnished with sliced truffles; coated with demi-glace sauce flavored with game fumet.

Pigeon Pigeon.

— en compote Trussed and browned in lard; deglazed with white wine and stock and simmered in tomato-flavored demi-glace sauce; garnished with mushrooms, pearl onions, and chopped bacon; served in sauce.

—, pâté de Roasted and cut in sections; set in pie dish with sliced bacon, garlic, shallots, hard-cooked egg yolks, and thickened stock; covered with pastry and baked.

LÉGUMES — VEGETABLES

Artichauts Artichokes.

—, *fonds d'* Artichoke bottoms.

— *à la grecque* Poached and quartered; marinated in oil, vinegar, fennel, coriander, and onions.

— *à la lyonnaise* Poached in white wine and stock; served with caramelized onions and chopped parsley.

— *au naturel* Poached in salted water with a dash of lemon; served with melted butter and hollandaise sauce.

— *à la Varenne* Poached in salted water and lemon juice and stuffed with chopped broccoli; coated with hollandaise sauce and glazed under the broiler.

Asperges Asparagus.

— *à la flamande* Poached; dressed with crushed hard-cooked eggs mixed with hot melted butter.

— *au naturel* Poached in salted water; served with hollandaise sauce or melted butter.

— *à la polonaise* Poached in salted water; topped with chopped hard-cooked eggs combined with toasted bread crumbs, parsley, and melted butter.

— *Villeroi* Poached; dipped in *sauce Villeroi* and coated with bread crumbs; deep-fried.

Aubergines Eggplants.

— *à la crème* Sautéed in butter; coated with cream sauce.

— *farcies* Halved and scooped out; filled with the chopped pulp sautéed with tomatoes, garlic, onions, mushrooms, and bread crumbs; baked.

— *au gratin à la catalane* Halved and scooped out; stuffed with the chopped pulp sautéed with onions and chopped hard-cooked eggs; topped with bread crumbs seasoned with garlic and baked until golden brown.

— *à la turque* Stuffed with ground mutton, pilaf, and duxelles; coated with demi-glace sauce and sprinkled with bread crumbs; baked.

Betteraves Beetroots.

— *à la béchamel* Cooked slices sautéed in butter and coated with béchamel sauce.

— *à la crème* Slices sautéed in butter and removed from pan; pan juices thickened with cream and finished with butter; poured over beets.

Carottes Carrots.

— *au beurre* Boiled; drained and tossed with butter.

— *à la crème* Boiled in salted water with a pinch of butter and sugar; coated with some of the cooking liquid thickened with cream.

— *glacées* Boiled in stock with butter, sugar, salt, and pepper; cooked until carrots are tender and stock has been reduced to a syrupy glaze; tossed with glaze.

—, *purée de* Boiled in water with salt, butter, and sugar; passed through a sieve and enriched with butter and cream.

-, *Crécy* Boiled in salted water with a pinch of butter and sugar; puréed with cooked rice.

— *à la Vichy* Slices covered with a small amount of cold water with salt and sugar; cooked covered until liquid is absorbed and carrots are tender.

Cèpes Cèpes.
— *à la crème* Sautéed with onions; thickened with cream.
— *farcis au gratin* Cèpes stuffed with chicken forcemeat; sprinkled with butter and Parmesan cheese and baked.
— *à la provençale* Sautéed in olive oil with garlic and onions.

Champignons Mushrooms.
— *farcis* Caps coated with seasoned butter; filled with various stuffings and sprinkled with Parmesan cheese and butter; baked.
— *à la grecque* Poached in white wine, olive oil, lemon juice, stock, and spices; cooled and preserved in the cooking liquid.
— *grillés* Caps tossed in seasoned butter and grilled under the broiler; served on tiny croutons and sprinkled with lemon juice.
— *à la périgourdine* Sautéed in oil with truffles, shallots, parsley, salt, and pepper; sprinkled with lemon juice.

Chou Cabbage.
— *-croute* Sauerkraut; sliced cabbage simmered in stock and white wine with onions, carrots, bacon, juniper berries, peppercorns, and seasonings.
— *farci* Stuffed with veal forcemeat and poached in stock.
— *à la flamande* Sliced; cooked in butter and vinegar with diced apples.
— *à la limousine* Sliced; cooked in stock with chestnuts, bacon fat, butter, and vinegar.
— *rouge à la limousine* Braised in red wine and stock with salt pork, chestnuts, vinegar, and spices.

Chou-fleur Cauliflower.
— *à l'anglaise* Boiled in salted water; served with melted butter.
— *au beurre noir* Boiled in salted water; sprinkled with lemon juice,

chopped parsley, and *beurre noir*.
— *au gratin* Blanched; coated with *sauce Mornay* and sprinkled with Parmesan cheese; browned in a hot oven.

Choux de Bruxelles Brussels sprouts.
— *à l'indienne* Poached in stock; tossed with *sauce au cari* and served over rice.
— *Mornay* Blanched; sautéed in butter; arranged in a baking dish and coated with *sauce Mornay* and sprinkled with Parmesan cheese; baked au gratin.

Concombres Cucumbers.
— *à la crème* Cut into strips; sautéed in butter and thickened with cream.
— *farcis* Peeled, cut lengthwise, and seeded; stuffed with chicken forcemeat mixed with duxelles.

Courgettes Zucchini.
— *farcies* Cut lengthwise and hollowed out; stuffed with duxelles and baked.
— *à la niçoise* Slices dredged in flour and sautéed; arranged in casserole with sliced tomatoes and drizzled with garlic-oil; baked.
— *à la provençale* Slices dredged in flour and sautéed; arranged in casserole with rice, chopped sautéed tomatoes, garlic, and onions; sprinkled with Parmesan cheese and baked.
— *à la romaine* Marinated slices dipped in batter and fried or baked; with tomato sauce.

Épinards Spinach.
— *à l'anglaise* Blanched; drained well and served with melted butter.
— *à la crème* Blanched; sautéed in butter until dry; thickened with cream.
— *au gratin* Blanched; tossed with *sauce Mornay* and sprinkled with Parmesan cheese; baked au gratin.

Haricots blancs White navy beans.
— *à la bretonne* Simmered in seasoned water until tender; tossed with *sauce bretonne* and sprinkled with chopped parsley.
— *à la lyonnaise* Simmered in salted water until tender; tossed in butter with sliced sautéed onions.
Haricots verts Green beans.
— *à la bonne-femme* Par-boiled; sautéed in butter with bacon; moistened with stock and cooked covered; served with melted butter and chopped parsley.
— *au naturel* Cooked in salted water until tender; served with melted butter and seasoned with salt and pepper.
— *à la normande* Par-boiled; sautéed in butter; cream added to thicken and enriched with butter and egg yolks.
Oignons Onions.
— *farcis* Blanched; hollowed out and stuffed with veal forcemeat; baked, basting frequently; when nearly done, sprinkled with crumbs and browned.
— *en fritot* Sliced; dipped in batter and deep-fried; seasoned with salt.
— *frits* Thinly sliced; tossed in seasoned flour and fried in hot butter mixed with oil.
— *à la lyonnaise* Thin slices browned in butter; moistened with beef stock and vinegar.
Petits pois Peas.
— *à l'allemande* Boiled until tender; drained and tossed with *sauce à l'allemande*.
— *à l'anglaise* Boiled in salted water; drained and served with butter.
— *au beurre* Boiled until tender; drained and tossed with butter; seasoned with salt and sugar.

— *frais à la française* Simmered with lettuce and onions in water seasoned with butter, salt, and sugar; cooked until peas are tender; stock reduced to a glaze and finished with butter.
— *à la hollandaise* Cooked until tender; drained and tossed with hollandaise sauce.
Pommes de terre Potatoes.
— *allumettes* Matchsticks; deep-fried.
— *à l'alsacienne* New potatoes cooked in butter with bacon and onions; seasoned with chopped parsley.
— *à l'anglaise* Steamed; seasoned with salt and pepper and served with butter.
— *Anna* A potato cake made by layering thin potato slices in a round, well buttered pan and baked in a hot oven; can also be cooked in a frying pan.
— *Annette* Anna potatoes prepared with julienne strips instead of rounds.
— *Berny* Boiled and sieved; mixed with egg yolks, butter and chopped truffles; dipped in egg and minced almonds and deep-fried.
— *Byron* Baked; pulp removed and mashed with cheese; coated with cream and baked au gratin.
— *à la cancalaise* Baked and hollowed out; stuffed with poached oysters and mushrooms bound with *sauce vin blanc*.
— *chasseur* Baked and hollowed out; stuffed with chopped chicken livers and mushrooms bound with *sauce chasseur*.
— *château* Olive-shaped; par-boiled; browned in butter.
— *Châteaubriand* *Pommes de terre château* coated with meat glaze and sprinkled with chopped parsley.

— *copeaux* Cut in ribbons and deep-fried.

— *cordon de soulier* Long thin strips deep-fried.

— *à la Crécy Pommes de terre Anna* prepared with a layer of carrot purée.

— *à la crème* Boiled, peeled, and sliced; sautéed briefly in butter and simmered in cream until thick.

—, *croquettes de* Boiled, peeled, and sieved; bound with butter and egg yolks; dipped in egg and crumbs and deep-fried.

— *Cussy* Coin-sized slices sautéed in butter with truffle slices; deglazed with Madeira wine and chicken stock.

— *dauphine* See Part II, *Dauphine, pommes de terre.*

— *dauphinoises* See Part II, *Dauphinoise, pommes de terre.*

— *Delmonico* Peeled, diced, boiled, and drained; simmered in butter and cream and sprinkled with crumbs; browned in the oven.

— *duchesse* See Part II, *Duchesse, pommes de terre.*

— *fondantes* Small ovals cooked in a covered pan in butter until golden brown.

— *au four* Baked potatoes; whole potatoes baked in the oven.

— *frites* Thin strips deep-fried.

—, *galette de* Mashed potatoes bound with egg yolks and formed into patties; brushed with egg yolks and baked in the oven.

—, *gaufrettes de* Waffle-cut chips deep-fried.

— *Georgette* Baked potato cup filled with *écrevisses à la Nantua.*

— *Godard Pommes de terre dauphine* mixture shaped in small ovals and deep-fried.

— *gratinées* 1) Mashed potatoes topped with cheese and browned. 2) (Also called *pommes de terre*

Jackson) Baked potato cups stuffed with its pulp and topped with cheese; browned in the oven.

— *irlandaises* Ribbon-cut; steamed.

— *Jackson* See *Pommes de terre gratinées,* this section.

— *Lafitte* Duchesse potatoes formed into sticks and dipped in egg and bread crumbs; deep-fried.

— *à la landaise* Cut in a large dice; cooked in a covered pan with chopped onions, diced Bayonne ham, and goose fat.

— *Lorette Pommes de terre dauphine* formed into small crescents and deep-fried.

— *à la lyonnaise* Boiled, peeled, and sliced; sautéed in butter with thinly sliced onions.

— *Macaire* Baked potato pulp mashed with butter and shaped into a pattie; cooked in butter on a griddle.

— *Maintenon* Baked potato cup filled with a *salpicon* of chicken, tongue, truffles, and mushrooms bound with *sauce Soubise;* sprinkled with Parmesan and browned in the oven.

— *maire* Same as *Pommes de terre à la crème.*

— *à la maître d'hôtel Pommes de terre à la crème* prepared with chopped parsley.

— *marquise* See Part II, *Marquis, pommes de terre.*

— *mirette* See Part II, *Mirette, pommes de terre.*

— *Mont-Doré* Mashed potatoes mixed with grated cheese and mounded in a casserole; dusted with grated cheese and browned.

— *mousseline* Mashed potatoes lightened with whipped cream.

— *au naturel* Boiled potatoes.

— *noisette* Small balls cooked in butter until golden brown.

— *paille* Short, very thin strips; deep-fried.

— *en paniers* See Part II, *Panier, pommes de terre.*

— *à la parisienne* Small balls cooked in butter until browned; tossed in meat glaze.

— *Parmentier* See Part II. *Parmentier, pommes de terre.*

— *Pont-Neuf* Cut into rectangles; deep-fried.

— *à la provençale* Raw or cooked slices sautéed in butter with garlic until golden brown.

—, *purée de* Peeled; cooked in salted water and passed through a sieve; enriched with butter and cream.

— *rissolées* Small ovals well browned in butter.

— *rôties* Cut uniformly; tossed with butter and roasted in the oven.

— *Saint-Florentin* See Part II, *Saint Florentin, pommes de terre.*

— *à la sarladaise* See Part II, *Sarladaise, pommes de terre.*

— *sautées* Boiled, peeled, and sliced; sautéed in butter.

— *à la savoyarde* See Part II, *Savoyarde, pommes de terre à la.*

— *soufflées* See Part II, *Soufflé, pommes de terre.*

— *Soubise* Baked potato cups filled with white onion purée mixed with cream; sprinkled with bread crumbs and baked.

— *surprise* See Part II, *Surprise, pommes de terre.*

— *à la toulousaine* Cut in quarters and sautéed with garlic in goose fat; *sauce velouté* added; covered and cooked in the oven until tender.

— *à la Vichy* Same as *Pommes de terre à la Crécy.*

— *voisin* *Pommes de terre Anna* sprinkled with grated cheese.

— *Yvette* Same as *Pommes de terre Annette.*

Tomates Tomatoes.

— *farcies à la niçoise* Hollowed out and stuffed with pilaf, diced sautéed eggplant, garlic, and bread crumbs; baked.

— *farcies à la parisienne* Par-cooked; hollowed out and stuffed with chopped truffles and mushrooms; sprinkled with bread crumbs and browned under the broiler.

—, *fondu de* Peeled, chopped and pressed; sautéed in butter until very well cooked.

-, *à la portugaise* *Fondu de tomate* with the addition of chopped garlic.

— *grillées* Thick slices brushed with oil and seasoned; cooked on very hot grill.

— *à la provençale* Large dice sautéed in olive oil with parsley and plenty of garlic.

— *sautées à la lyonnaise* Halved, seeded, and sautéed in butter; topped with thinly sliced onions fried in butter.

— *à la sicilienne* See Part II, *Sicilienne, tomates à la.*

Truffes Truffles.

— *au champagne* Cooked with champagne and *mirepoix* in covered pot; uncovered; liquid reduced and combined with demi-glace sauce.

— *au Madère* *Truffes au champagne* substituting Madeira wine for champagne.

— *sautées à la provençale* Slices sautéed in olive oil with chopped garlic.

— *à la serviette* Poached in Madeira wine and served on a folded napkin.

— *sous les cendres* Seasoned and moistened with Cognac; wrapped in pork fat then in foil or waxed paper; tucked under glowing embers.

SALADE — SALAD

Salade Salad.
— *Aïda* Sliced artichoke bottoms, tomatoes, green peppers, chickory, and chopped hard-cooked eggs; tossed with vinaigrette.
— *à l'allemande* Diced apples, potatoes, gherkins, pickled herring, chopped hard-cooked eggs, beets, and onions; tossed with vinaigrette.
— *américaine* Slices of potato and tomato, drizzled with vinaigrette; garnished with hard-cooked eggs, celery, and onions.
— *andalouse* Tomatoes, red pepper, rice; tossed with vinaigrette mixed with garlic, onions, and parsley.
— *Bagration* Strips of artichoke bottoms, celery, and tongue; garnished with macaroni, chopped hard-cooked eggs, and truffles; dressed with mayonnaise sauce mixed with tomato purée.
— *Danicheff* Sliced celeriac, artichoke bottoms, potatoes, asparagus tips and mushrooms; dressed with mayonnaise sauce; garnished with crayfish tails, chopped hard-cooked eggs, and truffles.
— *demi-deuil* Julienne truffles and potatoes; drizzled with mustard enriched with cream.
— *francillon* Mussels and potatoes cooked in white wine; garnished with truffles and tossed with vinaigrette.
— *impériale* Julienne of apples, carrots, truffles, and French beans; tossed with vinaigrette and chopped parsley.
— *à l'indienne* Red pepper strips, asparagus tips, and diced apples over rice; coated with curry cream.
— *mikado* See Part II, *Mikado, salade*.
— *mimosa* See Part II, *Mimosa, salade*.
— *niçoise* See Part II, *Niçoise, salade*.
— *orientale* Rice, red pepper, tomatoes, black olives, and green beans tossed with vinaigrette.
— *Rachel* Julienne of truffles, potatoes, artichoke bottoms, and celery; garnished with asparagus tips and tossed with mayonnaise sauce.
— *russe* See Part II, *Russe, salade*.
— *salmigondis* See Part II, *Salmigondis, salade*.
— *Waldorf* Diced apples, celery, and chopped walnuts; tossed with mayonnaise sauce.

DESSERTS — DESSERTS

Bavarois A custard or fruit purée flavored and lightened with whipped cream.
— *à la normande* Apple purée mixed with gelatin and poured in a mold to set; topped with pastry cream.
— *rubané* Different colors and flavors layered in a mold.
Bombe A frozen dessert featuring a bombe mold lined with ice cream or fruit ice and filled with a custard-like mixture.
— *Aïda* Lined with strawberry ice cream and filled with cherry-flavored bombe mixture.
— *duchesse* Lined with pineapple ice and filled with pear-flavored mixture.
— *mousseline* Lined with strawberry ice cream and filled with whipped cream flavored with strawberry purée.
— *tutti-frutti* Lined with strawberry ice cream and filled with lemon mixture containing bits of candied fruit.

Bourdaloue Various fruits halved and filled with frangipane cream and sprinkled with crushed macaroons.

Cerises jubilé See Part II, *Jubilé, Cerises.*

Charlotte russe Bavarois custard poured into a mold lined with ladyfingers; chilled to set; unmolded.

Clafouti See Part II.

Compote de fruits Apples, pears, peaches, and apricots poached in syrup.

Coupe Ice creams, whipped creams, ices, and so on, served in a cup or glass and decorated with various sweet sauces and garnishes.

Crème caramel Custard poured into a caramel-lined mold and chilled to set; unmold and serve.

Crème glacée Ice creams.

Crêpes à la normande Thin pancakes filled with diced apples cooked in butter and Calvados; folded and served hot.

Crêpes Suzette See Part II, *Suzette, crêpes.*

Diplomate A ladyfinger-lined mold layered with pastry cream (which has been lightened with whipped cream) and ladyfingers brushed with flavored syrup.

Éclairs au chocolat Oval *choux* pastries filled with pastry cream and glazed with chocolate.

Gâteau Saint-Honoré See Part II, *Saint-Honoré, gâteau.*

Glace au four See Part II.

Île flottante See Part II.

Marguerite See Part II.

Marquis au chocolat See Part II.

Pêche Melba See Part II, *Melba, pêche.*

Mont-Blanc See Part II.

Mousse au chocolat See Part II.

Omelette norvégienne See Part II, *Norvégienne, omelette.*

Oranges en suprise See Part II, *Suprise, oranges, en.*

Paris-Brest *Choux* paste piped into a ring and baked; sliced in half length-wise and filled with pastry cream and almonds.

Poires Belle-Hélène See Part II, *Belle Hélène, poires.*

Poires pochées au vin rouge Halved, peeled pears poached in red wine which has been sweetened with sugar and flavored with cinnamon.

Pommes en charlotte Charlotte mold lined with buttered bread slices; filled with cooked apple purée flavored with cinnamon and lemon; baked.

Riz Condé Rice baked in milk, sugar, and butter; finished with egg yolks.

Riz à l'impératrice Rice baked in milk, butter, and sugar; mixed with fruit soaked in liqueur; bavarois custard folded in and poured into molds to set.

Soufflé au Grand Marnier Pastry cream enriched with egg yolks and lightened with beaten egg whites; flavored with Grand Marnier and baked; sprinkled with powdered sugar and served immediately.

Soufflé Montmorency Pastry cream enriched with egg yolks and lightened with beaten egg whites; flavored with cherries and cherry liqueur; baked and served immediately.

Soufflé Rothschild See Part II, *Rothschild, soufflé.*

Tarte alsacienne See Part II.

Tarte bourbonnais See Part II.

Tarte des Demoiselles Tatin See Part II.

Vacherin à la Chantilly See Part II.

Vacherin aux marrons glacés See Part II.

Part II

French Food and Beverage Vocabulary

FRENCH PRONUNCIATION KEY

VOWELS

a, â .... **(ah)** *a* as in *harp;* ex. *chat* (shah)
e, eu, œu .... **(uh)** *u* as in *mug;* ex. *beurre* (buhr)
er, é .... **(eh)** *a* as in *bake;* ex. *légal* (leh-gahl)
ê, è .... **(e)** *e* as in *get;* ex. *Grèce* (gres0
i, y .... **(ee)** *ee* as in *beet;* ex. *diner* (dee-neh)
i .... (before a vowel) **(y)** y as in yell; ex. *pied* (pyeh)
o .... **(o)** *o* as in *toy;* ex. *sole* (sol)
oi .... **(wah)** *wa* as in *watch;* ex. *bois* (bwah)
o, eau, au ... **(oh)** *o* as in *no;* ex. *château* (shah-toh)
ou .... **(oo)** *oo* as in *groom;* ex. *nous* (noo)
u .... **(ü)** no English sound; *ee* followed by *oo;* ex. *pur* (pür)

CONSONANTS

c....... **(k)** *k* as in *kite;* ex. *canot* (kah-noh)
c....... **(s)** (before e and i) *s* as in *sea;* ex. *cire* (seer)
ç....... **(s)** *s* as in *surf;* ex. *ça* (sah)
ch .... **(sh)** *sh* as in *ship;* ex. *château* (shah-toh)
g ...... **(g)** *g* as in *gift;* ex. *grotte* (grot)
g ...... **(zh)** (before e and i) *zh* as in *Jacques;* ex. *gilet* (zhee-le)
gn .... **(ny)** *ny* as in *canyon;* ex. *cognac* (koh-nyahk)
j .... **(zh)** *zh* as in *Jacques;* ex. *jus* (zhü)
qu .... **(k)** *k* as in *king;* ex. *quai* (keh)
s....... **(s)** *s* as in *saw;* ex. *scie* (see)
s....... **(z)** (between vowels) *z* as in *zoo;* ex. *réseau* (reh-zoh)
y ...... **(y)** *y* as in *yell;* ex. *payer* (peh-yeh)
ll ...... **(yuh)** *yuh* as in *young;* ex. *malliot* (mayuh-yah)

Notes:

There is no accent mark in the pronunciation of French words. The last syllable may be somewhat more pronounced than the preceding ones, but, in general, each syllable is equally stressed.

Words that appear several times throughout the book, such as *sauce* and *garniture*, are not pronounced when combined with other words—i.e., *sauce béarnaise* or *garniture Agnès Sorel*.

When an entry word appears two or three times in a row, it is marked with a plus sign (+)—i.e., *Agneau* [ah-nyoh], *Agneau de lait* [+ duh leh], *Agneau de pauillac* [+ duh poh-yahk], and so on.

A capitalized vowel in a pronunciation—i.e., *blanc* [bla], *bondon* [bO-dO], *lapin* [lah-pI]—indicates it is to be pronounced with a slight nasal sound.

Abaisse [ah-beh-seh] A rolled out sheet of pastry.

Abaisser [ah-beh-seh] A term meaning to roll out thinly (pastry).

Abat-faim [ah-bah-fA] Literally "hunger killer," this outdated term referred to dishes served first or early in the meal.

Abatis/Abattis [ah-bah-tee] Poultry giblets.

— *de volaille* [+ de vo-lah-yuh] Chicken giblets.

— *en croûte* [+ E kroot] Poultry giblets baked in a pastry.

— *en ragoût* [+ E rah-goo] Stewed poultry giblets.

Abats (de boucherie) [ah-baht de boo-shree] Variety meats of an animal.

— *d'agneau* [+ dah-nyoh] Variety meats of lamb.

Abatte [ah-baht] A heavy double-edged knife used for flattening meats.

Ablette/Blette [ah-blet/blet] A small (5–7 in.) freshwater fish with thin, silvery scales. It is also referred to as *bleak* and is usually served fried.

Aboukir, amandes d' [ah-mahnd dah-boo-keer] A petit four of blanched almonds coated with green or pink almond paste and caramel.

Abricot [ah-bree-koh] Apricot.

Abricoter [ah-bree-koh-teh] To glaze. Usually refers to coating a pastry with apricot jam.

Absinthe [ahb-sIth] A green, bitter liqueur distilled from wormwood and flavored with anise. Banned in many countries, there are now several substitutes.

Acajou [ah-kah-zhoo] Cashew nut.

Acarne [ah-kahrn] Sea bream.

Accolade, en [E ah-koh-lahd] A term referring to foods that are shingled on a plate for decorative purposes.

Accuncciatu [ah-koon-syah-too] A Corsican stew consisting of mutton, lamb, horsemeat, and potatoes.

Acétomel [ah-seh-toh-mehl] A sweet-sour syrup made from vinegar and honey.

Ache [ahsh] Wild celery.

Achigan [ah-shee-gA] Black bass.

Acide, sauce [ah-seed] A white wine sauce combined with shallots and grated horseradish.

Affrioler [ah-freeoh-leh] A culinary term meaning to tempt by means of the decorative appearance of a dish.

Affriter [ah-free-teh] Term meaning to season a pan by rubbing salt over the base or by heating oil in the pan until very hot and then wiping clean. This process prevents foods from sticking to the pan.

Africaine, à l' [ah-lah-free-ken] "African style." Describes food prepared with eggplants, tomatoes, cucumbers, olive-shaped potatoes (*olivettes*), and herbs and spices such as cloves, cumin, and coriander. Dishes served *à l'africaine* are often accompanied with a tomato flavored demi-glace.

Africaine, sauce Tomatoes, onions, and peppers reduced in white wine and seasoned with garlic, parsley, bay, thyme, and hot paprika; combined with demi-glace sauce.

Agneau [ah-nyoh] Lamb less than one-year old.

— *de lait* [+ duh leh] Suckling lamb about a month old.

— *de pauillac* [+ duh poh-yahk] Lamb raised in coastal Médoc, in France's Bordeaux region.

— *de pré-salé* [+ duh preh sah-leh] Lamb that has grazed on northern coastal grasslands (Brittany, Vendée, Guienne). The flesh of these animals are very tender and delicately flavored.

Agnès Sorel [ah-nyeh soh-rel] The mistress of Charles VII of France; the name given to several culinary dishes.

—, *garniture* Julienne chicken breast, mushrooms, and pickled beef tongue; used mainly with poultry dishes.

Agoursi [ah-goor-see] Ridge cucumber.

Agur [ah-gür] A grating cheese from French Basque made from ewe's milk.

Aïda, sauce [ah-yee-dah] *Sauce Mornay* combined with spinach and paprika. Served with fish.

Aiglefin [eg-leh-fI] Haddock.

Aiglon [eg-lO] A dessert consisting of fruit (apricot, apple, peach, etc.) poached in vanilla syrup, arranged on vanilla ice cream, sprinkled with crystallized violets, and topped with spun sugar.

Aïgo à la ménagère [ah-yee-goh ah-lah meh-nah-ger] A specialty of Provence, it is a garlic soup with tomatoes, leeks, cloves, fennel, and orange peel. Garnished with quartered potatoes and poached egg.

Aïgo boulïdo [+ boo-ee-doh] A garlic soup from Provence seasoned with sage, bay, and thyme. Thickened with egg yolks and served over slices of bread sprinkled with olive oil and grated cheese.

Aïgo San d'Iou [+ sahn dyoo] A fish soup from Provence similar to bouillabaisse with the addition of potatoes, which are eaten separately; served with aïoli.

Aïgo-sau [+ soh] A Provençal fish and vegetable soup heavily flavored with garlic.

Aigre-douce, sauce [eg-ruh doos] A sweet-sour sauce composed of sugar, white wine, shallots, vinegar, and finished with demi-glace sauce. Garnished with raisins and capers.

Aigre-doux [+ doo] Sweet and sour.

Aiguebelle [eh-guh-bel] A monastery in Provence (Montélimar) where the liqueur of the same name is made.

Aiguillette [eg-gwee-yet] A thin strip of any meat, usually duck or poultry.

— *baronne* [+ bah-ruhn] The tip of a beef rump.

Aiguillon [eg-gwee-yO] A spicy sausage or meat.

Aiguiseur [eg-gwee-zhur] Knife sharpener.

Aiguisoir [eg-gwee-zwahr] Knife sharpener.

Ail [ahy] Garlic.

—, *purée d'* Puréed garlic.

— *rose* [+ rohz] Red-skinned garlic.

— *vert* [+ vehr] "Green garlic" harvested before the cloves have formed.

Aile [el] Wing.

Ailerons (Aile) de poulet [ah-yuh-rO de poo-leh] Chicken wings.

Aillade [ah-yahd] (1) (*Provence*) A *sauce vinaigrette* with garlic. (2) (*Languedoc*) A mayonnaise based sauce with garlic and walnuts. (3) (*Albi*) Synonymous with aïoli.

Ailée [ah-yeh] A thick, spreadable condiment composed of bread crumbs, ground almonds, garlic, and stock.

Aillloli [ah-loh-lee] See *Aïoli*.

Aïoli [ah-yoh-lee] A garlic flavored mayonnaise thought to have originated in Provence. Also spelled *aillloli*.

Airelle [eh-rel] Cranberry.

Aisy [eh-zee] A town in France in which *cendré d'Armencon* cheese is produced. See *Cendré d'Armencon*.

à la/à l' [ah-lah/ahl] In the style of/ with.

— *carte* [ah-lah kahrt] Each item priced separately on a menu.

— *mode* [ah-lah mod] "In the manner of."

Albacore [ahl-bah-kohr] The French name for the yellow-fin tuna.

Alberge [ahl-behrzh] A variety of peach mainly used in jam making.

Albertine, à l' [ahl ahl-behr-teen] Describes fish dishes garnished with asparagus tips, tomatoes, and mushroom caps, and coated with a white wine sauce.

Albi [ahl-bee] A town in Languedoc famous for stuffed goose necks, pork liver, juniper berries, and local confections and pastries.

Albigeoise, à l' [ah-lah ahl-bee-zhwahz] A garnish for large joints of beef featuring stuffed tomatoes and potato croquettes.

Albigeoise, pot-au-feu à l' [poh-toh-fuh +] A hearty soup of veal and pork knuckles, ham, sausage, root vegetables, and cabbage. *Confit d'oie* (preserved goose) is added at the last minute.

Albufera, d' [dahl-bü-feh-rah] The name of many culinary dishes named after Marshal Suchet, the duke of Albufera.

—, *garniture* (*For poultry*) Rice, truffles, foie gras; puff pastry tartlets filled with truffles, sliced calf's sweetbreads, pickled ox tongue, and mushrooms; served with sauce Albufera.

—, *sauce* Suprême sauce with the addition of meat glaze (*glace de viande*) and pimento butter.

Alcarazas [ahl-kah-ra] A porous earthenware pitcher used to cool liquids by evaporation.

Alcool [ahl-kol] Alcohol.

Alfonse, sauce [ahl-fOs] *Sauce velouté* combined with *glace de viande*, cayenne pepper, and pimento butter.

Algérienne, à l' [ah-lahl-zheh-ree-yen] A garnish consisting of sweet potato croquettes, tomatoes cooked in oil with garlic, and julienne red pepper.

Alhambra, à l' [ah-lahl-ham-brah] A garnish of sautéed artichoke bottoms, chopped tomatoes, and small green peppers.

Alicot/Alicuit [ah-lee-koh/ah-lee-kwee] A ragoût of poultry giblets, garlic, potatoes, and carrots. This specialty of the Rouergue is traditionally served with cèpes and roasted chestnuts.

Aligot [ah-lee-goh] (*Auvergne*) A potato dish consisting of fresh garlic and Cantal cheese combined with mashed potatoes. Also spelled *aligout*.

Aligoté [ah-lee-goh-teh] A white Burgundy wine.

Aligout [ah-lee-goo] See *Aligot*.

Alimentation générale [ah-lee-mE-tah-shuhn zheh-neh-rahl] French word for grocery store.

Alise pacaude [ah-leez pah-kohd] A traditional Easter cake from Vendée.

Allemagne [ah-luh-mahn-yuh] Germany.

Allemande, à l' [ah-luh-mAd] "German style." Denotes the dish is served with *sauce allemande*.

Allemande, sauce *Sauce velouté* flavored with white wine and mushroom essence; thickened with egg yolks and cream.

Alliance, à l' [ah lah-lee-yAs] Garnish of glazed carrots, onions, artichoke bottoms, and demi-glace sauce.

Alliance, sauce Hollandaise sauce made with tarragon vinegar and fresh chopped chives.

Allonger [ah-lO-zheh] French culinary term meaning to thin out a sauce with the addition of a liquid.

Allumettes [ahl-loo-met] Baked puff pastry strips, usually topped with a sweet or savory spread.

Alose [ah-lohz] Shad.

Alouettes [ah-loo-et] Lark. Also known in France as *maviettes*.

Aloumère [ah-loo-mer] A type of fungus. Prepared like mushrooms.

Aloxe-corton [ah-loks kor-tO] An area of the côte de Beaune producing outstanding red and white Burgundies.

Aloyau [ah-loy-oh] Beef sirloin.

Alphonse, à l' [ah-lahl-fOs] A garnish for butcher's meat consisting of artichoke bottoms, mushrooms, and *sauce Madeira*.

Alsace [ahl-sahs] A province in north eastern France bordering Germany; famous for cabbage, pork products, foie gras, *baeckeoffe*, and *kugelhopf*. Alsatian wines are of superb quality (Rieslings, Gewürztraminers, and Tokay).

Alsacienne, à l' [ah-lahl-sah-syen] Denotes the use of the natural resources of Alsace in preparation of a dish, particularly sauerkraut and sausage.

Alsacienne, sauce A cold sauce of calf's brains ground with oil, flavored with mustard, vinegar, and lemon.

Alumelle/Allumette [ah-loo-mel/ah-loo-met] See *Amelette*.

Amande [ah-mahnd] Almond.

— *amère* [+ ah-mehr] Bitter almond. Illegal in the United States. Contains prussic acid, which is lethal but is destroyed when heated. Used in almond liqueurs and confections outside the U.S.

— *verte* [+ vehr] "Green almond." This is a soft, unripe almond sour in taste.

Amandine [ah-mah-deen] This American-French term describes almonds used in the preparation of a dish.

Amanite [ah-mah-neet] A genus of mushroom grown in southern France. Some varieties are poisonous.

Amaugette/Amauguète [ah-moh-zhet/ah-moh-get] (*Landes*) A ragoût of sheep's offal.

Amazone, à l' [ah-lah-mah-zon] A garnish for various meats composed of lentil croquettes filled with chestnut purée and morels. Served with *sauce chasseur*.

Ambassadeur [ahm-bah-sah-duhr] A garnish consisting of duchess potatoes and artichoke bottoms stuffed with duxelles. Accompanied by grated horseradish which is served on the side.

Ambassadrice, à l' [ahm-bah-sah-drees] A garnish composed of: (1) (*For beef*) Mushrooms sautéed with chicken livers, braised lettuce, potatoes *parisienne*, and *sauce Madeira*. (2) (*For poultry*) Asparagus tips, lamb sweetbreads, truffles, and suprême sauce.

Ambigu [ahm-bee-goo] A cold buffet usually served late in the evening.

Améléon [ah-meh-leh-O] A type of cider from Normandy.

Amelette [ah-meh-let] A word once used for omelette.

Amélie, à l' [ah-lah-meh-lee] A garnish for fish composed of mushrooms, truffles, and potato croquettes; with *sauce cardinal*.

Amer [ah-mer] Bitter.

Américaine, à l' [ah-lah-meh-ree-ken] Pertains to dishes prepared or garnished with lobster and/or *sauce américaine.* Also applies to grilled meats garnished with tomatoes, bacon, and fried sweet potatoes.

Américaine, sauce à l' Lobster shells sautéed in butter, reduced with white wine, brandy, and fish fumet; finished with butter and lobster coral.

Amiens [ah-myen] A town in Picardy renowned for its duck pâté, macaroons, and sausages.

Amiral, à l' [ah lah-mee-rahl] A garnish for poached fish comprised of fried oysters, mussels, fluted mushroom caps, and sliced truffles; coated with *sauce Nantua* enriched with crayfish butter.

Amou [ah-moo] A ewe's-milk cheese produced in Bearn and Gascony.

Amourettes [ah-moo-ret] The spinal marrow of veal, beef, or mutton. Delicately flavored, they are used for fillings in pâtés, vol-au-vent, savory pies, and so forth.

Amphitryon [am-fi-tree-yO] Dinner host.

Amuse-gueules [ah-müz-guhl] Small, bite-sized savory snacks.

Amygdalin [ah-meeg-dah-lI] A now obsolete term for sweets containing almonds.

Ananas [ah-nah-nahs] Pineapple.

Anchoïade/Anchoyade [ahn-shwah-yahd/A-shwah-yahd] (*Provence*) A condiment composed of anchovies puréed with garlic, shallots, and parsley in olive oil. Used as a bread spread or served with raw vegetables.

— **à la dracenoise** [+ ah-lah drah-suh-nwahz] *Anchoïade* with the addition of onions and hard-cooked eggs in the purée.

Anchois [A-shwah] Anchovies.

—, **sauce** (1) *Sauce normande* with the addition of anchovy butter and anchovy fillets. (2) Anchovies puréed with oil, lemon juice, capers, garlic, and seasonings. Served cold with crudities. (3) Any sauce featuring anchovies.

Ancienne, à l' [ah-lA-syen] A garnish for white (poultry or fish) stews featuring sliced onion and mushroom caps. Also applies to savory dishes (ragoûts) served in a pastry crust.

Ancienne, blanquette à l' [blA-ket +] A white stew (veal, lamb, or poultry) with onions, potatoes, and mushrooms.

Andalouse, à l' [ahn-dah-looz] A garnish for meats and poultry consisting of peppers stuffed with rice, chopped pimento, chorizo sausage, fried eggplant, and sausage.

—, **sauce** (1) *Sauce velouté* with the addition of tomato purée, chopped pimento, and parsley. (2) Mayonnaise with the addition of tomato purée, chopped pimento, and parsley.

Andouille [ahn-doo-yuh] A spicy cooked sausage made from pork chitterlings and tripe. A specialty of Vire, Vouvray, and Chinon.

Andouillette [ahn-doo-yet] A small raw pork sausage; some of France's finest come from the towns of Caen, Cambrai, Troyes.

— **de ficelle** [+ duh fee-sel] Andouillette made from long sections of chitterling as opposed to the ordinary type that is made from chopped pieces. Highly prized and expensive.

— **de Lyon** [duh lyO] Andouillette made from a pork and veal mixture.

— **à la strasbourgeoise** [ah-lah strahz-boor-zhwahz] Grilled andouillette sausages served on a

Andouillette à la strasbourgeoise
(cont.)
bed of braised saurkraut and garnished with boiled potatoes.
— *de Vire* [duh veer] From Vire (Normandy); grilled andouillette sausage accompanied with sorrel purée.
Aneth [A-neth] Dill.
Ange de mer [Azh duh mer] A type of shark found off European coasts. Prepared as for skate.
Angélique [A-zheh-leek] Angelica.
Anges à cheval [Ahn-zheh ah she-vahl] "Angels on horseback"; an appetizer of oysters wrapped in bacon, broiled, and served on small rounds of toast.
Anglaise, à l' [ah-lA-glez] "English style." (1) (*For fish*) Dipped in eggs and bread crumbs and fried. (2) (*For meats and vegetables*) Boiled and served with various cold sauces.
Anglaise, crème [krem +] A custard composed of sugar, egg yolks, milk, and vanilla that is heated until thickened.
Anglaise, sauce *Sauce velouté* with the addition of chopped hard-cooked egg yolks, pepper, lemon, nutmeg, and finished with anchovy-butter.
Anglaise, taverne [tah-vehrn +] Parisian restaurants that feature English food.
Anglet [A-gleh] Town near Bayonne renowned for its white wine.
Angoulême [A-goo-lem] Town located in the Charente; well-known for its brandies, seafood, and game.
Angoumois [A-goo-mwah] An area of the Charente famous for its game, stuffed cabbage (*farée*), stuffed snails, preserved duck, and pigs feet ragoût (*gigorit*).
Anguille [A-gwee-yuh] Eel.

Anguries [A-goh-ree] Antilles cucumber.
Animelles [ahn-i-mel] Animal testicles, usually from the ram, bull, or lamb.
Anis étoilé [ah-nis eh-twah-leh] "Star anise." Also referred to as *badiane* in France.
Anis vert [+ vehr] Aniseed.
Anisette [ah-nee-set] An anise-flavored liqueur.
Anjou [A-zhoo] An area of the Loire Valley particularly famous for its charcuterie and green cabbages (*piochous*).
Antiboise, à l' [ah-lA-tee-bwahz] Describes dishes using resources of Antibes (Provence), particularly eggs, sardines, olive oil, tomatoes, and garlic.
Antillaise, à l' [ah-lA-tee-yez] Describes dishes served with rice mixed with tomato sauce and *macédoine* vegetables. Also describes certain dishes containing pineapple, banana, or coconut.
Antin, sauce [A-tI] *Sauce Madeira* with the addition of a white wine, shallots, and fines herbes; garnished with truffles and quartered mushroom caps.
Anversoise, à l' [ah-lA-ver-swahz] A garnish made up of hop shoots cooked in butter or cream and served in a pastry shell.
AOC See *Appellation d'Origine Contrôllée*.
Apéritif [ah-peh-ree-teef] An alcoholic beverage served before the meal to stimulate the appetite.
Aplatir [ah-plah-teer] French culinary term meaning to flatten meat with a mallet. This process breaks down the fibers, making the meat more tender, and decreases cooking time.
A point [ah pwI] Term describing meat cooked medium rare.

Appareil [ah-pah-rey] Mixture; typically refers to batters, pastes, pastry doughs, and so forth.

— *a bombe* [+ ah bO-b] A light, airy filling for bombes consisting of egg yolks, syrup, and whipped cream. This basic filling is then flavored with the desired ingredients.

Appellation d'Origine Contrôllée [ah-pel-ah-syO doh-ree-zheen kO-troh-leh] French law regulating the production of food products, most notably wine, insuring high quality. Other products, such as certain cheeses, butters, and poultry are also protected. Often abbreviated AOC.

Appert, François [frA-swah ah-per] (1750–1841) French chef credited with the invention of the tin can.

Appétence [ah-peh-tEs] A desire for food.

Appétit [ah-peh-tee] Appetite.

Appigret [ah-pee-greh] An obsolete term for seasonings, condiments, and so forth.

Apprêt [ap-pre] A term meaning the steps involved in preparing a dish.

Apron [ah-prO] Small freshwater fish related to the perch. Usually eaten fried.

Arachide [ar-rah-sheed] Peanut.

—, *huile d'* [+ weel] Peanut oil.

Araignée [ah-reh-nyeh] The hock muscle of an ox; considered a delicacy.

Araignée à friture [+ ah free tür] A mesh or wire basket used to contain foods while deep-frying.

Arapède [ah-rah-ped] The French name for a type of univalve shellfish similar to the cockle.

Arbois [ahr-bwah] A town in the Franche-Comté noted for producing excellent wines.

Arborlade [ahr-bor-lahd] Refers to two dishes now rarely prepared:

(1) An omelette sweetened with fruit juice and sugar. (2) An herb and cheese omelette; also known as *arbourlastre*.

Arboulastre [ahr-boo-lah-struh] See *Arborlade*.

— *d'œufs* [+ duhf] The word for omelette during the middle ages.

Arbouse [ahr-booz] A berry grown in France used primarily for making jam and producing liqueurs.

Arca [ahr-kah] A bivalve mollusk found along France's shorelines.

Arcachon [ahr-kah-shO] Town in Gascony famous for its oysters.

Arcachonnaises [ahr-kah-shun-ez] A type of oyster found in Arcachon Bay in southwest France.

Arcanette [ahr-kah-net] The name given to a small teal (a type of wild duck) found in Lorraine.

Archiduc à l' [ah-lahr-shee-dük] Name given to several culinary dishes; usually denoting the use of onions, paprika or Hungarian red pepper, cream, and *sauce hongroise*.

Archiduc, sauce Suprême sauce prepared with reduced champagne.

Ardennaise, à l' [ah-lahr-den-nez] Refers to game dishes prepared with juniper berries.

Ardennes [ahr-den] A Belgian ham of exceptional quality.

Argenteuil [ahr-zhuhn-tuh-yuh] (1) A town in the Île-de-France, near Paris, world renowned for its asparagus. (2) A variety of asparagus. (3) Term denoting the presence of asparagus in a dish.

Ariège [ahr-yezh] An area in Languedoc famous for its mineral water, charcuterie, and *confit d'oie* (preserved goose).

Ariègeoise, à l' [ahr-yezh-wah] Describes dishes using the natural food resources of southwestern France, including green cabbage,

Ariègeoise, à l' (cont.)
pickled pork, poultry breast, sausage, and kidney beans.

Arlequin [ahr-luh-kI] (1) Leftovers. (2) A highly colorful dish.

Arles [ahrl] A town in Provence noted for *saucisson d'Arles* (Arles sausage), oils, snails, and pastries.

Arlésienne, à l' [ah-lahr-leh-zyen] A garnish for tournedos and noisettes of fried eggplant slices, sautéed tomatoes, and fried onion rings. Also used as a garnish for sole.

Arlésienne, sauce Béarnaise sauce with the addition of tomato purée and anchovy paste.

Armagnac [ahr-mah-nyahk] An area in Gascony producing brandy of the same name. Brandy from Armagnac is considered second only to cognac in quality.

Armand, à l' [ah-lahr-mahnd] Describes dishes garnished with soufflé potatoes, truffles, foie gras, and *sauce bordelaise*.

Armenoville, à l' [ah-lahr-muh-noh-veel] A garnish for roasted meats composed of anna potatoes and creamed morel mushrooms.

Armoricaine, à l' [ah-lahr-mor-ee-ken] Describes dishes served with *sauce velouté* to which garlic, tomatoes, and shrimp have been added.

Armottes [ahr-mot] (*Gascony*) Cornmeal mush mixed with pork or goose meat and grilled.

Aromates [ar-ro-maht] Aromatics; an herb or spice used to enhance the aroma (and taste) of a dish.

—, *sauce aux* (1) A reduction of aromatic herbs (thyme, marjoram, sage, tarragon) in red wine and added to demi-glace sauce. (2) A reduction of aromatic herbs in white wine and added to *sauce velouté*.

Arquebuse [ahr-kuh-büz] An aromatic liqueur made from various herbs.

Arrêter [ah-re-teh] Literally "stop" or "arrest," this cooking term refers to the stopping of cooking of a particular item, often by plunging it in ice water.

Arroser [ah-roh-zeh] To baste.

Artagnan, à l' [ah-lahr-tah-nyA] A garnish for large roasts consisting of cèpes coated in béarnaise sauce, stuffed cherry tomatoes, and olive-shaped potato croquettes.

Artichaut [ahr-tee-shoh] Artichoke.

—, *fonds d'* [fO dahr-tee-shoh] Artichoke hearts.

Artois [ahr-twah] A region in northern France close to the English Channel credited with numerous seafood specialties and noted for its abundance of top-quality vegetables.

—, *d'* [dahr-twah] (*For tournedos and noisettes*) A garnish of potato croustade filled with peas and served with *sauce Madeira*.

Asco [ah-skoh] A winter cheese from Corsica.

Asperge [ah-spehrzh] Asparagus.

Aspic (gelée de cuisine) [ahs-peek (zheh-leh duh kwee-zeen)] A natural gelatinous substance derived from simmering certain cuts of beef, chicken, or fish in water. Aspic jelly is used to coat foods, giving a smooth shiny surface. Gelatin is sometimes added to insure proper setting.

Assaisonnement [ah-sez-uhn-mO] (1) Seasonings. (2) The act of seasoning.

— *aromatique* [+ ah-ro-mah-teek] Aromatic seasonings such as garlic, onions, sage, and cloves.

— *au lard* [+ oh lahr] A salad dressing made up of bacon fat, vinegar, diced bacon, and seasonings. This dressing is often used in dandelion salad.

— *des salades* [+ deh sah-lahd] Salad dressing.

Assation [ah-sah-syO] Cooking food in its natural juices.

Assiette [ah-syet] "Plate/platter." Also refers to an assortment of foods on a platter.

— *anglaise* [+ A-glez] An assortment of cold, cooked meats arranged on a plate.

— *assortie* [+ ah-sor-tee] An assortment of cold appetizers arranged on a plate.

— *froide* [+ frwah] See *Assiette anglaise.*

Assiettes parisiennes [+ pah-ree-zyen] A assortment of appetizers served on a small plate.

Athénienne, à l' [ah-lah-teh-nyen] Describes dishes perpared with olive oil, eggplant, olives, stuffed peppers, and *riz pilaf à la grecque.*

Attelet [ah-tuh-leh] A small decorative skewer.

Attereau [ah-tuh-roh] Refers to food items skewered, coated in bread crumbs, and fried.

Attignole [ah-tee-nyohl] (*Normandy*) A type of cold meatball made from pork and pork fat.

Attriau [ah-tre-yoh] A flat sausage made from pork, pork liver, and veal.

Aubenas [oh-buh-nah] Town in Ardèche noted for its chestnut products and truffles.

Auber, à l' [ah-loh-ber] A garnish of artichoke bottoms stuffed with a chicken forcemeat and topped with *sauce Madeira.* Served with grilled meats and poultry.

Auberge [oh-berzh] Inn; eating place.

Aubergines [oh-behr-zheen] Eggplant.

Augusta, à l' [ah-loh-güs-tah] De-

scribes poached fish garnished with cèpes and topped with *sauce Mornay.*

Aunis [oh-nee] (1) A part of the Charente region in western France famous for its shellfish, particularly oysters; also recognized for first-rate fruits, vegetables (peas), and lamb. (2) The name of a cow's- or goat's-milk cheese from western France; rarely produced today.

Aurillac [or-ree-yahk] A town in the Auvergne region of central France most famous for the Cantal cheese produced there.

Auriol [oh-ryohl] (*Marseilles*) The local name for mackerel.

Aurore à l' [ah-loh-rohr-uh] (1) Denotes the use of tomato purée in certain dishes. (2) Denotes the use of *sauce aurore* in a dish. (3) Describes dishes reddish in color.

— *Lenten, sauce* [lehn-tehn] *Sauce aurore* prepared with fish *velouté.*

—, *sauce Velouté* (chicken) with the addition of tomato purée.

Autriche [oh-treesh] Austria.

Autrichienne, à l' [ah-loh-tree-shyen] Describes dishes prepared with paprika or Hungarian pepper, onions, fennel, sour cream, and tomatoes.

Autun [oh-tU] A French cow's-milk cheese.

Auvergnate, à l' [ah-loh-ver-nyaht] Describes dishes prepared with the resources of the Auvergne, particularly pork products and cheese.

Auvergne [oh-ver-nyuh] A province in central France; charcuterie, cabbage dishes, Cantal and Fourme cheese, and *clafouti* are among the specialties of Auvergne.

Avec peau [ah-vek poh] "With skin." Refers to fruits, vegetables, poultry, and so forth.

Aveline [ah-vuh-leen] Filbert. A nut very similar to the hazlenut.

Avignonnaise, sauce [ah-vee-nyuhn-nez] Béchamel seasoned with garlic and Parmesan cheese; enriched with egg yolks and cream.

Aviner [ah-vee-neh] French wine-term referring to the process of destroying the wood taste from new wine casks.

Avocat [ah-voh-kah] Avocado.

Avoine [ah-vwahn] Oats.

Axoa [ahks-oh-ah] Ground veal cooked with onions, garlic, and assorted peppers; a specialty of Gascony.

Axonge [ahks-Ozh] A high-quality lard rendered from the fat of hog's kidneys.

Aydes, les [leh ah-eed] A cheese from the Orléanais region best eaten in the winter and spring months.

Azi/Azy [ah-zee] A type of rennet made from whey and vinegar.

Azyme [ah-zeem] Unleavened bread.

B & B A bottled liqueur consisting of Bénédictine mixed with brandy.

Baba [bah-bah] A yeast cake made with raisins and moistened with rum or kirsch. Usually baked in a baba mold (a tall cylindrical receptacle about the size of an eight-ounce measuring cup).

— *au rhum* [+ oh rU] A baba moistened with rum.

Babeurre [bah-buhr] Buttermilk.

Backenoffe [bah-kuh-nof] (*Alsace*) A baked stew prepared with mutton, pork, and potatoes; also spelled *beckenoffe* and *baekenofe*.

Baconique [bah-kO-neek] An obsolete term refering to pork dishes.

Badoise, à la [ah-lah bah-dwahz] A term describing both small game roasts garnished with pitted cherries and a cherry-cream sauce and large game roasts garnished with braised red cabbage, puréed potatoes, and bacon.

Baekenofe [bah-ek-uh-nohf] See *backenoffe*.

Bagna [bah-nyah] See *Pain-Bagnat*.

Bagration [bah-grah-syO] Name given to several culinary dishes. Various garnishes include artichoke hearts and julienne of celeriac, macaroni, truffles, and pickled ox-tongue.

Baguette [bah-get] A long crusty loaf of bread.

Baguette de thiérache [+ duh tyeh-rash] A soft cow's-milk cheese.

Bahama, à la [ah-lah bah-hah-mah] A garnish for fish composed of shrimp, julienne red pepper, diced turtle meat, and béchamel sauce.

Bahut [bah-hüt] A two-handled container used for holding sauces or soups.

Baie [bah-yee] Berry.

Baies de ronce [+ duh rOs] Blackberry. Also called *mûre* in France.

Bain-marie [bA-mah-ree] A hot-water bath. Metal containers holding various foods are placed in a hot water container to prevent scorching while keeping food hot.

Baiser [be-zeh] Two tiny meringue puffs coupled together with butter cream. See *Tête de nègre*.

Balance [bah-lAs] The French word for a (kitchen) scale.

Balaou [bah-lah-oo] The French name for a small sardinelike fish.

Ballon [bah-lO] A boned, rolled beef shoulder.

Ballottine [bah-lot-teen] Boned meat, fish, or poultry stuffed, rolled, and poached. Coated in aspic, and sliced; served hot or cold.

Bâloise, à la [ah-lah bah-lwahz]

Fried fish garnished with fried onion rings and *sauce bâloise*.

Bâloise, sauce A white butter sauce composed of white wine, shallots, Worcestershire sauce, butter, and chopped chervil and parsley.

Bamboche, en [E bA-bosh] Describes certain dishes garnished with fried cod.

Bamia/Bamya [bah-myah] The French word for a variety of okra.

Banane [bah-nahn] Banana.

Bandol [bA-dol] A town in southeast France (Provence) known for a red AOC wine sharing the same name.

Banilles [bah-neel] A small fragrant pod sometimes used as a substitute for vanilla.

Banneton [bahn-tO] A basket without hands.

Banon [bah-nO] A cow's-milk cheese from Provence wrapped and cured in chestnut leaves.

Banquière, à la [ah-lah bA-kyer] Describes foods richly garnished "banker's style."

Banquière, garniture Garnish for steaks, poultry, and sweetbreads composed of quenelles of mushrooms, chicken, and truffles.

Banquière, sauce Sauce *suprême* with the addition of Madeira wine and chopped black truffles.

Banyuls [ba-nee-lüs] Town in southern France (Roussillon) producing an excellent dessert wine of the same name.

Bar [bahr] Bass.

— *grillé* [+ gree-yeh] Broiled sea bass.

— *rayé* [+ reh] Striped bass.

Baraquilles [bah-rah-keel] Small pastries stuffed with a *salpicon* of calf's sweetbreads, foie gras, diced partridge or pheasant, and truffles. Served as an appetizer.

Barbantane [bahr-bA-tahn] A

sweet wine from a region of the same name in the Bouches-du-Rhône.

Barbarin [bahr-bah-rI] A variety of squash.

Barbeau [bahr-boh] Barbel. A European river fish related to the carp. It is usually poached or braised.

Barberey [bahr-bur-reh] A French cow's-milk cheese similar to Camembert, made in Troyes (Champagne). Also known as *Fromage de Troyes*.

Barberon [bahr-buh-rO] A word for *salsify* used in parts of France.

Barbe-de-capucin [bahrb-duh-kah-püsheen] Wild chicory; a bitter salad green.

Barbillons [bahr-bee-yO] Small barbels (*barbeaux*), usually fried.

Barboteur [bahr-bo-tuhr] A local French name for duck.

Barbotte [bar-bot] Burbot.

Barbouille, en [E bahr-boo-yuh] Describes rabbit or poultry prepared with red wine and the animal's blood.

Barbue [bahr-bü] Brill; a flat saltwater fish compared to turbot.

Barde [bahr] The process of wrapping fat (bacon, pork fat) around very lean meat to prevent drying out during cooking and to add flavor.

Bardatte [bahr-daht] (*Brittany*) Braised cabbage stuffed with rabbit meat and wrapped in bacon.

Barèges [bah-rezh] A region in southwestern France noted for the fine-quality mutton raised there.

Bar-le-Duc [bahr-luh-dük] A town in Lorraine most famous for its red currant and gooseberry jams.

Baron [bah-rO] The hind quarters and saddle of lamb, mutton, or beef.

Barquette [bahr-ket] A small canoe-shaped pastry shell. Barquettes contain either a sweet or savory filling and are served as an hors d'œuvre or a dessert.

Barrique [bahr-reek] A barrel used for carrying wine.

Barrot [bahr-roht] An anchovy cask.

Barsac [bahr-sahk] A sweet white Bordeaux of excellent quality.

Bartavelle [bahr-tah-vel] Rock partridge. It is commonly roasted with cabbage or used in *chartreuse*.

Basilic [bah-seel-eek] Basil. In France it is known as the royal herb.

—, *au* Refers to dishes prepared with basil.

Basquaise, à la [ah-lah bask-wez] "Basque style"; a garnish for large roasts consisting of Bayonne ham, mushroom caps, and anna potatoes. Also describes dishes prepared with roasted red peppers, tomatoes, and garlic.

Basque [bahsk] A region in southwest France bordering Spain. Red peppers, tomatoes, garlic, and ham (Bayonne) are typical ingredients of French-Basque cookery.

Basse venaison [bahs vuh-ne-zO] A French term for hare and rabbit meat.

Bastella [bahs-tel-luh] (*Corsica*) A savory turnover of meat—usually pork—and vegetables. See *Inarbittate, Inzuchatte, Incivulate.*

Bastion [bah-styO] The arrangement of cold food—usually eel—in cylindrical fashion and coated in aspic.

Ba-ta-clan [bah-tah-klA] A pastry made with almonds and rum and topped with fondant icing.

Bâtard [bah-tahr] A long, thin, crusty loaf of bread.

Bâtarde, sauce Béchamel sauce with the addition of egg yolks, lemon juice, and butter.

Bateaux [bah-toh] Boat-shaped containers used to serve appetizers.

Bâtelière, à la [ah-lah bah-tuhl-yer] Literally "boatman's style"; a broad term referring to dishes garnished with seafood.

Bâton [bah-tO] (1) See *Bâtonnet.* (2) Long, somewhat thin loaves of crusty bread.

Bâton de Jacob [+ duh zhah-kohb] "Jacob's baton"; a small baton-shaped éclair filled with cream and glazed with fondant.

Bâtonnet [bah-tuhn-neh] Also called *bâtons.* Various foods in the form of small sticks, usually pastries or vegetables.

Bâtonnets aux amandes [+ oh ah-mahnd] A stick-shaped almond pastry topped with almond paste.

Batterie de cuisine [bah-tree-duh kwee-zeen] The French term for kitchen equipment.

Battre [bah-treh] To whip or beat (*eggs, cream*).

Baudroie [boh-drwah] Monkfish.

Bavarois [bah-vah-rwah] A sweet custard made up of eggs, heavy cream, gelatin, and milk. Fresh fruit and liqueurs often added as flavorings. Also called Bavarian cream.

Bavaroise [bah-vah-rwahz] A hot beverage composed of egg yolks, tea, milk, and alcohol (kirsch, Marachino, Cointreau, or rum).

Bavaroise aux choux [+ oh shoo] An obsolete term for a mixture of absinthe and orgeat.

Bavette [bah-vet] The French word for *flank,* the abdominal muscle of beef.

Baveux/Baveuse [bah-vuh/bah-vuhz] A term usually meaning runny or soft, usually referring to omelettes.

Bayonnaise, à la [ah-lah bah-yuhn-nez] Refers to dishes using the natural resorces of Bayonne, particularly ham.

Bayonnaise, garniture A garnish for various meat dishes, it consists of macaroni and julienne of Bayonne ham in béchamel sauce.

Bayonne [bah-yuhn] A southwestern port town in the French Basque, Bayonne is credited with the production of the world famous Bayonne ham, though it is actually made in Orthez, a nearby town.

Béarn [beh-ahrn] French province located in southwest France; specialties include *ouliat, garbure,* béarnaise sauce, and various pork products.

Béarnaise, sauce [behr-nez] An emulsion sauce consisting of a reduction of shallots, tarragon, and vinegar combined with beaten egg yolks and whisked in butter. Finished with fresh tarragon and served with grilled meats and poached fish.

Béatilles [beh-ah-tee-yuh] A *salpicon* of small ingredients (sweetbreads, kidneys, mushrooms, *mirepoix,* foie gras) used as a filling for vol-au-vent.

Béatilles, ragoût de [rah-goo duh +] A fricassée of poultry offal.

Béatrix [beh-ah-treeks] A garnish for large roasts consisting of sautéed morels, quartered artichoke bottoms, baby carrots, and roasted potatoes.

Beaucaire [boh-ker] A garnish for various meats composed of braised cabbage, boiled new potatoes, sliced apples, and mushroom caps.

Beaucuit [boh-kwee] A French word for *buckwheat;* also called *blénoir, bucail,* and *sarrasin.*

Beaufort [boh-for] (1) A type of French Gruyère cheese, it is made from cow's-milk and has a firm, fruity flavor. (2) A garnish for fish comprised of poached oysters, lobster meat, and *sauce américaine.*

Beaugency [boh-zhE-see] (*For grilled meats*) A garnish of quartered artichoke bottoms, stewed tomatoes, poached beef marrow, and béarnaise sauce.

Beauharnais [boh-ahr-neh] (*For grilled meats*) A garnish of stuffed mushroom caps, quartered artichoke bottoms, and *sauce beauharnais.* Also applies to sweet dishes using bananas and rum.

—, sauce à la Béarnaise sauce with the addition of tarragon butter. Served with grilled meats or fish.

Beaujeu [boh-zhuh] (*For large roasts of beef, roebuck, mutton*) A garnish of sautéed artichoke bottoms, puréed lentils, and glazed chestnuts.

Beaujolais [boh-zhoh-leh] A world-famous red wine produced from the Gamay grape.

— nouveau [+ noo-voh] New Beaujolais wine.

Beaune [bohn] A town in Burgundy famous for its white wines.

Beaupré de Roybon [boh-preh duh roee-bO] A French cheese produced in Dauphiné; best eaten in the winter months.

Beauvilliers [boh-vee-yeh] A garnish of spinach *cromesqui,* stuffed tomatoes, and sautéed salsify; served with large cuts of meat. Also the name of a heavy almond cake.

Beauvilliers, Antoine [A-twahn +] (1754–1817) Great French chef credited with opening the first restaurant.

Bécasse [beh-kahs] Woodcock. A game bird prized in France for its entrails.

Bécasseau [beh-kah-soh] Young woodcock.

Bécassine [beh-kah-seen] Snipe.

Béchameil, Louis de [loo-ees duh beh-shah-mel] (1630–1703) A French financier and food lover. Lends his name to the classic béchamel sauce, though it's doubtful he created it.

Béchenoffe [be-she-nof] A mutton and potato stew from Alsace.

Becqueter [bek-kuh-teh] To play with or peck at one's dinner.

Bêche-de-mer [besh duh mehr] The French word for the sea cucumber, a sea creature related to the starfish and sea urchin; commonly used in soups in France.

Becfigue [be-feeg] See *Becs-Fins.*

Becs-fins [bek-fI] A small game bird similar in appearance and preparation to the lark.

Bedeù [be-duh] (*Nice*) The word for a local variety of tripe.

Beignets [be-nyeh] Small pieces of vegetables or meat dipped in batter and fried; a fritter.

Beignets venteux [+ vE-tuh] See *Soupirs de nonne.*

Belgique [bel-zheek] Belgium. Country bordering northeast France. Belgium's culinary influences on France include dishes featuring herring, pork products, rich breads and pastries, and the use of beer both as a beverage and a cooking ingredient.

Belle alliance [bel ahl-yAs] (1) A garnish for grilled meats composed of slices of goose liver, tomatoes, and truffles. Served with *sauce Madeira.* (2) A variety of winter pear reddish-yellow in color.

Belle angevine [+ A-zgeh-veen] A variety of winter pear.

Belle Chevreuse [+ shuh-vruhs] A variety of peach bright red in color.

Belle de Berry [+ duh ber-ree] See *Poire de Berry; Poire de curé.*

Belle dijonnaise [+ dee-zhon-nes] A dessert featuring fruit served on black currant ice, coated with black currant purée laced with cassis, and garnished with black currants.

Belle et bonne [eh buhn] A variety of pear used for baking or poaching.

Belle garde [+ gahrd] A type of firm-fleshed peach used for baking or poaching.

Belle-Hélène [+ eh-len] The name of several culinary dishes named after an Offenbach operetta.

—, poires [pwahr +] A dessert of poached pears on vanilla ice cream topped with chocolate sauce.

—, poulet [poo-leh +] Sautéed chicken breast garnished with asparagus tips, mushrooms, and black truffles; coated with suprême sauce.

Bellet [bel-leh] An AOC wine from southwest France.

Belle-vue, en [E bel-vü] A term meaning to display beautifully.

Belle-vue garniture Cold, whole fish in aspic elaborately decorated.

Bellone [bel-lon] A variety of large figs.

Belmont, à la [ah-lah bel-mO] A garnish for large roasts composed of stuffed bell peppers and tomatoes au gratin.

Belon huîtres [beh-lO wee-truh] A variety of oysters, excellent in quality, found along the northwest coast of France.

Bénédictin [beh-neh-deek-teh] A cake made with almonds and Bénédictine.

Bénédictine [beh-neh-deek-teen] A famous liqueur first produced in 1510 at the Abbey of Fécamp in

Normandy. It is a cognac-based, sweet liqueur made with seventy-five herbs, spices, and flowers.

Bénédictine, à la A garnish for numerous dishes composed of puréed salt cod and creamed truffles in tartlet shells.

Berceau [ber-soh] A type of manual chopper consisting of a large curved blade with handles on each end. The food is minced using a rocking motion.

Berchoux, sauce *Sauce allemande* with the addition of heavy cream and chervil butter.

Bercy [ber-see] The name given to a number of culinary preparations that often include the use of Bercy butter and white wine. Also the name of a Parisian district.

—, *beurre* A butter sauce composed of white wine, shallots, poached marrow, pepper, lemon juice, and whole butter slowly whisked in.

—, *sauce* Fish *velouté* with the addition of chopped shallots, reduced white wine, parsley, and finished with whole butter.

Berdonneau [ber-don-noh] A French nickname for the Atlantic turbot.

Bergamote [ber-gah-mot] (1) A variety of bitter orange used in pâtisserie and confectionery. (2) An herb of the mint family used in salads, cordials, and in making Oswego tea. (3) A variety of pear. (4) An orange-flavored barley sugar.

Bergerac [ber-zheh-rak] A district in southwestern France noted for its white wines.

Bergère, à la [ah-lah ber-zher] "Shepherdess style"; denotes the use of butter, cream, and mushrooms in preparation of a dish.

Berlingot [ber-lI-go] A triangular-shaped, peppermint-flavored confection.

Berlinoise, sauce [ber-lee-nwahz] Mayonnaise sauce to which red currant jelly and lemon juice has been added. Used to garnish fruits.

Bernard, à la [ah-lah ber-nahr] A garnish for large cuts of meat composed of sliced boletus mushrooms, sautéed chopped tomatoes, and potato croquettes.

Bernard, Émile [eh-meel ber-nahr] A nineteenth century chef and author of *Culinary classique*.

Bernis [ber-nee] Refers to dishes (usually eggs) prepared with asparagus.

Berny [ber-nee] A garnish for game composed of small tarts filled with puréed lentils and sliced truffles.

Berrichonne, à la [ah-lah ber-ree-shun] Garnish for large cuts of meat comprised of cabbage sautéed with bacon, poached chestnuts, and glazed pearl onions.

Berry [ber-ree] A French province south of Touraine noted for fresh water fish (lampreys), wild game, and its high-quality mutton. Specialties include *sanguine* (a type of pancake), *citrouillat* (a pumpkin tart), and *truffiat* (a potato scone).

Besaigre [bes-seg-ruh] An obsolete term referring to sour wines.

Bête de compagnie [bet duh cO-pah-nyee] A wild boar between the ages of one and two.

Bête fauve [+ fohv] A term referring to a large game such as a deer; this term is now rarely used.

Bête rousse [+ roos] Wild boar between the ages of six months and one year.

Bêtise [beh-teez] A mint-flavored confection manufactured in France.

Bette [bet] (1) Swiss chard. (2) A variety of beet.

Bettelman [be-tel-mahn] A specialty dessert of Alsace consisting of bread crumbs combined with candied orange peel, cherries, sugar, and beaten egg whites. It is baked and sprinkled with cinnamon.

Betterave [bet-trahv] Beetroot.

Beurre [buhr] Butter.

— *à la meunière* [+ ah-lah muh-nyer] Melted butter combined with lemon juice; served with fish *à la meunière.*

— *à l' anglaise, sauce* [+ ah-lA-glez] See *Beurre, sauce au.*

— *blanc* [+ blA] Meaning white butter literally, this emulsion sauce is composed of white wine, vinegar, shallots, and butter.

— *bourguignon* [+ boor-gee-nO] Served with escargots, this sauce is made up of reduced red wine combined with shallots, parsley, and mushrooms; thickened with beurre manié, and finished with whole butter.

— *Châteaubriand* [+ shah-toh-bree-A] A white wine reduction combined with veal glaze and maître d'hôtel butter. Finished with chopped tarragon.

— *chivry* [+ shee-vree] See *Ravigote, beurre.*

— *clarifié* [+ klah-ree-fee-eh] Clarified butter.

— *Colbert* [+ kohl-ber] Maître d'hôtel butter to which a meat glaze and fresh tarragon has been added. Served with fish prepared *à la Colbert.*

— *composé* [+ kO-poh-zeh] Whole or melted butter combined with one or more ingredients and used as an accompaniment to various dishes.

— *d'ail* [+ dahy] Garlic butter.

— *d'anchois* [+ dA-shwah] Anchovy butter.

— *de cacao* [+ duh kah-kah-oh] Cocoa butter. The fatty substance derived from cocoa beans.

— *de citron* [+ duh see-truhn] Lemon butter.

— *de Gascogne* [+ duh gahs-koh-nyuh] Similar to *beurre de Provence*, this sauce contains veal fat combined with poached garlic rather than butter.

— *de pistache* [+ duh pees-tash] Pistachio butter.

— *de Provence* [+ duh pro-vEs] This is the term used for *aïoli* in the south of France.

— *d' échalote* [+ deh-shah-lot] Shallot butter.

— *d' escargot* [+ des-kahr-goh] Snail butter.

— *d' estragon* [+ des-trah-gO] Tarragon butter.

— *fondu* [+ fO-dü] Melted butter.

— *homard* [+ oh-mahr] Lobster butter.

— *hôtelière* [+ o-tel-yer] Whipped butter combined with lemon juice, parsley, and duxelles.

—, *maître d'hôtel* [me-truh-do-tel] Softened or melted butter flavored with chopped fresh parsley and fresh lemon juice. It is used to season numerous savory dishes.

— *manié* [+ mah-nyeh] This raw roux is made up of butter kneaded with flour. It is used to thicken sauces and should never come to a boil.

— *marchand de vin* [+ mahr-shA-duh-vin] See *Marchand de vin, beurre.*

— *Marseilles* [+ mahr-se-yuh] The name used for oil in some parts of France.

— *à la meunière* [+ ah-lah muh-nyer] Browned butter seasoned with lemon juice and parsley. Usually served over pan-fried fish.

— *Montpellier* [+ mO-puh-lyeh] Butter combined with blanched green herbs, gherkins, anchovies, egg yolks, and olive oil. It is used as an accompaniment to cold dishes.

— *nantais* [+ nA-teh] Beurre blanc with the addition of heavy cream.

— *noir* [+ nwahr] "Black butter"; whole butter cooked until it has reached a deep brown color, with chopped parsley added at the last minute; served with a variety of dishes.

-, *sauce* A sauce for fish composed of browned butter combined with lemon juice and parsley.

— *noisette* [+ nwah-zet] (1) Whole butter combined with crushed hazelnuts. (2) Butter cooked to a light-brown, hazelnut color; popularly served with eggs, skate, and brains.

— *printanier* [+ prI-tah-nyeh] Whole butter mixed with puréed green vegetables. Served with cold appetizers and used to thicken sauces.

— *rouge* [+ roozh] "Red butter"; pounded lobster shells and paprika combined with melted butter and strained.

—, *sauce au* Salted boiling water thickened with roux and combined with egg yolks, cream, lemon, and finished with a generous amount of butter.

— *vert* [+ vehr] "Green butter"; butter combined with puréed spinach.

— *vigneron, sauce au* [+ vee-nyuh-rO] Red wine, red wine vinegar, and shallots reduced by half and finished with whole butter.

— *vin rouge* [+ vin-roozh] Softened whole butter kneaded with red wine.

Beurrecks à la turque [buhr-reks-ah-lah-türk] An appetizer consisting of Gruyère cheese melted with béchamel sauce, wrapped in pastry, and rolled into cigar shapes; breaded and fried.

Beurrier [buhr-ryeh] Butter dish.

Béziers [beh-zyeh] A town in southern France recognized for the red table wines produced there.

Biarrotte, à la [ah-lah byahr-roht] Denotes the use of cèpe mushrooms in the preparation of a dish or the use of cèpes as a garnish.

Bien cuit [byE kwee] Cooked well-done.

Bière [byehr] Beer.

— *de gingembre* [+ zhI-zhahm-bruh] Ginger beer.

— *de ménage* [+ duh meh-nazh] Home-made beer.

Bifteck [bif-tek] Steak.

— *haché* [+ ah-sheh] Beef hash.

Bigarade, sauce [bee-gahr-rahd] (1) The thickened juices from a roasted duck, flavored with orange, lemon, and Grand Marnier. (2) A clear, reduced duck-stock flavored with orange and lemon and finished with carmelized sugar dissolved in vinegar.

Bigarreau [bee-gahr-roh] A large, sweet, variety of cherry.

Bignon [bee-nyO] A potato stuffed with seasoned ground pork and baked.

Bigorneau [bee-gor-noh] Winkle. A type of snail found along European coastlines. They are usually poached and eaten cold.

Bijane [bee-zhahn] A chilled soup common in the Anjou region consisting of bread moistened in red wine.

Bijou, à la [ah-lah bee-zhoo] Pastry shells stuffed with lamb sweetbreads; used as a garnish for meat entrées.

Bireweck [beer-wek] An Alsatian yeast pastry made with candied fruit and flavored with kirsch. Also spelled *birwecka*.

Biscotte [bees-kot] A twice-baked yeast biscuit popular throughout France.

Biscotte parisienne [+ pah-ree-zyen] A light pastry made with almonds, egg yolks, and beaten egg whites; flavored with kirsch.

Biscuit [bees-kwee] A small, dry pastry similar to a cracker; cookie.

Biscuit glacé [+ glah-seh] An ice cream cake.

Bisontine, à la [ah-lah bee-zO-teen] A garnish of duchesse potato crustades, cauliflower, and braised stuffed lettuce.

Bisque [beesk] A rich soup usually prepared with puréed shellfish and thickened with cream.

Bistrot [bees-troh] Bistro. A small tavern or café.

Bistrouille [bees-troo-ee-yuh] A mixture of coffee and brandy. Also spelled *bistouille*.

Blanc, à [ah blA] A term used to describe foods cooked without browning.

Blanc de blanc The term for white wines made from white grapes.

Blanc de cuisson [+ duh kwee-sO] A mixture of flour, water, lemon juice, and seasonings. It is used to thicken and prevent discoloration of the stock used for cooking offal.

Blanc de noir [+ duh nwahr] The term for white wines made from black grapes.

Blanc d'œufs [+ duhf] Egg whites.

Blanc fumé [+ fü-meh] The name for the Sauvignon Blanc grape in parts of the Loire Valley.

Blanchaille [blA-shah-yuh] Whitebait; small or young fish (particularly sprat) eaten whole.

Blanchir [blA-sheer] Blanch; cooking raw ingredients quickly in boiling water.

Blanc-manger [blA-mA-zheh] Traditionally an almond custard. The term is often now used to describe a custard or pudding made with cornstarch and milk.

Blanquette [blA-ket] A white stew of lamb, veal, or chicken thickened with egg yolks and cream.

Blayais [blah-yeh] A wine growing region in Bordeaux.

Blé [bleh] Wheat.

Blenny [bleh-nee] A small freshwater fish usually fried. Common in the south of France.

— *cagnette* [+ kah-nyet] Fried blenny.

Blé noir [bleh nwahr] A French word for buckwheat; see *Beaucuit*.

Blette [blet] A local French word for chard. See *Ablette*.

Bleu, au The method of cooking live or very fresh fish—usually trout—in boiling water or stock.

Bleu d'Auvergne [+ doh-ver-nyuh] A blue-veined cheese made from a combination of sheeps, goats, and cows milk. Produced in Auvergne.

Bleu, cuire au [kweer oh bluh] A term used to describe steak cooked extremely rare.

Bleu de Basillac [+ duh bah-see-yahk] A blue-veined cheese similar to Roquefort; produced in Limousin.

Bleu de Bresse [+ duh bres] A creamy, lightly-veined blue cheese made in Bresse, north of Lyons.

Bleu du Haut Gex [+ duh oh zhuhks] See *Septmoncel*.

Bleu du Haut Jura [+ zhü-rah] See *Septmoncel*.

Bleu de Salers [+ duh sah-leh] Similar to *Bleu d'Auvergne*, this blue cheese is made from the milk of the Salers cow.

Blond de veau [blOd duh voh] White veal stock.

Blond de volaille [duh vo-lah-yuh] White chicken stock.

Blondir [blO-deer] To very lightly brown food in fat.

Blondiner [blO-dee-neh] A term meaning to cook onions gently in butter without browning.

Bœuf [buhf] Beef.

— *haché* [+ Ahsh] Minced beef.

— *salé* [+ sah-leh] Salted beef.

Bohémienne, à la [ah-lah boh-heh-myen] A garnish of rice pilaf, fried onion rings, and tomato *concassée*; for poultry and certain game.

Bohémienne, sauce A cold sauce made up of mayonnaise sauce combined with béchamel sauce and seasoned with tarragon vinegar.

Boîte à épices [bwaht ah-eh-pees] Spice box.

Boitelle [bwah-tel] Refers to cooked fish garnished with sliced mushrooms.

Bol [bol] Bowl.

Bolée [boh-leh] A small vessel used for serving cider.

Bolet [boh-leh] Boletus; a genus of wild mushrooms.

Bolognaise, à la [ah-lah boh-lo-nyez] Describes dishes prepared in the style of Italy, particularly Bologna. Pasta, beef, tomatoes, and other vegetables are the primary ingredients used when cooking *à la bolognaise*.

Bolognaise, sauce A tomato sauce containing beef and seasoned with sage, rosemary, and red wine. It is very similar to Italy's classic Bolognese sauce.

Bombay, à la [ah-lah bO-beh] A garnish for fish comprised of brown rice, various chutneys, and curry sauce.

Bombe (glacée) [bO-b glahseh] A frozen dessert made up of ice cream or sherbet lined in a spherical mold. The center is filled with various ingredients.

Bombine [bO-been] A specialty of Ardèche, this is a type of salt pork stew with potatoes and blood sausage.

Bonbon [bO-bO] A candy or confection, usually fondant or nuts, coated with chocolate.

Bondon [bO-dO] Produced in Normandy, this is a soft textured cheese, similar to Neufchâtel.

Bonite [boh-neet] A type of saltwater fish related to the tuna.

Bonne-femme [buhn fahm] Simply prepared. This term usually indicates stock (for boiling foods) and vegetables have been used in the cooking process.

Bonne-dame [+ dahm] Orach. A green, leafy vegetable similar to spinach.

Bonnefoy, sauce [buhn-fwai] Bordelaise sauce made with white wine instead of red.

Bonnes-mares [buhn mahr] A very fine red Burgundy wine.

Bonnet-turc [buhn-neh türk] The name for a variety of pumpkin in some parts of France.

Bonnezeaux [buhn-nuh-zoh] A white wine from Anjou made from the Chenin Blanc grape.

Bontemps, sauce [bO-tE] Sauce for grilled meats made up of *velouté* combined with cider and finished with mustard and butter.

Bonvalet [bO-vah-leh] See *Beauvilliers*.

Bordeaux [bor-doh] A town in southwestern France famous for superior red and white wines.

Bordelaise, à la [ah-lah bor-dlez] "Bordeaux style." (1) The name given to several dishes prepared with red wine or served with

Bordelaise, à la (cont.)
bordelaise sauce. (2) Indicates cèpes are present in a dish. (3) Served or prepared with potatoes and artichokes.

Bordelaise, sauce A reduction of red wine with shallots, thyme, and bay added to demi-glace sauce; garnished with poached bone marrow.

Bordure [bor-dür] "Border." Food arranged around the edge of a platter used to contain the main dish.

Borgne [bor-nyuh] See *Aïgo San d'Iou.*

Bosson macérés [bos-sO mah-seh-reh] Soft goat's-milk cheeses produced in Vivarais.

Bossu [bos-sü] A cup of coffee to which Calvados has been added.

Bottereaux [bot-troh] Small yeast-pastries traditionally eaten during Lent. They are flavored with liqueur and fried; from western France.

Bouchée [boo-sheh] These are stuffed sweet or savory bite-sized pastries or confections.

Bouchées au chocolat [+ oh shoh-koh-lah] A term referring to several various chocolate confections.

Boucher [boo-sheh] Butcher.

Bouchère, à la [ah-lah boo-sher] Denotes a dish is prepared or garnished with bone marrow.

Bouchère, sauce A brown sauce with beef, tomatoes, and onions.

Boucherie [boo-shree] Butcher's shop.

Boucs [books] A local name for shrimp in parts of the Charente.

Boudin [boo-dI] A type of sausage.

Boudin blanc [+ blA] A delicate white sausage made from chicken, pork, or veal. Cream, eggs, and bread crumbs are sometimes added.

— *noir* [+ nwahr] A sausage composed of pig's blood, pork fat, bread crumbs, and seasonings; it is stuffed in caul and poached prior to eating.

Boudy [boo-dee] A variety of apple.

Bouffis [boo-fees] Lightly smoked herring.

Bougnette [boo-nyet] (1) (*Southern France*) A type of flat pork sausage. (2) (*Cévennes*) A small fritter. (3) (*Auvergne*) A thick pancake.

Bougon [boo-gO] See *Mothais.*

Bougras [boo-grah] (*Périgord*) A potato-cabbage soup with leeks and onions. The soup is traditionally prepared with the water in which blood sausages were cooked. Also called *soupe à l'eau de boudin.*

Bouillabaisse [boo-yah-bes] A fish stew from Marseilles. The stock is prepared with tomatoes, onions, white wine, and water, and is flavored with saffron and fennel. An assortment of seafood is added and is served over crusty slices of French bread.

— *Borgne* [+ bor-nyuh] See *Aigo San d'Iou.*

— *Corse* [+ kors] (*Corsican cookery*) A version of the classical bouillabaisse with the addition of red peppers and pimentoes.

— *de morue* [+ duh mo-rü] A cod and potato stew.

Bouillant [boo-yA] A small pastry filled with a *salpicon* of chicken. Served boiling hot.

Bouillante [boo-yAt] An obsolete term referring to soup served boiling hot.

Bouille [boo-yu] A milk container.

Bouille, la [lah boo-yuh] A double-cream cheese made from cow's-milk produced in Normandy; somewhat similar to Camembert.

Bouilleture [bwee-ye-tür] An eel stew from northwestern France prepared with mushrooms and wine; also spelled *bouilliture*.

— *d'Anguilles* [+ dA-gwee-yuh] (*Anjou*) A soup prepared with baby eels, white wine, garlic, mushrooms, and prunes. The soup is slowly simmered for hours and is finished with whole butter.

Bouilli [bwee-yee] Boiled beef.

Bouillinada [bwee-nee-nah-dah] A fish stew much like bouillabaise from the Roussillon region in the south of France.

Bouillir [bwee-yeer] To boil.

Bouilloire [bwee-wahr] Kettle.

Bouillon [bwee-yO] A clear, thin, seasoned stock acquired from simmering meat or vegetables for an extended period of time. Fried onions and vermicelli are served with the meal.

Bouis-abaisso d'épinards [bwee-ah-be-soh deh-pee-nahr] A potato-spinach casserole popular in Marseilles. The dish is seasoned with garlic, fennel, and saffron, and is topped with fried eggs.

Boulangère, à la [ah-lah boo-lA-zhyer] Term given to meat or poultry baked in the oven with a garnish of potatoes and onions.

Boulangerie [boo-lA-zhree] Bakery.

Boulaud [boo-loh] See *Rabotte*.

Boule-de-neige [bool-duh-nezh] (1) Small, ball-shaped cakes iced with whipped cream. (2) Bombe glacée coated with whipped cream. (3) A local French name for agaric (mushroom).

Boulette [boo-let] (1) Similar to croquettes, these are *salpicons* of meat, fish, or poultry dipped in egg and bread crumbs and then fried. (2) A version of Maroilles cheese.

— *d'Avesnes* [+ doh-vehz-nyuh] This pungent cow's-milk cheese results from combining Maroilles cheese with fresh herbs and spices; produced in Flanders.

— *de Cambrai* [+ duh kam-breh] A soft, ball-shaped cheese made from cow's-milk and flavored with herbs.

Boule de Lille [bool duh leel] A version of *mimolette*. See *Mimolette*.

Bouquet [boo-keh] The aroma of wine. It is produced by the evaporation of essential oils (which are extremely volatile) and is one of the main elements in determining the quality of a wine.

Bouquet garni [+ gahr-nee] An herb bundle consisting of peppercorns, bay leaves, thyme, and parsley. Used to flavor stocks and sauces.

Bouquetière, à la [boo-keh-tyehr] A garnish of colorful vegetables arranged in a bouquet form. Served with roasted meats and poultry.

Bourbonnais [boor-buhn-neh] A region in central France known for its hearty, country-style cooking.

Bourdaloue [boor-dah-loo] A dessert made up of poached fruit—usually pears, peaches, or apricots—coated with frangipane cream and crushed macaroons and browned in the oven.

Bourdelot normande [boor-duh-loh nor-mahnd] See *Rabotte*.

Bourgeoise, à la [boor-zhwahz] Describes dishes simply prepared with potatoes, onions, carrots, turnips, bacon, and demi-glace sauce.

Bourget, lac du [lahk duh boor-zheh] A lake in Savoy providing an abundance of freshwater fish.

Bourgogne [boor-goh-nyuh] Burgundy; an eastern French prov-

VOCABULARY

Bourgogne (cont.)
ince noted not only for world class wines but also for several culinary contributions, such as Dijon mustard and blackcurrants, Charolais beef, Cassis, and *sauce bourguignonne.*

Bourgueil [boor-guhl] Famous red and rosé wines from the Loire Valley produced from the Cabernet Franc grape.

Bourguignonne, à la [boor-gee-nyuhn] Dishes prepared with red wine.

Bourguignonne, boeuf à la [buhf ah-lah +] Famous dish from Burgundy consisting of beef cooked in red wine with button mushrooms, pearl onions, and bacon.

Bourguignonne, sauce Red wine reduced with shallots, parsley, bay, and mushrooms; strained and thickened with beurre manié. Served with snails, eggs, poultry, and beef.

Borre-geuele [bor-guhl] See *Torgoul.*

Bourguignotte, sauce [boor-gee-nyot] *Sauce espagnole* with the addition of reduced Volnay wine and finished with crayfish butter. Garnished with crayfish tails.

Bourrache [boo-rahsh] Borage.

Bourriche [boo-reesh] A basket used for carrying oysters.

Bourride [boo-reed] (*Provence*) A garlicky seafood stew similar to bouillabaisse. Aïoli is mixed with the fish stock to thicken and is served over crusty bread. It is argued that a classic bourride must never contain saffron (unlike bouillabaisse) or shellfish.

Bourriolles [boor-ryohl] A sweet, heavy pancake made from buckwheat flour and potato purée. A specialty of Aurillac.

Boursault [boor-soh] A very soft, triple-cream cheese from France.

Boursin [boor-sI] A soft, double-cream cheese flavored with herbs.

Boutargure [boo-tahr-zhür] See *Poutargue des Martigues.*

Bouteille [boo-teh-yuh] Bottle.

Bouteiller [boo-teh-yeh] An obsolete term synonymous with wine steward or sommelier.

Bouton de chèvre [boo-tO duh she-vruh] A small, ball-shaped goat's-milk cheese from France.

Bouton-de-culotte [+ duh kü-luht] A soft goat's cheese produced in Macon. Also called *Chevrotin de Macon.*

Bout-saigneux [boo-se-nyuh] A calf's or sheep's neck.

Bouzigues [boo-zeeg] A type of oyster from Sète, a Mediterranean port town in Languedoc.

Bouzy [boo-zee] A sparkling red wine from Champagne, of excellent quality.

Boyaux [bo-yoh] See *Bedeù.*

Brabançonne, à la [brah-A-son] "Brabant style"; denotes that a dish is garnished with fresh vegetables from Brabant—particularly Brussels sprouts—topped with *sauce Mornay.* Served with lamb or mutton and usually accompanied with croquette potatoes.

Bragrance [brah-grAs] (1) A garnish for grilled meats consisting of tomatoes topped with béarnaise sauce and potato croquettes. (2) An orange flavored génoise layer cake.

Braisage [bre-zhazh] Braising; cooking meat or vegetables by first browning in fat and then slowly cooking in a sealed vessel with a small amount of liquid.

Braisière [bre-zyer] Braising pan.

Brancas [brA-kah] A garnish of anna potatoes and chiffonade of lettuce. Served with small cuts of meat.

Brandade [brA-dahd] (*Provence*) A spread comprised of salt cod, garlic, and shallots pounded to a paste, into which olive oil is slowly incorporated.

— *de morue* [+ duh mo-rü] (*Languedoc*) Similar to the Provençal dish with the addition of sliced black truffles.

Brandade à la provençale, sauce [+ pro-vE-sahl] Nutmeg, garlic, and lemon are added to *sauce allemande* and finished with olive oil and chopped tarragon.

Brandevin [brAd-vI] Literally "burned wine," this is the name for spirits distilled from wine.

Brandy [brA-dee] A spirit distilled from fermented fruit. The Cognac and Armagnac regions of France are regarded as the world's finest producers of brandy.

Branicka, à la [bra-nee-kah] Tartlets filled with duxelles, sautéed asparagus tips, and *sauce Madeira.* Served as a garnish for small cuts of beef.

Brantôme, sauce [brA-tom] A white wine sauce with julienne of turnips, carrots, and parsnips; sliced truffles, and chopped chervil. Served with fish.

Braou-bouffat [bra-oh-boo-fah] Literally "good eating," this soup is prepared from the stock used to cook blood sausage. Its contents include cabbage, rice, vermicelli, and onions. It is a specialty of Cerdagne.

Brassadeau [brah-sah-doh] A small ring-shaped pastry traditionally eaten on Palm Sunday. Other names include *tortillon, cordillon,* and *brassado*; from southern France.

Brassado [brah-sah-do] See *Brassadeau.*

Brasserie [brah-sree] An establishment where food and alcoholic beverages are served.

Brayaude [brah-yod] A term denoting that a dish is prepared with the food resources of Auvergne, including cabbage, potatoes, cheese, morels, Auvergne ham, and cream.

Brebis [breh-bee] Ewe.

Brèdes [bred] A dish made from the leaves of various green leafy plants—usually cabbage, lettuce, or watercress—which is sautéed with bacon and served with rice.

Bréhan [breh-A] A garnish for beef tournedos composed of stuffed artichoke bottoms, boiled potatoes and cauliflower, sliced truffles, and hollandaise sauce.

Bréjaude [breh-zhohd] A cabbage and bacon soup from Limousin.

Brème [brem] Bream. A freshwater fish similar to carp used mostly in stews.

— *de mer* [duh mer] Sea bream.

Brésolles [breh-zol] A dish composed of alternating layers of thinly sliced meat and ham purée.

Bressane, à la [breh-sahn] Term denoting a dish prepared with Bresse chicken.

Bressane, sauce Sauce espagnole with the addition of orange juice, Madeira wine, and chicken livers. Served with chicken dishes.

Bresse [bres] A region in Burgundy famous for Bresse chicken, which is considered the finest in France.

Brestois [bres-twah] A génoise cake originating in Brest flavored with orange, lemon, and almonds.

Bretagne [bruh-tah-nyuh] Brittany. A province in northwest France noted for *agneau de pré-salé, galettes,* and white navy beans.

Breteuil [breh-tuh-yuh] A dish consisting of fried fish garnished with oysters and beurre noir.

VOCABULARY

Breton (gâteau) [bruh-tO] A thick, round, almond biscuit.

Bretonne à la [bruh-tuhn] Denotes a dish is prepared or garnished with white navy beans.

Bretonne purée Cooked, puréed, white navy beans.

Bretonne, sauce Velouté with the addition of white wine, mushrooms, carrots, and leeks, and finished with butter and cream.

Bretonneau [bruh-tuhn-noh] The name once used in Normandy for turbot.

Brie [bree] A very soft, creamy, cow's-milk cheese. Brie, which was first produced in the Île-de-France, is one of the great cheeses of the world. Types of Brie include: *Brie de Meaux*, which is the most famous, *Brie de Coulommiers*, *Brie de Melun*, and *Brie de Montereau*.

Brigade cuisine [bree-gahd-kwee-zeen] The kitchen staff of a restaurant.

Brignole [bree-nyol] A French town famous for a variety of prune made from the Perdrigon plum. See *Pruneau fleuri*.

Brillat-Savarin [bree-yah-sah-vah-rI] (1) The name of numerous culinary preparations named after Jean Anthelme Brillat-Savarin, a French politician and gastronome. (2) A soft, triple cream cheese produced in Normandy.

—, garniture Duchess potatoes stuffed with truffles and foie gras and bound with demi-glace sauce; blanched asparagus tips.

Brioli [bree-yoh-lee] A chestnut-flour cake from Corsica. It is traditionally served with hot milk.

Brioche [bree-osh] A very rich yeast bread made with generous amounts of eggs and butter.

— coulante [koo-lAt] See *Gâche améliorée*.

Brisolée [bree-zoh-leh] A dish featuring roasted chestnuts and cheese; from Valais.

Bristol [brees-tol] Served with beef or lamb, this garnish consists of risotto pancakes, sautéed flageolet beans, and potatoes *parisienne*.

Broccana [brok-kah-nah] A sausage and veal pâté from Limousin.

Broccio/Brucciu [bro-chyoh/broo-chyoo] A creamy goat's- or sheep's-milk cheese produced in Corsica.

Broche, à la [brosh] Describes food served or cooked on a skewer or spit.

Brochet [bro-sheh] Pike.

Brochette [bro-shet] Skewer.

—, en See *Broche, à la.*

Broglie, sauce [bro-ylee] A mushroom-flavored demi-glace sauce to which Madeira wine and diced ham have been added.

Brou de noix [broo duh nwah] A liqueur made from pulverized walnut husks; flavored with cinnamon.

Brouet [broo-eh] A now obsolete term meaning soup.

Broufado [broo-fah-doh] A beef and anchovy stew with capers; a specialty of Provence.

Brouillade [broo-ee-yahd] Scrambled eggs with chopped black truffles.

Brouilly [brooee-yee] A renowned red wine from Beaujolais.

Brousse/Broussa [broos/broo-sah] A fresh, unsalted, curd cheese produced in Provence. It is made from goat's or ewe's milk.

Brousse du rove [+ duh rohv] Brousse cheese made from sheep's milk.

Broutes [broot] (*Béarn*) Cabbage leaves boiled and served with oil and vinegar; a traditional Lenten meal. Also known as *broutons*.

Broutons [broo-tO] See *Broutes*.

Broyé [broh-yeh] A large shortbread pastry popular in Poitou.

Broyo [broh-yoh] A thick cornmeal mush from Béarn.

Brucciu [broo-chyoo] See *Broccio*.

Brugnon [brü-nyO] Nectarine.

Brûlé [brü-leh] French word meaning burned.

Brûlés, oignons [o-nyO +] Literally "burned onions." Whole onions roasted until dark brown; used mainly to color stocks as well as to add flavor.

Brûlot [brü-loh] This term describes alcohol that is ignited before being added to food or drink.

Brunoise [brü-nwahz] Vegetables cut into tiny cubes.

Brut [brü] Term applied to champagne indicating it is dry (little or no sweetness).

— *non dosé* [brü nO doh-zeh] Indicates champagne to which no sweetener has been added.

Bruxelloise, à la [brük-sel-lwahz] "Brussels style." This term describes a garnish of Brussels sprouts, chicory, and château potatoes.

Bucaille [bü-kah-yuhl] Obsolete French name for buckwheat.

Buccin [bü-kI] Whelk. A large edible marine gastropod.

Bûche [büsh] A rolled sponge cake filled with jelly or cream.

— *de Noël* [+ duh no-el] A rolled sponge cake frosted with chocolate cream and garnished to look like a log. A traditional Christmas cake.

Bûcheron [bü-shrohn] A type of log-shaped goat cheese produced in France.

Buffetier [büf-tyeh] Pantry cook.

Buglosse [bü-glos] A European herb similar to borage.

Bugnes [bü-nyuh] A yeast pastry

popular in Arles traditionally eaten on special occasions.

Bugnon [buh-nyO] A small, ring-shaped pastry fried in oil.

Buisson [bwee-sO] Describes food arranged in a pyramid.

Bulgare, sauce [bül-gahr] Mayonnaise combined with tomato paste and chopped celery.

Byrrh [beer] An aperitif from the Roussillon.

Cabaret [kah-bah-reh] An establishment serving food and drink as well as providing a floor show.

Cabassoles [kah-bah-sol] A local ragoût of the Larzac region of Rouergue composed of lamb's offal, veal knuckle, and vegetables.

Cabécou [kah-beh-koo] A soft cheese made from a combination of sheep's, goat's, and cow's milk.

Cabernet [kah-ber-neh] A famous black wine grape.

— *franc* [+ frA] A black grape used to make red Bordeaux, Chinon, and Saumur-Champigny wines.

— *sauvignon* [+ soh-vee-nyO] The major grape used in the production of red Bordeaux wines.

Cabessal, en [E kah-be-sal] Describes stuffed hare tied and cooked in a round pan.

Cabillaud [kah-bee-yoh] Cod.

Caboulot [kah-boo-loh] A small, rural café.

Cabri [kah-bree] Young goat; kid.

Cacahuète [kah-kah-wet] Peanut.

Cacalaus [kah-kah-loh] A Provençal dish of cooked snails served with aïoli or an herbed tomato sauce.

Cachat [kah-shah] A soft goat's- or ewe's-milk cheese produced in Provence.

Cachuse [kah-shüz] Braised pork and onions. This is a local specialty of Normandy and Picardy.

Cadillac [kah-dee-yah] A white dessert wine from Bordeaux.

Caen [kah-ehn] A town in Normandy having the distinction (along with Cambrai) of producing the best tripe sausage (andouillettes) in France.

Café [kah-feh] An establishment selling light food and drink.

Café Coffee.

— *allongé* [+ ah-lO-zheh] Regular coffee slightly diluted with water.

— *au lait* [+ oh leh] Coffee with hot milk.

— *brûlot* [+ brü-loh] Coffee flavored with orange and lemon peel and fortified with a splash of flaming brandy.

— *complet* [+ kO-pleh] A continental breakfast; coffee served with milk and with croissants, toast, jam, and so forth.

— *décaféiné* [+ deh-kah-fee-neh] Decaffeinated coffee.

— *express* [+ egs-pres] Espresso.

— *glacé* [+ glah-seh] Iced coffee. Also, coffee-flavored ice cream.

— *liégeois* [+ lee-ezh-wa] Café glacé topped with whipped cream.

— *noir* [+ nwahr] Black coffee.

— *noisette* [+ nwah-zet] Coffee to which a small amount of milk has been added, giving it a nut color.

Café anglais [+ A-gleh] Artichoke bottoms stuffed with truffles and mushrooms. This is used as a garnish for grilled meats.

Cafetière [kahf-tyer] Coffee pot.

Caghuse [kah-güs] (*Picardy*) A cold dish of braised pig knuckle and onions. Also spelled *Caqhuse*.

Cagnette [kah-nyet] Fried blenny (a river fish). Popular in the south of France.

Cagouillards [kah-goo-yahrd] The local name for snails in the Chartene region.

Cagouilles [kah-goo-yuh] The local name for snails in Marennes.

Sometimes called *petit gris*.

Cahors [kah-or] The name of a red wine; the capital of Quercy.

Caieu [kah-yuh] A giant mussel fished off the coast of Normandy.

Caille [kah-yuh] Quail.

Caillebotte [kah-yeh-boht] The name for fresh cheese or curds in western France.

Cailletot [kah-yuh-toh] The name for turbot in Normandy.

Caillette [kah-yet] A pork and vegetable sausage.

Caisse [kes] A small container used to bake *salpicons*, ragoûts, casseroles, and so forth.

Cajasse [kah-yahs] A *sarladais* pastry made with rum and fruit.

Calisson [kah-lee-sO] An almond and fruit pastry from Aix-en-Provence. Also known as *galichons*.

Calmar [kahl-mahr] Squid.

Calvados [kahl-vah-doh] An apple brandy from Normandy, the best coming from the *pays d'Auge*.

Cambacérès [kahm-bah-ser] A garnish for fish made up of crayfish tails, sliced mushrooms and truffles, and *sauce beurre blanc*.

Cambrai [kam-breh] A Flemish town regarded as producing the finest andouillettes in France. Also noted for its production of *bêtises*. See *Caen, bêtise*.

Camembert [ka-mE-ber] A soft cow's-milk cheese produced in Normandy similar to Brie. Camembert is also the name of a town in the *vallée d'Auge*.

Camérani [kah-muh-ra-nee] A garnish for poultry and sweetbreads made up of tartlets stuffed with foie gras, truffles, ox tongue, and macaroni mixed with duxelles and ham; with suprême sauce.

—, *sauce* Demi-glace sauce fortified with Madeira wine and truffle essence.

Canapés [kah-nah-peh] Small, variously shaped pieces of bread garnished with a variety of hot or cold toppings and served as an appetizer.

Canard [kah-nahr] Duck.
— *sauvage* [+ soh-vahzh] Wild duck.

Cancalaise, à la [kahn-kah-lez] Denotes a dish is prepared or garnished with Cancale oysters and *sauce normande.*

Cancoillotte [kahn-kwah-yot] (1) A soft, strong cheese made from combining Metton or St. Marcellin cheese with white wine and butter. (2) A dish from Franche-Comté consisting of melted Cancoillotte cheese served with crusty bread slices; similar to the English Welsh Rabbit. See *Fromage fort.*

Cane [kahn] A French name for a female duck.

Caneton [kan-nuh-tO] Young male duckling.

Canette [kah-net] Young female duck.

Canette A vessel used to contain beer or lemonade.

Canistrelli [kah-nee-strel-lee] (*Corsica*) An anise-flavored cookie.

Canneberge [kah-nuh-berzh] Cranberry.

Cannelle [kah-nel] Cinnamon.

Canole [kah-nol] A thick, crumbly biscuit from Limousin.

Canon [kah-nO] A local specialty of Provence consisting of pheasant liver and chestnuts wrapped in cabbage.

Canotière, à la [kah-noh-tyer] Describes poached fish garnished with sliced shallots, mushrooms, and crayfish tails; topped with *sauce canotière.*

Canotière, sauce Sauce bâtarde prepared with fish stock.

Cantal [kA-tahl] A hard, cow's-milk cheese from Auvergne, the best being produced in Laguiloe. Also known as *fourme du Cantal* and *fourme de Salers.*

Cantalet/Cantalon [kA-tah-leh/kA-tah-lO] Smaller versions of Cantal cheese.

Cantal, petit [puh-tee +] A smaller version of Cantal cheese. Larger than Cantalet.

Cantarèu [kA-tuh-ruh] Small gray snails, usually served in tomato sauce. A specialty of Nice.

Cantonnaise, à la [kA-tuhn-nez] Describes dishes garnished with Cantonese fried rice and shrimp.

Cap corse [kahp kors] A type of local cheese from Corsica.

Capendu [kah-pE-dü] A variety of red apple.

Capilotade [kah-pee-lo-tahd] A ragoût made from leftover meat (usually poultry).

Capone [kah-pon] See *Rascasse.*

Capoun [kah-poon] A Nice specialty of cabbage stuffed with rice and sausage.

Câpre [kah-pruh] Caper. The flower bud of a Mediterranean shrub that is pickled in brine or vinegar and used for a garnish or seasoning.

Câpres, sauce aux [oh kah-pruh] There are many versions of caper sauce; however, the most common is a hollandaise sauce or *sauce au beurre* with the addition of capers.

Capucin [kah-pü-sI] A Gruyère cheese tartlet. Also hare.

Capucine, à la [kah-pü-seen] A garnish for various dishes composed of stuffed cabbage and stuffed mushrooms.

Caqhuse [kah-küz] See *Caguse.*

Caquelon [kah-klO] A type of cooking dish used in southern France for simmering or poaching.

Carafe [kah-rahf] A glass container used for serving wine.

Caramel [kah-rah-mel] Sugar that has become brown and liquid by heating.

Caraméliser [kah-rah-mel-i-zeh] To slowly brown sugar or foods containing sugar (onions, carrots, etc.) by applying heat.

Caraque [kah-rahk] A term now rarely used referring to chocolate "straws" or "scrolls"; a decoration made by carefully scraping a chocolate block so the shavings curl. Also called *copeaux*.

Carbonade [kahr-bO-nahd] Beef braised in beer or red wine with seasonings.

Cardamome [kahr-dah-mom] Cardamom.

Carde [kahrd] Chard.

Cardeau [kahr-doh] The name for sardines in parts of northwestern France.

Cardinal [kahr-dee-nahl] Describes dishes having a reddish color. The most popular being fish garnished with lobster and lobster sauce.

—, *sauce* Velouté (fish) enriched with cream and lobster butter.

Cardine [kahr-deen] See *Merè de sole*.

Cardon [kahr-dO] Cardoon. A Mediterranean plant related to the globe artichoke. The stalks are similar to celery and are eaten as a vegetable in the south of France.

Carême (Marie-Antoine) [mah-ree A-twahn kah-rem] (1783–1833) Considered the founder and perhaps the greatest contributor of classic French cooking.

Carême, garniture (1) (*For fish*) Fish quenelles, sliced truffles, and béchamel sauce. (2) (*For grilled meats*) Potatoes *parisienne*, stuffed olives, and *sauce Madeira*.

Cargolade [kahr-go-lahd] The name for snails in the Roussillon region.

Cari [kah-ree] Curry.

Carmélite, à la [kahr-meh-leet] The name given to dishes inspired by the colors worn by the Carmélite nuns (black and white).

Carmélite, sauce Sauce *bourguignonne* to which diced ham and onions have been added.

Carmen [kahr-mE] Indicates tomatoes or pimentoes have been used in the preparation of the dish.

Carmencita, à la [kahr-mE-see-tah] Describes large roasts garnished with tomato *concassées* and red bell peppers.

Carnegie, à la [kahr-ne-gee] Grilled meats garnished with quartered artichoke bottoms, asparagus tips, and sliced truffles.

Carnot [kahr-noh] Indicates meat dishes garnished with sautéed cucumbers and topped with tarragon-flavored *sauce bordelaise*.

Carolines [kahr-roh-leen] Small éclairs of various savory fillings; served as an appetizer.

Carottes [kah-roht] Carrots.

Carré [kah-reh] A rack (ribs) of lamb or veal.

Carré de Bonneville [+ duh bohn-nuh-veel] A cow's-milk cheese from Normandy similar to Bondart.

Carré de l'Est [+ duh lest] A soft, cow's-milk cheese similar to Brie.

Carrelet [kahr-leh] Plaice; a saltwater fish prepared like sole.

Carte [kahrt] Menu.

Carte, à la Dishes individually priced on a menu.

Carthagène [kahr-thah-zhen] See *Vin doux natural*.

Cartoufle [kahr-toof-luh] A former name for the potato in parts of France.

Carvi [kahr-vee] Caraway.

Casanova, sauce [kah-sah-noh-vah] Mayonnaise combined with chopped hard-cooked egg yolks, diced truffles, and fresh tarragon.

Casse [kahs] A specialty of Rennes (Brittany) consisting of pork offal and vegetables.

— *-museau* [+ mü-zoh] A hard, double-cooked biscuit flavored with almonds.

— *-noix/-noisettes* [+ nwah/nwah-zet] Nut crackers.

Casserole [kahs-rohl] The name given to both an oven-proof cooking utensil and the food cooked in it—usually a ragoût or a sauce-bound dish.

Cassis [kah-sees] (1) Black currant. (2) A black currant liqueur. (3) A town in southern Provence producing excellent white wines.

Cassole [kah-sol] An obsolete word for the dish in which a cassoulet was prepared.

Cassolette [kah-soh-let] The name given to a small container used to serve certain foods as well as to the food contained in it.

Cassoulet [kah-soo-leh] A casserole or thick ragoût prepared with white beans and a variety of meats. A specialty of Languedoc.

— *carcassonnais* [+ kahr-kah-sohn-neh] A version of cassoulet made with pork, lamb, preserved goose, sausage, and beans. Partridge is sometimes added.

— *de Castelnaudary* [+ duh-kah-stel-noh-dree] This version of cassoulet contains pork, goose, sausage, and beans.

— *toulousain* [+ too-loo-zen] A type of cassoulet prepared with pork, Toulouse sausage, and a generous amount of preserved goose. Beans are also added.

Castagnaci [kahs-tah-nyah-chee] A pudding from Corsica made with chestnut flour. Also, a fritter or waffle made from chestnut flour.

Castiglione, garniture à la [kah-stee-lyoh-neh] Mushroom caps stuffed with ham and rice, sautéed eggplant, and poached marrow.

Castillane, à la [kah-stee-yahn] Describes tournedos or noisettes garnished with tomato *concassées*, croquette potatoes, fried onions and tomato sauce.

Catalane, à la [kah-tah-lahn] Refers to dishes cooked in the style of Catalonia, Spain. Ingredients often used when cooking à la Catalane include olive oil, tomatoes, eggplant, beans, garlic, saffron, and red pepper.

Catigau [kah-tee-goh] See *Catigot*.

Catigot [kah-tee-goh] A favorite dish of the Rhône Valley, it consists of eel and carp simmered in broth with potatoes, garlic, and tomatoes. Also spelled *catigau*.

Cauchoise, à la [koh-shwahz] Describes dishes prepared with the food resources of Caux, Normandy, including hare, apples, shrimp, potatoes, and ham.

Caudière [koh-dyer] A fish soup originating in Picardy consisting of sole, eel, and garlic cooked in white wine.

Caudrée [koh-dreh] A fish soup similar to *caudière*.

Cavagnats [kah-vah-nyah] A basket-shaped pastry containing eggs; a traditional Easter treat from Menton (*Provence*).

Cave à liqueurs [kah-vah lee-kuhrs] Liqueur cabinet.

Caviste [kah-veest] The person responsible for the wine cellar of an establishment.

Cavour, à la [kah-voor] A garnish for veal dishes composed of quartered mushrooms, sliced truffles, chicken liver purée, and small raviolis.

Cédrat [seh-dra] Citron.

Céleri [sehl-uh-ree] Celery.

Céleri bâtarde [+ bah-tahrd] "False celery"; a nickname for lovage in parts of France.

Céleri-rave [+ rahv] Celeriac.

Cendré [sA-dreh] The collective name for French cheeses ripened in ashes.

— *d'Argonne* [+ dahr-gohn] A cow's-milk cheese from Lorraine.

— *d'Armençon* [+ A dahr-mE-sO] Soft cow's-milk cheese from Aisy. See *Aisy.*

— *de la Brie* [+ duh la bree] A low fat cow's-milk cheese typically produced on farms in Île-de-France.

— *d'Orléanais* [+ dor-leh-ahn-ez] Soft farm cheeses made from cow's milk.

Cendre, sous la [soo-lah sA-druh] "Under the ashes"; refers to foods (potatoes, truffles, chestnuts) cooked beneath the embers of a fire, either wrapped in foil or its own protective shell.

Céracée [seh-rah-seh] A fresh cow's-milk cheese compared to ricotta; also called *Serac.*

Céréale [seh-reh-ahl] Cereal.

Cerise [suh-reez] Cherry.

Cérons [seh-rO] A town in the Bordeaux region known for peas.

Cervelle de Canut [sehr-vel duh kah-nü] An herbed cream cheese; also called *Claqueret* (*Lyonnais*).

Cévenole, à la [seh-vuh-nohl] Denotes that chestnuts are used in preparation of a dish.

Chabichou [shah-bee-shoo] A soft, slightly sweet, goat's-milk cheese produced in Poitou.

Chablis [shah-blee] A town in northern Burgundy famous for the white wine produced there.

Chaboisseau [shah-bwah-soh] A small Mediterranean fish used in bouillabaisse or matelote.

Chaingy [shen-zhee] A type of cheese made in Orléans.

Chambertin [shA-ber-tI] A renowned red wine from Burgundy.

—, *sauce* A sauce made from mushrooms, fish stock, and Chambertin wine. It is strained and finished with butter.

Chambolle-musigny [shA-bol-mü-see-nyee] A wine-growing region of Burgundy.

Chambord [shA-bor] A garnish of fish quenelles, mushrooms, roe, sliced truffles, and *sauce chambord.*

—, *sauce* Demi-glace sauce with the addition of reduced red wine and fish stock; finished with anchovy butter.

Chambrer [shA-breh] This term refers to wine (usually red wine) brought to room tempature before consumption.

Chamois [shA-mwah] A type of wild goat whose flesh is considered a delicacy.

Champagne [shA-pah-nyuh] An area of France producing the finest sparkling wine in the world. Though it is overshadowed by the wine industry, Champagne cuisine includes many fine items and specialties, including pork products (particularly pâtés and andouillettes), *gougères* (a *choux* pastry), cheeses, game, and pears.

Champagne fine [+ feen] Special brandies produced in the Charente region of France.

Champenois [shA-peh-nwah] Describes foods cooked in champagne.

Champenois See *Riceys-Cendré.*

Champignon [shA-pee-nyO] Mushroom.

—, *sauce* Demi-glace sauce flavored with mushroom essence and garnished with mushroom caps.

— *à la grecque* [+ grek] Pickled mushrooms.

— *de Paris* [+ duh pah-ree] A French name for button mushrooms.

Champigny [shA-pee-nyee] An apricot-flavored puff pastry tart.

Champoreau [shA-po-roh] Black coffee mixed with brandy.

Champvallon [shA-vah-lO] Mutton cooked *en casserole* with onions and potatoes.

Chancelier, à la [shA-suh-lyeh] Refers to dishes garnished with pearl onions, potatoes *parisienne*, and demi-glace sauce.

Chancy, à la [shA-see] A garnish for meat dishes consisting of sliced carrots, green baby peas, and sliced mushrooms.

Chanterelle [shA-trel] An edible, wild mushroom of excellent quality.

Chantilly (crème) [krem shA-tee-yee] The French word for sweetened whipped cream.

Chantilly, sauce Sauces into which whipped cream is folded are referred to as *chantilly* sauces; the most common being hollandaise, suprême, and mayonnaise.

Chaource [shah-oors] A soft, creamy, cow's-milk cheese produced in Champagne.

Chapelure [shah-plür] Bread crumbs and/or the process of making bread crumbs.

—, **sauce** Veal stock flavored with ham and black pepper and thickened with bread crumbs.

Chapon [shah-pO] (1) Capon; a young, castrated cock. (2) (*Provence*) Toasted bread brushed with olive oil and garlic.

Charbonnée [shahr-buhn-neh] (1) (*Berry and Bourbonnais*) A pork civet. (2) (*Île-de-France*) A beef stew prepared with red wine. (3)

Food that is barbecued over a charcoal fire.

Charbonnier [shahr-bohn-nyeh] A variety of wild mushroom found in France.

Charcuterie [shahr-koo-tree] Pork and pork products, i.e., bacon, ham, sausage, pâtés, and so forth.

—, **sauce** *Sauce Robert* garnished with gherkins.

Chardonnay [shahr-dO-neh] Grape used to produce excellent white Burgundies.

Charente [shah-rEt] A region of western France perhaps best known for the production of cognac. See *Aunis, Angoumois*, and *Saintonge*.

Charlotte [shahr-loht] A dessert made up of pastry cream, custard, mousse, or puréed fruit poured into a charlotte mold that has been lined with various pastries, chilled, and served unmolded. Another type of charlotte consists of puréed fruit—most commonly apples—placed in a bread-lined charlotte mold and baked; unmolded and served hot.

— *royale* [+ roh-yahl] Bavarian cream flavored with kirsch and poured into a mold lined with jelly roll slices; unmolded and served chilled.

— *russe* [+ rüs] Bavarian cream set in a mold that is lined with ladyfingers and chilled. It is unmolded before serving.

Charolais [shah-roh-lez] A high-quality breed of cattle originating in Charolles (Burgundy).

Charolaise, à la [shah-ro-lez] Beef dishes garnished with cauliflower *Villeroi* (breaded and fried) and tartlets filled with turnip purée.

Charolles [shah-rol] A town in Burgundy best known for *charolais* cattle.

Chartres, à la [shahr-truh] This term indicates the presence of tarragon in a preparation.

Chartres, sauce Demi-glace sauce flavored with tarragon.

Chartreuse [shahr-truhz] An herb-flavored liqueur first made by the Carthusian monks. There are two types of Chartreuse: a yellow variety, which is the sweeter of the two, and a green variety, which is drier and more aromatic.

Chartreuse A dish consisting of alternate layers of cabbage and partridge baked in a mold and turned out before serving.

Chasseur [shah-suh] This term indicates that a dish was prepared or garnished with mushrooms and shallots.

—, sauce Demi-glace sauce flavored with mushrooms, shallots, tomato purée, and white wine.

Chasseur du Saucisson [+ duh sohsee-sO] A type of smoked sausage made from pork belly and beef.

Châtaigne [shah-ten-yuh] A variety of chestnut. See *Marron*.

Châtaigne de mer [+ duh mehr] A French nickname for sea urchin. See *Oursin*.

Château [shah-toh] A vineyard plantation in Bordeaux. Some of the most famous chateaus include: Château Ausone, Château Lafite, Château Latour, and Château Mouton-Rothschild.

— bottled This term means a wine was bottled on the plantation or estate where the grapes were grown and wine made.

Chateaubriand [shah-toh-bree-A] A thick, very tender cut of beef fillet traditionally served with château potatoes and béarnaise sauce; named after 19th-century French statesman François Chateaubriand.

—, sauce Demi-glace sauce flavored with mushrooms, tarragon, and cayenne. The sauce is strained and finished with butter.

Châtelaine, à la [shah-tuh-len] This term describes meat dishes garnished with artichokes, chestnuts, and noisette potatoes. *Sauce soubise* often accompanies dishes served *à la châtelaine*.

Chatham, à la [shah-tahm] A garnish of buttered noodles, julienne of ox tongue, and sliced mushrooms. Served with veal dishes.

Chauchat [shoh-shah] This term describes poached fish topped with béchamel sauce and garnished with château potatoes.

Chaudemer [shoh-duh-mehr] A fish stew similar to matelote; a specialty of the Île-de-France.

Chaudèu [shoh-deh] (*Nice*) A hard, round biscuit flavored with orange flowers.

Chaud-froid [shoh-frwah] Describes food (usually poultry, but other meats and fish are also used) prepared hot (*chaud*), but served cold (*froid*) and coated with *sauce chaud-froid*.

—, sauce The name for several sauces that have been greatly reduced or to which aspic has been added, i.e., demi-glace, *velouté*, tomato, and so forth. The result is a gel-like sauce that adheres to foods. See *Chaud-froid*.

Chaudin [shoh-dI] A casing for chitterlings made from the large intestines of a pig.

Chaudrée [shoh-dreh] A famous fish stew from the coast of Poitou. It traditionally includes sole, eel, and plaice simmered in white wine with onions and garlic.

— de fouras [duh foo-rah] This method of serving *chaudrée* involves pouring the stock over crusty bread and serving the fish separately.

Chaudumé [shoh-dü-meh] A pike and eel stew.

Chaudumel [shoh-dü-mel] See *Chaudumé*.

Chaudumer [shoh-dü-meh] See *Chaudumé*.

Chausson [shoh-sO] Turnover.

Chavette [shah-vet] Describes poached fish garnished with artichoke bottoms and sliced truffles; topped with *sauce Mornay*.

Chef [shef] "Chief/leader." One who prepares quality food in a professional manner.

—, *commis* [kom-ee +] Kitchen assistant.

— *de cuisine* [+ duh kwee-zeen] The chef in charge of the kitchen.

— *de partie* [+ duh pahr-tee] The chef in charge of a shift. Also refers to a chef in charge of a specific section of the kitchen.

— *de service* [+ duh ser-vees] Dining room manager.

— *entremetier* [+ E-truh-meh-tye] Vegetable chef.

— *garde manger* [+ gahrd mAgeh] The person in charge of cold foods.

— *patissier* [+ pah-tee-syeh] Pastry chef.

— *patron* [+ pah-trO] The chef-proprietor of an establishment.

— *poissonier* [+ pwah-sO-nyeh] Fish and seafood chef.

— *potager* [+ po-tah-zheh] Soup chef.

— *saucier* [+ soh-syeh] "Sauce chef." Usually the second in command in the kitchen; also referred to as *sous chef*.

—, *sous* [soo +] See *Chef saucier*.

— *tourant* [+ too-rA] Relief chef. Capable of performing all kitchen tasks.

Chemise, en [E shuh-meez] Describes ingredients cooked in their natural skin; i.e., potatoes, onions, poultry. This term also refers to foods wrapped during cooking.

Chemisier [shuh-mee-zeh] Term meaning to coat a mold or pan with aspic or other substance (i.e., buttered parchment paper) to prevent from sticking.

Chemitrés [she-mee-treh] A waffle-type pastry from Lorraine.

Chenin Blanc [she-nI blA] The white wine grape of Touraine. Vouvray, Coteaux du Layon, and Saumur are some of the excellent wines produced from the *chenin blanc* grape.

Cherbourg [sher-boorg] A coastal town in Normandy famous for shrimp.

—, *à la* [sher-boorg] Oysters, shrimp, and mussels assembled as a garnish for fish dishes.

Cheron [she-rO] Describes dishes garnished with potatoes *parisienne* and artichoke bottoms stuffed with a vegetable *salpicon*.

Chester [ches-tuhr] A French cheese produced from cow's milk, similar to cheddar.

Cheval, à [ah shuh-vahl] Describes grilled steak garnished with fried eggs.

Chevaler [shuh-vah-leh] A shingled arrangement of food on a platter.

Chèvre [she-vruh] The generic term for goat's-milk cheeses. *Chèvre* is also the French word for *goat*.

—, *pur* [pür +] This term on a chèvre label indicates that the cheese is made entirely from goat's milk.

Chevreau [shuh-vroh] The French word for kid; a young goat.

Chevret [shuh-vreh] A goat's-milk cheese produced in Bresse.

Chevreton/Chevroton [shev-ruh-tO/shuh-vroh-tO] A soft cheese made from goat's milk; produced in Auvergne.

Chevrette [shev-ret] A local name for prawns in Aunis.

Chevreuil [shuh-vruhl] Venison.

—, *en* A term describing meat that is prepared like venison; i.e., marinated, larded, grilled, and so forth.

—, *sauce* (1) Prepared by adding red wine and cayenne pepper to *sauce poivrade*. (2) *Sauce espagnole* to which diced ham is added. The sauce is finished with Port and red currant jelly.

Chevreuse [shuh-vruhz] This term indicates a dish is prepared with the produce typical of the Chevreuse Valley—i.e., artichokes, mushrooms, chervil, and truffles.

Chevrier [shuh-vree-yer] A type of flagelot bean grown in the Arpajon region.

Chevrotin des Aravis [shuh-vroh-tI deh ah-rah-vee] A firm goat cheese made in Savoy.

Chevrotin du Bourbonnais [+ dü boor-bO-nez] The name for various goat cheeses produced in the Bourbonnais region of central France.

Chevrotin de Mâcon [+ duh mah-kO] See *Bouton-de-Culotte*.

Chialades [shee-ah-lahd] A local crêpe from Argonne.

Chiboust [shee-boost] French chef credited with creating the *gâteau Saint-Honoré*.

—, *crème* [krem +] A custard cream filling used in the *gâteau Saint-Honoré*.

Chichifregi [shee-shee-freh-zhee] A sweetened fried dough popular in Provence.

Chiffonnade [shee-foh-nahd] This term refers to leafy herbs and greens cut in fine, thin strips.

Chimay, à la [shee-meh] Describes stuffed chicken garnished with noodles and asparagus tips.

Chinois [shee-nwah] A cone shaped strainer.

Chinois confit [+ kO-fee] A candied Chinese orange.

Chinon [shee-nO] Red, white, and rosé wines produced in the Loire region from the *Cabernet franc* grape.

Chinonnaise, à la [shee-nO-ez] Refers to dishes garnished with stuffed cabbage and parslied potatoes.

Chipeau [shee-poh] A variety of wild duck.

Chipirones [shee-pee-rohn] The name given to inkfish or squid in the French Basque Provinces.

Chipolata [shee-po-lah-tuh] A small, spicy, pork sausage.

—, *à la* Denotes a dish is garnished with chestnuts, onions, and *chipolatas*.

Chique [sheek] An almond-fondant confection flavored with mint or anise.

Chiqueter [shee-kuh-teh] To decorate pastry shells before baking, usually by marking with a knife or fork.

Chiroubles [shee-roo-bluh] A Beaujolais wine.

Citron [see-trO] Lemon.

Chivry [shee-vree] See *Beurre Chivry*.

—, *sauce* Sauce velouté and white wine reduced and combined with green herbs. Finished with chivry butter.

Chocart [shoh-kahr] An apple turnover made with puff pastry. Also spelled *choquart*.

Chocolat [shoh-koh-lah] Chocolate.

Choiseul (garniture) [shwah-zuhl] (1) (*For poached sole*) Served with white wine sauce and garnished with sliced truffles. (2) (*Tournedos and noisettes*) Artichoke bottoms stuffed with foie gras and mushrooms and served with demi-glace sauce.

Choisy [shwah-zee] This term indicates that lettuce was used in preparation of a dish.

Choix [shwah] Literally "choice," this term refers to a grade of meat.

Chope [shop] A large, beer mug with handles.

Choquart [shok-ahr] See *Chocart*.

Choron, à la [shoh-rO] A garnish for various dishes featuring potatoes *parisienne*, artichoke bottoms filled with baby peas, and *sauce Choron*.

Choron, sauce Béarnaise sauce flavored with tomato purée.

Chou [shoo] (1) Cabbage. (2) A plain pastry case of various shapes and sizes made from *choux* paste; see *Pâte à chou*.

— *de Milan* [+ duh mee-lahn] Savoy cabbage.

— *Farci* [+ fahr-see] Stuffed cabbage.

— *-fleur* [+ fluhr] Cauliflower.

— *frisé* [+ free-zeh] Kale.

— *-rave* [+ rahv] Kohlrabi.

— *-rouge* [+ roozh] Red cabbage.

— *vert* [+ vehr] Green cabbage.

Choucroute [shoo-kroot] Sauerkraut.

Choucroute garnie [+ gahr-nee] An Alsatian specialty composed of sauerkraut cooked with smoked goose, ham, sausage, and pork. It is traditionally served with boiled potatoes.

Chouée [shoo-weh] (*Anjou*) A simple dish made up of boiled green cabbage tossed with butter.

Chou à la crème [+ krem] Cream puffs.

Choux brocolis [shoo-brok-oh-lee] Broccoli.

Choux de Bruxelles [+ duh brük-sel] Brussels sprouts.

Ciboule [see-bool] A type of green onion.

Ciboulette [see-boo-let] Chive.

Cidre [see-druh] Cider.

Cierp de Luchon [syerp duh loo-shO] A type of cheese from the Comté de Foix.

Cigale de mer [see-gahl duh mehr] A type of lobster found in warm waters.

Cimier [see-myeh] See *Cuissot*.

Cingalaise, à la [sI-gah-lez] Describes dishes accompanied with *sauce cingalaise*.

Cingalaise, sauce A cold sauce consisting of hard-boiled eggs, pimentoes, cucumbers, and tomatoes; combined with oil and seasoned with curry.

Cinq-épices [sAk-eh-pees] "Five spices"; a combination of cloves, fennel, cinnamon, pepper, and star anise. Used heavily in Asian cookery.

Ciseler [see-zleh] A term for making incisions on meat or fish to prevent cracking during cooking as well as to speed up the cooking time.

Citronner [see-truh-neh] This term means to add lemon or lemon juice to foods to prevent discoloration or to enhance flavor.

Citrouillat [see-troo-yaht] A pumpkin tart originating in Berry.

Citrouille [see-troo-yuh] Pumpkin.

—, *à la* With pumpkin.

Civet [see-veh] A game stew prepared with mushrooms, red wine, and blood. In some parts of France, the dish is highly spiced and thick cream is added.

— *de lièvre* [+ duh lye-vruh] Hare stew, also jugged hare.

Civette [see-vet] Chives. See *Ciboulette*.

Clafouti [klah-foo-tee] An unpitted black cherry tart. It is a specialty

Clafouti (cont.)
of Limousin and similar to the *milliard* of Auvergne.

Claires [klehr] Algae-rich marine enclosures where Marennes oysters are harvested. The oysters, which turn green, are considered a great delicacy.

Clairet [kleh-reh] Very light wines.

Clamart, à la [klah-mahr] This term refers to dishes prepared with green peas.

Claqueret (lyonnais) [klah-kreh (lyuhn-neh)] See *Cervelle de Canut*.

Claqueret [klah-kreh] A type of fruit jelly now rarely prepared.

Claremont [klahr-mO] Describes dishes garnished with braised onions, stuffed cucumbers, and stewed tomatoes.

Clavelat [klah-vuh-lah] A nickname in parts of France for the Mediterranean turbot.

Clermont [kler-mO] Describes dishes garnished with chestnuts and/or cabbage.

Clitocybe [klee-toh-keeb] A variety of edible mushrooms.

Clitopile Petite-Prune [klee-to-peel puh-teet-prün] A type of edible mushroom. Also called *mousseron* or *meunier*.

Cloche [klohsh] A dish cover used to keep food hot.

Clou de girofle [kloo duh gee-rof-luh] Clove.

Clouter [kloo-teh] Literally "to stud." The process of inserting small pieces of food—i.e., cloves, truffles, tongue, bacon—into the surface of other foods to add flavor and in some cases, moisture.

Clovisse [kloh-vees] A variety of clam popular in France.

Cochon [koh-shO] Pig.

— *de lait* [+ duh leh] Suckling pig; also called *porcelet*.

Cochonnaille [koh-shuhn-nah-yuh] Charcuterie; pork products.

Cocktail [kok-tel] Cocktail.

Cocos [koh-koh] A type of white haricot bean grown in Brittany.

Cocotte [ko-kot] A lidded earthenware cooking vessel used to slow-cook braised meats, and casseroles in the oven.

—, *en* Describes foods cooked in a cocotte.

Cœur à la crème [kuhr ah-lah-krem] A dessert consisting of sweetened, fresh cheese formed in the shape of a heart (*cœur*) and topped with fresh strawberries or cherries.

Cœur d'artichauts [+ dahr-tee-shoh] Artichoke hearts.

Cœur de bray [+ duh brah-yeh] A soft cheese made from cow's milk produced in Normandy.

Cœur de laitue [+ duh leh-tü] Hearts of lettuce.

Cœur de palmier [+ duh pahl-myeh] Hearts of palm.

Cognac [koh-nyahk] A town in western France on the Charente River producing the world-famous brandy of the same name. Folle Blanche, St. Emilion, and Colombard are the principal grapes used to produce cognac.

Coing [kwI] Quince.

Cointreau [kwahn-troh] A clear orange-flavored liqueur from France. An excellent product, it rivals the darker Grand Marnier in quality.

Colbert [kohl-ber] Describes fish, usually sole, that is coated with bread crumbs, fried and topped with Colbert butter.

—, *beurre* See *Beurre Colbert*.

—, *sauce* A sauce consisting of meat glaze flavored with lemon, parsley, and Madeira, and finished with a generous amount of butter.

Colère, en [E koh-ler] A preparation of whiting in which the fish's tail is inserted in its mouth, forming a circle; breaded and fried; served with tomato sauce.

Colin [koh-lI] The name given to hake in some parts of France.

Colinette [koh-lee-net] A method of preparing fish in which a fillet is stuffed with truffles and fish forcemeat, then breaded and fried. Tomato sauce is typically served with fish prepared in this fashion.

Colle [kohl] Gelatine or aspic used to thicken foods.

— *de couennes* [+ duh koo-wen] Pork gelatine.

Coller [ko-leh] Incoporating softened gelatine to foods to thicken. Also describes decoratively cut foods such as truffles, carrots, turnips, that are adhered to cold pâtés or *chauds-froids*.

Collet [ko-leh] Neck.

— *de mouton* [+ duh moo-tO] Neck of mutton.

Collier [kol-yeh] Neck.

Collioure, sauce [kol-lyoor] Puréed anchovies, chopped garlic, and fresh parsley combined with mayonnaise sauce.

Colombine [koh-lohm-been] A small croquette served as an hors d'œuvre. It is made up of a savory *salpicon* rolled in bread crumbs and Parmesan cheese and fried.

Colonne [ko-lon] A kitchen tool used to core fruits and cut vegetables into cylindrical shapes.

Colvert [kohl-vehr] The French name for the mallard duck.

Columbo, le [luh ko-lüm-boh] A type of curry mixture popular in the French West Indies composed of mustard seeds, garlic, hot peppers, saffron, coriander, black pepper, and cumin.

Colza [kol-zah] A cabbagelike vegetable used in soups and salads. Rapeseed oil is derived from the seeds of the vegetable.

Cominée de elines [ko-mee-neh deh-leen] An obsolete term referring to dishes containing cumin.

Commercy [ko-mehr-see] A town in Lorraine famous for madeleines.

Commis de rang [kom-mee duh rA] An assistant waiter.

Commodore [kom-mo-dor] A garnish for large poached fish consisting of crayfish croquettes, mussels Villeroi, and fish quenelles; with sauce normandy.

Compote (de fruits) [kO-poht (duh frwee)] Fresh or dried fruit poached in syrup.

Compote, à la Glazed pearl onions and mushroom caps sautéed with chopped bacon. Used as a garnish for poultry dishes.

Compoter, mettre en [kO-poh-teh] The process of stewing foods—i.e., fruits, vegetables, poultry, and game—to a very soft tender stage.

Compotier [kO-poh-tyeh] A large dish used for serving compotes or similar desserts.

Comté [kO-teh] A pale-yellow cow's-milk cheese from the Franche-Comté similar to Emmentaler. Also called *Gruyère de Comté*.

Comtesse [kO-tes] Describes beef or veal studded with truffles and garnished with braised lettuce, veal quenelles, and veal demiglace.

Concassées [kO-kah-seh] Peeled seeded tomatoes roughly chopped.

Concasser [kO-kah-seh] To roughly chop. Often refers to tomatoes that are skinned, seeded, and coarsely cut.

Concombre [kO-kohm-bruh] Cucumber.

Concorde [kO-kord] Describes large cuts of meat that are garnished with potatoes au gratin, whole baby carrots and peas glazed in butter.

Concordia [kO-kor-dyah] Indicates dishes garnished with French beans, baby carrots, potatoes, and demi-glace sauce.

Condé [kO-deh] (1) Indicates that purée of red kidney beans was used in preparation of a dish. (2) A cold dessert made with stewed fruit and sweetened rice. (3) A small cake made with puff pastry and almonds.

Confire [kO-feer] To put foodstuffs in a substance that preserves them.

Confiserie [kO-fee-sree] Confectionery; sweets and candies.

Confit [kO-fee] Preserved meat—usually goose, duck, and pork—that is cooked slowly and then stored in its own fat.

Confiture [kO-fee-tür] Jam.

Confiturier [kO-fee-tü-ryeh] Jam pot.

Congelé [kO-zhe-leh] Frozen.

Congolais [kO-goh-leh] A confection made with meringue and coconut.

Congre [kO-greh] Conger eel; a snakelike fish common in France where it is used mostly in soups and stews.

Concierge [kO-syerzh] A live-in superintendent of a building who also acts as a doorman.

Connaught [kahn-naht] Game birds prepared with roasted chestnuts.

Conserver [kO-ser-veh] To preserve.

Consommé [kO-so-meh] A clear concentrated meat, fish, or poultry stock. It can be served hot or cold and used as a soup or a sauce base.

Consoude [kO-sood] Comfrey. A green salad herb.

Contender [kO-tE-deh] A variety of snap bean (*mange-tout*).

Conti [kO-tee] This term indicates a dish is garnished with a purée of lentils.

Continentale, à la [kO-tee-nE-tahl] A garnish for noisettes and tournedos consisting of artichoke bottoms and lamb kidneys; with demi-glace sauce.

Contiser [kO-tee-zeh] To adhere or stud foods with truffles.

Contre-filet [kO-truh-fee-leh] A cut of beef from the last rib to the rump. It is of excellent quality and prepared like tenderloin.

Conversation [kO-ver-sah-syO] A puff pastry tartlet filled with almond cream and topped with royal icing.

Copa [ko-pah] A Corsican charcuterie specialty of thinly sliced spiced pork shoulder.

Copeaux [ko-poh] Small spiral-shaped pastries. See *Caraque*.

Coq [kok] Literally "cock"; also refers to chicken.

— *au vin* [+ oh vI] Chicken cooked in wine. An authentic *coq au vin* includes the animal's blood to thicken the sauce.

Coque [kok] A brioche cake flavored with citron and traditionally prepared for Easter in some parts of France.

Coque Cockle; a small, bivalve marine mollusc.

Coque, à la This term describes foods cooked without removing their natural outer coverings, i.e., fruits, vegetables, and eggs.

Coque du Lot [+ dü loh] A type of cake traditionally prepared for the Easter celebration in some parts of France.

Coque, œufs à la [uhf ah-lah +] Soft-boiled eggs.

Coqueret [koh-kur-reh] The French name for the strawberry tomato. The edible fruit is primarily used for preserves.

Coques à petits fours [kok ah puh-teet foor] Petits fours composed of small almond meringue cookies sandwiched together with various fillings.

Coquelet [kok-leh] A young cock weighing between 1–1$\frac{1}{2}$ pounds.

Coquelicot [kok-lee-koh] Red poppy; used as a natural food coloring.

Coquelicots de Nemours [+ duh ne-moor] A small rectangular confection made from cooked sugar. They derive their red color from the red poppy (*coquelicot*), hence the name.

Coquetier [koh-kuh-tyeh] A decorative cup used to serve eggs cooked in their shell. Also, a special utensil used to boil eggs.

Coquillages [ko-kee-yazh] Mollusk.

Coquille [koh-kee-yuh] Shell.

— *Saint-Jacques* [+ sA zhah] The French name for scallop.

Cordée [kor-deh] A term used to described a pastry that is tough because of overkneading or poor mixing.

Cordelier, sauce [kor-de-lyer] *Sauce Madeira* flavored with purée of goose liver and truffles.

Cordial [kor-dyahl] A sweet aromatic liqueur or brandy.

Cordillon [kor-dee-yO] See *Brassadeau*.

Cordon bleu [kor-dO bluh] Literally "blue ribbon," this honor is awarded to chefs (originally women only) for culinary excellence.

Cordon de soulier [+ duh soo-lyeh] Shoestring potatoes; long, thin potato strips fried in oil.

Coriandre [kor-yA-duh] Coriander.

Corne [korn] A variety of soft-shelled walnut grown in Sarladaise.

Corne d'abondance [korn dah-bO-dAs] See *Craterelle*.

Cornet [kor-neh] A pastry cone. Cornets are usually made with puff pastry and filled with pastry cream (cream horns). Ice cream cones are a type of cornet made with wafers; also refers to hors d'œuvres of ham or salmon rolled into a cone and stuffed.

Cornichon [kor-nee-shO] Small sour pickle, also known as *gherkin*.

Cornouille [kor-noo-yuh] Cornelian cherry; the small reddish fruit of the cornel shrub used mostly in jellies or preserves.

Corse [kors] Corsica. A Mediterranean island located about one hundred miles southeast of France. It is best known for its smoked pork products, chestnuts, and Broccio cheese. Because Corsica was long a part of Italy, Italian influences are still prominent in the island's cuisine.

Corsé [kohr-seh] Strong black coffee. Also refers to a strong fortified wine.

Cosaque [koh-zahk] In former days this referred to a confection wrapped in shiny colored paper.

Côte [koht] A pork or lamb chop containing the filet and the eye.

Coteaux [koh-toh] A now obsolete term for food and wine connoisseurs.

Côtelette [koht-let] A pork or lamb cutlet. This cut contains less meat that the *côte*.

Cotignac [ko-tee-nyahk] Quince paste. Cotignac d'Orléans is a famous brand, made in Orléans.

Côtoyer [ko-to-yeh] A term meaning to turn a roast while cooking to achieve maximum heat distribution.

Cotriade [ko-tree-ahd] A Breton fish stew. An authentic *cotriade* contains up to a dozen types of fish (lobster excluded) and is prepared with onions and potatoes. The broth is poured over crusty bread and served as a first course followed by the fish and vegetables.

Coucher [koo-sheh] Term meaning to squeeze out, with a pastry bag.

Coucoulelli [koo-koo-lel-lee] A Corsican pastry made with white wine, olive oil, sugar, and flour.

Coudenas/Coudenat [koo-dna/koo-dnah] The name for *sabodet* in southwestern France. See *Sabodet*.

Coudenou [koo-dnoh] A white sausage made from pork and bound with bread crumbs and egg.

Cou farci [koo fahr-see] Stuffed goose neck, usually with foie gras.

Cougnou [koo-nyoo] A traditional Christmas yeast cake made in Flanders; known by different names throughout France.

Couke [kook] See *Koucke*.

Couler [koo-leh] This term is used to describe the method of pouring aspic into a cold savory pie through a vent in the top of the crust. Its purpose is to fill the gap between the filling and the top (interior) crust to facilitate slicing and improve consistency.

Coulis [koo-lee] (1) Meat juices obtained during cooking. (2) A meat, fish, or vegetable purée. (3) A strained fruit sauce.

Coulommiers [koo-lom-myehr] A soft-ripened, Brie-like cheese made from cow's milk.

Coup de feu [kood-fuh] *Mise en place* means to ready the ingredients and equipment needed to prepare a dish. *Coup de feu* refers to the steps involved in making the dish.

Coup de milieu [kood mee-lyuh] See *Normand, le Trou*.

Coupe [koop] A rounded, stemmed dessert cup. Desserts served in these are referred to as *coupes*.

Couper [koo-peh] To cut.

— *en dés* [+ E deh] To dice.

Coupole [koo-pol] See *Taste-Vin*.

Couque [kook] See *Koucke*.

Courbet [koor-beh] A garnish for fish comprised of oysters and mushroom caps and served with a curry-flavored butter sauce.

Courbine [koor-been] A common Mediterranean fish.

Courgette [koor-zhet] Zucchini squash.

Couronne [koor-on] Food arranged in a ring or "crown." Also, a rounded, braided French bread loaf.

Courquinoise [koor-kee-nwahs] An eel and mussel soup; popular in northern France.

Court-bouillon [koor-boo-yO] A seasoned, aromatic poaching liquid used primarily for cooking fish. Water or fish stock, white wine, vegetables, and spices are the main ingredients.

Cousinat [koo-zee-nah] (1) A chestnut and onion soup from Auvergne. (2) In the French Basque region it is a thick stew made with Bayonne ham, beans, squash, and assorted local vegetables.

Cousinette [koo-zee-net] A soup from Béarn made with leafy green vegetables including spinach, lettuce, sorrel, swiss chard, chicory, and a local vegetable called mauve.

Couteau [koo-toh] Knife.

— *de cuisine* [+ duh kwee-zeen] Chef's knife.

— *de saigner* [+ duh say-nyeh] Boning knife.

— *du tranchelard* [+ dü trAsh-lahr] Slicing knife.

— *poisson* [+ fee-leh duh pwah-sO] Fillet knife.

Couvé [koo-veh] A vanilla-lemon-flavored cake made in Dauphiné.

Couvert [koo-ver] "Cover"; the reserved place at the table of a restaurant; also, a cover charge.

Couverture [koo-ver-tür] Literally "to coat," this term also describes chocolate with an increased cocoa butter content.

Crabe [krahb] Crab.

Cramique [krah-meek] A type of brioche made with Corinth raisins.

Crapaud de mer [krah-pohd] See *Rascasse.*

Crapaudine, à la [E krah-poh-deen] A method of preparing pigeon in which the bird is split and butterflied, brushed with oil, and grilled. Chicken may also be prepared *à la crapaudine.*

Crapaudine, sauce Sauce *diable* with the addition of mushrooms, mustard, and tarragon or tarragon vinegar.

Crapiau [krah-pyoh] A type of apple pancake made in Nivernais. In the Morvan region of Burgundy, it is a large pancake cooked in lard. Also spelled *grapiau.*

Craquelin [krah-kuh-lI] A small, dry, crunchy pastry often served as a petit four.

Craquelot [crah-kuh-loh] Young, smoked herring.

Craterelle [krah-trel] An edible mushroom common in France. It is used with other mushrooms, in sauces, or dried. Also called *trompette de-la-mort* or *corne d'abondance.*

Crécy [kreh-see] Denotes that carrots have been used in preparation of a dish. Named for the Crécy district of France, noted for perhaps the world's finest carrots.

Crémant [kreh-mA] A sparkling wine from the Champagne region of France.

Crème [krem] Cream. Also describes sweet, syrupy liqueurs such as *crème de cassis* (black currant liqueur) as well as pastry creams—i.e., *crème pâtissière, crème à l'anglaise,* and so forth.

— *à l'anglaise* [+ ah-lA-glez] A custard sauce made with milk, sugar, vanilla, and thickened with egg yolks. It is used for dessert sauces, pastry fillings, and as a base for ice cream and Bavarian creams.

— *brûlée* [brü-leh] A custard dessert consisting of the chilled molded custard topped with sugar and caramelized under a broiler.

— *caramel* [+ kah-rah-mel] See *Crème renversée.*

— *chiboust* [+ shee-boost] See *Crème Saint-Honoré.*

— *des Vosges* [+ deh vohzheh] A soft cream cheese produced in Alsace.

— *fleurette* [+ fluhr-ret] A thinner and less rich form of *crème fraîche.*

— *fouettée* [+ fweht-teh] Whipped cream.

— *fraîche* [+ fresh] A thick, rich, tangy dairy product made by adding a harmless bacteria to cream that gives it its flavor and texture. It is used to thicken savory sauces and can be sweetened and used as a dessert sauce.

— *frite* [+ freet] A sweet preparation composed of chilled *crème pâtissiere* cut into slices, dipped in egg and bread crumbs, and fried.

— *pâtissière* [+ pah-tee-syer] See *Pâtissière, crème.*

— *renversée* [+ rE-vehr-seh] Also called *crème caramel*, this dessert consists of custard poured in a caramel-lined mold and chilled. Once set, the custard is unmolded and coated with the caramel.

— *Saint-Honoré* [+ sA toh-noh-reh] *Crème pâtissière* lightened with whipped egg whites. Used as a filling for gâteau Saint-Honoré. It is also known as *crème chiboust*.

Crèmer [kreh-meh] The act of adding cream to a sauce or soup to obtain a thicker, richer, and more flavorful product.

Crèmerie [kreh-muh-ree] A dairy store.

Crèmet [kreh-meh] A soft cow's-milk cheese from Angers and Saumur. It is traditionally sweetened and eaten as a dessert.

Cremona, moutarde [kreh-moh-nah moo-tahrd] A type of mustard made with fruit; similar to chutney.

Créole, à la [kreh-ol] Indicates that a dish is garnished or served with tomatoes, rice, and green peppers.

Créole, sauce Tomato sauce to which sautéed onions, garlic, and red pepper are added; seasoned with cayenne pepper and white wine.

Crêpe [krep] A very thin pancake usually filled with various sweet or savory preparations.

Crêperie [kre-pree] A restaurant specializing in offering crêpes.

Crêpes dentelle [+ dE-tel] A very delicate lacelike pancake from Quimperlé (Brittany).

Crêpes suzette [+ sü-zet] A famous dessert of crêpes warmed in orange butter, folded in quarters, and ignited with curaçao.

Crêpière [kre-pyer] See *Poêle à crêpe*.

Crépine [kreh-peen] Caul used to wrap *crépinettes*.

Crépinettes [kreh-pee-net] Small pork sausage patties wrapped in caul (*crépine*). Mushrooms, truffles, cream, ground chicken, and beef are oftentimes added.

Crespet [krehs-peh] A local crêpe from Béarn.

Cresson [kre-sO] Watercress.

Cressonière, sauce [kres-sO-nyer] Mayonnaise sauce to which chopped watercress and diced hard-cooked eggs are added.

Cressonière, à la Indicates watercress has been used as the main ingredient of a dish.

Crête de coq [kret duh kohk] "Cockscomb"; the red main on the cock's head. In traditional French cooking these are used to garnish fancy dishes.

Cretonnée de pois [kruh-tuhn-neh duh pwah] A dish comprised of green pea purée combined with chicken and bread crumbs, and seasoned with ginger and saffron.

Creuse [kruhz] A type of Portuguese oyster.

Creusois [kruh-zwah] See *Guéret*.

Crever [kruh-veh] Literally "to burst," this term simply means to parcook rice.

Crevettes [kruh-vet] Shrimp.

—, *sauce aux* *Velouté*, fish essence, and cream reduced by half and finished with shrimp butter.

Crible [kree-bluh] A type of sieve used primarily for straining fruits for jam.

Crique [kreek] A potato pancake popular in parts of central and southern France.

Croissant [krwah-sA] A flaky, buttery, crescent-shaped pastry made from a raised, laminated dough similar to puff pastry.

Cromesqui [kroh-mes-kee] Originating in Poland but popular in France, *cromesquis* are a type of croquette; various *salpicons* are dipped in batter and deep-fried. Typically served as an hors d'œuvre in France.

Croquant [kroh-kA] A small crunchy petit four made with almonds, hazelnuts, sugar, and egg whites.

Croquante [kroh-kAt] A large elaborate pastry used (now rarely) as a centerpiece; similar to *croquembouche*.

Croque au sel [krohk oh-sel] This term describes fresh, uncooked vegetables seasoned only with salt.

Croque-madame [+ mah-dahm] A grilled sandwich made up of sliced ham and Gruyère cheese; topped with a fried egg.

Croquembouche [kroh-kE-boosh] An elaborate pyramid-shaped centerpiece constructed by adhering small pastry balls glazed with caramel to a nougat base.

Croque-monsieur [+ meh-suyh] A hot ham and Gruyère cheese sandwich. It can be served on grilled bread, topped with *sauce Mornay* and cooked au gratin or dipped in egg and deep-fried.

Croquet [kroh-keh] A thin, cylindrical-shaped petit four made with almond meringue.

Croquette [kroh-ket] A sweet or savory *salpicon* dipped in egg and bread crumbs and deep-fried. They are traditionally shaped into balls and served with a sauce.

Croquignolles parisiennes [kroh-kee-nyol pah-ree-zyen] Small meringue-based pastries topped with vanilla buttercream.

Crosne [kron] Japanese plant.

Crottin de Chavignol [kro-tI duh shah-vee-nyol] A semi-hard, strong goat's-milk cheese produced in the town of Chavignol, in Berry.

Croustes [kroost] Potato dumplings; served *en casserole* with Gruyère cheese; a specialty of Dauphiné.

Croustade [kroos-tahd] An edible casing or shell made from puff pastry, hollowed-out bread, rice, noodles, and duchess potatoes. Croustades are used to contain thick stews, vegetables, creamed foods, and any other suitable preparation.

Croûte [kroot] A pastry or bread crust.

—, *en* Baked in crust.

Croûton [kroo-tO] (1) Small cubes or rounds of toasted or fried bread used in soups, salads, or as a base for various presentations. (2) Small pieces of aspic cut in various shapes and used as a garnish.

Croûtonner [kroo-tuhn-neh] To garnish (cold preparations) with aspic. See *Crouton*.

Crozets [kroh-zet] See *Crousets*.

Cru [krü] (1) The soil in which a plant or a fruit has grown. This is applied particularly to wine. (2) Raw.

Cruchade [krü-shahd] A type of cornmeal porridge similar to polenta.

Crudités [krü-dee-teh] Raw vegetables sliced thin or julienned and served as an hors d'œuvre.

Crustacés krüs-tah-seh] Crustaceans; shellfish.

Cubaine, à la [koo-ben, ah-lah] "Cuban style"; indicates that tomatoes, red peppers, and garlic are present in a dish.

Cugnot [koo-nyoh] See *Cougnou*.

Cuignot [kwee-nyoh] Provençal name for *quignon;* see *Grignon*.

Cuillère [kwee-yer] Spoon.

Cuire [kweer] To cook.

— *au four* [+ oh foor] To bake.

Cuisine [kwee-zeen] Kitchen; style of cooking.

— *à la vapeur* [+ al-lah vah-puhr] Steam cooking.

— *bourgeoise* [+ boor-zhwahz] Describes the various cooking styles throughout France based on local ingredients and simple fare.

— *paysanne* [+ peh-yee-zahn] Rustic, peasant cuisine.

Cuisinière [kwee-zeen-yer] Cook; stove.

Cuisses de grenouilles [kwees duh gruh-noo-yuh] Frog's legs.

Cuisson [kwee-sO] Cooking; cooking time.

— *au bain-marie* [+ oa bA mah-ree] Water-bath cooking.

Cuissot [kwee-soh] Haunch; hindquarter; applies particularly to deer.

Cuit [kweet] Cooked.

—, *bien* [byE kweet] Well-done.

Cul-de-poule [kül-duh-pool] A large bowl used to whisk egg whites.

Cul-de-veau [kül-duh voh] See *Quasi.*

Culotte [kü-lot] Rump.

Cultivateur, soupe du [soop dü kül-tee-vah-tuhr] A thin vegetable and bacon soup.

Curaçao [kü-rah-sah-oh] An orange-flavored liqueur.

Curcuma [kü-koo-mah] Turmeric; a bright yellow spice from a variety of lily plant; used as an ingredient in curries, pickles, and so forth.

Curé, fromage de [fro-mahzh duh kü-reh] See *Nantaise.*

Curnonsky [kür-nO-skeh] (1872–1956) French writer and gastronome; founder of the Academy of Gastronomes.

Curry [kür-ree] See *Cari.*

—, *sauce au Velouté* reduced with *mirepoix* and apples; seasoned with curry powder and strained; finished with cream or coconut milk.

Cussy [küs-see] A garnish for meat or poultry comprised of mushroom caps stuffed with chestnut purée and truffles and laced with Madeira. Also indicates that truffles are present in a dish.

—, *Louis, marquis de* [mahr-kee duh loo-ee] (1766–1837) French gastronome. Published *Les Classiques de la table* in 1843; created three hundred sixty-six ways to prepare chicken.

Cyrano [see-rah-noh] Describes dishes garnished with artichoke bottoms stuffed with purée of mushrooms and served with veal demi-glace.

Dacquoise [dah-kwahz] A cake consisting of whipped cream (or butter cream) between layers of almond meringue and dusted with powered sugar. Fruit is often added to the cream center.

Dail [dail] The name for *pholade* in Royan. See *Pholade.*

Dame blanche [dahm blAsh] Describes cold desserts with ingredients such as meringue, white buttercream, vanilla ice cream, and chantilly cream in which white is the dominant color.

Dame-jeanne [zhahn] A large vessel used to carry wine.

Damier [dah-myeh] A rum-flavored gâteau filled with hazelnut butter cream and decorated with sliced almonds.

Darblay, Potage [dahr-bleh] A cream of potato soup garnished with a julienne of vegetables.

Dariole [dah-ryol] (1) A classic dessert composed of a pastry-lined mold filled with frangipane cream (flavored with kirsch) and baked. (2) A small cylindrical mold in which the dessert of the same name is baked. (3) Sweet or savory preparations cooked in a dariole mold.

Darne [dahrn] A thick, center-cut slice of fish; a fish steak.

Dartois [dahr-twahz] Two layers of puff pastry enclosing various sweet or savory fillings; served as an appetizer or petit four. See *Sausselis; Manon, gâteau à la.*

Datte [daht] Date.

Daube, en [E dohb] Meat, poultry, or game very slowly stewed in red wine and stock in a lidded pot.

Daubière [doh-byer] A pot used to make *daubes.*

Daumont, à la [doh-mO] An elaborate garnish for fish made up of sautéed mushroom caps, crayfish tails bound with *sauce Nantua*, fish quenelles, fried roe, and sliced truffles. Served with *sauce normande* combined with crayfish butter.

Daumont, sauce Hollandaise sauce combined with oyster essence and lemon juice and garnished with oysters, truffles, and mushrooms.

Dauphin [doh-fI] A highly seasoned, soft cow's-milk cheese produced in northern France.

Dauphiné [doh-feen] A region in southeastern France famous for its potatoes.

—, *à la* Describes dishes garnished with dauphiné potatoes.

—, *pommes de terre* [pom +] Potato purée combined with Gruyère cheese and *choux* paste and deep-fried. Other vegetables may be substituted for the potatoes, such as eggplant, celeriac, turnips, and so on.

Dauphinoise, à la [doh-fee-nwahz] Denotes that a dish is served with dauphinoise potatoes.

Dauphinoises, pommes de terre [pom duh ter +] Sliced potatoes baked *en casserole* with cream mixed with eggs and Gruyère cheese and seasoned with nutmeg and garlic.

Daurade/Dorade [doh-rahd] Sea bream.

Débarrasser [deh-bah-rah-seh] To clear away, i.e., guests, table, kitchen utensils, and so forth. Also refers to food transferred to a holding or cooling area.

Déboucher [deh-boo-sheh] To uncork a wine bottle.

Déca [deh-kah] Decaffeinated coffee. Also called *faux café* and *café décaféiné.*

Décanter [deh-kA-teh] To carefully pour a liquid (usually wine) from one container to another in order to separate any sediment that has settled on the bottom.

Decize [deh-seez] A soft cheese similar to Brie; from the Nivernais region of Bourgogne.

Décoction [deh-kok-syO] To boil meat, fish, or vegetables in water to obtain its flavor and nutritional properties; a stock.

Découpage [deh-koo-pazh] Carving; slicing.

Découpoir [deh-koo-pwahr] A tool used to cut various decorative shapes from foods.

Décuire [deh-kweer] To adjust the tempature and consistency of boiling sweet syrups by the addition of water.

Défarde/Deffarde [deh-fahrd/def-fahr-deh] A ragoût of lamb's feet and intestines cooked in a seasoned stock. A specialty of southeastern France.

Déglacer [deh-glah-seh] To add a liquid (wine, stock, water, liqueur) to a roasting or sauté pan in order to dissolve the caramelized sediment left over from cooking, thus incorporating that flavor into the sauce.

Dégorger [deh-gor-zheh] To remove impurities from meats and fish by soaking them in cold water.

Dégraisser [deh-greh-seh] To remove (skim) fat from stocks and sauces; to cut away any excess fat from meats, poultry, and so on.

Dégraissis [deh-greh-see] The skimmed, clarified fats from stocks and sauces.

Déjazet [deh-zhah-zeh] Describes fried fish served with tarragon butter and garnished with fresh tarragon leaves.

Déjeuner [deh-zhuh-neh] Lunch.

Délice [deh-lees] Delicacy; delight. A word used to describe various sweet pastries.

Délicieuse, à la [deh-lee-syuhz] Describes fish dishes served with hollandaise sauce flavored with tomato *concassée* and garnished with boiled potatoes.

Délicieux [deh-lee-syuh] Delicious.

De mer [duh mer] From the sea.

Demi-deuil, à la [duh-mee-duh-yuh] "Half-mourning." This term describes white dishes—i.e., poultry, potatoes, white sauces, and white fish—garnished with black ingredients, typically truffles.

Demidoff [duh-mee-dof] The name given to several dishes containing truffles.

—, sauce Sauce Madeira flavored with truffle essence and garnished with diced trufffles.

Demi-étuvé [duh-mee-eh-tü-veh] The French term for Dutch cheeses (Edam, Gouda) aged up to six months in dry storage.

Demi feuilletée [+ fuh-yuh-teh] A dough made from leftover puff pastry scraps (*rognures*) that can be used for various preparations.

Demi-glace, sauce [+ glahs] A concentrated, flavorful brown sauce resulting from a reduction of *sauce espagnole* and brown stock.

Demi-sec [+ sek] "Half-dry"; describes sweet wines containing up to 6 percent sugar.

Demi-sel [+ sel] A soft, spreadable cow's-milk cheese popular in Normandy.

Demi-tasse [+ tah-suh] "Half-cup." This term refers to black coffee served in a small cup or the small cup in which the coffee is served.

Demoiselle [duh-mwah-zel] A species of lobster found off France's northern coast.

Dénerver [deh-ner-veh] To remove any undesirable meat, fat, skin, and silverskin from uncooked meat, fish, or poultry.

Denier, en [A deh-nyeh] Round coin-shaped slices of fried potatoes.

Dénoyauteur [deh-nwah-yoh-tuhr] Fruit pitter. Also spelled *énoyauteur*.

Dent-de-lion [dE-duh-lyO] Dandelion; also called *pissenlit*.

Denté/Denti [dE-tel/dE-tee] A firm-fleshed Mediterranean fish related to the sea bream.

Dentelle, crêpes [krep dE-tel] A very thin lacelike crêpe.

Dents-de-loup [dE-duh-loo] Diamond or triangle-shaped croutons used as a garnish for a variety of dishes and presentations.

Dépeçage [deh-puh-sahzh] The cutting up of meats, poultry, game, and so on.

Dépouiller [deh-poo-yehr] To skim the scum that rises to the surface of simmering sauces and stocks.

Derby, à la [der-bee] Describes dishes, particularly poultry, that are garnished with boiled rice, foie gras, and truffles.

Dérober [deh-ro-beh] To remove the skin from nuts, vegetables, beans, and so on.

Derval [der-vahl] Denotes the presence of quartered artichoke hearts in a dish.

Dés [deh] Dice.

Descar [deh-kahr] A garnish of Dauphiné potatoes and artichoke bottoms stuffed with a chicken *salpicon*. Accompanies large beef roasts.

Descartes, à la [des-kahrt] A garnish for poultry and game birds comprised of tartlet shells stuffed with a quail-truffle forcemeat.

Désosser [deh-soh-seh] To bone; to remove bones from meat, fish, or poultry.

Désossé [deh-soh-seh] Boneless.

Dessalage [deh-sahl-azh] To desalt brined or preserved foods by soaking in cold water.

Dessécher [deh-se-sheh] To rid foods of any excess moisture by the use of heat. This term particularly pertains to *choux* paste and vegetables.

Dessert [deh-ser] Dessert.

Desserte [deh-sert] (1) Credenza. (2) Leftovers.

Détailler [deh-tah-yeh] To cut foods—typically meats, vegetables, and truffles—into various shapes.

Détendre [deh-tE-druh] To thin or soften a dough mixture by the addition of a liquid.

Détrempe [deh-trE-peh] A baking term for the plain flour and water mixture of a dough before the addition of other ingredients.

Diable [dyah-bluh] (1) "Devil"; refers to dishes that are highly spiced. (2) A lidden earthenware cooking pot used to cook vegetables.

— *de mer* [+ duh mer] "Sea devil." A French nickname for the monkfish and *rascasse*.

—, *sauce à la* Demi-glace sauce to which a red wine reduction, vinegar, and cayenne pepper is added. Chopped tomatoes are often added.

Diablotins [dyah-bloh-tI] (1) Bread rounds topped with *sauce Mornay* and browned under a broiler. (2) A fruit fritter. (3) A chocolate confection. (4) A spicy Parmesan cheese dumpling used to garnish soup.

Diane, à la [dyahn] Named after Diana, goddess of the hunt. This term applies to various game dishes, usually accompanied by *sauce Diane*.

Diane, sauce *Sauce poivrade* combined with game stock, cream, and sweet butter.

Dieppe [dyep] A seaport in Normandy on the English Channel famous for the sole fished there.

Dieppoise, garniture [dyep-pwahz] A garnish of shrimp, mussels, mushrooms, and *sauce dieppoise*. Served with various seafoods, notably sole, brill, and whiting.

Dieppoise, sauce Fish *velouté* enriched with shrimp butter. Also known as *sauce Marguery*.

Digestif [dee-zhes-teef] A cordial or liqueur served after a meal, i.e., Chartreuse and Bénédictine.

Dijon [dee-zhO] The capital of Burgundy famous for its black currants, gingerbread, and mustards. It is one of the finest eating cities in France.

—, *moutarde de* [moo-tahrd duh +] Dijon mustard.

Dijonnaise, à la [dee-zhon-nez] "Dijon style"; describes dishes utilizing the food resources of Dijon, particularly mustard or black currants; dishes accompanied with *sauce dijonnaise*.

Dijonnaise, sauce An emulsion sauce prepared by whisking olive oil into Dijon mustard and crushed hard-cooked egg yolks until it reaches a mayonnaiselike consistency.

Dinde [dId] The French word for turkey.

Dîner [dee-neh] Dinner.

Diot [dyot] A small pork and vegetable sausage popular in eastern France.

Diplomate, à la [dee-ploh-maht] Describes various dishes containing rich and luxurious ingredients, particularly lobster, cream, and truffles.

Diplomate, sauce *Sauce normande* garnished with diced lobster meat and truffles, flavored with cognac, and finished with lobster butter.

Dives sur mer [deev sür mer] A town in Normandy noted for a fine variety of oyster.

Divine, sauce [dee-veen] Whipped cream folded into hollandaise sauce and flavored with chicken glacé.

Dodine [doh-deen] A former method of preparing poultry (usually duck) in which the bird is boned with the skin intact, stuffed, and braised. In some areas of France, *dodine* is synonymous with *civet*.

D.O.M. Initials printed on bottles of Benedictine liqueur standing for *Deo Optimo Maximo* (To God, most good, most great).

Dom Pérignon A champagne of excellent quality named after the seventeenth century monk credited with inventing the process of champagne making.

Donzelle [dO-zel] A small sea fish resembling the eel used in bouillabaisse. Also called *girelle*.

Dorade [do-rahd] Sea bream.

Dorée [do-reh] The name given to foods that have been cooked (by various methods) to a golden color.

Dorer [do-reh] A pastry term meaning to brown in the oven by brushing the product with egg.

Doria [do-ryuh] (1) Denotes the use of cucumbers in a dish. (2) Describes dishes containing the colors of the Italian flag (red, white, and green). (3) Indicates Piedmontese truffles are present in a dish.

Dorine [do-reen] A small tartlet filled with chestnut-flavored *crème pâtisserie* and slivered almonds.

Dormeur [dor-muhr] The name for the common edible crab in parts of France; also called *tourteau*.

D'Orsay [dohr-seh] Describes meat dishes garnished with château potatoes, stuffed olives, and mushroom caps.

Dorure [dor-rür] Beaten eggs brushed on pastries enabling browning in the oven.

Dosage [do-sazh] The sugar syrup added to champagne, determining the degree of sweetness of the final product.

Double-crème [doo-bluh-krem] A cow's-milk cheese that has been enriched with cream.

Double-fond [+ fO] Double boiler.

Doucette [doo-set] See *Mâche*.

Douillon [dwee-yO] See *Rabotte*.

Doux [doo] Sweet.

Douzaine [doo-zen] Dozen.

Doyenne [doh-yen] A variety of pear.

Dragée [drah-zheh] A nut, usually an almond, dipped in chocolate and then covered with a hard sugar coating.

Du Barry [dü bahry] Describes dishes containing cauliflower.

Dubley [dü-blee] A garnish consisting of grilled mushrooms and duchess potato baskets filled with mushroom purée.

Dubois, Urbain François [ür-bA frA-swah dü-bwah] (1818–1901) French chef and author of several cookbooks including *La Cuisine Classique* and *Le Grand Livre des pâtissiers et des confiseurs.*

Dubonnet [dü-buhn-neh] An aromatic French wine served as an aperitif.

Duchesse [dü-shes] (1) Indicates a dish is garnished with duchess potatoes and *sauce Madeira.* (2) *Choux* pastry filled with a variety of sweet or savory fillings. (3) A type of macaroon from Rouen.

Duchesse, pommes de terre Seasoned puréed potatoes enriched with egg yolks, squeezed through a pastry bag into various shapes, and browned in the oven.

Dufferin, à la [düf-frin] A garnish for fish composed of lobster, prawns, and hollandaise sauce (mixed with lobster butter).

Dugléré, Adolphe [ah-dolf dü-lyeh] (1805–1884) Best known as chef at Café Anglais in Paris; credited with several culinary creations, including anna potatoes, *potage Germiny*, and *sauce Dugléré.*

Dugléré, sauce *Sauce poulette* with the addition of diced tomatoes; finished with butter.

Dumaine, Alexandre [ah-leks-sA-druh dü-men] (1895–1974) Chef/owner of Côte-d'Or in Saulieu and one of the great chefs of his time.

Dumas [dü-mah] A garnish for meat dishes named after the great French author of *The Three Musketeers;* comprised of carrots and cabbage sautéed with bacon.

Dunant, sauce [dü-nA] Hollandaise sauce flavored with truffles, enriched with lobster butter, and lightened with whipped cream.

Durance [dü-rahns] Describes fish dishes garnished with small shrimps, diced lobster tails, and hollandaise sauce.

Duroc [dü-rok] A garnish for various meat and poultry dishes composed of sautéed new potatoes, mushrooms, tomatoes *concasées*, and demi-glace sauce.

Duse [düs] A garnish for large meat joints made up of French beans, Parmentier potatoes, and *sauce Madeira.*

Duxelles [dük-sel] Chopped, seasoned mushrooms cooked to a paste consistency and used as a garnish, stuffing, and flavoring.

— **sèches** [+ sesh] "Dry duxelles"; duxelles before it has been combined with other ingredients, i.e., stuffings, sauces, and cream.

Eau [oh] Water.

— **-de-vie** [oh-duh-vee] "Water of life"; term referring to fine brandies or liqueurs.

Ébouillanter [eh-boo-yA-teh] Scald.

Ébullition [eh-bül-yee-syO] Boiling.

Écailler [eh-kah-yeh] To scale (a fish); to remove scales from a fish.

Écalure [eh-kah-lür] The outer skin of vegetables and fruits.

Écarlate, à l' [ah-leh-kahr-laht] Literally "scarlet," this term describes dishes reddish in color. Also refers to pickled ox tongue, which turns red while soaking in the brine.

Échalote [eh-sha-lot] Shallot.

Échaudé [eh-chod] A small, dry biscuit.

Éclade [eh-klahd] A specialty of western coastal France composed of mussels cooked with pine needles. Called *églade* in some areas of France. See *Fumée.*

Éclair [eh-kler] A pastry made from *choux* paste and filled with pastry cream; topped with chocolate glaze.

Éclanche [eh-klAsh] An obsolete term for mutton shoulder.

Écossaise, à l' [ah-leh-kos-sez] "Scottish style"; describes dishes served with *sauce écossaise*. The term also denotes that salmon has been used in preparation of certain dishes.

Écossaise, sauce (1) *Sauce normande* with the addition of diced carrots, celery, and green beans. (2) Béchamel sauce to which chopped hard-cooked eggs are added.

Écrevisse [eh-kruh-vees] Crayfish.

—, *sauce* Hollandaise sauce finished with crayfish butter. This sauce can also be made with béchamel sauce.

Écuelle [eh-kwel] A deep earthenware dish usually used to serve soups, stews, and vegetables.

Écume [eh-küm] The scum that rises to the surface during the simmering of stocks and sauces.

Écuemer [eh-kü-mer] Skim; to remove the scum that rises to the surface during simmering (of sauces, stocks, etc.).

Écumoire [eh-kü-mwahr] Skimming ladle.

Edam [eh-dahm] A famous Dutch cow's-milk cheese; a version of *Edam* is produced in France.

Edouard VII [eh-dwahrd] Describes chicken stuffed with risotto, truffles, and foie gras; garnished with creamed cucumbers and coated with a curry pimento sauce.

Effiler [ef-fee-leh] To clean, remove the tips of, and uniformly cut green beans before cooking.

Effilocher [ef-feel-o-sheh] To cut leeks or other vegetables into very thin strips.

Églade [eh-glahd] See *Éclade*.

Églefin [eh-gleh-fI] Haddock.

Égoutter [eh-goo-teh] To drain (excess water or liquids).

Égrugeoir [eh-grü-zhwahr] A salt or pepper mill.

Égruger [eh-grü-zheh] To grind foods, particularly coarse salt or peppercorns. This term is now rarely used.

Égyptienne, à l' [ah-leh-zheep-tyen] Dishes containing ingredients indigenous to Egypt, including eggplants, tomatoes, onions, and rice.

Eierkückas [ah-yuhr-kü-kahs] A type of pancake from Alsace.

El pa y all [el-pah-ee-ahl] A Catalan specialty of sliced bread spread with garlic and olive oil.

Elzekaria [el-zuh-ka-ryah] A cabbage and white bean soup originating in the French Basque region.

Emballer [E-bah-leh] To wrap or tie foods in order to keep their shape during cooking.

Embossoir [E-bos-swahr] A funnel used to fill sausage casings.

Embrucciate [E-brü-shyat] A Corsican cake flavored with vanilla and filled with a sweetened Broccio cheese mixture.

Émincé [eh-mI-seh] A thinly sliced piece of meat, generally beef, pork, or mutton.

Émincer [eh-mI-seh] To cut meat, fish (especially salmon), or vegetables into fine slices.

Émincés [eh-mI-seh] A dish made from leftover meat. The meat is cut into very thin slices and covered with a sauce in order to keep it tender and avoid drying out.

Emmental [em-mE-tahl] Emmentaler cheese.

Emmenthal [em-mE-thahl] Emmentaler. A fruity cow's-milk cheese from the valley of the Emme in Switzerland. Savoy and Franche-Comté produce a fine French Emmentaler.

— *français* [+ frA-sez] See *Emmenthal*.

Empereur, à l' [ah-lE-peh-ruhr] A garnish for meat dishes featuring truffled Parmentier potatoes, tomato *concassée* sautéed with marrow, and asparagus tips.

Empotage [E-po-tahzh] The contents of a braising or stock pot, i.e., meat, vegetables, and seasonings.

Empoter [E-po-teh] The adding of ingredients to a braising or stock pot.

Émulsion [eh-mül-syO] The suspending of two immiscible liquids, i.e., butter or oil with water, vinegar, wine by use of an emulsifier (typically an egg yolk). Hollandaise, béarnaise, and mayonnaise are examples of emulsion sauces.

En [E] In; into.

— *-cas* [E kas] Snack; food eaten between meals.

Enchaud [E-shoh] Braised pork tenderloin. This specialty of the Perigord is often served with truffles, as one would expect.

Encornet [E-kor-neh] The word for squid in parts of France.

Endaubage [E-doh-bazh] The additional components used for braising meats—lard, *mirepoix*, seasonings, water, wine, and so forth.

Enrober [E-roh-beh] To coat a food item with sauce, aspic, *chaud-froid*, and so on.

Entrecôte [E-truh-kot] Literally "between the ribs," this term refers to any steak cut from the rib or loin area.

Entrée [E-treh] The main course on a menu.

Entremets [E-truh-meh] Desserts; sweets.

Entremetier, chef [shef E-truh-meh-tye] The egg and vegetable chef.

Épauls [eh-pohl] Shoulder.

Éperlans [eh-per-lA] Smelts.

Épi [eh-pee] An "earred" or knobbed baguette.

Épice [eh-pees] Spice.

Épicerie [eh-pee-sree] Grocery store.

Épicure [eh-pee-kür] A connoisseur of fine food and wine.

Épigramme [eh-pee-grahm] A dish consisting of two cuts of lamb–usually a breast slice and chop–treated *à l'anglaise* (breaded) and fried.

Épinard [eh-pee-nahrd] Spinach.

Épine d'hiver [eh-peen dee-ver] A type of winter pear.

Époisses [eh-pwahs] A soft, ripened cow's-milk cheese produced in the village of Époisses, in Burgundy.

Éponger [eh-pO-geh] To towel-dry; the process of absorbing excess moisture or grease from boiled or fried foods by the use of a towel.

Érable [eh-rah-bluh] Maple.

—, *sirop d'* [see-rop deh-rah-bluh] Maple syrup.

Ercé [ehr-seh] A cow's-milk cheese produced in the Ariège Valley of southern France.

Ervy [ehr-vee] See *Troyes*.

Ésaü [eh-soh] Describes dishes containing lentil purée.

Escalope [es-kahl-op] A thin slice of meat or fish, usually panfried.

Escaloper [es-kah-lo-peh] To carve thin slices of meat of fish.

Escargot [es-kahr-goh] Snail.

Escauton [es-koh-tO] (1) Cornmeal gruel cooked in goose fat. (2) A ham and vegetable stock. Both are specialties of Gascony.

Escoffier, Auguste [oh-güst es-kof-fyeh] (1846–1935) Dubbed the Emperor of chefs by Emperor William II, Escoffier spent a large portion of his career in London at the Savoy and Carlton Hotels.

Escoffier, Auguste (cont.)
He is the author of several cookbooks, including *Le Guide culinaire*. Along with Carême, he is considered the greatest contributer to modern French cooking.

Escubac [es-kü-bahk] A sweetened, spiced brandy from Lorraine; also spelled *scubac*.

Espadon [es-pah-dO] Swordfish; a large, firm-fleshed ocean fish of excellent eating.

Espagne [es-pah-nyuh] Spain. See *Espagnole, à l'*.

Espagnole, à l' [ah-les-pah-nyol] "Spanish style"; describes dishes prepared with ingredients indigenous to Spain, including tomatoes, pimentoes, onions, garlic, and rice.

Espagnole, sauce One of the classic sauces prepared by thickening brown stock with brown roux; flavored with *mirepoix* and bouquet garni and reduced until proper consistency is achieved.

Espelette [es-pel-let] A mildly spicy red pepper grown in the French Basque region.

Esprot [es-proh] Sprat; a small sardinelike fish common in Europe.

Esquinado toulonais [es-kee-nah-doh too-lo-neh] A specialty of Toulon (Provence) composed of crab shells stuffed with a mussel and crabmeat filling bound with a sauce and baked au gratin.

Essence A concentrated, flavorful liquid extracted from virtually any food source (meat, vegetables, herbs, fish) by infusion, distillation, or reduction.

Estocaficada [es-to-ka-fee-kah-dah] A dried salt cod dish popular in southern France (particularly Provence); it is stewed in olive oil with potatoes, garlic, olives, tomatoes, peppers, onions, and aromatic herbs. Also called *estofinado, estoficado, stocaficado,* and *stoficado*.

Estofinado [es-to-fee-nah-doh] See *Estocaficado*.

Estouffat [es-too-fah] (1) In Languedoc it is a hearty pork and bean stew. (2) In Béarn it is beef cooked *en daube* with red wine, cognac, aromatic herbs and vegetables, and Bayonne ham.

Estouffade [es-too-fahd] "A stewed dish"; beef slowly cooked in red wine.

Estragon [es-trah-gO] Tarragon.

Esturgeon [es-tür-gyO] Sturgeon.

Et [eh] And.

Étamine [eh-tah-meen] See *Tamis*.

Étouffér [eh-too-feh] "To smother"; (*French Cajun*) refers to foods cooked in a thick, spicy sauce.

Étouffée, à l' [eh-too-feh] Food cooked with little or no liquid in a tightly sealed vessel. Also spelled *à l' etuvée*.

Étourdeau [eh-toor-doh] A local name for a young capon.

Étourneau [eh-toor-noh] Starling. See *Sansonnet*.

Etratat, sauce [et-rah-tah] *Sauce allemande* with fish fumet, flavored with tomatoes and mushrooms, and garnished with oysters.

Étuvé [eh-tü-veh] A French term for aged Dutch cheeses.

Étuvée [eh-tü-veh] See *Etouffée*.

Étuver [eh-tü-veh] To cook food in a covered pan without moistening.

Excelsior [eg-sel-syor] A mild, triple-cream cheese made in Normandy from cow's milk. This cheese was first made in 1890 in Rovray-Catillon (Normandy).

—, garniture (1) Lamb noisettes garnished with braised lettuce and potatoes *fondants*. (2) Stuffed sole garnished with a *salpicon* of lobster, sliced truffles, and shrimp, bound with sauce Newburg; topped with *sauce normande*.

Exceptionnel, cru [krü eg-sep-syonnel] A wine term meaning exceptional growth. See *Cru*.

Excitant [eg-see-tA] A word sometimes used to describe spicy foods.

Explorateur [eg-splo-rah-tuhr] A French triple-cream cheese made in La Trétoire, near Paris.

Exprimer [egs-pree-meh] To remove juice or excess liquid from fruits or vegetables by squeezing or pressing.

Exquisite [eg-skee-zeet] Describes fish dishes garnished with mushroom dumplings, truffles, and *sauce américaine*.

Extra sec [egs-trah sek] A champagne term meaning extra dry.

Extrait [egs-treh] Extract. See *Essence*.

Fagot [fah-go] An herb bundle. See *Bouquet garni*.

Fagoue [fah-goo] Calf's sweetbreads or pancreas.

Faire blondir [fer blO-deer] Describes the gentle cooking of flour and butter in order to make a blond roux.

Faire chabrot [+ shah-broh] A traditional ending to a meal of *garbure*. Red wine is added into the remaining broth of the soup and consumed.

Faire la cuisine [+ lah kwee-zeen] To cook.

Faire revenir [+ ruh-vuh-neer] To flavor (*food*); to brown (*meat*).

Faire ripaille [+ ree-pah-yuh] A French expression used in the mountains of Savoy meaning to feast.

Faisan [feh-sA] Pheasant.

Faisandage [feh-sA-dazh] Describes highly flavored and tender game resulting from the animal being hung for an appropriate amount of time.

Faisandé [feh-zahndeh] See *Faisandage*.

Fait tout [fe-too] A small lidded pot. See *Marmite*.

Falculella [fahl-kü-lel-lah] A Corsican cheesecake made with Broccio cheese.

Falette [fah-let] A specialty of central France consisting of braised mutton with vegetables and white beans.

Fallue [fah-lü] See *Gâche améliorée*.

Fanchette [fA-shet] A puff pastry tartlet filled with pastry cream, frosted with meringue, and browned in the oven; also spelled *fanchonnette*.

Far [fahr] (1) A type of buckwheat porridge eaten with prunes or other dried fruit. (2) The name for a type of *farci* from Poitou made with various greens, bacon, eggs, and cream wrapped in cabbage leaves. (3) A prune flan from Brittany; see *Far breton*.

— **au gras** [+ oh gra] See *Farçon*.

— **au maigre** [+ oh meh-gruh] A type of meatless *farci* from Poitou.

— **brteon** [+ bruh-tO] A prune flan from Brittany.

Farce/Farci [fahrs/fahr-see] A stuffing or forcemeat.

Farcement [fahr-smA] (*Savoy*) A type of potato cake sweetened with pears and prunes.

Farci [fahr-see] Stuffed greens, most commonly cabbage (*chou farci*). A typical stuffing consists of chopped greens, herbs, pork, eggs, and cream; usually cooked in stock or fried.

— **au pot** [+ oh poh] See *Farçon*.

— **de veau en vessie** [+ duh voh E ves-see] A veal sausage from Lyonnaise.

Farcidure [fahr-see-dür] (*Limousin*) Small balls of cabbage stuffed with a mixture of buckwheat flour, sorrel, Swiss chard, and beets. The balls are fried or boiled and used to garnish various dishes and soups.

Farçon [fahr-sO] In Savoy, *farçon* is a sweetened potato cake. In other parts of France, *farçon* refers to certain preparations of sausage or sausage forcemeats.

Fardels [fahr-del] See *Tripoux*.

Far du poitou [fahr dü pwah-too] A specialty of Poitou consisting of lettuce leaves stuffed with lean pork meat, sorrel, garlic, lettuce, and eggs. It is seasoned, slowly simmered, and eaten hot or cold. Also called *farci au pot, far au gras,* or *far poitevin*.

Farée [fah-reh] (*Angoumois*) Cabbage stuffed with pork and greens.

Farigoule [fah-ree-gool] Also *farigoulette,* this is the Provençal name for thyme.

Farigoulette [fah-ree-goo-let] See *Farigoule*.

Farinade [fah-ree-nahd] A Corsican version of the Italian polenta made with chestnut flour instead of corn flour. It is traditionaly served with warm milk and Broccio cheese; see *Farniette*.

Farinage [fah-ree-nahd] This term refers to starchy food items such as pasta, gnocchi, polenta, and dumplings.

Farine [fah-reen] Flour.
— **de blé** [+ duh bleh] Flour made from hard wheat.
— **de gâteau** [+ duh gah-toh] Cake flour.
— **grise** [+ gree] A coarse grey flour. It is very flavorful and used to make *levains* and other types of bread.

Farinette [fah-ree-net] A local name for pancake in some regions of France, with each region having its own version. Also known as *omelette enfarinée* and *farinade*.

Farineux [fah-ree-nuh] Any natural or prepared food containing a high flour or starch content—i.e., beans, lentils, grains, pasta, and so forth.

Farinière [fah-ree-nyer] A flour bin.

Faséole [fah-zeh-ohl] A variety of haricot bean.

Faubonne [foh-buhn] A vegetable and white bean purée soup.

Faux café [foh kah-feh] Decaffeinated coffee.

Faux filet [+ fee-leh] See *Contre-Filet*.

Faux mousseron [+ moo-suh-rO] A variety of mushroom often dried, pulverized, and used as a seasoning.

Favart [fah-vahr] (1) Sweetbreads garnished with chicken quenelles flavored with tarragon and creamed cèpes in tartlet shells; served with chicken *velouté* finished with crayfish butter. (2) Beef or lamb garnished with noodles, truffles, and demi-glace sauce. (3) Poached eggs served in a tartlet shell over a *salpicon* of lambs sweetbreads and truffles.

Faverolles [fah-vuh-rol] The name for haricot beans in parts of southern France.

Faverottes [fah-vuh-rot] See *Faverolles*.

Favioles [fah-vyol] See *Faverolles*.

Favorite, à la [fah-voh-reet] The name given to several dishes garnished with artichokes or asparagus.

Féchuns [feh-shU] Stuffed cabbage with various fillings; a specialty of Montbéliard.

Fécule [feh-kül] A fine potato flour; yam or cassava starch. Also spelled *fecula*.

— *de maïs* [+ duh mah-ees] Cornstarch or cornflour.

Fédora [feh-doh-rah] (*For large roasts*) A garnish composed of roasted chestnuts, orange slices, and pastry shells filled with asparagus tips, diced carrots and turnips.

Fela [feh-lah] The name for conger (eel) in some parts of France.

Fenouli [fe-noo-lee] Fennel.

—, *sauce* Sauce *beurre blanc* garnished with sliced, cooked fennel.

Fenugrec [fe-noo-grek] Fenugreek; a Middle Eastern plant. The seeds are ground and popularly used as a spice in curries, chutneys, and pickles.

Féouse [feh-ooz] A local name for quiche in Alsace-Lorraine.

Fer [fer] Iron.

Féra [feh-rah] A scarce, highly regarded freshwater fish related to the salmon found only in a few European lakes, including Lake Geneva and Lake Bourget, in Savoy.

Ferchuse [fer-shooz] (*Burgundy*) Braised pigs offal simmered in red wine with onions and seasonings.

Fermière, à la [fer-myer] Describes various dishes garnished with vegetables cooked in butter.

Ferval [fer-vahl] A garnish for various dishes made up of quartered artichoke hearts and duchess potatoes mixed with chopped ham.

Festonner [fes-tuhn-neh] To decorate a serving platter by arranging various foods around its border in half-moon-like patterns (festoons).

Feuillantine [fuh-yA-teen] Puff pastry strips brushed with egg, sprinkled with sugar, and baked.

They often contain fruit, such as apples or prunes, and are traditionally served with coffee or tea.

Feuille [fuh-yuh] Leaf.

— *de Dreux* [duh druh] A flat, round cow's-milk cheese from the Île-de-France. It is often wrapped in chestnut leaves.

Feuilletage [fuh-yuh-tazh] Puff pastry; a (yeastless) laminated dough that rises or puffs when baked, because of the several layers of butter folded into the raw dough. Also known as *pâte feuilletée*.

Feuilleté [fuh-yuh-teh] Small strips or wedges of puff pastry filled with various cheeses, meats, or *salpicons*.

— *aux morilles* [+ oh mor-eel] Puff pastry stuffed with morel mushrooms. A specialty of the Morvan region of Burgundy.

Feuilleton [fuh-yuh-tO] A meat dish consisting of alternate layers of thinly sliced pork and/or veal and forcemeat. After constructing several layers, it is wrapped in bacon, tied, and braised.

Fève [fev] Broad bean; fava bean.

Féverole [feh-vrol] A white bean similar to the broad bean (*féve*).

Fèves de Marais [fev duh mah-reh] Broad bean.

Fèvettes [fuh-vet] Tiny, young *fèves*.

Fiadone [fyah-don] (*Corsica*) A vanilla-lemon-flavored cake made with Broccio cheese.

Fiatole [fyah-tol] The French name for a Mediterranean fish similar to the turbot.

Ficelle [fee-sel] Literally "string"; a long, thin loaf of bread (baguette).

Ficelles picardes [pee-kahrd] (*Northern France*) Savory crêpes filled with a *salpicon* of pork or ham, mushrooms, and cheese. They are covered with sauce and Gruyère cheese and baked au gratin.

Fiélas [fyeh-lahs] The Provençal name for conger eel.

Figatelli [fee-gah-tel-lee] A spicy sausage from Corsica made with pork and pork liver. It is grilled and eaten between slices of bread in order to absorb the grease.

Figer [fee-zheh] To coagulate; congeal. To go from a liquid to a solid state, e.g., butter and lard.

Figue [feeg] Fig.

— *de mer* [+ duh mer] An oysterlike shellfish with a brown, soft shell. Also called *violet*.

Figuette [fee-get] A beverage made from juniper berries and figs.

Filet [fee-leh] Tenderloin; pertains to beef, pork, lamb, and veal.

— *de Saxe* [+ duh sahks] Similar to bacon, it is a smoked pork filet.

— *Mignon* [+ mee-nyO] A small, very tender, prime cut of beef from the small end of the tenderloin. Although the term usually refers to beef, filet mignons can be cut from veal, pork, and lamb as well.

Filets de volaille [+ duh vo-lah-yuh] Chicken filets; located underneath the breast.

Fileter [fee-luh-teh] To fillet fish; to remove bones and other inedible portions.

Financier [fee-nA-syeh] An almond sponge cake used as a base for petits fours or gateaux.

Financière, à la [fee-nA-syer] (1) A rich (hence the name) garnish made up of truffled chicken quenelles, cockscombs and kidneys, olives, mushroom caps, and *sauce financière*. (2) A *salpicon* (made with the above ingredients) used as a filling for *croûtes*, vol-au-vents, and so on.

Financière, sauce Demi-glace sauce flavored with Madeira and truffle essence.

Fin de Bagnol [fI duh bah-nyol] A long thin variety of green French bean grown in the Roussillon.

Fin de siècle [fI duh sye-kluh] A triple-cream cheese produced in Normandy from cow's milk.

Fine [feen] Brandy made from wine.

— *champagne* [+ shA-pah-nyuh] Brandy coming from the Grande and Petite Champagne regions, including Cognac, Segonzac, and Jarnac.

Fine fleur de froment [+ fluhr duh froh-mE] A high-quality wheat flour.

Fines herbes [+ erb] A chopped herb mixture of chives, chervil, tarragon, and parsley. It is used to flavor a variety of preparations.

—, sauce aux (1) (*For fish*) Fines herbes reduced with white wine, strained, and finished with whole butter. (2) (*For beef*) Fines herbes reduced with white wine, added to demi-glace sauce, and strained.

Fine, huile d'olive [weel do-leev +] "Fine olive oil"; refers to oil rendered from the second pressing.

Finir [fee-neer] Finish; to put the final touches on a dish, sauce, soup, and so on.

Finnoise, à la [ah-lah feen-nwahz] Dishes prepared "Finnish style"; a garnish made of stuffed tomatoes, red peppers, and white wine sauce.

Finnoise, sauce Chicken *velouté* garnished with bell peppers and flavored with paprika, chervil, and parsley.

Fitou [fi-too] (*Languedoc*) A red AOC wine made from the Grenache and Carignan grapes.

Fixin [fick-sin] A red AOC wine from Burgundy.

Flageolet [flah-zhuh-leh] A tender, pale green or white kidney bean from France.

Flagnarde [flah-nyahrd] A local pastry from Clermont-Ferrand (Auvergne) resembling a large pancake with apples or prunes. Similar to *clafoutis* and *flamusse*.

Flamande, à la [flah-mahnd] "Flemish style"; denotes a garnish of cabbage, root vegetables, bacon, and sausage.

Flambé [flA-beh] Describes foods served or prepared with flaming alcohol.

Flamber [flA-beh] To prepare or serve dishes with flaming alcohol.

Flamery [flah-muh-ree] A rice or semolina pudding served chilled with puréed fruit.

Flamiche [flah-meesh] A savory tart from northern France made with various cheeses and/or vegetables. Also spelled *Flamique*.

— *à porions* [+ ah por-yO] A leek and squash tart from Picardy.

— *aux poireaux* [+ oh pwah-roh] A savory leek tart.

Flamique [flah-meek] See *Flamiche*.

Flammenküche [flah-men-koo-kuh] (*Alsace*) An open tart made with yeast dough and filled with onions and bacon.

Flamri [flam-ree] See *Flamery*.

Flamusse [flah-müs] (*Burgundy*) An apple custard tart; also, a type of cheese flan.

Flan [flA] An open tart filled with a variety of sweet or savory fillings—i.e., fruit, custard, vegetables, forcemeats, and so on.

Flanchet [flA-sheh] A piece of meat cut from the flank.

Flandre [flA-druh] Flanders; France's northernmost province bordering Belgium and the North Sea. See *Flamande, à la*.

Flangnarde [floh-nyahrd] See *Flagnarde*.

Flaquer [fla-keh] To remove the backbone of a fish.

Flaugnarde [floh-nyahrd] See *Flagnarde*.

Flaune [flohn] A pastry from Lodéve (Languedoc) made with ewe's-milk cheese, flour, and eggs; flavored with orange. Also called *flauzonnes* and *flônes*.

Flauzonnes [floh-zuhn-neh] See *Flaune*.

Flet [fleh] Flounder.

Flétan [fleh-tA] Halibut.

Fleurs de courgettes [fluhr duh koor-zhet] Zucchini flowers.

Fleur de Decauville [+ duh deh-koh-veel] A cheese from the Île-de-France.

Fleur de maïs [+ duh mah-ees] Cornstarch.

Fleuriste, à la [fluhr-reest] A garnish made from château potatoes and tomatoes stuffed with mixed vegetables; for various dishes.

Fleuron [flur-rO] Small crescent-shaped puff pastry used as a garnish.

Fleurs pralinées [+ prah-lee-neh] Candied flower petals made in Grasse, a city in Provence famous for its flowers.

Fleury, à la [fluhr-ree] Describes beef and lamb dishes garnished with potato croquettes stuffed with diced calves kidneys; served with demi-glace sauce flavored with tomato.

Floc [flohk] A strong aperitif made from Armagnac mixed with grape juice.

Flognarde [floh-nyahr] See *Flagnarde*.

Flône [flohn] See *Flaunes*.

Florentine, à la [floh-rE-teen] A term indicating spinach has been used in preparation of a dish.

Florian [floh-ryA] A garnish made up of braised lettuce, glazed pearl onions, baby carrots, and potato *fondants*.

Florida, moutarde de [moo-tahrd duh floh-ree-dah] A mild mustard flavored with wine; from champagne.

Flougnarde [floo-nyahrd] See *Flagnarde*.

Floutes [floot] (*Alsace*) Quenelles made from mashed potatoes and semolina. Also spelled *pflutters*.

Flûte [floht] A thin baguette.

Foie [fwah] Liver.

— *d'oie* [+ dwah] Liver from an ordinary goose.

— *gras* [+ grah] The expensive, highly prized livers of fattened geese or duck, obtained by force feeding the animals. The finest foie gras comes from Toulouse, Strasbourg, Périgord, and Landes.

- *cru* [+ krü] Raw foie gras.

Fol d'amour [fohl dah-moor] A soft cow's-milk cheese similar to Brie and Camembert.

Folle blanche [fuhl blAsh] One of the three principal varieties of grape—along with Colombard and St. Emilion—used in the production of cognac.

Foncer [fO-seh] To line the inside of a timbale or mold with plastic wrap, foil, bacon, pastry, or aspic.

Fond [fO] Stock; a liquid resulting from the prolonged simmering of animal's meat and bones with vegetables (*mirepoix*) and herbs (bouquet garni).

— *blanc* [+ blAk] "White stock"; made from chicken, pork, or veal bones that are not browned in the oven prior to simmering.

— *brun* [+ brU] "Brown stock"; made from bones, usually of beef, which are browned in the oven before simmering.

Fondant [fO-dA] An icing or candy made by heating sugar to the soft-ball stage (240°F) and then kneading it on a marble slab until pliable. The heated sugar can be formed into small balls and coated with chocolate for bon bons or heated and used to glaze cakes and petit fours.

Fondant A small croquette made from a *salpicon* of meat, poultry, or fish; served as an hors d'œuvre.

Fond de pâtisserie [+ duh pah-tees-ree] The base or foundation of a pastry—i.e., tart or flan shell, shortcrust, génoise, meringue shells, and so on.

Fondants, pommes de terre [pom duh ter +] Oval-shaped potatoes cooked in a lidded pan with butter until golden brown and tender.

Fond Lié [+ lyeh] See *Jus lié*.

Fondre [fO-dreh] To cook vegetables in a covered pan with a small amount of butter.

Fondu [fO-dü] Flawed cheeses (broken, misshapen) that are melted down and reformed into smaller cheeses; cream is often added for richness.

Fondu au marc de raisin [+ oh mahrk duh reh-zI] A processed French cheese with a crust formed from dried grape seeds. Also called *Fromage affiné dans le marc de raisin*.

Fondu creusois [+ kruh-zwah] (*Limousin*) A dish composed of melted cheese served with fried potatoes.

Fondue [fO-dü] Vegetables cooked to a pulp in a small amount of water and butter. It is seasoned and served as a garnish with poached fish, poultry, and eggs.

Fondue A famous Swiss dish of melted seasoned cheese in which bread cubes are dipped. There are several French versions, each named for the region from which it is made, i.e., *fondue savoyarde*, *fondue normande,* and so on.

— *à la française* [ah-lah FrA-sez +] "Fondue prepared the French way." It differs from the Swiss method in that the dish is finished with egg yolks.

— *bourguignonne* [+ boor-gee-nyohn] A dish comprised of cubed sautéed beef accompanied with various sauces.

— *nantuatienne* [+ nA-twah-tyen] A French fondue dish prepared with Bleu de Sassenage cheese.

Fontainebleau [fO-ten-bluh] A fresh, triple-cream cow's-milk cheese from Fontainebleau (Île-de-France); it is often sweetened and served with fresh fruit.

— Town in the Île-de-France noted for the Chasselas grape, one of the finest dessert grapes in France.

—, *garniture* Duchess potato nests filled with a macédoine of creamed vegetables. Accompanies lamb and beef dishes.

Forestière, à la [foh-res-tyer] This term denotes the presence of mushrooms in a dish.

Fouace [fwahs] A coarse, somewhat bland yeast pastry made in several parts of France with many variations, although it is typically flavored with orange and brandy; also known as *fouasse* and *fougasse.*

Fouasse [foo-wahs] See *Fouace.*

Fouée [foo-weh] A savory pastry from Burgundy made with bacon, walnut juice, and cream.

Fouet [fweh] A wire whisk.

Fougasse [fou-gah-seh] See *Fouace.*

Fougassette [foo-gah-set] A small brioche loaf flavored with orange and saffron; a specialty of Nice.

Fougeru [foo-guh-rü] A cow's-milk cheese similar to Coulommiers produced in Tournan-en-Brie.

The finished cheese is wrapped in fern leaves.

Four [foor] Oven.

—, *au* Baked in the oven.

Fourchette [foor-shet] Fork.

Fourme [foor-meh] The name for a variety of cheeses from the Limagne region of Auvergne, including Mézenc, Forez, and Ambert.

— *d'Ambert* [+ dam-ber] A famous blue-veined cheese made from cow's milk. Also known as *Fourme de pierre sur haute* and *Fourme de Montbrison.*

— *de Laguiole* [+ duh lah-gwee-yohl] See *Laguiole-Aubrac.*

— *du Cantal* [+ dü kA-tahl] See *Cantal.*

— *de Salers* [+ duh sah-leh] See *Cantal.*

Fourrer [foor-reh] To stuff or fill a food item (pastries, omelettes, breads).

Foyot, sauce [fwah-yo] Béarnaise sauce flavored with meat glaze.

Frais [freh] Fresh; cool.

Fraise [frez] Mesentery; a membrane from the abdomen of animals used in specialty dishes. See *Fricassin.*

Fraisage [freh-sazh] Kneading of dough.

Fraises [frez] Strawberries.

— *des bois* [+ deh bwah] Small, extremely sweet wild strawberries.

Fraisette des bois [fre-zet deh +] Describes fresh, pared fruit poached in syrup and served with wild strawberry purée.

Fraisier [fre-zyeh] A strawberry-kirsch-flavored génoise sponge cake.

Framboise [frA-bwahz] (1) Raspberry. (2) A raspberry brandy, the finest coming from Strasbourg (Alsace).

Française, à la [frA-sez] This broad term describes numerous dishes prepared French style.

Franche-Comté [frAsh-kO-teh] A mountainous province in western France; smoked hams, sausages, trout, Comté cheese, and Bresse chicken are among the specialties from the Franche-Comté; Jura produces some outstanding wines.

Frangipane [frA-gee-pahn] A rich pastry cream/custard containing crushed almonds or macaroons.

Frappé [frah-peh] Fruit, juice, or liqueur mixed with shaved ice.

Frascati, à la [frahs-kah-tee] A garnish for meat dishes composed of large mushroom caps stuffed with various fillings, such as asparagus tips, foie gras, and truffles.

Fréchure [freh-shür] See *Levadou*.

Frémir [freh-meer] To simmer; describes the bare simmering of water, which is the ideal temperature for poaching.

Frémissement [freh-mees-mE] Simmering.

Fressure [fres-sür] "Pluck"; the heart, liver, lungs, and spleen of an animal. See *Vendée, fressure*.

Friand [free-A] (1) Small puff pastry shells stuffed with various fillings and served hot as an hors d'œuvre. (2) A small almond-cream tartlet.

Friandise [free-A-deez] Any fancy petit four or confection. Also referred to as *friandise de confiseur* or *mignardise*.

Fribourg [free-boorgh] The name for Gruyère cheese in parts of France.

Fricadelles [free-kA-del] Small meatballs made from a combination of various meats.

Fricandeau [free-kA-doh] A larded, braised veal loin served with cooked greens. In Auvergne, *fricandeau* is a type of cold pork pâté.

Fricassée [free-kah-seh] A white stew. The meat (chicken, pork, or veal) is first browned in butter, cooked in stock, and finished with cream..

— *périgourdine* [+ peh-ree-goor-deen] Refers to vegetables that are browned in butter and used to flavor pot-au-feu, soups, ragoûts, and so on.

Fricassin [free-kah-sI] A dish comprised of sautéed goat *fraise* served in cream. A local dish from Bourbonnais.

Fricasson [free-kah-sO] Goat offal in cream. It is a specialty of Montlucon (Bourbonnais) similar to *fricassin*.

Frinot [free-noh] A French cheese produced in Orléans.

Frit [free] Fried.

Friteau [free-toh] Small pieces of battered and fried meat or vegetables.

Fritelle [free-tel] A sweet or savory fritter from Corsica. Savory fritelles are often made with Corsican sausage and cheese.

Frites [freet] French fries; fried potato sticks, also called *pommes de terre frites*.

Fritton [free-tO] See *Gratterons*.

Friton A dish consisting of sautéed pork and pork offal ground to a paste.

Fritot [free-toh] See *Friteau*.

Friture [free-tür] Deep-frying. *Friture* also refers to whole small fish or fish chunks breaded and deep-fried.

Frivolités [free-vol-ee-teh] A term used by Escoffier to describe small, elegant preparations such as barquettes and tartlets.

Froid [frwah] Cold.

Fromage [fro-mahzh] Cheese.

— *affiné dans le marc de raisin* [+ ah-fee-neh dA luh mahrk duh reh-zI] See *Fondu au marc de raisin.*

— *à la crème* [+ ah-lah krem] *Fromage blanc* to which cream and sugar are added.

— *à l'écarlate* [+ ah leh-kahr-laht] Crayfish butter.

— *blanc* [+ blA] "White cheese"; a bland, low-fat, fresh cheese made from cow's milk.

— *de cochon* [+ duh koh-shO] See *Fromage de tête.*

— *de tête* [+ duh tet] "Head-cheese"; a type of sausage made from the meat from the head of a pig or calf bound in its natural gelatin. Also called *fromage de cochon* and *pâté de tête.*

— *de Troyes* [+ duh trwah] See *Barberey.*

— *du pays* [+ dü peh-yee] Local cheeses.

— *fondu* [+ fO-dü] See *Gourmandises.*

— *fort* [+ fohr] Another name for *Cancoillotte* cheese.

— *frais* [+ freh] Fresh cheese.

— *glacé* [+ glahs] An obsolete term for flavored ices or ice cream frozen in a conical mold.

— *persillés* [+ per-see-yeh] The nickname for cheeses of the Roquefort type (blue-veined) used in parts of France. Although parsley (*persil*) is not present, the name is used to describe greenish streaks developed in the cheese.

— *râpé* [+ rah-peh] Grated or shredded cheese.

Fromager [froh-mah-zheh] (1) The word used for the adding of grated cheese to dishes, sauces, savory pastries, and so on. (2) Cheese maker or cheese strainer.

Fromagère [froh-mah-zhehr] A utensil used to serve grated cheese.

Fromagerie [froh-mah-zhuh-ree] A cheese/dairy shop.

Froment [froh-mE] Referring to wheat. See *Fine fleur de froment.*

Fromentée [froh-mE-teh] A type of sweet wheat porridge made with milk or cream.

Fromgey [frO-zhee] A fresh cheese from Lorraine.

Fruit [frwee] Fruit.

Fruiterie [frwee-tree] A storage room for fruit. Also spelled *fruitier.*

Fruitière [frwee-tyehr] Cheese factory.

Fruit givré [frwee zhee-vreh] A fruit-flavored ice or sherbet served in the scooped-out skin of the fruit from which it was made.

Fruits secs [frwee-sek] Dried fruits.

Fruits de mer [frwee de mer] Literally, "fruits of the sea," this term refers to seafood.

Fumage [fü-mahzh] Smoking; a method of preserving and flavoring foods (seafood, poultry, sausages) by exposing to smoke for a specific period of time.

Fumé [fü-meh] Smoked.

Fumée [foo-meh] A heavy slab of olive wood used in the preparation of *éclade.* The mussels are placed on the slab, covered with pine needles, and set alight.

Fumet [foo-meh] A highly concentrated, aromatic stock. The term commonly refers to extracts of fish, mushrooms, or truffles.

Fusil [fü-zeel] Sharpening steel.

Gaburatye [gah-boo-rah-tee] In Béarn *gaburatye* means a mixture of fresh vegetables.

Gâche [gahsh] A small yeast cake. In some parts of France (Normandy, Vendée) it is a type of brioche.

— *améliorée* [+ ah-meh-lyo-reh]

Gâche améliorée (cont.)
A traditional holiday brioche from Normandy. Also called *fallue* and *brioche coulante*.

Gade [gah-duh] The name for the red currant in Normandy.

Gadelle [gah-del] The name for the red currant in parts of western France.

Galabart [gahl-ah-bahr] A type of blood sausage made from pig offal; from southwestern France.

Galantine [gah-lA-teen] Boned rolled meat or poultry stuffed with forcemeat and tied; poached in stock and served cold.

Galette [gah-let] A broad term for a flat, round, sweet or savory ovencake or pancake; also the name for a shortbread cookie from Brittany.

— *de pommes de terre* [+ duh pom duh ter] A potato pancake.

— *des rois* [+ deh rwah] "Twelfth-Night cake"; a traditional cake served on Twelfth Night composed of puff pastry with a frangipane cream center. A coin or bean is placed in the cake bringing the recipient good luck.

— *de sarrasin* [+ duh sah-rah-sE] A buckwheat pancake.

Galettoire [gah-let-twahr] Griddle.

Galichons [gah-lee-shO] See *Calissons*.

Galicien [gah-lee-syE] A gâteau made with génoise sponge flavored with pistachios.

Galimafrée [gah-lee-mah-free] A once popular dish from the Île-de-France comprised of chicken hash with gravy.

Galopins [gahl-lo-pI] Fried sweetened bread strips; a local dish of Flanders.

Galutres [gah-lü-truh] Pork stuffed with mutton tripe and simmered in seasoned broth; a specialty of southwestern France. Also called *trescat*.

Gamay [gah-meh] The principal grape used in the production of Beaujolais, Pinot Noir, and red Burgundy wines.

Gambetta, à la [gahm-bet-tah] A discription for dishes garnished with stuffed eggplant and stewed tomatoes.

Ganache [gah-nahsh] A mixture of chocolate, heavy cream, butter, and flavoring (usually a liqueur). It can be used as a cake topping or filling, rolled into truffles, or heated and used as a sauce.

— *soufflé* [+ soof-fleh] *Ganache* beaten to double its volume. Used as a topping or filling for gâteaux, tortes, and pastries.

Ganses [gahns] A specialty cookie of Nice; it is deep-fried and sprinkled with powered sugar.

Gape [gahp] The word for *buttermilk* in parts of Auvergne.

Gaperon [gah-puh-rohn] A semi-hard cows'-milk or buttermilk cheese produced in Auvergne. Also spelled *gapron*.

Garbure [gahr-bür] A hearty meat and vegetable soup from Béarn. Potatoes and cabbage are always included as is some type of charcuterie. On special occasions *confit d'oie* is added. Traditionally, *garbure* is served over stale bread and is often topped with cheese and cooked au gratin.

Garde-manger [gahrd-mA-geh] The area of the kitchen or crew responsible for cold food items, including pâtés, savory mousses, aspics, *galantines*, and *ballottines*.

Gardon [gahr-dO] A freshwater fish related to the carp. Usually eaten fried.

Garniture [gahr-nee-tür] Garnish. A decorative accompaniment enhancing the taste and appearance of a dish.

Gascogne [gahs-koh-nyuh] Gascony. Food specialties of Gascony include cèpes, pâtés, charcuterie, *gasconnade*, matelote, *garbure*, and goose and duck products; the famous brandy Armagnac is produced in Gascony.

Gasconnade [gahs-koh-nahd] A specialty of Gascony featuring duck roasted with garlic and anchovies.

Gasconne, sauce [gahs-kohn] Veal *velouté* with the addition of white wine and herbs and finished with anchovy butter.

Gaspo [gahs-poh] The word for *buttermilk* in parts of Auvergne.

Gastrique [gahs-treek] Caramelized sugar that has been dissolved in vinegar. It is used to intensify sauces containing fruit, i.e., *sauce bigarade*.

Gastronome [gahs-tro-nohm] An expert of good food and fine dining.

—, **à la** A term for poultry dishes garnished with glazed chestnuts, truffles, sautéed morels, and cockscomb and kidneys. The dish is served with demi-glace sauce flavored with truffles.

—, **sauce** Demi-glace sauce to which a reduction of Madeira, champagne, and shallots has been added; seasoned with cayenne pepper.

Gastronomie [gahs-tro-no-mee] The art and science of food and fine dining.

Gâteau [gah-toh] The French word for *cake*.

Gâtis [gah-tee] Brioche baked with Roquefort and/or Cantal cheeses; a specialty of the Rouergue.

Gaudebrillaux [goh-duh-bree-yoh] A dish based on oxen tripe.

Gaudes [gohd] A cornmeal porridge similar to polenta.

Gaufres [goh-fruh] Waffles.

Gaufrettes, Pommes [pom goh-fret] Thin potato slices cut on a mandoline in a criss-cross pattern.

Gaufreuse [goh-fruhz] Pastry wheel; used to pinch the ends of pies, tarts, and so on.

Gaufrier [goh-free-yeh] Waffle iron.

Gauloise, à la [goh-lwahz] Denotes cockscombs and kidneys are present in a dish.

Gautier, à la [goh-tyeh] Describes fish dishes garnished with fish quenelles, mushrooms, and oysters.

Gayette [gah-yet] (*Provence*) A pork liver sausage usually served cold as an hors d'œurve.

Gélatine [zheh-lah-teen] Gelatin; a glutinous substance derived from animal bones and tissue. It is used to set or partially solidify liquid or thin preparations—i.e., jellies, mousses, pâtés, and so on. Sold in powdered form or in clear sheets.

Gelée [zheh-leh] Jelly; aspic.

Gélinotte [zheh-lee-noht] Hazel hen; a game bird native to Europe. Also called hazel grouse.

Gendarme [zhA-dahrm] Smoked, pickled herring. Also the name of a hard smoked sausage.

Général, sauce [zheh-neh-rahl] Demi-glace sauce reduced with tarragon vinegar, garlic, and orange peel. Finished with a dash of sherry.

Genevoise, à la [zheh-nuh-vwahz] Fish served with *sauce genevoise*.

Genevoise, sauce A sauce made up of fish fumet and red wine added to *sauce espagnole*; garnished with mushrooms and finished with anchovy butter.

Genièvre [zheh-nyev-ruh] Juniper berries.

Génoise [zheh-nwahz] A light, buttery sponge cake used as the base for a variety of gâteaux.

—, **sauce** (1) A combination of *sauce espagnole*, fish stock, and red wine; flavored with truffles and mushrooms and finished with anchovy butter. Similar to *sauce genevoise*. (2) A cold sauce combining Mayonnaise sauce with béchamel sauce and puréed pistachios and almonds; flavored with parsley and tarragon. Served with cold fish.

Gentiane [zhE-tyAn] A plant found in the French Alps used in the production of various aperitifs.

Georgienne, à la [zhyor-zhyen] Meat dishes accompanied with rice croquettes and tomato *concassée*.

Gérardmer [zheh-rahrd-mehr] See *Lorraine*.

Gerbaudes [zher-bohd] A traditional banquet in central France celebrating the end of the grape harvest.

Germon [zher-mO] Albacore; a member of the tuna family; also called *thon blanc* in France.

Géromé [zheh-rohm] A soft, strong-smelling cow's-milk cheese produced in Gérardmer (Lorraine); one of the oldest French cheeses.

Gervais [zher-veh] A double-cream, cow's-milk cheese. It is often sweetened and eaten with fruit as a dessert.

Gésier [zheh-zee-yeh] Gizzard; the muscular, digestive pouch of a bird's stomach. Gizzards are usually fried, stewed in a ragoût, or used in a stuffing.

Gewurz [guh-vurts] The word for *spicy* in Alsatian dialect.

Gewurztraminer [guh-vürts-trahm-mee-nuhr] A famous white Alsatian wine made from the Traminer grape.

Gex [zheks] A blue-veined, cow's-milk cheese produced in Gex in the Jura. It is pure white save for the greenish-blue streaks. Also called *Bleu du Haut-Jura*.

Gibassié [zhee-bah-see] (*Provence*) An orange-anise-flavored brioche traditionally prepared for the holidays. Also referred to as *pompe (à l'huile)*.

Gibassier [zhee-bah-syeh] See *Gibassié*.

Gibelotte, en [zhee-buh-lot] A rabbit and mushroom stew.

Gibier [zhee-byeh] Game.

Gigorit [zhee-goh-ree] A local dish of Pitou and Angoumois composed of pigs head and/or offal stewed in red wine and blood. Also known as *tantouillet* and *tantouillée*.

Gigot [zhee-goh] Leg of lamb or stew.

Gigue [zheeg] See *Cuissot*.

Gilbert, Philéas [feel-yahs zheel-behr] (1857–1942) French chef and author of several cookbooks and magazine articles. Worked with Escoffier on the classic *Guide culinaire*.

Gimblette [zhI-blet] "Ring biscuit"; a ring-shaped cookie flavored with almond and orange. *Gimblettes* are made throughout France; the most famous are those from Albi.

Gingembre [zhI-zhahm-bruh] Ginger. See *Pain d'epice*.

Girardi [ghee-rahr-dee] (*For fish*) A garnish of oysters, mushroom caps, and shrimp; with *sauce aux fines herbes*.

Girelle [ghee-rel] See *Donzelle*.

Girolle [ghee-rol] A French word for *chanterelle*. See *Chanterelle*.

Girondin, sauce [zhee-rO-dI] Hollandaise sauce seasoned with Dijon mustard.

Gite [zheet] The word for *pholade* in Arcachon (Bordeaux). See *Pholade.*

— *à la noix* [+ ah-lah nwah] A round of beef cut from the upper part of the leg.

— *-gîte* [zheet-zheet] A cut of meat from the shin of oxen.

Glaçage [glah-sahzh] Glazing; see *Glace.*

Glace [glahs] Ice/ice cream.

— *au four* [+ oh foor] Baked Alaska; a dessert consisting of molded ice cream covered with sponge cake and iced with meringue. The preparation is frozen and then baked in a hot oven to quickly brown. Also called *omelette norvégienne.*

— *de sucre* [+ duh soo-kruh] Icing.

— *de viande* [+ duh vyAd] "Meat glaze"; a highly reduced meat stock.

Glacé [glah-seh] Glazed; describes substances such as reduced meat stock, aspic, icing, and sugar that are used to coat foods. Also refers to foods that have been browned under the broiler.

Glacière [glah-syehr] (1) Refrigerator or freezer. (2) A sugar shaker.

Glux [glüks] A type of cheese produced in Nivernais.

Gobie [goh-bee] A small saltwater fish common in Europe; usually served fried; also called *goujon de mer.*

Godard [goh-dahr] A garnish for meat and poultry consisting of truffled chicken quenelles, cockscomb and kidneys, mushroom caps, and lamb sweetbreads; with *sauce Godard.*

—, *sauce* Demi-glace sauce fortified

with white wine and flavored with mushroom essence.

Godiveau [goh-dee-voh] Forcemeat used to make quenelles. Although the name refers to veal (*veau*), *godiveau* can be made from fish (usually pike) and poultry as well.

Goère [gwer] See *Goyère.*

Gogues [gohg] A dish from Anjou featuring sliced blood sausages fried in fat.

Goguette [goh-get] A highly seasoned pork sausage.

Gombaut [gO-boh] Okra.

Gombo [gO-boh] Okra.

Gondole [gO-dohl] A decoratively folded napkin used to adorn a table setting.

Gorenflot [gor-A-floh] Describes dishes garnished with a chiffonnade of red cabbage, sausage slices, and potatoes *fondants.*

—, *gâteau* [gah-toh +] A hexagon-shaped baba cake.

Goret [goh-reh] The French word for a piglet over six months old.

Goudale [goo-dahl] The remaining broth from a *garbure* after consumption; see *Faire chabrot.*

Gouère [goo-ehr] See *Gouerre.*

Gouéron [goh-eh-rohn] See *Tarte bourbonnaise.*

Gouerre [goo-ehr] A simple cake with several variations made throughout central France. Also spelled *gouéron* and *gouère.*

— *au cirage* [+ oh see-rahzh] (*Nivernais*) A variation of *gouerre* made with prunes.

Gouffé, garniture [goo-feh] (*For meat dishes*) (1) Duchess potato baskets filled with creamed morels and asparagus tips; with demi-glace sauce. (2) Risotto, truffles, veal quenelles, and mushrooms; with demi-glace sauce.

Gougelhopf [goo-guhl-hopf] See *Kugelhupf* or *Gougelhof.*

Gougère [goo-zhehr] An unsweet-ened *chou* pastry made with cheese; a specialty of Burgundy.

Gougnettes [goo-nyet] A type of yeast doughnut.

Goujon [goo-zhO] Gudgeon; a freshwater fish common in France related to the carp. Also known as *goujonnière* and *perche goujonnière*.

— *de mer* [+ duh mer] See *Gobie*.

—, *en* Describes whitefish, particu-larly sole, cut into thin strips, breaded, and deep-fried. Served with *sauce rémoulade* or (cold) *ravigote*. Also known as *goujon-nettes*.

Goujonnette [goo-zhoh-net] See *Goujon, en.*

Gounerre [goo-nehr] A type of po-tato pâté from Bourbonnais prov-ince.

Gourmand [goor-mAd] One who enjoys good food.

Gourmandise [goor-mA-deez] A processed cheese produced from cow's milk flavored with kirsch and walnuts.

Gourmandises [goor-mA-deez] Small fancy tidbits such as hors d'œuvres, petits fours, and so on.

Gourmet [goor-meh] A person with a refined palate; a connoisseur of good food and wine. Considered a step above a gourmand.

—, *sauce* Sauce espagnole combined with red wine and fish fumet, garnished with lobster tails, and finished with lobster butter.

Gournay [goor-neh] (*Normandy*) A fresh cream cheese made from cow's milk; similar to Camembert.

Gouster [goo-steh] A type of cow's-milk cheese resembling a cross between Gouda and Munster.

Goyère [go-yer] A cow's-milk cheese produced in Denain. Also spelled *goère*.

— (*Flanders*) A cheese flan made with Maroilles cheese.

Grain de café [grI duh kah-feh] Coffee bean.

Grain de poivre [+ duh pwah-vruh] Peppercorn.

Graisse [gres] Fat.

— *de cherbourg* [+ duh sher-boorg] See *Graisse normande*.

— *normande* [+ nor-mAd] A re-fined cooking fat used in Nor-mandy composed of pork and beef (*kidney*) fat flavored with herbs and vegetables. Sometimes calles *graisse de Cherbourg.*

Graisser [gre-seh] To grease; to coat a pan with fat, i.e., butter, grease, oil, and so on.

Gramolate [grah-mo-laht] A sorbet served between meal courses to cleanse the palate.

Grand [grA] Large.

— *cru* [+ krü] "Great growths." See *Cru.*

— *-duc, garniture* Dishes prepared with asparagus tips and truffles.

— *marnier* [+ mahr-nyer] A very fine orange-flavored liqueur. There are two types: Cordon Rouge (*cognac based*) is aged for at least 18 months and deep orange in color; and Cordon Jaune is pale and less potent.

— *veneur* [+ vuh-nuhr] Described game dishes served with *sauce grand veneur* and chestnut purée.

—, *sauce* Sauce poivrade combined with game essence and flavored with red currant jelly; thick-ened with cream.

Grande-Bretagne [+ bruh-tah-nyuh] Great Britain.

Grand-mère, à la [+ ah-lah mehr] Describes dishes garnished with fried pearl onions, sautéed mush-rooms, and potatoes *fondants*.

Grappe, la [lah grahp] A processed cheese made in France; grape skins and seeds form the rind.

Grapiau [grah-pyoh] See *Crapiau.*

Gras (au) [oh gra] With meat.

Gras double [+ doo-bluh] Tripe.

— *à la lyonnaise* [+ ah-lah lyuhn-nez] A specialty dish from Lyons featuring tripe sautéed with onions and parsley.

Grasse [grahs] A perfume-producing town in Provence; also known for its candied flowers.

Gratin [grah-tI] (1) The collective name for savory dishes—typically cooked in a type of casserole—that have been baked or broiled until a golden crust forms on the surface. (2) The golden brown crust formed on foods when baked or broiled.

—, *au* Describes dishes cooked (usually in a casserole dish) to a golden brown color.

— *dauphinois* [+ doh-fee-nwah] Potatoes simmered in cream, sprinkled with cheese, and baked au gratin.

— *de queues d'écrevisses* [+ duh kü deh-kruh-vees] A famous dish featuring crayfish tails cooked in tomato-cream sauce and topped with Gruyère cheese; browned under the broiler.

— *languedocien* [+ lA-guh-doh-syen] A specialty of Languedoc/Dauphiné composed of tomatoes and eggplant topped with bread crumbs and browned in the oven.

—, *sauce* White wine, duxelles, and fish fumet added to demiglace sauce.

— *savoyard* [+ sah-voh-yahrd] (*Savoy*) Alternating layers of sliced potatoes and Beaufort cheese baked au gratin.

Gratte-Cul [graht-kül] Rose hip; the "fruit" of the rose used to flavor liqueurs, jams, and so on.

Gratinée [grah-tee-neh] Baked onion soup. The soup is poured into a crock, topped with dried bread slices and Gruyère cheese, and baked au gratin.

Gratterons [graht-trohn] The small pieces of meat leftover from rendering pork or goose fat. The meat is seasoned, pressed, and eaten hot or cold. A specialty of southwestern France. Also known as *grattons* and *fritons.*

Grattons [grah-tO] See *Gratterons.*

Gratte paille [graht-pah-yuh] A triple-cream cheese from France similar to Brillat-Savarin.

Gravenche [gra-vEsh] A scarce, freshwater fish related to the salmon.

Graves [grahv] A wine-growing district of Bordeaux—named for its gravelly soil—producing both red and white AOC wines.

Grèce [gres] Greece.

Grecque, à la [grek] "Greek style"; dishes prepared with olive oil, lemon, wine, and herbs (coriander, fennel, oregano). Also describes certain entrées accompanied with rice pilaf.

Gremille [gre-mee-yuh] A European river fish related to the *goujon.*

Grenade [gre-nahd] Pomegranate; a fruit native to Persia used in the production of grenadine syrup.

Grenadin [gre-nah-dI] Small strips of veal or poultry that are larded and braised.

Grenadine [gre-nah-deen] (1) Usually a nonalcoholic syrup made from pomegranates used to flavor cocktails. (2) The pulp extract of pomegranate. (3) A beverage made from water and grenadine syrup.

Grenailles [gre-nah-yuh] A variety of small new potatoes.

Grenobloise, à la [gre-noh-blawz] Describes fish lightly floured and panfried in butter; garnished with capers and lemon.

Grenouille [gruh-noo-yuh] Frog.

—, cuisses de [kwees duh +] Frogs' legs; also called *nymphes.*

Grésale [greh-zahl] An earthenware container used to marinate goose meat in preparation of *confit d'oie.*

Gribiche [gree-beesh] A cold sauce prepared by combining oil, mustard, vinegar, and hard-boiled egg yolks. The mayonnaise is seasoned with capers, fines herbes, and hard-boiled egg whites; served with cold meat and fish.

Griffe [greef] A cut of beef from the shoulder area.

Grignon/Quignon [gree-nyO/kee-nyO] An end crust or dry piece of bread.

Gril [greel] Grill; broiler.

Grille-pain [gree-yuh pA] Toaster.

Grillade [gree-yahd] Grilled meats or vegetables; grilling.

Grillardin [gree-yahr-dI] Chef in charge of grilling/broiling.

Grillé [gree-yeh] Grilled; broiled.

— au fenouil [+ oh feh-nool] A method of grilling fish over smoking fennel.

Griller [gree-yeh] To grill.

Grillettes [gree-yet] An obsolete term for thinly sliced pork fried in butter.

Grimod de La Reynière [gree-moh duh lah reh-nyer] (1758–1837) A famous French gastronome and cookbook author.

Gris de Lille [gree-duh-leel] See *Vieux Lille; Puant macéré.*

Grive [greev] Thrush; a small game bird related to the blackbird. Prepared like quail.

Grondin [grO-dI] Gurnard/sea robin; a spiny, armor-scaled Mediterranean fish of which there are several species. Best eaten baked or braised.

Gros-blanquet [grohs blA-keh] A variety of sweet pear.

Groseille (à maquereau) [groh-syel (ah mah-kroh)] Gooseberry.

Grous/Groux [groo/groo] A thick porridge made from buckwheat flour; a specialty of Brittany.

Gruau d'avoine [groo-oh dah-vwahn] Oatmeal.

Grumeau [groo-moh] The lumps found in gravies, batters, sauces, and so on.

Gruyère de Beaufort [grü-yer duh boh-for] See *Beaufort.*

Gruyère de Comté [+ duh kO-teh] See *Comté.*

Guerbigny [gwehr-bee-nyee] (*Picardy*) A heart-shaped cheese made from cow's milk; similar to Rollot.

Guéret [gweh-reh] A cheese produced in Guéret en Marche. Sometimes called *creusois.*

Guéridon [gweh-ree-dO] A wheeled cart used in the dining room to serve food.

Guglhupf/Gugelhopf [goo-guhl-hüph/gü-gel-hohf] See *Kugelhof.*

Guigne [gee-nyuh] A variety of cherry used mainly in the production of *guignolet.*

Guignolet [gee-nyoh-leh] A liqueur made from the *guignes* cherry; a specialty of Angers.

Guignon [gee-nyO] See *Grignon.*

Guillaret [gee-yah-reh] A plain coarse pastry from Anjou.

Guillauneu [gee-yoh-nuh] A type of cake traditionally baked on Christmas Eve; from Touraine.

Guinguette [gwI-gwet] A popular gathering place for people to eat and drink and be entertained with music and dance.

Habillage [ah-bee-yahzh] Dressing; preparing fish and birds for consumption: plucking, scaling, gutting, and cleaning.

Hachage [ah-shazh] Chopping.

Hache [ahsh] Chopped; minced.

Hachée, sauce [ah-sheh] Demi-glace sauce combined with tomato purée, gherkins, capers, and duxelles; and added to a reduction of onions, shallots, and vinegar.

Hachis de bœuf [ah-shee duh buhf] Beef hash.

Hachua [ah-shwah] (*Béarn/Basque*) Beef braised in wine with Bayonne ham, vegetables, and seasonings.

Halévy [ah-leh-vee] A descriptive name for certain dishes featuring two sauces; typically refers to fish and egg preparations.

Halicot [ah-lee-koh] A mutton and vegetable stew from the Île-de-France. It is also called *haricot de mouton*, although there are no beans present in the dish.

Hareng [a-rA] Herring.

— *fumé* [+ foo-meh] Smoked herring.

— *salés* [+ sah-leh] Salt herring.

— *saur* [+ sor] Smoked salt herring.

Harenguet [ah-rE-geh] A name for the sardine in parts of northwestern France.

Haricot [ah-ree-koh] Bean.

— *aiguille* [+ eg-gwee-yuh] Young, tender, dwarf French bean; also known as *haricot filet*.

— *blanc* [+ blA] White navy beans.

— *de mouton* [+ duh moo-tO] See *Halicot*.

— *de Soissons* [+ duh swah-sO] Small white beans.

— *filet* [+ fee-leh] See *Haricot aiguilles*.

— *large* [+ lahrzh] A French word for *broad bean*.

— *rouge* [+ roozh] Red kidney bean.

— *vert* [+ vehr] Green bean; French bean.

Harle [ahrl] A variety of wild duck once popular in France.

Hâtereau [at-roh] An obsolete name for little balls of roasted pork liver.

Hauser, à la [oh-zeh] A descriptive phrase for meat and poultry dishes garnished with deep-fried onions, noisette potatoes, and *sauce Colbert*.

Haut-Brion [oh-bree-O] A highly regarded red wine from Bordeaux.

Haute cuisine [oht kwee-zeen] Term used to define the finest food available and expertly prepared.

Haut-Médoc [oh-meh-dok] (*Bordeaux*) The home of some of the finest vineyards in the world, producing red AOC wines.

Havanaise, à la [ah-vah-nez] "Havana style"; term for fish dishes prepared with tomatoes, bell peppers, mushrooms, and onions.

Havir [ah-veer] Describes meats grilled over high heat in order to sear the outside while keeping the middle rare.

Havraise, sauce [ah-vrez] Mussel and shrimp fumet reduced with white wine and finished with butter and egg yolks. Served with fish dishes.

Helder [hel-duhr] Denotes tomatoes or tomato sauce is used in preparation of the dish. Dishes prepared in this fashion are often accompanied with potatoes *parisienne*.

Hénons [eh-nO] The local name for cockles in Picardy. Found in the Bay of Somme, they are of excellent quality.

VOCABULARY

Henry IV, garniture [E-ree] (*For grilled meats and offal*) Artichoke bottoms stuffed with potatoes *parisienne*; watercress, and béarnaise sauce.

Henry IV, sauce Béarnaise sauce combined with *glace de viande*.

Herbe, herbes Herb, herbs.

— *de provence* [+ duh pro-vEs] An herb mixture consisting of thyme, rosemary, bay, basil, and savory.

— *royale* [+ roh-yahl] Literally "royal herb," this is the nickname for basil in France.

— *à soupe* [erb ah soop] A combination of leafy greens (spinach, sorrel, chard, orache, lettuce) served as a salad or used to flavor soups and stews.

— *à tortue* [+ tor-tü] "Turtle herbs"; a combination of basil, sage, thyme, coriander seeds, peppercorns, bay leaves, rosemary, and marjoram; used in preparation of *sauce tortue* and *tête de veau en tortue*. See *Tortue, en*.

— *vénitiennes* [+ veh-nee-syen] Tarragon, parsley, chervil, and sorrel chopped and combined with softened butter.

Hérisson de mer [eh-ree-sohn duh mer] A French nickname for sea urchin. See *Oursin*.

Historier [ees-toh-ryeh] To garnish or decorate a dish with small food items such as tomato or orange crowns, fluted mushrooms, truffle rounds, and so forth.

Hochepot [osh-poh] A rich Flemish soup consisting of pig's ears and tails, mutton, salt pork, cabbage, and root vegetables.

Hollandaise, à la [ohl-lA-dez] The name given to certain dishes served with hollandaise sauce.

Hollandaise, sauce An emulsion sauce composed of hot butter incorporated into beaten egg yolks

and lightly seasoned with lemon and tabasco.

Homard [oh-mahr] Lobster.

— *à l'américaine* [+ ah-meh-ree-ken] Lobster chunks sautéed with onions, shallots, and tomatoes; flavored with cognac and white wine and enriched with butter.

— *à l'anglaise, sauce de* [+ ah-lA-glez] Béchamel sauce flavored with anchovy essence and garnished with diced lobster.

—, *sauce* Sauce au vin blanc seasoned with cayenne, finished with lobster butter, and garnished with diced lobster.

Hongroise, à la [O-grwahz] "Hungarian style"; denotes paprika has been used in the preparation of a dish.

Hongroise, sauce Sauce velouté combined with a white wine reduction and seasoned with paprika.

Hors-d'œuvre [ohr duh-vruh] The first course of a meal or finger food served with cocktails.

Hôtelière, à la [o-tel-yer] A descriptive term for grilled meats served with *beurre hôtelière*. See *Beurre hôtelière*.

Huguenote [üg-not] A type of eartherware pot with short legs.

Huile [weel] Oil.

— *blanche* [+ blAsh] Literally "white oil"; refers to poppy seed oil in northern France.

— *de noix* [+ duh nwah] "Walnut oil"; produced in various parts of France, particularly in Périgord and Anjou.

— *vierge* [+ vyeh-gruh] "Virgin oil"; refers to olive oil.

Huilier [weel-yeh] Cruet; a small stand holding vessels of oil and vinegar, salt and pepper, or other condiments. Also called *ménagère*.

Huîtres [wee-truh] Oysters.

— *à l'anglaise, sauce aux* [+ ah-lA-glez] Oyster-flavored *velouté* enriched with cream.

—, *sauce aux* Oyster essence added to *sauce normande* or béchamel sauce.

Huppemeau [up-puh-moh] A cheese made in Huppemeau, Loive, and Cher regions with a slight resemblence to Brie.

Hure [ür] A type of headcheese (*pig*); the head of certain fish.

Hussarde, à la [ü-sahrd] Describes dishes prepared with tomatoes and horseradish.

Hussarde, garniture (*Large roasts*) Eggplant stuffed with mushrooms; stuffed tomatoes, duchesse potatoes, and grated horseradish.

Hussarde, sauce Demi-glace sauce combined with a white wine reduction, tomato purée, ham, and horseradish. Served with roasted meats.

Hydne [eed-nuh] A type of wild mushroom; used like chanterelles.

Hysope [ee-sop] Hyssop; an aromatic herb used mainly in the distillation of liqueurs such as Bénédictine and Chartreuse.

Igname [ee-nyahm] Yam.

Île-de-France [eel-duh-frAs] A province in north-central France blessed with an abundance of food resources. The finest produce of France is grown here, as well as superb cheeses (Brie, Coulommiers), charcuterie, meat and poultry, and game; several of the classic French sauces have originated in the Île-de-France area (béarnaise, Choron, Bercy, Ravigote).

Île flottante [eel-flot-tAt] "Floating island"; a classic dessert consisting of meringue puffs (islands) floating in custard cream and topped with caramel sauce.

Imbrucciata [I-broo-shyah-tah] The collective name for Corsican pastries made with Broccio cheese.

Impératrice, à l' [ah-lI-per-ah-trees] (1) A descriptive name applied to several dishes prepared with rich and/or expensive ingredients. (2) Various desserts based on vanilla custard with candied fruit and kirsch; refers in particular to a molded rice dessert.

Impériale, à l' [ah-lI-per-yahl] Describes dishes prepared with imperial ingredients such as foie gras, truffles, caviar, cockscombs and kidneys, and so forth.

Inarbittate [I-ahr-bi-taht] A savory Corsican pastry made with pork and swiss chard and/or spinach. See *Bastella*.

Incheville [Ich-uh-veel] A fresh cow's-milk cheese made in Normandy.

Incivulate [I-see-vü-laht] *Bastella* made with pork and onions. See *Bastella*.

Indépendance, à l' [ah-lI-deh-pE-dAs] Identifies various dishes garnished with artichoke bottoms stuffed with a *salpicon* of chicken and green peas; tomato *concassées*.

Indienne, garniture [I-dyen] (*For meat and fish*) Curried rice and *sauce indienne*.

Indienne, sauce (1) *Sauce allemande* seasoned with curry. (2) A cold mayonnaise based sauce with apples and seasoned with curry powder. (3) *Sauce velouté* to which apples, curry powder, and coconut milk has been added.

Infante, à l' [ah-lI-fAt] Describes poached fish served on a bed of duxelles and coated with *sauce Mornay* and grated Gruyère; baked au gratin.

Infuser [I-fü-zeh] To steep an ingredient (typically herbs) in a liquid to extract the flavor.

Insigny [I-see-nyee] A town in Normandy producing some of the finest butter in France.

Insigny, sauce Hollandaise sauce enriched with cream.

Inzuchatte [een-tsoo-shat-tuh] A Corsican pastry filled with pork and pumpkin or squash. See *Bastella*.

Iraty [ee-rah-tee] A cow's- or sheep's-milk cheese from Iraty, a town in the Pyrenees (Basque). Also known as *Ossau-Iraty* and *Oloron*.

Irouléguy [eer-oo-leh-gee] Red, white, and rosé AOC wines from the Basque region.

Isard [ee-zahr] A type of wild goat (chamios) found in the Pyrénées. The meat of the *isard* is tender and highly flavorful.

Ismail Bayaldi, garniture [ees-mah-eel bah-yahl-dee] (*For grilled meats*) Fried eggplant, stewed tomatoes, and pilaf. Often served with *sauce portugaise*.

Isoline, velouté [ee-zoh-leen] Chicken *velouté* garnished with sago and enriched with crayfish butter; served as a soup.

Issues [ee-sü] The inedible parts of a animal, i.e., hair, feathers, hoofs, and so forth.

Italie [ee-tah-lee] Italy. France's neighbor to the east; the cuisines of Provence, Savoy, and particularly Corsica are influenced by Italian cookery.

Italienne, à l' [ah-lee-tahl-yen] (1) Refers to various dishes made of meat, poultry, fish, and vegetables served with mushrooms. (2) Served with pasta croquettes and artichoke bottoms. (3) Served with duxelles and *sauce italienne*.

Italienne, sauce (*For meat dishes*) Demi-glace sauce flavored with tomato purée and garnished with duxelles and ham. (*For fish*) Omit the ham and add fish fumet.

Ivoire [ee-vwahr] A descriptive name for dishes white in color; refers particularly to chicken.

—, *sauce* Glace de viande added to suprême sauce.

Izzarra [ee-zah-rah] A local Basque liqueur made from wild flowers.

Jacques, à la [zhahk] Describes poultry or game birds stuffed with a forcemeat of chicken livers, mushrooms, and bread crumbs.

Jailles [zhah-yuhl] A spicy pork stew from the French Alps seasoned with apples and vinegar.

Jalousie [zhah-loo-zee] A marzipan or fruit tart resembling window blinds, hence the name.

Jambe de bois [zhAb-duh-bwah] A term now rarely used referring to beef shank that is used specifically for soups or pot-au-feu.

Jambon [zhA-bO] Fresh ham.

— *à l'alsacienne* [+ ah-lahl-sah-syen] (*Alsace*) Ham with Strasbourg sausage, sauerkraut, and boiled potatoes.

— *à la bayonnaise* [+ bah-yohn-nez] A specialty of the Bayonne region made up of braised ham served with pilaf garnished with *chipolata* sausage, tomatoes, and mushrooms.

— *de bayonne* [+ duh bah-yohn] Bayonne ham; the most famous product of the French Basque region; considered the finest of French hams. See *Bayonne*.

— *de gibier* [+ duh zhee-byeh] Leg of various game cured and smoked like ham. A specialty of Richelieu (Touraine).

— *de volaille* [+ duh vo-lah-yuh] A dish resembling pork leg (hence the name) consisting of stuffed, boned chicken legs served cold; from Richelieu (Touraine).

Jambonneau [zhA-bon-noh] Fore-leg ham; the lower portion of a pork leg. *Jambonneau* is also used for a stuffed chicken leg. See *Jambon de volaille.*

Jambonnette [zhA-bon-net] A sausage-like dish made from chopped seasoned pork and bacon.

Jambonnière [zhA-bon-nyer] A special pot used to cook whole ham.

Janot [zhah-noh] A type of candy from Albi.

Japonaise, à la [zha-pon-ez] Denotes a dish is garnished or prepared with Chinese artichokes.

Jardinière [zhahr-dee-nyer] A term indicating mixed vegetables are served with an entrée.

Jarret [zhah-reh] Knuckle; the lower portion of the rear leg of an animal. Typically refers to pork or veal.

Jau [zhoh] A type of *civet* made with young chickens; a specialty of the Burgundy and Nivernaise regions.

Jaune d'œuf [zhohn duhf] A French word for egg yolk.

Jaune longue de hollande [+ long duh ohl-lA] The French name for the Dutch yellow long potato.

Jessica, garniture [zhes-ee-kuh] Artichoke bottoms stuffed with marrow, sautéed morels, anna potatoes, and *sauce allemande*; for poultry or veal.

Jésuite [zheh-zweet] A baked delicacy composed of puff pastry filled with marzipan and glazed with royal icing.

Jésus [zheh-züs] A large pork sausage from Franche-Comté.

Jointoyer [zhwI-twah-yeh] A pastry term meaning to smooth out (icings, fillings, and so forth).

Joinville, garniture à la [zhwI-veel] (*For fish*) A garnish for fillets of sole comprised of shrimp, mushrooms, truffles, and *sauce normande* (which is finished with shrimp butter).

Joinville, sauce Sauce normande garnished with julienne truffles and finished with shrimp butter. Crayfish butter is sometimes substituted for the shrimp butter.

Jonchée [zho-sheh] A fresh cow's-, goat's-, or ewes'-milk cream cheese; sold in woven baskets.

Jubilé, cerises [suh-reez zhü-bee-leh] Cherries jubilee; a classic dessert featuring stoned cherries poached in syrup, set aflame with kirsch; served over vanilla ice cream.

Judic, garniture [zhü-eek] (*For various meats*) (1) Stuffed tomatoes, sautéed lettuce, and château potatoes. (2) Cockscombs and kidneys, sautéed lettuce, and sliced truffles. Both variations are served with Madeira flavored demi-glace.

Julienne [zhü-lyen] Food cut into thin strips; refers particularly to vegetables.

Jules verne, garniture [zhool-vehrn] (*Meat*) Sautéed turnips, potatoes, and mushrooms.

Jura [zhü-rah] A department and mountain chain in eastern France; famous for cheeses, charcuterie, and trout; *Jura* also produces some outstanding wines.

Jurançon [zhü-rA-sO] A popular sweet white wine from southwestern France (Pyrénées).

Jus [zhü] Juice; often refers to natural pan juices of roasted meats.

— *de singe* [+ duh sIzh] Literally "monkey juice"; a French culinary nickname for caramel coloring.

— *lié* [+ lee] Gravy; also *fond lié.*

Jussière, garniture [zhüs-syer] (*For various meats*) Stuffed braised onions, sautéed lettuce, and château potatoes.

Juter [zhü-teh] To drip juice/to be juicy.

Kaffee krantz [kah-feh krahnts] A coffee cake from Alsace.

Kaki [kah-kee] Persimmon; a reddish-orange fruit eaten fresh or used for a variety of sweet preparations.

Kälerei [kel-rahy] A pickled pork specialty from Alsace.

Kerstbroden [keerst-broh-duhn] A traditional Christmas yeast cake from Flanders.

Khedive [keh-deev] A garnish for various dishes consisting of asparagus tips, stewed tomatoes, mushrooms, and foie gras.

Kik à farz [keek-ah-fahrz] A buckwheat pudding from Brittany.

Kir [keer] An aperitif from Dijon made from a combination of Aligoté wine and cassis.

Kirsch [keersh] Cherry brandy; the finest comes from Germany and Alsace.

— **artificiel** [+ ahr-tee-fee-syel] Artificially flavored kirsch.

— **commerce** [+ ko-mers] Kirsch to which additional alcohol has been added.

— **fantaisie** [+ fA-teh-zee] Kirsch with additional flavoring.

— **pur** [+ pür] A pure cherry liqueur.

Klevner [klev-nuhr] The name sometimes used in Alsace for the Pinot Blanc grape.

Knepfles [knep-fluh] Another name for noque; see *Noque*.

Koeckbotteram [kü-kuh-bot-trahm] See *Kokeboterom*.

Kokeboterom [ko-kuh-bot-trom] A sweet brioche made with raisins; a specialty of Dunkirk (Flanders).

Also spelled *koeckbotteram*.

Koucke [kook] A sweetened brioche cake made with currants; a specialty of Flanders. Also called *couque* and *couke*.

Kouglof [koo-glof] See *Kugelhopf*.

Kouing-aman [kwI-gah-mahn] A sweet cake from Brittany made from butter and flour.

Kromesky [kro-mes-kee] See *Cromesqui*.

Kugelhof [kü-guhl-hof] (*Alsace*) A briochelike cake baked in a bundt mold with raisins, currants, and almonds; spelling may vary.

Kümmel [kü-muhl] A famous liqueur flavored with caraway.

Lady Curzon [lay-dee kü-zO] Descriptive name indicating that curry has been used in the preparation of a dish.

Laguiole-Aubrac [lah-gee-yohl oh-brahk] A Cantal-like cheese from Aubrac in the Rouergue region of southern France.

Laguipière, sauce [lah-gee-pyer] (1) (*For fish*) Sauce bâtarde with the addition of fish fumet, lemon juice, and truffles. (2) (*For various entrées*) Sauce bâtarde seasoned with chicken glaze and finished with whole butter.

Lait [leh] Milk.

— **de poule** [+ duh pool] Eggnog.

— **condensé** [+ kO-dE-seh] Condensed milk; whole, sweetened milk in which the water is evaporated by about 60 percent.

— **de coco** [+ duh koh-koh] Coconut milk.

— **desséché en poudre** [+ deh-se-sheh] Powdered milk.

— **écrémé** [+ eh-kreh-meh] Skim milk.

Laitance/Laite [+ leh-tAs/let] Soft roe or milt; the sperm of male fish.

Laitiat [le-tyah] A beverage made with whey and wild berries from

Franche-Comté.

Laiton [leh-tO] Refers to milk-fed lamb 70–150 days old. Also known as *agneau blanc.*

Laitue [leh-tü] Lettuce.

Lakmé [lahk-meh] A garnish for grilled meats made up of fave tartlet, mushroom caps, and tomato *concassée.*

La-mothe-Bougon [lah-mot-boo-gO] See *Mothais.*

La-mothe-Saint-Héraye [lah-mot-sA-teh-reh] See *Mothais,* also *Lamothe-Bougon.*

Lamproie [lA-prwah] Lamprey; an eel-like fish popular in France.

Landaise [lA-dez] A brioche-like cake from western France.

Landaise, à la Prepared in the style of the Landes region; indicates the use of items such as Bayonne ham, mushrooms, and duck and goose products (foie gras, confits, fat).

Landais, beurre [buhr +] Whole butter formed into rounds and rolled in bread crumbs. It forms a crust when melted under a broiler; served with fish.

Landes [lAd] A region in Gascony along the Atlantic coast. Landes is best known for its abundance of feathered game (pigeon, wild doves, woodcock, quail, ortolans), goose and duck confits, and foie gras; fish (pike, shad, and lampreys) and potato products.

Langouste [lahn-goost] Spiny lobster.

Langoustine [lahn-goo-steen] A crayfish-like marine crustacean.

Langres [lahn-gruh] A sharp, strong smelling cow's-milk cheese produced in Bassigny (Champagne).

Langue [lAg] Tongue.

Langue d'avocat [lAg-dah-voh-kah] The nickname for a variety of sole in Bordeaux.

Langue-de-chat [lAg-duh-shah] "Cat's tongue"; a delicate finger-shaped cookie used as a dessert garnish or as an accompaniment to sweet wines or champagne.

Langue-de-bœuf [lAg-duh-buhf] (1) Beef tongue. (2) Beefsteak mushroom; a type of wild mushroom.

Languedoc [lA-guh-dok] A province in southern France known for its robust peasant cooking. The region is quite rich with natural (culinary) resources and local dishes including: pot-au-feu, cassoulet, fish stews, *brandade,* garlic, poultry, lamb, asparagus, tomatoes, pastries, sparkling water, and wines.

Languedocienne, à la [lA-guh-doh-syen] Indicates that eggplants, cèpes, and tomatoes—referred to as the Languedoc trinity—are present in a dish.

Laon [lah-ohn] A town in Île-de-France famous for the exceptional asparagus and artichokes that are grown there.

Lapereau [lah-puh-roh] Young rabbit.

Lapin [lah-pI] Rabbit.

Lapin huppé [+ up-peh] A snack (*mâchon*) featuring thinly sliced *cervelas* sprinkled with vinaigrette.

Lapostole, sauce [lah-pos-tohl] A dessert sauce composed of sweetened apricot purée flavored with white wine, orange zest, and Grand Maniér.

Lard [lahr] A word sometimes used in France for bacon. Lard (pork fat) is called *saindoux* in French.

Lard fumé [lahr-fü-meh] Smoked bacon.

Lard maîgre [+ meg-ruh] See *Poitrine.*

Lard à piquer [+ ah pee-keh] Pork fat used to lard lean cuts of meat.

Larder [lahr-deh] The act of inserting pork fat into lean pieces of meat, usually with the aid of a larding needle (*lardoire*).

Lardoire [lahr-dwahr] Larding needle; an instrument used to insert fat into lean pieces of meat.

Lardons [lahr-dO] Strips of pork fat or bacon inserted into lean pieces of meat to add flavor and moisture.

Lardoons [lahr-doonz] See *Lardons*.

Larousse gastronomique [lah-roos gah-stro-no-meek] Culinary dictionary written by Prosper Montagné in 1938. It is perhaps the most famous and impressive culinary work of all times.

Larron [lah-rO] A version of Maroilles cheese.

Laumes, les [leh lohm] An aromatic cow's-milk cheese from the Côte d'Or in Burgundy. It is washed with Burgundy wine and has a slightly smoked flavor.

Lavallière, garniture [lah-vahl-yer] (*For grilled meats*) Artichokes stuffed with puréed asparagus, château potatoes, and *sauce bordelaise*.

La Varenne [lah vah-ren] (1618–1678) Great French chef credited with the first organized cookbook (*Le cuisinier francais*); considered by many to be the father of French cuisine.

—, garniture Indicates that mushrooms have been used in the preparation of a dish.

—, sauce Mayonnaise sauce with the addition of duxelles, parsley, and chervil.

Lavaret [lah-vah-ret] A freshwater fish related to the salmon found in the Lac du Bourget in Savoy.

Laver [lah-veh] Washing; cleaning impurities from foods.

Layon, Coteaux du [koh-toh dü lah-yO] White AOC wines from Anjou.

Lèche [le-cheh] Sliver; a thin slice.

Leclerc, sauce [luh-klerk] Demi-glace sauce with the addition of white wine, mushrooms, mustard, and red pepper.

Légumes [leh-güm] The French word for vegetables.

Légumier [leh-gü-myeh] A lidded dish used to serve vegetables.

Lentille [lE-tee-yuh] Lentil.

Lentilles vertes du puy [+ ver dü peh-yee] Small green lentils.

Léopold, garniture [leh-oh-pohld] Mushroom and shallot tartlets, sliced foie gras, and *sauce Madeira*; for grilled meats.

Lescher [les-shuhr] To cut meat into thin strips.

L'Étoile [leh-twahl] A white AOC wine from Jura.

Levadou [lev-ah-doo] (*Languedoc*) A stew featuring pork lungs; also called *fréchure*.

Levain [luh-vI] Leaven; sourdough to which flour and water have been added to create a new dough. The fermented dough causes the bread to rise prior to baking. *Levain* is also the name of the finished bread.

Levraut [luh-vroh] A hare between the ages of 2 and 4 months.

Levretaut [luh-vruh-too] A young hare less than 2 months old.

Levroux [luh-vroo] A goat's-milk cheese from Berry shaped like a flat-topped pyramid.

Levure [luh-vür] Yeast.

— chimique [+ shee-meek] Baking powder.

— de bière [+ duh byehr] Brewer's yeast.

Liaison [lee-ay-zO] A thickening/binding agent (beurre manié, roux, egg yolks, cornstarch, cream) for soups and sauces.

Liard [lee-yahr] Coin-shaped slice. (Refers particularly to potatoes.)

Lichette [lee-shet] A thin slice of food.

Lié [lyeh] A sauce that has been slightly thickened.

Liégeoise, à la [lee-ezh-waz] Named after the Belgian city of Liège, this term denotes the presence of juniper berries in a dish.

Lier [lyeh] To bind or thicken.

Lièvre [lye-vruh] Hare.

Lièvre farci en cabessal [+ fahr-see E kah-be-sol] (*Limousin*) A dish composed of hare stuffed with a spicy forcemeat of veal, pork, and garlic. Braised in red wine and served with the braising liquid thickened with the animal's blood and liver.

Ligurienne, à la [lee-gür-yen] (*For large roasts*) Stuffed tomatoes, risotto seasoned with saffron, and duchess potatoes.

Lilly, garniture [lee-lee] Artichoke bottoms stuffed with foie gras; truffles, and anna potatoes; for grilled beef and lamb.

Limandelle [lee-mA-del] See *Mère de sole*.

Limoner [lee-moh-neh] To clean foods by washing in fresh water.

Limousin [lee-moo-zI] *Bréjaude, clafoutis, lièvre farci en cabessal,* chestnuts, cabbage, and wild mushrooms are among the culinary contributions of this province situated in central France.

Limousine, à la A descriptive term indicating that red cabbage and/or chestnuts are present in a dish.

Limousine, chou rouge à la [shoo roosh ah-lah +] A classic Limousin dish of red cabbage cooked in stock with potatoes and chestnuts.

Lingots [lI-goh] White beans grown in the Vendée region and in parts of northern France.

Liqueur [lee-kür] Neutral spirits (brandy, whiskey, rum) mixed or redistilled with flavoring ingredients such as fruits, flowers, herbs, seeds, and so on. Chartreuse, Bénédictine, Grand Marnier, and Cointreau are examples of fine French liqueurs.

Lison, garniture [lee-zO] Creamed lettuce, duchess potato pancakes, and ox tongue; for various meats.

Lisses [lees] Term referring to early peas.

Listrac [lees-trahk] An excellent red Bordeaux wine.

Lithuanienne, à la [lee-twahn-nyen] Describes dishes garnished with cooked button mushrooms in sour cream.

Livarot [lee-vah-roh] A popular cow's-milk cheese from Livarot (Normandy).

Livèche [lee-vesh] Lovage; an herb that looks and tastes like celery.

Livournaise, à la [lee-voor-nez] Named after the Italian city of Livorno, this term indicates that chestnuts and/or ham are prevalent in a dish.

Livournaise, sauce A cold sauce composed of oil and vinegar combined with hard-cooked egg yolks, and anchovies; seasoned with nutmeg and parsley.

Lochois [lo-shwah] A type of sweet pastry made in Loches-en-Touraine.

Lombarde, sauce [lO-bahr] Hollandaise sauce mixed with chopped mushrooms and parsley.

Lombarde, garniture [lO-bahrd] (*For grilled meats*) Tomatoes filled with white Piedmont truffles; risotto topped with Parmesan cheese.

Longe [lOg] A French term for the top part of the veal loin.

VOCABULARY

Longeole [lO-zhyohl] A vegetable and pork sausage from Savoy.

Longuet [lO-gweh] A long, thin, rather dry loaf of bread.

Lonzo [lO-zoh] A highly spiced, pickled pork filet; cut thin and served as an hors d'œuvre or ground for sausage.

Lorette [lo-ret] A garnish for lamb or beef consisting of chicken croquettes, asparagus, and sliced truffles. Served with demi-glace sauce.

Lorraine [lo-ren] Province in northeast France bordering Belgium, Luxembourg, and Germany. Area resources and specialties include: red currant jam (Bar-le-Duc), charcuterie, pâté de foie gras, *potée*, and quiche.

— A type of cheese from Lorraine; see *Gérardmer*.

—, *à la* Indicates a dish is garnished with braised red cabbage and potatoes *fondants*; also describes dishes prepared with bacon and Gruyère cheese.

Lotier [lo-tyeh] An aromatic plant used to flavor marinades, rabbit dishes, and certain cheeses. Also known in France as *mélilot*, *mirlirot*, and *trèfle de cheval*.

Lotte (de mer) [lot-duh mer] Monkfish.

Lotte de rivière [+ duh ree-vyer] Burbot; a freshwater fish prized in France for its liver.

Loubine [loo-been] The name for gray mullet in some parts of France.

Louche [loosh] Ladle.

Lou fassum [loo-fah-suhm] A specialty of Antibes (Provence) featuring cabbage stuffed with sausage, tomatoes, green peas, and rice. Also spelled *sou fassum*.

Louisiane, garniture [lwee-zyahn] With sweet corn and fried bananas.

Louis XIV, garniture [loo-ee] (*For grilled meats*) Artichoke bottoms stuffed with duxelles, anna potatoes, and sliced truffles.

Louis XV, garniture (*For various entrées*) Truffle and mushroom *salpicon* in artichoke bottoms.

Lou kencous [loo ken-koos] A type of spicy sausage from Bordelais.

Lou linka [+ kin-kah] A small garlic sausage from the Basque Provinces.

Lou magret [+ mah-greh] See *Magret*.

Loup (de mer) [loo (duh mer)] Sea bass.

Louquenka [loo-kA-kah] A garlic and pepper sausage from the Basque Provinces.

Lourdes [loord] A city in Gascony famous for the miraculous cures that have taken place there; less known for its production of fine chocolate.

Lou sar [loo sahr] A Mediterranean fish related to the sea bream found off the coast of Provence; best cooked grilled or broiled.

Lucullus, garniture [luh-koo-luhs] Describes dishes richly garnished with items such as truffles, cockscomb and kidneys, and foie gras.

Lumas [lü-mah] The word for snails in Poitou.

Lunel [loo-nel] A local Muscat wine from Languedoc.

Lunettes [loo-net] Small cookies spread with jam; also known as *sablés milanais*.

Lut [lüt] A paste made from flour and water used to seal the lid of a cooking vessel prior to baking. Sometimes referred to as *repère*.

Lyonnais [lyuhn-neh] A small province in central France with an excellent culinary reputation; best known for onion and egg dishes.

Lyonnaise, à la [lyuhn-nez] Indicates onions are present in a dish.

Lyonnaise, sauce Demi-glace sauce to which a reduction of white wine with sautéed onions and vinegar are added.

Macaron [mah-kah-rO] Macaroon; an almond-meringue biscuit (cookie).

Macaroni [mah-kah-ro-nee] Macaroni.

Macédoine [mah-seh-dwahn] A mixture of diced fruits (in syrup and liqueur) or vegetables (typically potatoes, carrots, peas, French beans, and turnips). The vegetables are used as an entrée accompaniment, garnish, or flavoring agent for soups and sauces.

—, *à la* Describes dishes garnished with a macédoine of vegetables.

Macérer [mah-seh-reh] Macerate; to flavor foods—typically fruits—by soaking in a liquid (liqueur, wine, syrup).

Maceron [mah-seh-rO] A celery-/parsley-like plant once popularly used as a flavoring.

Mâche [mahsh] A winter salad green native to Europe. Also known as corn salad, lamb's lettuce, or in France as *doucette*.

Mâchon [mah-shO] (*Lyon*) The local word for snack; a typical daily snack consists of various salads and/or charcuterie.

Macis [mah-see] Mace.

Mâcon [mah-kO] A region in southern Burgundy known not only for the excellent wines (red, white, rosé) produced there, but also for top quality beef, poultry, and vegetables.

Mâconnaise, à la [mah-kon-nez] Indicates that dishes (typically fish) have been prepared with red Mâcon wine.

Macquée [mah-keh] A fresh Belgian cheese used extensively in France for a popular savory tart.

Macreuse à pot-au-feu [mah-kruhz ah poh-tuh-fuh] A cut of beef used specifically for pot-au-feu.

Macvin [mahk-vI] A spicy, potent liquor wine from the Haut-Jura region.

Madeleine [mahd-len] A small, dry, sponge cake baked in a scallop-shell-like mold. The madeleines of Commercy and St. Yrieix are famous.

Madère [mah-der] Madeira; a fortified wine from the island of Madeira (Portugal) used extensively in the kitchen to flavor sauces, soups, and various dishes.

—, *sauce* Demi-glace sauce flavored with Maderia.

Madiran [mah-dee-rA] Red AOC wine from southern France.

Magenta, sauce [mah-zhen-tuh] Béarnaise sauce flavored with tomato *concassée*.

Magistère [mah-zhuh-ster] A very concentrated and flavorful consommé served with various garnishes.

Magret [mah-greh] The French term for the breast meat of fattened ducks.

Maigre [meh-gruh] Lean.

Maigre-gras [+ gra] A double-spouted pitcher used to pour off excess fat from gravies.

Maillot, garniture [meh-yoh] Oval-shaped carrots and turnips, braised lettuce, and French beans; served with demi-glace sauce; for various dishes.

Maillot, sauce Sauce Madeira with the addition of white wine, hard-cooked egg yolks, and cayenne pepper.

Maingaux [mA-goh] A local cream cheese from Rennes (Brittany). Also spelled *Mingaux*.

VOCABULARY

Maintenon [mA-tuh-nO] A discriptive term for dishes prepared or garnished with *appareil à maintenon*; see *Maintenon, appareil à.*

—, *appareil à* [ah-pah-rey ah +] A mixture of béchamel sauce, onion purée, and mushrooms fortified with egg yolks. The mixture sometimes contains truffles and tongue and is used in various culinary preparations.

Maïs [mah-ees] Corn.

Maison [meh-zO] A term used in describing a dish to indicate that it is a specialty or a creation of a particular establishment.

Maître-cuisinier [me-truh-kwee-zeen-yeh] A word sometimes used for the chef of a large establishment.

Maître de shai [+ duh shah-ee] The person in charge of the vineyards.

Maître d'hôtel [+ do-tel] (1) Headwaiter. (2) The person in charge of all restaurant or hotel dining room operations. (3) Formerly, the proprietor of an establishment.

—, *à la* Describes grilled meats garnished with maître d'hôtel butter and soufflé potatoes.

—, *beurre* See *Beurre, maître d'hôtel.*

Malaga, sauce [mah-lah-gah] Demi-glace sauce with a white wine-shallot reduction; seasoned with red pepper and lemon and finished with malaga wine.

Malakoff [mahl-ah-kof] (1) A type of gâteau of which there are several versions. (2) A type of Neufchâtel cheese made from cow's milk.

Malaxer [mah-lahk-seh] To soften a food item; i.e., butter, by kneading.

Malsat [mahl-sah] A type of white pork sausage from southern France. Also spelled *melsat.*

Maltais [mahl-teh] A diamond-shaped petit four flavored with almonds and candied orange.

Maltaise, à la [mahl-tez] Describes sweet and savory dishes flavored with orange.

Maltaise, sauce Hollandaise sauce to which the juice of blood oranges is added.

Mancelle, à la [mA-sel] (*For poultry and game*) Tartlets filled with duxelles and game purée.

Manche [mAsh] "Handle"; the bone extending from the cutlet or leg of an animal, which aids in eating or carving.

Manchette [mA-shet] A paper or foil crown used to decorate the *manche.*

Manchon [mA-shO] Small marzipan cups filled with praline cream and dipped in ground pistachios. Served as a petit four.

Mandarin [mA-dah-rI] A cognac-based liqueur flavored with mandarin orange.

Mandarine [mA-dah-reen] Tangerine.

Mandoline [mA-doh-leen] An all-purpose manual slicing machine.

Mange-tout [mAzh-toot] Snap bean.

Mangue [mahng] Mango; a tropical fruit with an orange-colored pulp.

Manicamp [mah-nee-kA] A strong cow's-milk cheese from Picardy.

Maniér [mah-nyeh] (1) To make a mixture by hand. (2) To prepare a beurre manié. (3) To knead butter into flour in the preparation of a raw roux.

Manouls [mah-nool] Stuffed tripe (veal or lamb, depending on the region) from the south of France.

Manqué [mA-keh] An almond-praline sponge cake popular in Paris.

Mantua [mA-twah] Describes fish

coated with Parmesan bread crumbs and fried; coated with *sauce italienne*.

Maquereau [mah-kroh] Mackerel.

Maraîchère, à la [mah-re-sher] Indicates that fresh vegetables have been used in the preparation of a dish.

Marasquin [mah-rahs-kI] Maraschino; a clear liqueur produced mainly in Italy from marasca cherries. Used in the French kitchen to flavor pastries and desserts.

Marbrade [mahr-brahd] A type of *fromage de tête* from southwestern France.

Marc [mahrk] (1) The remains of the grapes pressed for wine. (2) A spirit distilled from *marc*. The *marc* of Alsace, Champagne, Burgundy, Haut-Jura, and Savoy are highly regarded.

Marcassin [mahr-kah-sI] A young wild boar under the age of 6 months.

Marcelin [mahr-suh-lI] A type of pastry flavored with strawberries and almonds.

Marchand de vin, à la [mahr-shA duh vin] Literally "in the manner of the wine merchant," this term indicates that red wine and shallots are used in a preparation.

Marchand de vin, beurre [+ buhr] Reduced red wine and shallots, *glace de viande*, chopped parsley, and lemon juice incorporated into softened butter.

Marchand de vin, sauce A reduction of red wine, shallots, and a bouquet garni combined with demi-glace sauce and garnished with poached marrow.

Marche [mahr-sheh] A former province in central France; the dishes and resources of Marche are nearly identical to those of its immediate neighbor to the south, Limousin. See *Limousin*.

Marché [mahr-sheh] Market.

Maréchale, à la [mah-reh-shahl] Describes meats treated *à l'anglaise* (breaded), pan fried, and garnished with asparagus tips and truffles.

Marée [mah-reh] Seafood at a French fish market.

Marengo [mah-rE-goh] A classic dish featuring chicken or veal sautéed with chopped tomatoes, mushrooms, and garlic and garnished with croutons, crayfish tails, and fried eggs.

Marennes [mah-ren] A coastal town in the Charente region renowned for oysters.

Margarine [mahr-gah-reen] A fat substitute developed in 1869 originally composed of beef suet and skim milk. Margarine is now made from vegetable oil.

Marguerite [mahr-ge-reet] A dessert preparation consisting of strawberries macerated in kirsch, served over grenadine-flavored sorbet, and topped with maraschino cream.

Marguery [mahr-ge-ree] The name given to several preparations named after French chef and restaurant owner Nicholas Marguery.

—, *filets de sole* [fee-leh duh sol +] A classic dish made of sole poached in fish fumet, garnished with mussels and shrimp, and topped with the thickened poaching liquid.

—, *sauce* (1) Hollandaise sauce flavored with oyster juice and garnished with oysters. (2) Another name for *sauce dieppoise*.

—, *tournedos* [toor-ne-doh] Beef tournedos garnished with artichoke hearts filled with creamed truffles and morels; mushrooms,

Marguery, tournedos (cont.) and cockscombs, and kidneys. Topped with the pan juices deglazed with port and beef stock and enriched with cream.

Marianne [mah-ree-ahn] Describes poached fish served on a bed of spinach and garnished with mussels; coated with white wine sauce.

Marie-Jeanne, garniture [mah-ree zhahn-neh] A classic garnish for touredos and noisettes composed of tartlets filled with duxelles and sliced truffles; potatoes *parisenne*.

Marie-Louise, garniture [+ loo-eez] (*For various meats*) (1) Artichoke hearts filled with duxelles and coated with *sauce Soubise*; noisette potatoes. (2) Tartlets filled with a vegetables *brunoise*.

Marie Stuart, garniture [+ stü-ahrt] A garnish of onion purée in tartlet shells, beef marrow, and demi-glace sauce for various meats.

Marie Thérèse, garniture [+ teh-rez] (*For grilled meats*) Croquettes made from risotto and truffles and served with demi-glace sauce flavored with tomato.

Marietta [mah-ree-et-tuh] Describes meat and poultry dishes garnished with noodle nests filled with tomato *concassée* and cockscombs; served with *sauce Madeira*.

Mariette [mah-ryet] A fruit preparation composed of poached apples or pears set on a bed of chestnut purée and topped with apricot-rum sauce.

Marignan [mah-ree-nyA] Savarin cake layered with cherry-flavored meringue and glazed with apricot jam.

Marigny, garniture [mah-ree-nyee] Small tarts filled with French beans and green peas; potatoes *fondants*.

Marigny, sauce Tomato *concassée* and mushroom essence combined with demi-glace sauce, finished with a splash of white wine, and garnished with mushroom caps and olives.

Marinade [mah-ree-nahd] A seasoned liquid in which meats, fish, and vegetables are soaked in order to absorb the liquid's flavor. The marinade can be cooked or uncooked and is made up of an acid (wine, lemon juice, vinegar), oil, and seasonings. A marinade also acts as a tenderizer and preservative.

— **à chaud** [+ ah shoh] A cooked marinade composed of wine, vinegar, water, *mirepoix*, and seasonings; used to season venison.

Mariner [mah-ree-neh] To marinate; to soak foods in a marinade. See *Marinade*.

Marinetta, garniture [mah-ree-net-tuh] (*For meat and poultry*) Tartlets filled with creamed spinach and crescent-shaped puff pastries (*fleurons*).

Marinette [mah-ree-net] An apple-raisin tart.

Marinière, à la [mah-ree-nyer] (1) Describes shellfish cooked in white wine with shallots and butter. (2) Describes fish poached in white wine and garnished with mussels.

Marinière, moules à la [mool +] A classic French dish featuring mussels cooked in white wine, butter, shallots, and garlic. The cooking liquid is strained, fortified with whole butter, and poured over the mussels.

Marinière, sauce Sauce Bercy flavored with mussel essence and thickened with egg yolks.

Marivaux [mah-ree-voh] Descriptive term for large roasts garnished with duchess potato baskets filled with French beans and a *salpicon* of diced vegetables.

Marjolaine [mahr-zhoh-len] Marjoram; an herb of the mint family used extensively in European kitchens. Wild marjoram is also known as oregano.

Marjolaine A three-layered cake featuring chocolate, vanilla, and praline buttercreams.

Marjolin [mahr-zhol-lI] A variety of potato.

Marmande [mahr-mAd] A town in western France noted for the fine tomatoes and asparagus grown there.

Marmelade [mahr-me-lahd] A sweetened purée made from stewed fruit. Used as a spread or in pastries.

Marmite [mahr-meet] A tall, narrow pot used to cook pot-au-feu, cassoulets, stews, large cuts of meat, and so on.

— *dieppoise* [+ dyep-pwahz] A creamy fish stew from Dieppe (Normandy) made with local seafood and vegetables.

— *norvégienne* [+ nor-veh-zhyen] A type of insulated double boiler.

—, *petite* [puh-teet +] See *Petite marmite.*

Marocaine, à la [mah-ro-ken] (*For noisettes and tournedos*) Sautéed zucchini, rice pilaf with saffron, and tomato sauce.

Maroilles/Marolles [mah-rwal/ mah-rol] A famous French cow's-milk cheese first made in the Abbey of Maroilles in Picardy. Nicknamed "Vieux Puant" (Old Stinker) because of its strong aroma and flavor.

Marquer [mahr-keh] A French cooking term referring to a preparation that is completely finished except for cooking.

Marquise [mahr-keez] (1) A pineapple- or strawberry-flavored sherbet with kirsch; topped with Chantilly cream and fruit purée. (2) The name given to various light mousse- or custard-like desserts.

— *au chocolat* [+ oh shoh-koh-lah] A famous mousse-like dessert made with melted chocolate and butter to which beaten egg yolks and whites are (separately) folded in.

Marquise A variety of pear.

Marquise, garniture (*For various meats*) Truffle and asparagus tarts, poached beef marrow, and marquise potatoes.

Marquise, pommes de terre [pom duh ter +] Cooked potatoes milled and combined with butter, egg yolks, and tomato purée; piped in decorative shapes and baked.

Marrons [mah-rohn] Chestnuts.

—, *glacés* [glah-seh +] (1) Shelled chestnuts poached in sweet syrup and glazed with liquified sugar. (2) Shelled chestnuts simmered in veal stock until tender with the stock reduced to a glaze, coating the chestnuts.

—, *purée de* [pü-reh duh +] A purée of chestnuts; used in poultry and game stuffings or in sweet preparations.

Marsala [mahr-sah-luh] A fortified wine from Sicily used in numerous sweet and savory preparations in the French kitchen.

Marseillaise, à la [mahr-se-yez] (*For various meat dishes*) Tomatoes sautéed with garlic, pitted olives stuffed with anchovies; *sauce Provençal.*

Marseille [mahr-se-yuh] A seaport town in southeastern France (Provence) known as the birthplace of bouillabaisse.

VOCABULARY

—, *sauce* Mayonnaise sauce combined with a purée of *oursin* (sea urchin).

— *vanille* [+ vah-nee-yuh] A nickname for garlic in some parts of France.

Martin-sec [mahr-tI-sek] A variety of sweet winter pear.

Martin-sire [+ seer] See *Rouville.*

Mascotte [mahs-kot] A gâteau composed of génoise sponge layered with mocha butter cream and decorated with almonds. Praline butter cream sometimes substitutes for the mocha.

Mascotte, à la Describes meats cooked *en cocotte* and garnished with *olivettes*, sautéed artichoke bottoms, sliced truffles, and tomatoes *concassée*; with demi-glace sauce.

Masquer [mahs-keh] "Mask"; to coat foods with sauce, aspic, glaze, icing, cream, and so forth.

Massacanat [mahs-sah-kah-na] An over-sized omelette from southern France traditionally served as a holiday breakfast treat.

Masséna, à la [mah-seh-nah] Describes certain dishes garnished with artichoke bottoms filled with béarnaise sauce and poached beef marrow.

—, *œufs* [uhf +] Poached eggs on artichoke bottoms, topped with béarnaise sauce and beef marrow.

—, *tournedos* [toor-ne-doh +] Grilled tournedos garnished with artichoke hearts and beef marrow and served with *sauce Périgourdine.*

Massenet, garniture [mah-suh-neh] (1) (*For various meats*) Poached beef marrow in artichoke bottoms, French beans, and anna potatoes; with *sauce Madeira.* (2) Describes egg dishes garnished with artichokes and asparagus tips.

Massepain [mah-se-pI] Marzipan; a sweet paste made from ground almonds, sugar, and egg whites. Used heavily in the pastry kitchen as a flavoring for cakes, icings, petits fours, and confections.

Massillon [mah-see-yO] A short dough tartlet filled with marzipan and glazed with kirsch icing.

Matafan [mah-tah-fA] The local name for *matefaim* in Berry. See *Matefaim.*

Matefaim [mah-tuh-fI] A large sweet or savory pancake from western France.

Matelote [maht-loht] A freshwater fish stew prepared with wine, garlic, mushrooms, and herbs; from the Île-de-France.

— *à la normande* [+ ah-lah nor-mAd] (*Normandy*) A stew prepared with cider, Calvados, local freshwater fish, and cream.

Matelote, sauce (1) Demi-glace sauce combined with a red wine and fish fumet reduction; seasoned with mushrooms and cayenne pepper and finished with anchovy butter. (2) Same as above, omitting the demi-glace sauce.

Matignon [mah-tee-nyO] A mixture of chopped aromatic vegetables (and sometimes ham) cooked to a pulp. It is used as a garnish or to coat meats as they roast to provide moisture and flavor.

—, *garniture* Describes dishes garnished with artichokes stuffed with a vegetable fondue.

— *au gras* [+ oh gra] *Matignon* prepared with meat, usually ham or bacon.

— *au maigre* [oh meh-gruh] *Matignon* prepared without meat.

Maury [mohr-ree] An area of the Roussillon producing a very sweet, potent wine of the same name. It is used in the production of Byrrh, a local aperitif.

Mauve [mohv] Mallow; a plant common in France. The leaves are used in salads or as a vegetable.

Mauviettes [moh-vyet] Lark; also known in France as *alouette*.

Maximilien, sauce [mahk-see-meel-yah] Hollandaise sauce seasoned with anchovy purée.

Mayonnaise, sauce [mah-yuhn-nez] A cold emulsion sauce made by whisking oil into egg yolks and mustard and seasoned with vinegar, salt, and pepper; the base for several cold sauces.

Mazarin [mah-zah-rI] A small, round short dough pastry baked in a special mold and filled with *mazarin* mixture. See *Mazarin, appareil à.*

—, *appareil à* [ah-pah-rey ah +] A pastry filling made from almond paste, sugar, butter, eggs, and flour. It is used to make *mazarins* and other pastries.

Mazarin, à la (1) (*For meat dishes*) Artichoke hearts stuffed with a diced vegetables, rice croquettes, mushrooms, and quenelles. (2) (*For fish*) Barquettes alternately filled with truffles and tiny shrimp. Served with *sauce écrevisse*.

Mazarin, petites pâte à la [puh-teet paht ah-lah +] Small savory puff pastries filled with chopped veal and bacon and enriched with eggs and cream. The pastries are baked and served as a garnish or hors d'œuvre.

Mecque, pain de la [pA duh lah-mek] A small, plain tea pastry made from *chou* dough and topped with sugar and almonds.

Médaillon [meh-dee-yO] Medallion; a small round cut of meat or fish. Lamb medallions are commonly referred to as noisettes and beef medallions as tournedos.

— *composé* [+ kO-poh-zeh] A mixture of various chopped meats shaped in a flat circle, breaded, and fried.

Médicis [meh-dee-chee] A descriptive term for meat medallions garnished with vegetable tartlets and noisette potatoes; served with *sauce Madeira* or béarnaise sauce.

Médicis, sauce Béarnaise sauce flavored with tomato purée and red wine.

Médoc [meh-dok] An exclusive red wine district of Bordeaux. It is divided into two parts; the Haut-Médoc in the southern part of the peninsula and Bas-Médoc to the north. Some of the world's great red wines are produced there.

Mélange [meh-lAzh] Mixture.

— *des îles* [+ deh eel] French term for a mixture of dried red, green, white, and black peppercorns.

Mélanger [meh-lA-zheh] To mix.

Mélasse [meh-lahs] Molasses; a thick dark syrup produced during the refining of sugar.

Melba [mel-bah] The name given to several culinary preparations named after the famous opera singer Dame Nellie Melba. The term *Melba toast* describes thin slices of toast used as a base for canapés and hors d'œuvres.

—, *pêche* [pesh +] A famous dessert created by Escoffier consisting of vanilla ice cream covered with fresh sliced peaches and topped with raspberry sauce.

—, *sauce* Lobster butter and chunks incorporated into sauce Newburg.

Mélilot [meh-lee-loh] See *Lotier*.

Melon [muh-lO] Sweet fragrant fruits related to the gourd family.

Melongène [muh-lO-zhen] A French word for eggplant. See *Aubergine*.

Melsat [mel-sah] See *Malsat*.

Melunoise, à la [muh-lü-nwahz] Describes poached fish in *sauce Robert*.

Ménegère [meh-nuh-zher] See *Huilier*.

Ménegère, à la Describes simply prepared dishes; similar to *à la bonnefemme*.

Mendiants [mE-dyA] (1) A dessert whose colors (white, purple, brown, and gray) are those of the dress of the four Roman Catholic mendicant orders. The dish is composed of raisins, figs, hazelnuts, and almonds. (2) (*Alsace*) A dessert composed of bread stuffed with apples, nuts, and cinnamon; dipped in egg and fried.

Menon [muh-nO] An eighteenth-century French chef and author of several highly acclaimed cookbooks, including *La Cuisinière bourgeoise* and *Les Soupers de la cour*. Considered one of the great French chefs.

Menon In Nice, a roasted young goat.

Menthe [mEt] Mint.

— *douce* [+ doos] Spearmint.

— *à l'eau* [+ ah loh] A beverage made up of mint syrup and carbonated water.

— *poivrée* [+ pwah-vruh] Peppermint.

— *vert* [+ vehr] Spearmint.

Mentonnaise, à la [mE-tuhn-nez] (1) Describes fish prepared with black olives, tomatoes, and garlic. (2) Describes meat dishes accompanied with stuffed zucchini, tomato-flavored rice, and potatoes *parisienne*.

Menu [me-nü] A list of dishes served at a specific meal or available at an eating establishment.

— *à la carte* See *à la carte*.

— *dégustation* [+ deh-goos-tah-syO] A sampling menu, usually made up of several small courses.

—, *table d'hôte* [tah-bluh-doht] Refers to a complete meal for a set price. Also called *prix-fixe*.

Menu-droit [+ drwah] A strip of poultry breast; grilled and served with sauce. *Menu-droit* was once the name for a type of stew made from the variety meats of a deer.

Mephiso [meh-fee-soh] Describes grilled fish served with *sauce diable*.

Meringage [meh-rI-gazh] A term referring to the meringue part of a dessert; i.e., crust, topping, decorations, and so on.

Meringue [mur-rIg] A light, fluffy combination of stiffly beaten egg whites and sugar. It is used raw to lighten delicate mixtures—i.e., mousses and soufflés—or it can be cooked and used for a topping or base for pastries.

— *à l'italienne* [+ ah-lee-tahl-yen] Italian-style meringue; a method of making meringue in which hot sugar syrup is slowly whisked into egg whites.

— *ordinaire* [+ or-dee-ner] A simple method of making meringue in which granulated or powered sugar is added to beaten egg whites. Also called French meringue.

— *suisse* [+ swees] "Swiss meringue"; a combination of egg whites and sugar heated in a *bainmarie*. When very warm, the mixture is placed in a bowl and beaten until stiff.

Meringuer [muh-rI-geh] (1) To decorate sweet preparations with meringue. (2) To lighten a sorbet or mousse mixture by incorporating beaten egg whites.

Merlan [mer-lA] Whiting; a saltwater fish similar to cod found in the

North Atlantic and the Mediterranean.

Merle [merl] Blackbird; a member of the thrush family, merles are very popular in Corsica where they are used in *salmis* and pâtés.

Mérou [meh-roo] Grouper; a large salt-water fish found in the Atlantic and Medtierranean.

Merveille [mer-veel] A simple pastry composed of flour, eggs, butter, and sugar; cut into various shapes and deep-fried. The pastries are sprinkled generously with sugar and served warm or cold.

Mescladisse [mes-klah-dees] A salad composed of various greens and sprouts tossed with vinaigrette and goat cheese. Referred to as *mesclun* in Provençe.

Mesclun [mes-klU] See *Mescladisse*.

Messire-jean [mes-seer zhA] A variety of pear found in France.

Méteil [meh-tehl] A mixed-grain flour. This term also describes bread made from such flour.

Méthode [meh-tuhd] In Bayonne *methode* is synonymous with *confit de porc* (preserved pork).

Metro [meh-troh] A garnish for large roasts composed of artichoke bottoms stuffed with *brunoise* vegetables; potatoes *parisienne*.

Mets [me] Refers to tableside preparations; dishes prepared at the guests table.

Metton [me-tO] A hard, grainy cow's-milk cheese from Jura.

Méture [meh-tür] This term refers to various cornmeal products from eastern France; i.e., cornmeal pudding (Gascony and Béarn), cornmeal bread (Landes), and cornmeal wheat bread (Normandy).

Meuille [muh-yuh] A local name for the gray mullet in Charentes.

Meunière, à la [muh-nyer] Describes fish lightly floured and panfried in butter. The fish is served with the butter to which lemon juice and parsley have been added.

Meunière, beurre à la [buhr ah-lah +] See *Beurre à la meunière*.

Meunster [muhn-stuhr] See *Munster*.

Meurette, en [E muh-ret] Burgundian dishes cooked in red wine sauce.

Méursault An area in Beaune (Burgundy) producing full-bodied, dry white wines of high quality.

Mexicaine, à la [mek-see-ken] Describes dishes prepared or garnished with mushroom caps, roasted sweet peppers, and tomatoes. A spicy demi-glace sauce often accompanies dishes served *à la mexicaine*.

Miche [meesh] A large, round loaf of wheat bread.

— *noir* [+ nwahr] Black bread from Limousin and other parts of France.

Mie de pain [mee-duh pA] Bread crumbs; also called *chapelure* and *panure*.

Miel [myel] Honey.

Migaine [mee-gren] A mixture of cream and eggs used as a base for quiches, custards, and so on.

Migliassis [mee-glee-ah-sees] A type of sweet Corsican cake made with chestnut flour, milk, sugar, and eggs.

Mignardises [mee-nyahr-deez] See *Friandise*.

Mignon [mee-nyO] A flat *tuile*. See *Tuile*.

Mignon, garniture Refers to dishes garnished with artichoke hearts filled with green peas and truffled poultry quenelles. Often served with demi-glace sauce laced with Madeira.

Mignonnette [mee-nyon-et] (1) Coarsley ground white peppercorns used heavily in the French kitchen. (2) Refers to round pieces of meat or poultry prepared in various manners. (3) Matchstick potatoes.

Migourée [mee-goo-reh] A local fish stew of the Charente.

Mijoter [mee-zhoh-teh] A very slow simmer.

Mikado [mee-kah-doh] Describes dishes prepared with a Japanese flavor.

—, consommé [kO-suh-meh +] Chicken consommé garnished with tomato *concassée* and strips of chicken breast.

—, garniture Broiled tomatoes and sautéed Chinese artichokes; accompanies grilled meats.

—, salade [sah-lahd +] A classic salad composed of boiled potatoes bound with mayonnaise and seasoned with soy sauce; garnished with diced tomatoes and sweet peppers, cooked shrimp, and Chinese artichokes.

Milanais [mee-lah-neh] An anise-flavored génoise cake. *Milanais* is also a type of small almond and citrus-flavored cookie.

Milanais, sablés [sah-bleh +] See *Lunettes.*

Milanaise, à la [mee-lah-nez] "In the style of Milan (Italy)" (1) Describes foods dipped in Parmesan bread crumbs and deep-fried or panfried. (2) Refers to dishes topped with Parmesan cheese and baked au gratin.

Milanaise, garniture A garnish for various entrées composed of pasta, sliced ox tongue, and truffles; with tomato sauce and Parmesan cheese.

Milhassou [meel-ah-soo] A type of cornmeal pudding; a specialty

dessert from the French Basque Provinces.

Miliasse [meel-yahs] A cornmeal porridge—prepared sweet or savory—made in several parts of southern France. There are several variations of the spelling.

Millas [mee-ya] See *Miliasse.*

Millasse [mee-yas] See *Miliasse.*

Mille-feuille [mee-yuh-fuh-yuh] Literally "thousand leaves," this name describes a dessert consisting of puff pastry alternately stacked with layers of whipped cream and fruit jam.

Milles [meel] A simple, local pastry from Sarladais (Périgord) featuring corn flour or other grain flour. See *Milliassous.*

Millésime [mee-yeh-seem] A term referring to the vintage year of a wine.

Milliard [mee-yahd] A cherry tart from Clermont-Ferrand (Auvergne).

Millias [mee-yahs] See *Miliasse.*

Milliassous/Milliessou [mee-yuh-soo/mee-yuh-soo] The name for a pastry of Périgord outside of Sarladais.

Millière [mee-yer] A rice and corn porridge (sweet or savory) from Anjou.

Milton [meel-tO] A *salpicon* of truffles, cockscombs and kidneys, and asparagus tips bound with béchamel sauce; a garnish for poultry dishes.

Mimolette [mee-moh-let] A soft-textured, mild-flavored cow's-milk cheese. *Mimolette* is produced in many parts of northern Europe, including Flanders. Also known as *Boule de Lille.*

Mimosa [mee-moh-sah] Describes dishes garnished with hard-cooked eggs.

—, consommé [kO-suh-meh +]

Chicken consommé garnished with diced *royale* and sieved hard-cooked egg yolks.

—, *salade* [sah-lahd +] Describes various salads garnished with sieved egg yolks or hard-boiled eggs.

Mingaux [mI-goh] See *Maingaux*.

Miques [meek] Boiled dumplings made from corn and wheat flour and pork fat; a specialty of Sarladais.

Mirabeau [mee-rah-boh] A garnish for certain dishes composed of anchovy filets, pitted olives, and tarragon leaves.

—, *sauce* *Sauce allemande* enriched with garlic-herb butter.

Mirabelle [mee-rah-bel] A small golden-yellow plum grown in the Alsace-Lorraine region; usually used in tarts or jams.

— A plum brandy made in Lorraine from the *mirabelle* plum.

Mireille [mee-reh-yuh] Usually, a preparation for peaches, which are sprinkled with sugar, topped with strawberry purée, and garnished with Chantilly cream and chopped almonds.

Mireille Describes dishes served with *mireille* potatoes.

Mirepoix [meer-pwah] A mixture of roughly chopped aromatic vegetables—carrots, onions, celery, and leeks—and used to flavor stocks, sauces, soups, braised and roasted meats, and so forth.

— *au gras* [+ oh gra] *Mirepoix* with the addition of ham or bacon used to enhance the flavor of meat stocks and sauces.

— *au maigre* [+ oh meh-gruh] Meatless *mirepoix* typically used for fish sauces.

— *bordelaise* [+ bor-dlez] See *Mirepoix fine*.

— *fine* [+ feen] Finely diced

mirepoix used mainly as a garnish for certain meats and fish. Also referred to as *mirepoix bordelaise*.

—, *sauce* A reduction of vegetables (*mirepoix*), white wine, ham, and herbs; enriched with butter or cream.

Mirette [mee-ret] Term denoting that *mirette* potatoes accompany an entrée.

—, *pommes de terre* [pom-duh-ter +] Julienne potatoes sautéed in butter with truffles. *Glace de viande* is added to the pan when nearly complete and the finished dish is garnished with Parmesan cheese.

Mirlirot [meer-le-roh] See *Lotier*.

Mirliton [meer-le-tO] A small tart featuring *pâte feuilletée* (puff pastry) filled with frangipane and garnished with almonds.

Miroir, au [oh mee-rwahr] Describes dishes having a glossy, mirrorlike, finish, particularly eggs.

Miroton [mee-roh-tO] Sliced leftover beef and sautéed onions topped with *sauce Lyonnaise* and bread crumbs and baked *en casserole*.

Miroton, sauce Demi-glace sauce flavored with tomato, mustard, and fried onions.

Mise en place [meez-E-plahs] "In its place"; a restaurant term meaning to organize all the food and equipment needed to perform a particular task.

Missiasoga [mees-syah-so-gah] Air-cured pieces of goat meat; a Corsican specialty.

Mississa [mee-see-sah] A Corsican specialty of smoked marinated pork; usually cooked on the grill.

Mitan [mee-tA] A center cut steak or filet of salmon.

Mitonner [mee-tuhn-neh] To cook at slow simmer.

Mitron [mee-trO] A French word for baker's assistant.

Mode, bœuf, à la [buhf ah-lah mod] A famous beef dish composed of marinated top or bottom round braised in red wine, vegetables, stock, and herbs; served with pan juices.

Moderne, à la [mo-dern] (*For various meats*) Braised cabbage and/or lettuce, sliced truffles, and veal quenelles.

Moelle [moh-el] Bone marrow; the soft interior of (beef) bones. It it usually poached and used as a garnish or to flavor stocks and sauces.

—, **à la** Refers to dishes garnished with poached bone marrow.

—, **sauce** Prepared like *sauce bordelaise* with white wine replacing the red. The sauce is garnished with chopped parsley and sliced marrow.

Mogador [mo-guh-dor] The name given to certain dishes dedicated to the Moroccan seaport of the same name. Goose liver appears in many of these dishes.

—, **consommé** [kO-suh-meh] Chicken consommé garnished with goose liver, julienne of chicken breast, diced ox tongue, and sliced truffles.

—, **sauce** Brown sauce to which black truffles and goose liver have been added.

Mogettes [moh-zhet] Large white beans grown in southeastern France. Also called *cocos*.

Moïna [moh-ee-nah] Describes poached sole garnished with creamed morels and artichoke hearts.

Moka [moh-kah] Mocha; a type of coffee bean grown in Arabia. *Mocha* also refers to a combination of coffee and chocolate.

Mokatine [moh-kah-teen] Small mocha-flavored cakes or petits fours.

Mollusque [mol-lüsk] Mollusk; a type of soft-bodied shellfish protected by a single shell (univalve) or two connecting shells (bivalve). Cephalopods, which are also mollusks, have no shell; i.e., octopus and squid.

Monaco [moh-nah-koh] (1) Describes various dishes garnished with sliced calfs' brains, mushroom caps, and truffles. (2) A descriptive term for poached fish garnished with oysters, tomatoes, and croutons and served with a white wine sauce.

Monégasque, à la [moh-neh-gahsk] Refers to dishes garnished with *oignons monégasque*. Also an hors d'œurve made from small tomatoes stuffed with flaked tuna.

Monégasque, oignons [o-nyO +] Small onions simmered in water, olive oil, vinegar, and seasonings. Tomato purée and raisins are added to the mixture and reduced until thick. Used as a garnish.

Monie borgne [moh-nee bor-nyuh] The name in France for a variety of cod; also called *officier* and *tacaud*.

Monseigneur [mO-seh-nyuhr] Describes fish fillets stuffed with fish mousse and garnished with tartlets filled with creamed shrimp.

Monselet, à la [mO-suh-leh] A garnish for grilled meats consisting of stuffed eggplant, noisette potatoes, and béarnaise sauce. Also refers to dishes garnished with quartered artichoke hearts and truffles.

Monsieur [muh-syuh] A double-cream, cow's-milk cheese from Normandy.

Montagné [mO-tah-nyuh] A descriptive term for filet mignons garnished with stuffed tomatoes, artichoke hearts, and mushroom caps.

Montagné, Prosper [pros-puhr mO-tah-nyuh] (1864–1948) French chef and author of several cookbooks including the masterpiece *Larousse gastronomique*.

Montagny [mO-tA-nyee] A white AOC Burgundy wine from the Côte Chalonnaise in southern Burgundy.

Montansier [mO-tA-zyeh] The name given to a preparation of poached fish in which the fish is coated with two sauces: white wine sauce and red wine sauce.

Montbazon [mO-bah-zO] A garnish composed of lamb sweetbreads, chicken quenelles, mushroom caps, and sliced truffles; accompanies poultry dishes.

Mont-blanc [mO-blA] A classic dessert composed of Chantilly cream mounded on a bed of chestnut purée that has been laced with brandy.

Mont-bry [+ bree] A garnish for a variety of entrées made up of creamed ceps and spinach purée seasoned with Parmesan cheese; demi-glace sauce is served with the dish.

Mont-cenis [+ seh-nees] A blue-veined cheese made from cow's or goat's milk from Savoy.

Mont-d'or [+ dohr] A soft goat's-milk (sometimes made with goat's and cow's milk) cheese from Lyon.

Monte Carlo [mO-teh kahr-loh] A garnish composed of cucumbers, green beans and peas, and potato croquettes.

Montebello [mO-teh-bel-loh] A garnish for beef and lamb filets composed of a *salpicon* of truffles and ox tongue bound with *sauce Choron*.

Monte-Cristo [+ kree-stoh] See *Montpensier*.

Montélimar [mO-teh-lee-mahr] A city in southern France (Dauphiné) known as the nougat capital of France.

Monter [mO-teh] To incorporate egg whites, egg yolks, cream, butter, and so forth into a preparation in order to give it more body and/or richness.

Monter au beurre [+ oh buhr] To swirl whole butter into a sauce to add flavor and body.

Montglas [mO-glah] Describes dishes prepared or garnished with *salpicon montglas*. See *Montglas, appareil à*.

—, *appareil à* [ah-pah-rey ah +] Ox tongue, goose liver, mushrooms, and truffles bound with *sauce Madeira*. The mixture is used as a garnish or filling for savory pastries, or as a flavoring agent for sauces.

Montigny, sauce [mO-tee-nyee] *Sauce velouté* flavored with *glace de viande* (meat glaze) and tomatoes.

Montmorency [mO-moh-rA-see] (1) A town near Paris renowned for the fine quality of cherries grown there. (2) Refers to dishes prepared with Montmorency cherries.

Montpensier [mO-pE-syeh] (*For meat dishes*) Asparagus tips, sliced truffles, and Madeira-flavored demi-glace.

—, *gâteau* [gah-toh +] A génoise sponge made or garnished with almonds and dried and candied fruit.

Montrachet [mO-trah-sheh] A popular, creamy goat cheese produced in Burgundy.

Montrachet, puligny [pü-lee-ynee +] A dry white wine from Burgundy considered one of the finest in France.

Montreuil, garniture [mO-tre-yuh] (1) Describes fish served with white wine sauce and garnished with potatoes *parisienne* mixed with shrimp *velouté*. (2) Refers to dishes garnished with artichoke bottoms filled with vegetables *brunoise*. (3) A dessert featuring vanilla ice cream topped with pears and coated half with raspberry and apricot purée.

Montrouge [mO-roozh] Denotes the presence of mushrooms in a preparation.

Monvoisin [mO-vwah-sI] Describes poached fish coated with white wine sauce and garnished with shrimp, tomatoes, and chopped parsley.

Moque [mohk] The traditional cup for serving cider in Normandy and beer in other parts of northern France.

Morbier [mor-byeh] (*Jura*) A distinctive cheese made from cow's milk. A blackish-gray streak of edible ash runs through the center of the cheese.

Morille [mor-eel] Morel; an edible mushroom related to the truffle and distinguished by its spongy, cone-shaped cap. Morels can be dried, preserved in oil, or used fresh.

Morlaisienne, à la [mor-le-zyen] Indicates a garnish of shrimp and mussels; for fish cooked au gratin.

Mornay, sauce [mor-neh] Béchamel sauce to which Gruyère and Parmesan cheeses are added. Cream or egg yolks are incorporated just before serving.

Morteau [mor-toh] A large smoked pork sausage from a village in the Jura area of the same name. Also called *jésus de morteau*.

Mortier [mor-tyeh] Mortar; a bowl, made from various materials, in which foods (with the aid of a pestle) are ground.

Morue [mo-rü] Salted dried cod.

— **à la languedocienne** [+ ah-lah lA-guh-doh-syen] A traditional dish of Languedoc featuring salt cod, potatoes, and garlic simmered to a creamy paste. Also known as *morue à la provençale*.

— **à la provençale** [+ ah-lah pro-vE-sahl] See *Morue à la languedocienne*.

— **verte** [+ vehr] Salted cod that is not dried.

Morvan [mor-vA] An area in and around Burgundy known for its fine pork products, particularly ham and sausage. Honey, goat cheese, and mushrooms are also Morvan specialties.

Morvandelle, à la [mor-vA-del] "In the style of Morvan"; describes dishes prepared with the natural food resources of Morvan (Burgundy), particularly ham; see *Morvan*.

Mosaïque [moh-zah-eek] Foods (vegetables, aspic, truffles, and so on) cut in various decorative shapes used to adorn pâtés, terrines, *chaud-froids*, and so forth. It is also a type of gâteau flavored with apricot and red currant jam.

Moscovite [mohs-koh-veet] The name given to several sweet preparations.

— **aux fruits** [+ oh frwee] (1) A hot preparation of poached apples hollowed out and filled with fruit purée; flavored with kirsch. (2) Bavarian cream prepared with fruit purée flavored with kirsch and poured into a special mold to set.

Moscovite, à la "In the Moscovite or Russian style"; describes dishes prepared with ingredients such as caviar, beets, cabbage, sour cream, sturgeon, and potatoes.

Mostelle [moh-tel] Rockling; a fish related to the whiting found in Mediterranean and North Atlantic waters. Prepared like whiting.

Mothais [moo-teh] A type of goat cheese produced in Poitou. Also called *La-Mothe-Saint-Héray* and *La-Mothe-Bougon*.

Mouclade [moo-klahd] A specialty of Bordeaux featuring mussels simmered in white wine with garlic, shallots, cream, and butter. The mussels are arranged on a platter and drizzled with the sauce.

Mouflon [moo-flO] A now rare wild mountain sheep found in Corsica. *Ragoût de moufflon* was once a popular Corsican specialty.

Mouillette [moo-yet] Small strips of bread used for dipping.

Moule [mool] Mussel; a thin-shelled bivalve mollusc with tannish-orange flesh and most commonly, a dark blue shell.

Moules [mool] Molds; decorative containers of various shapes and sizes used to bake cakes, tarts, pâtés, and so forth.

Moulin [moo-lI] Mill; an instrument used to pulverize grains, coffee beans, spices, and so forth.

— **à légume** [moo-lee-leh-güm] Vegetable mill; a metal strainer through which fruits and vegetables are pressed, separating the inedible seeds and skin from the pulp.

— **à poivre** [+ ah pwah-vruh] Pepper mill.

Mounjetado [moon-zhe-tah-doh] A dish composed of navy beans, tomatoes, garlic, and pork; cooked *en casserole*.

Mourtaïrol/Maurtayrol [moor-tah-eer-ohl] A local Rouergue specialty; chicken soup seasoned with saffron.

Mousquetaire, sauce [moos-kuh-ter] (1) Tomatoes, garlic, and fine herbs seasonings sautéed in oil. (2) A cold sauce of mayonnaise, shallots, chives, cayenne pepper, garlic, and vinegar.

Mousse [moos] A sweet or savory preparation to which beaten egg whites or whipped cream are incorporated into a soft base (such as melted chocolate, ground meat or fish, and so forth) to lighten the mixture. Mousses are usually served cold.

— **au chocolat** [+ oh shoh-koh-lah] A classic dessert prepared by folding meringue and whipped cream into melted chocolate. Rum or flavored liqueurs are often added to heighten the flavor.

— **d'écrevisses** [+ deh-kruh-vees] Crayfish mousse; puréed crayfish is combined with egg whites, heavy cream, chopped crayfish tails, and seasonings; baked in a water bath and served hot or cold with various sauces.

Mousseline [moos-leen] Savory forcemeats lightened with whipped cream and egg whites; similar to mousse. This term also refers to small delicate pastries.

Mousseline, sauce (1) Hollandaise sauce to which whipped heavy cream is added. (2) Any sauce to which whipped cream is added.

Mousseron [moo-suh-rO] Fairy-ring mushroom; a small edible mushroom with a pale stem and reddish cap.

— **à la crème** [+ ah-lah krem] A local Burgundian specialty of creamed mushrooms. See *Mousseron*.

Mousseuse, sauce A cold sauce for fish and vegetables made by whisking water and lemon juice into creamed butter; finished with cream.

Mousseux [moo-suh] "Sparkling"; sparkling wines.

Moût [moo] Must; unfermented grape juice.

Moutarde [moo-tahrd] Mustard.

— *de dijon* [+ duh dee-zhO] A mustard made in Dijon, France, from brown mustard seeds, white wine, and must (*moût*); considered the finest mustard in France.

— *de florida* [+ duh floh-ree-dah] A type of mild mustard from the Champagne region.

— *de meaux* [+ duh moh] A type of hot Dijon mustard made with whole mustard seeds and vinegar.

—, *sauce* Hollandaise sauce with the addition of Dijon mustard.

— *à la crème, sauce* [+ ah-lah krem] Prepared mustard combined with salt, pepper, lemon juice, and cream.

Moutardelle [moo-tahr-del] A type of horseradish.

Moutardier [moo-tahr-dyeh] Mustard pot; a small receptacle used to serve mustard at the table.

Mouton [moo-tO] Mutton; a lamb over one year old.

— *pré salé* [+ preh-sah-leh] See *Pré salé.*

Mouvette [moo-vet] A type of wooden spoon used in former times.

Moyeu [moh-yuh] An obsolete French word for egg yolk.

Mozart, garniture [moh-zahrt] (*For small cuts of meat*) Artichoke hearts filled with celery purée, fried potatoes, poached egg, and sliced black truffle.

Muge [müzh] See *Mulet.*

Mulet [mü-leh] Gray mullet; a firm-fleshed, mild-flavored, saltwater fish.

— *cabot* [+ kah-boh] Striped mullet.

Munster/Meunster [mün-stahr] A famous cheese made from cow's milk produced in Alsace. The production of this strong smelling, semi-soft cheese is regulated by French law. See *Meunster.*

Muntanacciu [mU-tahn-ah-choo] A type of Corsican cheese made from cow's milk.

Murat [mü-rah] A town in Auvergne famous for its cornets.

Mûre [mür] Blackberry.

Murols [mü-rohl] A flat, mild-flavored cow's-milk cheese from Auvergne characterized by an indentation in its center.

Muscade [müs-kahd] Nutmeg.

Muscadelle [müs-kah-del] (1) Vine plant of Bordelais. (2) A variety of pear.

Muscadet müs-kah-deh] A famous white AOC wine from the Muscadet region of Anjou. Also the name of the grape from which the wine is made.

Muscat [müs-kah] White or black grapes with a musky flavor.

Muscatel [müs-kah-tel] A sweet dessert wine produced from the muscat grape; also called *Muscat.*

Museau [mü-zoh] The muzzle of an animal; most commonly from the pig (*museau de porc*) and ox (*museau de bœuf*). The meat from the muzzle is usually simmered and boned and used in various hors d'œuvres.

Musette, en [E mü-zet] Rolled beef shoulder. This term is now rarely used.

Musigny [mü-zee-nyee] Among the finest and most fragrant of the red Burgundy wines from Chambolle-Musigny.

Mynster [mün-steh] An alternate spelling for Munster cheese.

Myrte [meert] Myrtle; a fragrant European shrub used to flavor liqueurs and smoked meats.

Myrtille [meer-tee-yuh] Blueberry.

Nage [nahzh] A fragrant stock in which shellfish is cooked; similar to court bouillon.

—, *à la* "Swimming"; describes shellfish served in the stock in which it was cooked.

Nancy [nahn-see] A city in Lorraine famous for its charcuterie, particularly blood pudding (*boudin noir*). Macaroons are also a renowned specialty.

Nanette, garniture [nah-net] Refers to certain dishes garnished with stuffed artichokes, creamed lettuce, mushroom caps, and sliced black truffles; served with *sauce Madeira* or suprême sauce.

Nantais [nA-teh] See *Curé, fromage de.*

Nantais Shortdough cookies made with almonds and candied fruit.

Nantaise, à la [nA-tyahz] (1) (*For meats*) Glazed turnips; peas, and creamed potatoes. (2) (*Fish and shellfish*) With *sauce beurre blanc.*

Nantes [nAt] A town in Brittany famous for duck. Macaroons and *petit-beurres* (butter cookies) are also local specialties of Nantes.

—, *pain de* [pA duh +] A small almond cookie glazed with apricot jam and fondant icing.

Nantua [nA-twah] A town in the Franche-Comté region famous for freshwater crayfish.

—, *à la* Indicates crayfish is present in a dish.

—, *sauce* Béchamel sauce flavored with crayfish fumet and tomato purée and finished with crayfish butter.

Napoléon [nah-poh-leh-A] (1) Puff pastry strips layered with pastry cream (*crème pâtissèrie*) and sprinkled with powdered sugar. (2) This term on a bottle of cognac indicates the brandy is of superior quality and aged for several years.

Napolitain [nah-poh-lee-ten] (1) A large elaborate cake once used as a centerpiece for fancy buffets. (2) Small pieces of bitter chocolate.

Napolitain, fonds [fO +] Sweet almond biscuits iced with butter cream and jam.

Napolitaine, à la (*For meat dishes*) Served with spaghetti tossed with chopped tomatoes and Parmesan cheese.

Napolitaine, sauce Demi-glace sauce flavored with diced ham, bouquet garni, cloves, red currant jelly, and Madeira wine.

Nappe [nahp] Tablecloth.

Napper [nah-peh] To lightly coat with sauce.

Narbonne [nahr-buhn] A coastal town in Languedoc whose renowned food resources include honey and tripe.

Natte [naht] "Braid"; the design for various pastries.

Natté pain [+ pA] A braided loaf of bread.

Nature [na-tür] Refers to dishes served as simply and plainly as possible.

Naulet [noh-let] A yeast cake traditionally baked at Christmas time in Berry.

Navarin [nah-vah-rI] (1) A lamb or mutton stew. (2) Describes dishes that contain turnips, carrots, and so on.

— *printanier* [+ prI-tah-nyer] A lamb or mutton stew prepared with fresh garden vegetables; i.e., potatoes, peas, carrots, celery, onions, beans, herbs, and so forth.

— *provençale* [+ pro-vE-sahl] *Navarin printanier* with the addition of chopped peeled tomatoes and garlic.

Navarraise, sauce [nah-vahr-rez] Tomato-garlic sauce infused with fresh herbs.

Navet [nah-veh] Turnip.

Navette [nah-vet] A type of butter cake. *Navettes* are famous in Albi where they are made with almonds.

Nègre en chemise [neg-rE shmeez] (1) A rich mousse-like chocolate dessert chilled in a mold and decorated with whipped cream. (2) A combination of whipped cream (*crème chantilly*) and chestnut purée.

Négus [neh-gü] Sweetened wine flavored with lemon and spices.

Neige [nezh] (1) Egg whites beaten to a stiff consistency. (2) A red fruit sorbet.

Neige de florence [+ duh floh-rEs] Delicate flakes of pasta used to garnish consommés.

Nélusko [neh-lüs-koh] (1) A petit four composed of cherries stuffed with red currant jelly. (2) A frozen chocolate bombe flavored with praline. (3) *Velouté* soup garnished with diced chicken and chicken quenelles; enriched with hazelnut butter.

Nemours [ne-moor] (1) A puff pastry tartlet filled with plum jam. (2) A garnish for various meat dishes composed of duchess potatoes, green peas, and glazed carrots.

Nemrod, garniture (*For game*) Mushroom caps filled with chestnut purée, potato croquettes, and cranberry tartlets.

Néroli [neh-roh-lee] (1) Orange blossom oil used in pastries, confections, and liqueurs. (2) A small almond pastry flavored with orange.

Nesselrode [neh-suhl-rod] Indicates that chestnuts are present in a dish.

Neufchâtel [nuhf-shah-tel] A town in Normandy producing some of the finest butter and cream cheeses in France, including Neufchâtel, a mild cream cheese made with cow's milk from the town of Neufchâtel-en-Bray.

Nevers [nuh-vehr] A city in Nivernais known for its *nougatine*. Excellent poultry is raised in Nevers.

Nice [nees] A Provençale city in close proximity to Italy. Nice cookery is characterized by the use of tomatoes, black olives, basil, green peppers, capers, lemon, anchovies, and tuna. Fresh vegetables—artichokes, eggplant, and zucchini—are also emphasized.

Nichette, garniture [nee-shet] A garnish for meat or poultry composed of mushroom caps filled with cockscombs and kidneys; grated horseradish. Served with *sauce moelle*.

Niçoise, à la [nee-swahz] Describes dishes prepared in the style of Nice. See *Nice*.

Niçoise, salade [sah-lahd +] French beans, diced cooked potatoes, and quartered tomatoes tossed with oil and vinegar and garnished with capers, black olives, anchovy filets, and hard-cooked eggs.

Nieule [nyahl] A small, plain pastry from northern France.

Niflette [nee-flet] A cake made with puff pastry and filled with pastry cream; from the Île-de-France.

Nigelle [nee-zhel] The tiny, dried black seeds of an herbaceous plant of the genus Nigella. This peppery spice is also known as black cumin or black onion seed. In France, because of its complex aroma, it is sometimes called *quatre-épices, toute-épice,* or *poivrette.*

Nîmes [neem] A town in Langeodoc recognized for its pastries and confections and preserved green olives.

Nina [nee-nah] A dessert composed of pineapple sorbet topped with strawberries (which have been macerated in kirsch) and whipped cream.

Ninon, garniture [nee-nO] (*For various entrées*) Duchess potatoes, cockscombs, and kidneys bound with *sauce velouté,* tartlets filled with asparagus tips, and sliced truffles.

Niolo [nyo-loh] A cured Corsican cream cheese made from goat's or sheep's milk.

Nivernais [nee-ver-neh] A province in central France bordering Burgundy that includes the Morvan and Charolais regions. The cattle of Charolais produce the finest beef in France and Morvan yields excellent pork products as well as honey and mushrooms. The finest root vegetables in France are said to be grown in Nivernais. See *Nevers.*

Nivernaise, à la [nee-ver-nehz] Describes dishes prepared with root vegetables; i.e., carrots, turnips, potatoes, and so forth.

Nivernaise, sauce *Sauce allemande* garnished with diced turnips and carrots.

Noces [nos] A type of porridge from northern France made from oat flour.

Noël [no-el] Christmas. See *Réveillon.*

Noir [nwahr] Black.

Noisette [nwah-zet] A small tender

steak cut from the rib or loin area; usually refers to lamb, although the term can be applied to describe similar cuts of beef or veal.

Noisette Hazelnut.

Noisette, sauce Hollandaise sauce finished with hazelnut butter.

Noisettines [nwah-ze-teen] Small shortbread pastries spread with hazelnut cream.

Noix [nwah] Nuts.

— *du brésil* [+ dü bree-seel] Brazil nut.

— *de macadam* [+ duh mah-kah-dahm] Macadamia nut.

Noix A lean tender cut of meat from the fillet of veal; also called *sous-noix.*

Noix muscade [+ müs-kahd] Nutmeg; an aromatic seed from an East Indian tree. The outer covering of this sweet spice is mace, which is also used as a spice.

Nonnat [nO-nah] A type of small sea fish best prepared deep-fried; served as a light meal or as an hors d'œuvre.

Nonnette [nO-net] A light gingerbread cake; a specialty of Dijon.

Nonpareille [nO-pah-rah-yuh] (1) Small pickled capers. (2) Colored granulated sugar used for decorating cakes and pastries. (3) A flat chocolate chip dipped in white sugar beads. (4) A variety of French pear.

Nonpareille, sauce Hollandaise sauce made with lobster butter and garnished with diced lobster tail and truffles. Crayfish butter and tails may substitute for the lobster.

Noques [nohk] Sweet or savory dumplings; the Alsatian version of the Austrian *nockerln.*

— *à l'allemande* [+ ah lah-luh-mAd] A savory dumpling prepared with flour, butter, egg yolks,

Noques à l'allemande (cont.) beaten egg whites and cooked in boiling stock; ground veal or pork livers are sometimes added to the mixture.

— *à la viennoise* [+ ah-lah vyen-nwahz] A type of sweet dumpling made with butter, cream, egg whites, sugar, and flour. The dumplings are poached in sweetened milk and served with sauce or custard.

Nora, sauce [no-rah] *Sauce poivrade* combined with cranberry purée.

Norbertes [nor-bert] A variety of small black plums from Champagne used in jams.

Normande, à la [nor-mAd] "Normandy style." Usually refers to dishes prepared with apples, cider, and/or Calvados but can also indicate dishes utilizing butter, cream, or seafood.

Normande, sauce A rich sauce combining fish fumet with fish *velouté*, mushrooms, and cream; enriched with egg yolks, butter, and more cream; served with fish.

Normandie [nor-mA-dee] Normandy; a coastal province in northern France. Although some of the finest apples and apple products (cider, Calvados) in Europe are produced here, Normandy is equally noted for the production of cheeses: Camembert, Neufchâtel, Excelsior, Livarot, Pont l'Évêque, and Trappiste. Butter (Isigny), cream (Bayeux), and duck (Rouen) are among the other major food resources of Normandy.

Normand, le trou [luh troo +] A shot of Calvados taken between the courses of a large meal as a *digestif*. *Le coup du milieu* or *le trou du milieu* is the term used when a liqueur other than Calvados is used.

Norvégien [nor-veh-zhyE] A type of rich almond confection.

Norvégienne, à la [nor-veh-zhyen] "Norwegian style"; (1) Describes cold fish coated with aspic and garnished with such items as chilled shrimp, cucumbers stuffed with smoked salmon, beets filled with shrimp *salpicon*, hard-cooked eggs, cherry tomatoes, and so on. (2) Describes various hot fish dishes prepared or garnished with anchovies. (3) (*For meat entrées*) Served with *sauce Madeira* and buttered noodles.

Norvégienne, omelette [om-let +] Baked Alaska; a molded dessert consisting of ice cream wrapped with sponge cake, coated with meringue, and quickly browned in a very hot oven. Also called *glace au four*.

Nougat [noo-gah] A confection used for candy filling and petits fours made from sugar, nuts, and honey. See *Montélimar*.

— *blanc* [+ blA] White nougat; nougat with the addition of egg whites, which gives the candy a lighter and softer texture.

Nougatine [noo-gah-teen] (1) A confection similar to nougat made from caramelized sugar, glucose, and almonds. The mixture is rolled out when soft and broken into small pieces. (2) Small pieces of nougat. See *Nevers*. (3) A four-layer génoise cake filled with praline cream and glazed with chocolate fondant icing.

Nouilles [noo-yuh] Noodles.

— *à l'alsacienne* [+ ah-lahl-sah-syen] A specialty of Alsace featuring egg noodles combined with Gruyère cheese. The mixture is topped with fried noodles and baked.

Nouillettes [noo-yet] Very thin short noodles.

Nouvelle cuisine [noo-vel kwee-zeen] "New cooking"; a style of cooking stressing lighter, simpler, lower calorie meals. Healthier cooking techniques (steaming, boiling) and ingredients replace traditional, higher caloric methods.

Noyau [no-yoh] The kernel of a fruit (cherries, plums, apricots, peaches, and so forth) found inside the hard shell or pit.

— *de poissy* [+ duh pwah-see] A famous French liqueur from the Île-de-France flavored with the kernels of cherries.

Noyaux, crème de [krem-duh no-yoh] The collective name for various liqueurs flavored with fruit kernels.

Nulle [nül] A custard scented with musk.

Nymphes [neemf] Frog legs. See *Grenouilles, cuisses de.*

Nyons [nee-yO] A town in Dauphiné whose specialties include preserves of *grives* (thrush) and pickled truffles.

Nyons Oil-cured black olives from Provence.

Odalisque, à l' [oh-dah-leesk] A garnish for meat dishes composed of sliced eggplant and green peas.

Oelenberg [ü-lE-burg] A mild type of Trappist cheese from Alsace made from cow's milk.

Œuf(s) [uhf] Egg(s).

— *à la coque* [+ ah-lah kok] Soft-cooked (boiled) eggs.

— *à la neige* [+ ah-lah nezh] A dessert composed of meringue poached in milk and served with custard sauce.

— *au plat* [+ oh plah] Fried eggs.

— *brouillés* [+ broo-ee-yeh] Scrambled eggs.

— *de poisson* [+ duh pwah-sO] Roe; refers to the eggs of female fish. See *Laitance.*

— *durs* [+ dür] Hard-boiled eggs.

— *miroir* [+ mee-rwahr] Synonymous with *œufs au plat.*

— *mollet* [+ moh-le] Medium boiled eggs.

— *pochés* [+ po-sheh] Poached eggs.

—, *sauce aux* (1) Hollandaise sauce garnished with chopped hard-cooked eggs. (2) Chopped hard-cooked eggs combined with chopped parsley, lemon, and butter.

— *sur le plat* [+ sür luh plah] Shirred eggs; cooked in a warm oven.

Officier [uh-fee-syeh] See *Monie borgne.*

Ognonnade/Oignonade [O-nyO-nahd/wA-nyO-nahd] (1) A stew heavily flavored with onions. (2) Chopped onions slowly cooked in butter.

Oie [wah] Goose.

Oignon [o-nyO] Onion.

— *clouté* [+ kloo-teh] an onion studded with cloves; used to flavor sauces.

—, *sauce à l'* See *Soubise, sauce.*

—, *soupe à l'* [soop ah-lo-nyO] A classic French soup made with thinly sliced onions sautéed in butter and added to beef consommé and white wine; topped with croutons and grated Gruyère cheese and baked au gratin.

Oignonade See *Ognonnade.*

Oille [wa-yuh] Derived from the Spanish *olla*, this term refers to a hearty soup.

Oiseau [wah-zoh] Bird; refers to any edible poultry or game bird.

Oiseaux sans tête [+ sA tet] Although this term means "headless birds," it refers to boneless stuffed meat (beef or mutton).

Oison [wa-zO] Gosling; young goose.

VOCABULARY

Olive [o-leev] The small, pitted fruit of the olive tree. Olives are widely grown in Provence and along with tomatoes and garlic characterize that province's cookery.

—, *huile d'* [weel do-leev] Olive oil. See *Huile viegre* and *Fine huile d'olive*.

Olives, sauce aux Demi-glace sauce garnished with diced olives.

Olivet [o-lee-veh] A town in the Loire Valley producing Olivet cheese.

— *bleu* [+ bluh] A soft cow's-milk cheese made in the Loire Valley.

— *cendré* [+ sA-dreh] A harder type of Olivet coated with ash.

Olivette [o-lee-vet] (1) An olive-shaped potato. (2) The word in and around northern France for poppy seed oil.

Oloron [o-lo-rO] A ewe's-milk cheese from Béarn. See *Iraty*.

Omble chevalier [O-bluh shuh-vah-lyeh] Considered a delicacy, this troutlike fish (related to the salmon) is found in France only in Lake Bourget and Lake Annecy, both in Savoy.

Ombre [O-bruh] Grayling; a relative of the trout, this freshwater fish is best prepared *au bleu* or stuffed and baked.

Ombrine [O-breen] A saltwater fish compared to bass.

Omega, sauce [oh-meh-gah] Hollandaise sauce flavored with chervil.

Omelette [om-let] An egg dish made by cooking a mixture of beaten eggs, cream, and seasonings in a pan until set. Various fillings—i.e., cheese, vegetables, meat—may be added. The omelette is usually folded to enclose the fillings before serving.

— *à la gasconne* [+ ah-lah gahs-kuhn] A specialty of Gascony, this flat omelette combines beaten eggs with ham, onions, garlic, and herbs and is cooked in goose fat.

— *à la normande* [+ ah-lah nor-mAd] (*Normandy*) A sweetened omelette topped with apples cooked in cream and flavored with Calvados.

Omelette enfarinée [+ E-fah-ree-neh] See *Farinette*.

Omelette surprise [+ soo-preez] *Omelette norvegienne* garnished with poached fruit. See *Norvégienne, omelette*.

Omnibus [om-nee-büs] The name for a chef's or waiter's assistant.

Onglet [O-glet] A French term for a cut of beef from the diaphragm area.

Opéra, à l' [ah-lo-peh-rah] (1) (*For noisettes and tournedos*) Small tarts filled with chicken liver and potato nests filled with asparagus tips. (2) (*For fish*) Asparagus bundles and *sauce beurre blanc*.

Ophelia, garniture [o-feel-yuh] (*For fish*) Fried potatoes and salsify; served with *sauce aurore*.

Orade [o-rahd] A fish considered essential to a classic bouillabaisse.

Orange [o-rAzh] Orange.

Orangeat [o-rA-zhah] A coin-shaped confection made from marzipan and orange peel.

— *perlé* [+ per-leh] A confection made up of orange peel coated with sugar which has been cooked between 224-228°F ("pearl" stage).

Orangine [o-rA-zheen] An orange-génoise cake layered with pastry cream and glazed with fondant icing.

Oreille-de-lièvre [o-reh-yuh-duh-lye-vruh] The word for *lamb's lettuce* in parts of France; see *Mâche*.

Oreille de mer [+ duh mer] Abalone;

a variety of large snail. Also called *ormeau*, *ormier*, and *six-yeux*; best cooked braised or quickly sautéed with garlic.

Oreille de porc [+ duh pork] Pig's ears; usually poached and fried or chopped and used in sausages and forcemeats.

Oreiller de la belle aurore [+ duh lah bel oh-rohr-uh] A classic savory pie filled with a hearty combination of veal, pork, partridge, duck, chicken livers, and hare.

Oreillettes [o-reh-yet] (*Languedoc*) Pastry dough deep-fried and sprinkled with sugar.

Orge [orzh] Barley; an ancient grain used in making beer and animal feed.

— *perlé* [+ per-leh] Pearl barley; husked, polished barley used in soups stews, casseroles, and other sweet and savory preparations.

Orgeat [or-zhah] A syrup made from sweet and bitter almonds, sugar, lemon, and water. It is used to flavor pastries and cocktails.

Orientale, à l' [ah-lo-ryE-tahl] A descriptive term for dishes served with tomatoes, white rice, and saffron.

Orientale, garniture (*For various meat dishes*) Tomato halves stuffed with saffron risotto, fried okra and peppers.

Orientale, sauce *Sauce américaine* flavored with curry and enriched with cream.

Origan [o-ree-gahn] Oregano; an herb related to the mint family which is also known as wild marjoram.

Orléanais [or-leh-ahn-eh] A historic province located in the center of France renowned for its superb dining. Orléanais is pehaps best known for game pâtés; poultry, flour, and asparagus are other notable products.

Orléanaise, à l' [ah-lor-leh-ahn-ez] Describes meat dishes garnished with braised endive and *maître d'hôtel* potatoes.

Orléans [or-leh-A] The capital city of Orléanais, where some of the finest mustard and wine vinegar in France is produced. Quince paste is also a well-known product of Orléans.

—, *sauce* Fish *velouté* added to a white wine reduction, flavored with mushrooms and enriched with crayfish butter.

Orloff [or-lof] See *Orlov*.

Orlov [or-lof] The name of several dishes in honor of the Russian prince Grigori Grigoryvich Orlov.

—, *garniture* (*For large cuts of meat*) Braised celery and lettuce; château potatoes.

—, *selle de veau* [sel-duh-voh +] An elaborate dish featuring saddle of veal in which the loin is removed, sliced lengthwise, and stuffed with mushrooms and truffles; coated with *sauce soubise* and Parmesan cheese and browned under the broiler.

—, *tournedos* Grilled tournedos garnished with anchovy filets and pearl onions; served with *sauce Madeira*.

Orly [or-lee] Describes batter-fried fish served with tomato sauce.

Ormeau [or-moh] See *Oreille de mer*.

Ormier [or-myeh] See *Oreille de mer*.

Oronge [or-rAzh] A rare, white-fleshed, red-capped edible mushroom.

Orratza [or-raht-sah] The word for the conger eel in Gascony. See *Congre*.

Ortolan [or-toh-lA] A small, rare wild bird considered a great delicacy. It is now protected in several parts of France.

Ortolans à la landaise [+ ah-lah lA-dez] In Landes this prized bird is prepared by roasting on a spit over an open fire or wrapped in wax paper and placed near the fire so as to cook in its own fat and juices.

Os [oh] Bone; hard tissue forming the skeleton of vertebrate animals. Beef, lamb, poultry, and fish bones are used to make stock. Beef bones contain marrow and are used in a variety of preparations. See *Moelle*.

Oseille [oh-zeh-yuh] Sorrel; a green leafy herb having a slightly bitter taste. Prepared like spinach, sorrel is used as a vegetable or to flavor soups and salads.

Ossau-iraty [os-soh-ee-rah-tee] See *Iraty*.

Ostendaise, à l' [ah-los-tE-dez] Describes stuffed poached fish garnished with oysters, sliced truffles, and fish croquettes; served with *sauce normande*.

Otero [o-teh-roh] A descriptive term for poached sole coated with *sauce Mornay* and Parmesan cheese and cooked au gratin; garnished with a baked potato cup filled with shrimp.

Othello [o-tel-loh] A garnish for tournedos and noisettes composed of *pailles* potatoes (see *Pailles, pommes*), and green peas.

Oublie [oo-blee-yeh] A small wafflelike cookie sometimes formed into cornets (cones).

Ouillade [wee-yahd] (*Roussillon*) A pork stew made with cabbage and beans. *Ouillade* also refers to a garlic and egg soup.

Ouillat [wee-yah] An onion and bean soup from Béarn. Also called *Tourri, Soupe du berger*, and *Toulia*; see *Ouille*.

Ouille [wee-yuh] A pot used in parts of France for various soups and stews (*ouillade, ouilat*).

Oulade [oo-lahd] A hearty peasant soup of the Cevennes region featuring cabbage, potato, and sausage. In Languedoc, white beans replace the potatoes.

Oule [ool] A copper pot used to prepare *oulade* and other soups and stews.

Oursin [oor-sI] Sea urchin; a spiny sea creature. Although sometimes smelling strongly of iodine, its roe is considered a delicacy.

—, purée d' [pü-reh door-sI] Purée of sea urchin; used to garnish certain fish dishes.

Ourteto [oor-teh-toh] (*Provence*) A type of spread made from cooked greens, onions, and garlic.

Oxymel [oks-ee-mel] A thick combination of honey and vinegar.

Oyonnade [o-yuhn-nahd] A Bourbonnais (Burgundy) specialty of goose stew with red wine.

Pachade [pah-chahd] (*Auvergne*) A thick pancakelike dessert with fruit, baked in the oven; similar to *clafoutis*.

Pageau/Pageot [pah-zhoh/pah-zhoh] The French name for the red sea bream; best poached or baked.

Pagel [pah-zhel] A sea fish said to be essential to an authentic bouillabaisse.

Paillarde [pah-yahrd] Refers to a piece of meat (veal, beef, lamb) pounded into thin slices.

Paillasse [pah-yahs] A term describing glowing charcoals, indicating the fire is ready (for cooking).

Paillassons [pah-yah-sO] Potato pancakes made from thinly cut potatoes.

Pailles, pommes [pom pah-yuh] "Straw potatoes"; cut in very thin strips and deep-fried.

Paillette [pah-yet] The French word for gold flakes used in the bottling of Goldwasser (a German herb liqueur) and for decorating pastries.

Paillette au Parmesan [+ oh pahr-me-zahn] Puff pastry flavored with Parmesan cheese and cut into thin strips.

Pain [pA] Bread.

— *à cacheter* [+ ah kah-shuh-teh] A small waferlike cookie.

— *au chocolat* [+ oh shoh-koh-lah] Chocolate-filled puff pastries.

— *baigné* [+ be-nyeh] See *Pan bagna(t)*.

— *bis* [+ bee] Brown bread.

— *complet* [+ kO-pleh] (1) A loaf of whole wheat or meal bread. (2) An almond-flavored cake baked in the form of a loaf.

— *de campagne* [+ duh kahm-pah-nyuh] A large, round loaf of bread made from coarse flour.

— *(de cuisine)* [pA (duh kwee-zeen)] A molded forcemeat loaf made from meat, poultry, chicken, and so on.

— *de foie gras* [+ duh fwah gra] An old method of preparing foie gras in which the liver is puréed and bound with butter, eggs, and bread crumbs.

— *de gênes* [+ duh zhen] An almond sponge cake.

— *de maïs* [+ duh mah-ees] Cornbread.

— *de mie* [+ duh mee] A long rectangular loaf of bread.

— *de seigle* [+ duh seh-gluh] A loaf of crusty rye bread, usually oval in shape.

— *d'épice* [+ deh-pees] Gingerbread.

— *frit, sauce* [+ free] Beef or poultry stock thickened with fried bread crumbs and flavored with ham, shallots, parsley, and lemon.

— *frotté* [+ fro-teh] Sliced bread fried in lard and seasoned with fresh garlic.

— *grillé* [+ gree-yuh] Toasted bread.

— *ordinaire* [+ or-dee-ner] Plain bread.

— *perdu* [+ per-dü] Sliced bread dipped in egg and fried on the griddle; French toast.

—, *sauce au* Boiled milk flavored with onion *cloute*, and thickened with bread crumbs, butter, and cream.

Paladru [pah-lah-droo] A type of cheese from Savoy.

Palais [pah-leh] Palate; refers to the soft, edible, muscular portion of the roof of the mouth of animals.

Palermitaine, à la [pah-luhr-mee-ten] "In the style of Palermo (*Sicily*)"; describes dishes garnished with ingredients such as eggplant, tomatoes, macaroni, Parmesan cheese, and so on.

Palermitaine, sauce (1) Mayonnaise sauce seasoned with lemon, red pepper, and garlic. (2) Demi-glace sauce flavored with red wine and orange and finished with shallot butter.

Paleron [pah-luh-rO] A French style cut of beef from the shoulder and neck area.

Palestine, à la [pah-les-teen] A garnish for meat and poultry consisting of small boiled onions, fried dumplings, and buttered artichoke hearts.

Palet de dames [pa-leh-duh-dahm] Small fancy currant cookies.

Paletot [pah-luh-toh] The remains of a goose from which the liver (foie gras) has been removed.

Palette [pah-let] French style shoulder cut of pork.

Palette A type of spatula having a long, thin, flexible steel blade that is used to frost cakes.

Palmier [pahl-myeh] Sweetened puff pastry baked in the shape of palm leaves.

Palmier, cœurs de [kuhr duh +] "Hearts of palm"; the edible shoots of certain palm trees.

Palois [pah-lwah] The word for *dacquoise* in Pau (Béarn). See *Dacquoise*.

Paloise, à la Describes dishes prepared in the fashion of Pau (Béarn), which includes the use of fresh vegetables, French beans, and potatoes. Béarnaise sauce or *sauce Paloise* are the traditional accompanying sauces.

Paloise, sauce Béarnaise sauce prepared with fresh mint instead of tarragon.

Palombe [pah-lOb] The name given to the woodpigeon in southwest France. See *Ramier*.

Palourde [pah-loord] Carpet-shell clam; one of the finest and most popular type of clams in France.

Pampaillet [pA-pah-yeh] A traditional annual celebration in Bordeaux signifying the end of the grape harvest.

Pamplemousse [pA-pluh-moos] Grapefruit.

Panade [pah-nahd] A paste made from a liquid (stock, water, cream, eggs) combined with flour, bread, rice, or potatoes; used to thicken forcemeats, quenelles, and other similar preparations.

— A peasant soup from the Jura area consisting of seasoned stock thickened with bread and cream.

Panais [pah-neh] Parsnip; a large white root vegetable.

Pan-bagnat [pA-bah-nyah] A Nice specialty of sliced crusty bread moistened with olive oil and spread with various foods: tomatoes, green peppers, black olives, radishes, hard-cooked eggs, anchovies, onions, and so on. *Pan-bagnat* is also referred to as *bagna* and *pain baigné*.

Paner [pah-neh] To coat foods with bread crumbs.

Panetier [pah-nuh-tyeh] In the Middle Ages, this was the person in charge of making and distributing bread.

Panetière [pah-ne-tyer] A sideboard dresser in which bread is stored.

—, *à la* The descriptive term for dishes featuring *salpicons*, ragoûts, fish, or other appropriate preparations served inside a hollowed-out bread loaf.

Panette [pah-net] A sweet raisin bun traditionally served on Easter Sunday in Corsica.

Panier [pah-nyeh] Basket.

Paniers en pommes de terre [+ E pom duh ter] Edible baskets made from shredded potatoes; filled with various foods and served as a garnish.

Panisse/Panisso [pah-nees] A Provençal dish similar to polenta featuring chickpea or corn flour boiled to a mush. Once chilled, it is sliced and fried and topped with Parmesan cheese; it can also be sweetened and served as a dessert.

Panizze [pah-nee-suh] A Corsican version of the Italian polenta made with chestnut flour. It is traditionally fried and topped with Broccio cheese.

Panne [pahn-neh] The fat surrounding the kidneys of a hog. It is used to make various forcemeats and sausages.

Pannequet [pahn-e-keh] Thick crêpe spread with various sweet or savory fillings.

Panoufle [pah-noo-fluh] A fine cut of meat from the top of the sirloin.

Pantin [pA-tI] A small (pork) force-meat patty, sometimes containing truffles.

Panure (à l'anglaise) [pah-nyür] The egg and bread crumb coating for dishes prepared *à l'anglaise.*

Panzarotti [pA-zah-rot-tee] Sweet rice fritters traditionally served on special (religious) occasions; from Corsica.

Papeton [pah-puh-tO] A quichelike dish from Avignon (Provence) composed of eggplant, eggs, and milk.

Papillote [pah-pee-yot] (1) A small paper crown used to adorn the exposed bone of a steamship round, rack of lamb or pork, poultry drumsticks, and so on. (2) A small chocolate candy.

Papillote, en Describes fish and sometimes meat baked inside parchment paper. The fish or meat is topped with herbs, vegetables, and butter; and it is sealed in the paper.

Pâques [pahk] Easter; the celebration of the Resurrection of Jesus on the third day after his crucifixion. Great feasts and traditional Easter treats are prepared throughout France.

—, *œufs de* [uhf duh +] Easter eggs; hard-cooked eggs decoratively dyed or painted in celebration of Easter. This term also refers to egg-shaped confections prepared for Easter.

Paquette [pah-ket] The French term for a female lobster carrying mature eggs. Considered a delicacy.

Paquerette [pah-kuh-ret] Daisy; a common flower. The leaves and bud are eaten in salads.

Parfait [pahr-feh] A frozen custard dessert folded with sweetened whipped cream and flavored with various liqueurs or fruits.

Parfumé [pahr-fU] Flavoring; natu-ral food additives (herbs, spices, wine, liqueurs, stocks, extracts) used to increase the taste and aroma of a dish.

Paris [pah-ree] France's capital city located in the Île-de-France and home to some of the world's finest restaurants.

— *ail* [+ ahy] A type of garlic sausage typically sliced and served with sauerkraut.

— *-Brest* [+ bre] Originating in Paris in the late 1800s, this dessert consists of praline butter cream sandwiched between two large rings of almond *chou* pastry.

Parisien [pah-ree-zyE] A ring-shaped sponge cake layered with pastry cream. The center is filled with thick apricot jam and sealed with sponge cake; iced with meringue and browned in the oven.

Parisienne, à la [pah-ree-zyen] "In the style of Paris"; describes a number of garnishes for various hot and cold dishes. Common ingredients used in dishes prepared this way include truffles, mushrooms, artichokes, crayfish, hard-cooked eggs, ox tongue, and potatoes *parisienne.*

Parisienne, sauce (1) Creamed *petit-suisse* cheese to which oil is added. Seasoned with lemon and chevril, it is served with cold asparagus. (2) Demi-glace sauce combined with a white wine–shallot reduction and *glace de viande*; seasoned with lemon and chervil.

Paris-Nice [+ nees] *Paris-Brest* in which the praline butter cream is substituted with cream *Saint-Honoré.*

Parmentier, à la [pahr-mE-tyeh] Refers to a variety of preparations that use potatoes.

Parmentier, Antoine Augustin [A-twahn o-güs-tI +] (1737–1813)

Parmentier, Antoine Augustin (cont.)
French agronomist and zealous promoter of the potato to a then unaccepting France. The name Parmentier is now synonymous with potato.

Parmentière [pahr-mE-tyer] An early name for the potato in France, named after Antoine Augustin Parmentier.

Parmentier, pommes de terre [pom-duh ter +] Cubed potatoes sautéed in butter and sprinkled with chopped parsley.

Parmentier, potage A thick purée of potato and leek soup.

Parmesan [pahr-me-zO] One of the world's great cheeses, this hard, grainy Italian cheese is widely used in the French kitchen. The true Parmesan cheese—*parmigiano reggiano*—is produced in the areas of Parma (originally), Bologna, Mantua, and Modena.

Parmesane, à la Describes a number of preparations utilizing Parmesan cheese.

Parures [pah-rür] The remains of meats, fish, poultry, or vegetables after being trimmed prior to cooking (skin, parings, fat); trimmings.

Pascade [pahs-kahd] A type of savory pancake from the Rouergue region of southern France.

Pascaline [pahs-kah-leen] Roasted lamb stuffed with lamb forcemeat.

Passarelle [pah-sah-rel] Raisins made from muscatel grapes.

Passarillage/Passerillage [pah-sah-ree-yahzh/pah-se-ree-yahzh] The process of drying (muscatel) grapes; see *Passarelle*.

Passe-bouillon [pahs bwee-yO] Stock strainer.

Passe-crassane [+ krah-san] A type of fragrant pear.

Passe-pomme [+ pom] The French name for a variety of apple.

Passe-tout-grain [+ too-grI] A red Burgundy wine made from the gamay and pinot noir grape.

Passe-purée [+ pü-reh] A strainer used to press through puréed foods.

Passerillage [pah-se-ree-yazh] See *Passarillage*.

Passoire [pah-swahr] The French word for strainer.

Pastillage [pah-stee-yahzh] A combination of powdered sugar, powdered starch, gum tragacanth, and water. This paste can be formed into various shapes and decorations or used to adorn cakes, pastries, confections, and so forth.

Pastille [pah-stee-yuh] A small disk-shaped confection made from sugar, syrup, and various flavorings.

Pastis [pahs-tees] The name given to a type of sweet brioche-like pastry; a specialty of Béarn and Gascony.

Pastis A potent anise-flavored liqueur similar to *Pernod*; popular in southwestern France and Corsica.

Pastèque [pahs-tek] Watermelon; not particularly popular in France, although fairly common in Provençe.

Patate (douce) [pah-taht (doos)] Sweet potato.

Pâte [paht] The collective French term for any type of dough, batter, paste, and so forth.

— **à chou** [+ ah shoo] Puff pastry made by adding flour to boiling water and butter and slowly adding eggs. The paste is piped into various shapes and baked until dry; used for numerous sweet or savory pastries.

— **à foncer** [+ ah fO-seh] An all-purpose pastry lining for pies and tarts. *Ordinaire* is made without eggs, *fine* with eggs.

— *à frire* [+ ah freer] Frying batter; a basic mixture for deep-frying or panfrying foods made up of flour, baking powder, milk, eggs, and seasonings. The batter should be well chilled and thick.

— *à l'eau* [+ ah loh] A flour and water paste used to patch or seal crusts.

— *à pâté* [+ ah pah-teh] The pastry crust used for *pâté en croûte*; made up of flour, butter or lard, eggs, and water.

— *anglais* [+ A-glez] See *Pie*.

— *aux anchois de collioure* [+ oh A-shwah duh kol-lyoo] A specialty of the Roussillon region composed of anchovies baked in pastry.

— *brisée* [+ bree-zeh] Short pastry; a rich, flakey, versatile dough used for tarts, pies, quiches; made with butter, sugar, flour, and water.

— *d'amandes* [+ dah-mahnd] Almond paste; a mixture of ground almonds, sugar, and syrup; used to make marzipan (*massepain*).

— *de bécherel* [+ duh beh-she-rel] A garlic pie from Brittany.

— *sablée* [+ sah-bleh] See *Pâte sucrée*.

— *sucrée* [+ soo-kreh] *Pâte brisée* enriched with eggs. Also called *pâte sablée*, it is used for pies, tarts, cookies, and so forth.

Pâté [pah-teh] A forcemeat spread of meat, poultry, fish, or vegetables baked in a crust or terrine and served hot or cold. Pâté can be very smooth or somewhat coarse in texture.

— *de campagne* [+ de kahm-pah-nyuh] A coarsely ground pork and liver terrine.

— *de cedrat* [+ duh seh-drah] A citron preserve from Bayonne.

— *de courres* [+ duh koor] Offal pâté; a specialty of Brittany.

— *de foie gras* [+ duh fwah-gra] Goose- or duck-liver pâté. By law it must contain 80 percent liver and is usually combined with truffles, pork liver, cognac, or Armagnac. Duck liver is considered superior to goose liver.

— *de tête* [+ duh tet] See *Fromage de tête*.

— *en croûte* [+ E kroot] Pâté baked in a pastry-lined mold.

— *en terrine* [+ E teh-reen] Pâté cooked in a terrine. See *Terrine*.

— *feuilletée* [+ fuh-yuh-teh] See *Feuilletage*.

— *maison* [+ meh-zO] A pâté that is considered a specialty of a particular establishment. See *Maison*.

— *minute* [+ mee-nüt] Chicken livers simmered for a minute in stock and puréed with butter.

— *pantin* [+ pA-tI] Pâté wrapped in pastry crust and baked free-standing (without the aid of a pan or mold) in the oven.

Pâtes alimentaires [+ ah-lee-mE-tehr] Pasta dough.

Pâtisserie [pah-tees-ree] (1) The art of pastry cooking. (2) A pastry shop or kitchen. (3) The items sold in a pastry shop; pastries (cakes, tarts, cookies, eclairs).

Pâtissier [pah-tee-syeh] Pastry chef.

Pâtissière, crème [krem pah-tee-syer] Pastry cream; a custard filling for pastries composed of flour, sugar, eggs, milk, and vanilla.

Pâtissière, noix [nwah +] Part of the upper leg of veal. It is usually larded and roasted or used for escalops and roulades.

Patranque [pah-trAk] A sort of mush consisting of old bread soaked in milk and bound with Cantal cheese; panfried in butter.

V O C A B U L A R Y

Patronnet [pah-tro-neh] A pastry chef's young apprentice.

Pauchouse [poh-chooz] A freshwater fish stew made with red or white wine and thickened with beurre manié; bacon is sometimes added for extra flavor; a specialty of eastern France, particularly Burgundy and Franche-Comté.

Pauillac [poh-yahk] A wine-growing region of Bordeaux producing perhaps the finest red wines in the world; e.g., Châteaux Lafite-Rothschild, Mouton-Rothschild, Latour, Grand-Puy-Lacoste. Pauillac is also renowned for the excellent milk-fed lamb raised there.

Paulée [poh-leh] A festive gathering celebrating the closing of the grape harvest in Burgundy.

Paupiette [poh-pyet] A small flattened piece of meat that is stuffed, rolled, and braised.

Pauvre homme, à la [poh-vruh om] "In the poor man's style"; In the past this term described leftover meats served with *sauce pauvre homme*.

Pauvre homme, sauce (1) Demiglace sauce flavored with parsley and shallots and thickened with bread crumbs. (2) Reduced vinegar added to boiling stock, seasoned with shallots, chives, and parsley and thickened with roux and bread crumbs.

Pavé [pah-veh] (1) The name for various sweet or savory mousselike preparations formed into square or rectancular shapes. (2) A square génoise cake layered with buttercream. (3) A square piece of gingerbread.

— **au chocolat** [+ oh shoh-koh-lah] Génoise sponge cake layered with chocolate buttercream and trimmed into a square shape.

— **du roi** [+ dü rwah] Pâté de foie gras studded with truffles and baked *en croûte* in a rectangular pan; served cold.

Pavé d'Auge [+ dazh] See *Pavé de moyaux.*

Pavé de bœuf [+ duh buhf] A thick piece of grilled beef.

Pavé de moyaux [+ duh mo-yoh] A cow's-milk cheese from Normandy similar to Pont l'Évêque. Also called *pavé d'Auge.*

Pavie [pah-vee] A variety of peach.

Pavot [pah-voh] Poppy seed; the nonnarcotic seed of the opium poppy used as a bread topping and pastry filling.

Paysanne, à la [peh-yee-zahn] (1) Describes dishes accompanied by a *paysanne* garnish or *paysanne* potatoes. (2) Describes foods cut into triangles.

Paysanne, garniture (*For meats and poultry*) The same as *à la fermière* with the addition of cocotte potatoes and diced bacon.

Pêche [pesh] Peach.

Pêche-Abricot [pesh ah-bree-koh] Nectarine.

Pékinoise, à la [peh-kee-nwahz] (*For fried fish*) Garnished with Chinese mushrooms and scallions and served with a dipping sauce composed of garlic, ginger, soy sauce, and onions.

Pélamide [peh-lah-meed] Bonito; a member of the tuna family found in the Atlantic and Mediterranean; also called *bonite.*

Pélardon [peh-lahrp-dO] A goat's-milk cheese from the Cévennes region of Languedoc. *Pélardon de Ruoms* and *pélardon d'Anduze* are local varieties.

Pellaprat, Henri Paul [E-ree pol pellah-prah] (1869–1950) French chef and culinary teacher and author of several cookbooks, including *L'Art culinaire moderne.*

Pelle [pel] Literally "shovel," this term describes shovel-like kitchen tools; i.e., scoops, oven peels, spatulas, large spoons, and so forth.

— *à frire* [+ ah freer] A heavy mesh-like basket used to contain foods being deep-fried.

— *à poisson* [+ ah pwah-sO] A spatula-like utensil used to serve fish.

Pelure d'oignon [puh-lür do-nyO] "Onion peel"; refers to the color of some red and rosé wines.

Pelures The skins or peels of vegetables; used to flavor stocks.

Peraldou [per-ahl-doo] Another name for pélardon d'Anduze cheese. See *Pélardon.*

Perche [pehrsh] Perch; a spiny-finned freshwater fish of the genus Perca. The river perch is highly regarded in France.

— *de mer* [+ duh mer] Ocean perch; a saltwater fish related to the rockfish.

— *goujonnière* [+ goo-zhoh-nyer] See *Goujon.*

Perdreau [per-droh] Partridge under one year of age.

— *à la catalane* [+ ah-lah kah-tah-lahn] A local specialty of the Roussillon region of braised partridge with bitter oranges.

—, *chartreuse de* [shahr-truhz duh +] A famous dish composed of partridge, cabbage, bacon, and root vegetables layered in a casserole dish and baked. When slightly cooled it is turned out on a platter before serving.

Perdrix [per-dreeks] A mature partridge more than one year old.

Père janvier [per jA-vyeh] A traditional Christmas cake from Ardèche.

Pergamon, garniture [per-gah-mO] (*For filet mignons*) Sliced truffles

and croquette potatoes served with demi-glace sauce flavored with *Madeira.*

Périgord [peh-ree-gor] A gastronomically esteemed region in western France synonymous with truffles.

Périgourdine, à la [peh-ree-goor-deen] Describes dishes prepared or garnished with sliced black Perigord truffles and sometimes foie gras. See *Périgueux, à la.*

Périgourdine/Périgueux, sauce [peh-ree-gwuh] Demi-glace sauce flavored with truffle essence and Madeira and garnished with chopped or sliced truffles.

Périgueux, à la Named for the capital city of Perigord, this term is nearly synonymous with *à la périgordine* except that the truffles are chopped instead of sliced.

Périgueux, sauce See *Périgourdine, sauce.*

Perlés du Japon [per-leh de zhah-pO] (1) Tapioca pellets; see *Tapioca.* (2) The name for oysters in some parts of France.

Pernod [per-noh] A famous licorice-flavored liqueur produced in France.

Persane, à la [per-zahn] "Persian style"; (1) (*For meat and poultry*) Bell peppers stuffed with pilaf, sliced bananas, and stewed tomatoes. (2) (*For lamb and mutton*) Sautéed onions and peppers, stewed tomatoes, and grilled eggplant.

Persicot [per-see-koh] A sweet, spicy liqueur flavored with almonds and peaches.

Persil [per-seel] Parsley; an aromatic herb heavily used in the French kitchen to flavor or garnish dishes.

—, *sauce* *Sauce au beurre* with the addition of chopped parsley.

— *pour poisson, sauce* [+ poor pwah-sO] Fish *velouté* flavored with chopped parsley; served with fish.

Persillade [per-see-yahd] A seasoning combination of chopped parsley and garlic.

Persillé [per-see-yeh] (1) A high-quality cut of beef marbled with specks of fat. (2) Describes dishes seasoned with *persillade*. (3) The collective name given to certain blue cheeses produced in Savoy and the French Alps.

Persiller [per-see-yeh] To garnish a dish with chopped parsley.

Péruvienne, à la [peh-rü-vyen] Describes a *salpicon* of ham, chicken, and oxtail meat bound with tomato sauce; used as a garnish for various entrées.

Pessac [pe-sahk] A town in the Bordeaux region noted for strawberries.

Pétafine [peh-tah-feen] A fresh cheese product from the Dauphiné region seasoned with anisette.

Pétéram/Pétéran [peh-teh-rA] A hearty stew from Luchon (Gascony) made with mutton, pork, veal, potatoes, and garlic.

Pétillant [peh-tee-yA] Said of wines with a light sparkle.

Petit [puh-tee] Small.

— *-beurre* [+ buhr] A small butter cookie. Particularly famous are the *petits-beurre* from Nantes (Brittany).

— *-carré* [+ kah-reh] A type of cream cheese similar to Neufchâtel.

— *déjeuner* [+ deh-zhuh-neh] Breakfast.

— *-duc, garniture* [puh-tee dük] (*For various meats*) Small tarts filled with creamed chicken, asparagus spears, and sliced truffles.

— *four* [+ foor] Elegant bite-sized iced cakes, pastries, or confections.

— *gris* [+ gri] See *Cagouilles*.

— *-lait* [+ leh] Whey; the clear liquid that separates from the curd of curdled milk or when cheese is made.

— *lisieux* [+ lee-syuh] Similar to Livarot, this cow's-milk cheese is one of Normandy's oldest cheeses.

— *pain* [+ pA] Roll.

— *pois* [+ pwah] Green peas.

— *-suisse* [+ swees] A fresh cheese from Normandy made from cow's milk and fortified with cream.

Petite huile [+ weel] The name for poppy seed oil in parts of France.

Petite marmite [puh-teet mahr-meet] A hearty soup comprised of beef, vegetables, chicken, oxtail, and marrow in stock. It is traditionally served with sliced French bread and Gruyère cheese.

Petites [puh-teet] The name for *tripoux* in parts of France. See *Tripoux*.

Petits légumes [+ leh-güm] Cooked vegetables served as a side dish.

Petits pâtés chauds [+ pah-teh shoh] Hot, savory, individual pies filled with meat and/or vegetables.

Petits-pieds [+ pyed] Refers to small winged game.

Pétoncle [peh-tO-kluh] The French word for a type of small scallop.

Pets de nonne [peh-duh-non] See *Soupirs de nonne*.

Pflutters [fluh-tuhrs] See *Floutes*.

Pholade [fo-lahd] A shellfish related to the clam found on France's Atlantic coast. It is popular in Brittany, particularly Brest, where it is called *bonne-soeur* and *religieuse*. See *Dail* and *Gite*.

Pibronata [pee-broh-nah-tah] Wild boar that is roasted and served in a highly spiced sauce. A local Corsican specialty.

Pic, André [A-dreh peek] (1893–1984) French chef and successful restaurateur; with Alexandre Dumaine and Fernand Point, considered one of the finest culinary masters of his time.

Picanchâgne [peek-A-shah-nyuh] A dessert composed of puff pastry filled with sliced pears and formed into a ring shape. A local Bourbonnais specialty.

Picardie [pee-kahr-dee] Picardy; a northern province bordering Normandy and the English Channel. Picardy is pehaps best known for salt-meadow sheep and Maroilles and Rollot cheeses.

Pichet [pee-shet] A serving pitcher.

Picholine [pee-shoh-leen] A French word for large green olives.

Picodon [pee-koh-dO] The collective name for various goat's-milk cheeses produced throughout France; i.e., Picodon de Dieulefit (Dauphiné), Picodon de Saint-Agrève (Languedoc), and so forth.

Picoussel [pee-koo-sel] A type of plum pancake flavored with herbs. It is a specialty of Mur-de-Barrez in Auvergne; also spelled *pique-aousel*.

Pie [pee] A dish composed of a sweet or savory filling baked in a pastry crust.

Pièce de bœuf [pyes duh buhf] The French name for the top of the rump of beef. This prime cut of meat is sometimes called *pointe de culotte*.

Pièce de résistance [+ duh reh-zees-stAs] The specialty of the chef or of the house; the climax of the dinner.

Pièces montées [+ mO-teh] A centerpiece or decoration of a banquet table.

Piech [pyesh] A veal or mutton brisket stuffed with rice and greens; from Nice.

Pied [pyeh] Foot.

Pied de cheval [+ duh shuh-vahl] A variety of large oyster.

Pieds de cedrillon [+ duh seh-dree-yO] A type of *crepinette* (sausage) made with pig's feet, mushrooms, and truffles.

Pieds de mouton [+ duh moo-to] (1) Sheep's trotters. (2) A type of wild mushroom similar to chanterelles.

Pieds de porc [+ duh pork] Pig's feet.

Pieds et paquet [+ duh pah-keh] A specialty of Marseilles featuring sheep's tripe stuffed with bacon, onions, and herbs and simmered in white wine and tomato sauce.

Piémontaise, à la [pyeh-mO-tez] "In the style of Piedmont"; indicates that white truffles are present in a dish.

Piémontaise, sauce Sauce *velouté* flavored with white truffles and enriched with anchovy butter.

Pigeon [pee-zhO] A wild or domesticated bird of excellent eating.

Pigeonneau [pee-zhyO-noh] Squab; a young, tender pigeon 3–5 weeks old.

Pignoles, sauce aux [pee-nyohl] Demi-glace sauce to which a reduction of sugar, peppercorns, and vinegar is added. The sauce is strained and garnished with pine nuts.

Pignon [pee-nyO] Pine nut; the seed of the stone pine, common in Mediterranean countries. It is eaten raw or roasted and used in sauces, charcuterie, salads, and so forth.

Pilchard [peel-shahr] A southern European sea fish related to the herring. Young pilchards (sardines) are sold canned in oil or tomato sauce; fresh pilchards are usually grilled or smoked.

Pilon [pee-lO] Pestle; a hand utensil used to pound or crush foods in a mortar.

Piment [pee-mE] Pimento or pimiento; a large, sweet red pepper.

Piment (de la Jamaïque) [+ (duh lah zhah-mah-eek)] Allspice; a spice resembling a combination of cinnamon, cloves, and nutmeg; ground from the berry of the tropical American tree *pimenta officinalis*. Also called *toute-épice* and *poivre giroflée* in France.

Piment doux [pee-mE doo] Sweet red pepper.

Pince [pIs] Tongs; a two-arm hinged serving utensil used to grasp foods; i.e., ice or sugar cubes, green salads, olives, and so forth.

Pinceau [pI-soh] A pastry brush.

Pincée [pI-seh] Pinch; an approximate measure of $1/16$ teaspoon.

Pincer [pI-seh] To brown foods in fat before adding liquid.

Pineau [pee-noh] Another name for Pinot grapes; see *Pinot*.

— *des charentes* [+ duh shahr-rEt] An aperitif from Charentes composed of wine must fortified with cognac.

Pinée [pee-neh] Fine-quality dried cod.

Pinot [pee-noh] A variety of black and white grapes used in making red Burgundy, Champagne, and white Alsatian wines.

— *blanc* [+ blA] A white grape—sometimes referred to as Klevner—used in making some white Alsatian and a small percentage of white Burgundy wines.

— *gris* [+ gri] A white grape, also called *Tokay d'Alsace*, used in the production of a small amount of white Alsatian wines.

— *meunier* [+ muh-nyeh] One of the black grapes (along with Pinot Noir) used in the production of champagne wines.

— *noir* [+ nwah] A black grape used to produce the finest red Burgundy wines. See *Pinot meunier*.

Pintade [peen-tahd] Guinea hen; a domestic bird related to and prepared like pheasant.

Pintadeau [peen-tah-doh] Young guinea hen.

Piochons [pyo-shO] A variety of green cabbage.

Piper [pee-peh] The name for sweet peppers in Béarn.

Piperade [pee-puh-rahd] A Basque specialty featuring tomatoes, onions, and sweet peppers sautéed in oil and combined with beaten eggs. Bayonne ham is often added to this famous scrambled egg dish.

Pipo créme [pee-poh krem] A blue-veined, cow's-milk cheese similar to *bleu de Bresse*.

Piquante, sauce [pee-kahnt] Demiglace sauce combined with a reduction of white wine, vinegar, onions, and shallots. The sauce is garnished with chopped gherkins and seasoned with tarragon, parsley, and chervil.

Pique-aousel [peek-ah-oo-zel] See *Picoussel*.

Pique-nique [+ neek] Picnic.

Piquer [pee-keh] To insert fat into lean pieces of meat with the aid of a special needle.

Piquette [pee-ket] A weak wine of little character.

Pirot [pee-roht] A local *poitevin* dish featuring *chevreau* (young goat) sautéed with garlic and sorrel.

Pis [pee] The meat from the underside of cattle; brisket.

Pisane, à la [pee-zahn] Describes stuffed, rolled fish garnished with spinach, anchovies, tomatoes, diced hard-cooked eggs; with *sauce Mornay.*

Pissala/Pissalat [pee-sah-lah] Anchovies ground with olive oil. Used as a condiment. See *Pissaladière.*

Pissaladière [pee-sah-lah-dyer] A famous Niçoise specialty made up of cooked onions, anchovies, black olives, and *pissala* baked in a pastry shell.

Pissenlit [pee-sahn-lee] Dandelion; a wild field plant having edible leaves that are used fresh in salads or cooked as a vegetable.

Pistache [pees-tash] Pistachio nut.

Pistache, en Prepared with garlic.

Pistole [pees-tol] A variety of plum usually dried and sold as prunes.

Pistou [pees-too] A Provençal sauce similar to pesto composed of basil and garlic pounded together with olive oil.

—, soupe au [soop oh +] A soup from Provence having several variations; essentially a vegetable soup with white beans, tomatoes, vermicelli, and seasoned with *pistou*; served with crusty bread.

Pithiviers [pee-thee-vyer] A town in Orléans famous for Pithiviers cheese and *gâteau de Pithiviers.*

— au foin [+ oh fwI] A soft Orléanais cheese made from cow's milk.

—, gâteau de [gah-toh duh +] An almond-cream tart; from Pithiviers.

Plafond [plah-fO] A copper baking pan used in former times.

Plaisir [ple-zeer] Another name for *oublie.*

Planche à découper [plA-shah dee-koo-peh] Cutting board.

Planche à hacher [+ ah-sheh] Cutting board.

Plaque à rôtir [plah-kah roh-teer] Roasting pan.

Plat-de-côte [plah-duh-koht] Corned beef; cured beef brisket preserved in brine.

Plateau [plah-toh] Tray.

Platine [plah-teen] A short-sided baking pan.

Plat principal [plah prE-see-pahl] The main dish.

Pleurote [pluhr-oht] Mushroom; an edible wild mushroom of excellent quality.

Plie [plee] Plaice; a European flatfish related to the flounder.

Plisson [plys-sO] Sweet thickened milk used as a dessert topping.

Plombières [plO-byer] An almond ice cream mixed with candied fruit and lightened with whipped cream.

Plombières, crème [krem +] Custard cream flavored with kirsch and lightened with whipped cream. Used as a filling for pastries or as a dessert topping.

Plongeur [plO-zhuhr] Pot washer.

Pluches [plüsh] The leaves of fresh herbs.

Pluvier [plü-vyeh] Plover; a small European shore bird considered excellent game.

Poché [posh] Poached; food cooked in barely simmering water.

Pocher [poh-sheh] To poach.

Pocheteau (blanc) [poh-shtoh (blA)] A French name for skate. See *Raie.*

Pochon [poh-shon] Ladle.

Pochouse [poh-hahz] See *Pauchouse.*

Poêlage [poh-el-ahzh] A method of pot roasting in which the meat is cooked in butter with vegetables in a lidded pan.

Poêle [poh-el] Frying pan.

— à crêpe [+ ah krep] Crêpe pan; a small frying pan used for making crêpes. Also called *crêpière.*

Poêle à omelette [+ ah om-let] Omelette pan.

Poêlon [poh-el-O] A small saucepan.

Pogne/Pognon [poh-nyuh/poh-nyO] In the French Alps (Dauphiné) it is a fruit or squash tart. In western Dauphiné and surrounding areas it means brioche.

Pogne de romans [+ duh roh-mA] A sweet brioche traditionally served with red currant jelly.

Poingclos [pwA-kloh] The name for *tourteau* in Brittany.

Point, à [ah pwI] (1) Applies to foods that have attained the desired temperature or doneness (particularly refers to steak cooked medium). (2) The finished dish, completely prepared and garnished.

Point de culotte [+ duh kü-luht] See *Pièce de bœuf.*

Point, Fernand [fer-nA pwI] (1897–1955) French restaurateur regarded not only as one of France's great chefs but also as a fine teacher and personality.

Pointes d'amour [+ dah-moor] Name sometimes used for asparagus tips.

Pointes d'asperge [+ dah-spehrzh] Asparagus tips.

Poirat [pwah-rah] A pear pie from central France; served with fresh cream.

Poire [pwahr] (1) Pear. (2) A lean, tender, high-quality steak from the leg of beef.

— *de curé* [+ duh kü-reh] A variety of pear also called *belle-de-Berry.*

— *William* [+ wil-yuhm] A high-quality *alcool blanc* made from the William pear.

Poiré Fermented pear juice similar to cider; the *poiré* of Normandy is famous.

Poires belle-hélène [+ bel eh-len] A famous dessert featuring vanilla ice cream topped with poached

pears and garnished with crystallized violets; coated with chocolate sauce.

Poires tapées [+ tah-peh] Dried pears.

Poireau [pwah-roh] Leek; a variety of green onion.

Pois [pwah] Peas.

— *cassés* [+ kah-seh] Split peas; small yellow or green dried peas split in half.

— *chiche* [+ sheesh] Chickpeas; large beige peas having a nutlike flavor.

Poisson [pwah-sO] The French word for fish.

— *-chat* [+ shah] Catfish.

Poissonnier [pwah-sO-nyeh] The chef in charge of preparing and cooking fish.

Poissonnerie [pwah-suhn-nree] A fish market.

Poissonnière [pwah-suhn-nyer] Fish kettle; a long, narrow, deep pan used to poach whole fish.

Poitou [pwah-too] A coastal province in western France bordering the Atlantic. Seafood, cattle, game, and dairy products (particularly butter and cheese) are of excellent quality.

Poitrine [pwah-treen] Breast; the meat from the chest area of an animal.

— *de bœuf* [+ duh buhf] Beef brisket.

— *fumée* [+ foo-meh] Smoked pork belly.

Poivrade [pwah-vrahd] Describes dishes prepared with black pepper or accompanied by *sauce poivrade.* This term sometimes refers to small artichokes seasoned only with salt.

—, *sauce* Although this name describes a variety of sauces featuring ground or whole peppercorns, it is typically demi-glace sauce seasoned with white wine, vinegar, and peppercorns.

Poivre blanc [pwah-ruh blA] White pepper; ripe peppercorns with the outer husk removed; milder then black pepper (*poive noir*).

Poivre d'ane [+ dahn] A local cheese from Provence made from goat's milk and sometimes from cow's or ewe's milk; formed in small balls and seasoned with rosemary and savory.

— A nickname in Provence for winter savory.

Poivre de cayenne [+ duh kah-yen] (1) Cayenne pepper. (2) A hot powder made from ground cayenne chili peppers.

Poivre, entrecôte au [+ oh E-truh-kot] Pepper steak; beefsteak coated with crushed peppercorns and grilled.

Poivre gris [+ gri] Gray pepper; a combination of white and black pepper.

Poivre noir [+ nwahr] Black pepper; whole peppercorns picked while green and sundried. Very pungent.

Poivre rosé [+ ro-zeh] Pink peppercorns; the dried berries from the Baies rose flower. These mildly pungent berries are not true peppercorns.

Poivrette [pwah-vret] See *Nigelle*.

Poivre vert [+ vehr] Green peppercorns; unripe peppercorns usually pickled or dried.

Poivron [pwah-vrO] Red pepper; pimento.

Poivrons doux [+ doo] Sweet peppers.

Pojarski, à la [poh-hahr-skee] (1) Chopped beef or veal mixed with bread crumbs and fried. (2) Chicken breast or salmon dredged in flour and panfried.

Polenta [poh-len-tah] A thick corn-meal porridge that can be eaten as a mush or chilled (which will cause it to firm up), sliced, and grilled. In France there are several versions of this classic Italian dish, including *panizze* (Corsica), *polente* (Nice), *milliasse* (Gascony), *gaudes* (Franche-Comté), *panisso* (Provence), and *broyo* (Béarn).

Polignac [poh-lee-nyahk] The name for various preparations that usually include mushrooms or truffles.

—, *sauce* White wine sauce flavored with mushrooms and enriched with cream.

Polka [pohl-kah] Refers to breads and pastries decorated with zigzag patterns on top representing the brisk, lively Polish dance.

Polonaise, à la [poh-loh-nez] Refers to dishes prepared with a mixture of chopped hard-cooked eggs, parsley, and fried bread crumbs. Cauliflower and asparagus are perhaps the most popular foods prepared *à la polonaise*.

Polonaise, sauce (1) Veal stock thickened with sour cream, seasoned with fennel and grated horseradish, and garnished with chopped hard-cooked eggs. (2) Demi-glace sauce combined with a red wine and vinegar reduction and garnished with raisins and chopped almonds.

Pommes [pom] Apples; the finest in France are grown in Normandy.

—, *sauce aux* Puréed apples sweetened with cinnamon sugar.

Pommes de terre [pom-duh-ter] Potatoes.

Pompadour [pO-pah-door] The name give to several food preparations in honor of Mme. de Pompadour, mistress of King Louis XIV.

—, *filets de sole* [fee-leh duh sol]

Pompadour filets de sole (cont.) Breaded panfried sole garnished with truffles and served with *sauce Choron*. Potatoes *parisienne* are a typical accompaniment.

—, *salpicon* [sahl-pee-kO +] A mixture composed of diced tongue, foie gras, mushrooms, and truffles bound with *sauce Madeira*. Used as a filling for vols-au-vent, tartlets, *croûtes*, barquettes, and so forth.

—, *sauce* White wine sauce enriched with crayfish butter and garnished with crayfish tails and truffles.

—, *tournedos* [toor-ne-doh +] Grilled tournedos topped with *sauce périgourdine* and garnished with artichoke bottoms filled with small noisette potatoes.

Pompe [pOp] The collective name for a variety of sweet or savory pastries from various parts of France.

— *à la huile* [+ ah-lah weel] A term now rarely used, synonymous with *gibassier*.

— *aux poires* [+ oh pwahr] A pear pie from Nivernais.

— *aux pommes* [+ oh pom] A dessert made with puff pastry sweetened with cinnamon sugar and filled with plums.

Pompon [pom-pom] A larger version of *pomponette*.

Pomponnette [pO-puhn-net] A very small savory turnover containing various fillings; served as an hors d'œuvre.

Pont-l'Évêque [pO-leh-vek] A soft-ripened cow's-milk cheese produced in the Pays d'Auge. It matures in special cellars whose walls are covered with a unique fungus found only in this region; one of Normandy's oldest cheeses.

Pontigny [pO-tee-nyee] Describes

fish entrées garnished with fish quenelles, mushroom caps, crayfish tails, and *sauce matelote*.

Pont-Neuf [pO-nuhf] Small puff pastry tartlets filled with frangipane cream mixed with crushed macaroons and topped with strips of pastry.

Porc [por] Pork; the meat of a pig.

Porcelet [por-seh-leh] A suckling pig up to the age of 2 months.

Porchetta [por-shet-ta] A large sausage made from the meat (all edible parts) of a young pig. The meat is combined with bread crumbs and heavily flavored with garlic; served cold.

Portefeuille, en [por-tuh-fuh-yuh] Term referring to certain dishes that are usually stuffed.

Porto [por-toh] Port; a fortified dessert wine from the Douro Valley in northern Portugal. In France it is used in numerous culinary preparations.

—, *sauce au* Demi-glace sauce flavored with Port wine and the zest of orange and lemon.

Port-salut [por-sahl-loo] A well-known French cheese created by Trappist monks in Brittany. It is made from cow's milk and has a soft, smooth texture.

Portugaise, à la [por-tü-gez] Indicates that tomatoes are used in the preparation of a dish.

Portugaise, sauce Tomato sauce reduced with veal glaze, seasoned with garlic and parsley, and finished with butter.

Pots [poh] Cooking vessels of various sizes and shapes.

Potage [po-tahzh] Soup; generally refers to puréed soups slightly thickened with egg yolks or cream. See *Soupe*.

Potager [po-tah-zheh] Soup cook.

Potagère [po-tah-zher] The name

for lamb's lettuce in parts of France; see *Mâche*.

Pot-à-oille [poh-tah-ahl] In former times it referred to a large soup pot.

Pot-au-feu [poh-tuh-fuh] A French national dish featuring meat and root vegetables slowly cooked in seasoned stock. Traditionally, the broth is eaten first; and then it is followed by the meat and vegetables.

Potée [po-teh] A dish composed of meat (traditionally pork) and vegetables that are cooked in stock in an earthenware pot. There are numerous versions of this hearty souplike dish.

Potiron [po-tee-rO] Pumpkin.

Pot-je-vleese [poh-zhe-vlees] A terrine composed of veal, rabbit, and pork. Also spelled *potjevfleisch*; a specialty of Flanders.

Pots de crème [+ duh krem] A custard dessert baked in small, lidded cups.

Pouding [poo-dI] Pudding.

Poudre, au [oh poo-druh] Powdered.

Pougnon [poo-nyo] See *Pogne*.

Pouillard [poo-yard] Young partridge.

Poularde [poo-lard] Pullet; a female chicken under one year old.

Poule [pool] Hen.

— **-au-pot** [+ oh-poh] A specialty of southwest France featuring whole chicken stuffed with Bayonne ham, chicken livers, and bread crumbs; simmered in stock with beef and vegetables.

— **sans os** [+ sA-zoh] A mixture of chicken, pork, sorrel, and wheat flour. The mixture is formed into small balls and deep-fried. A specialty of Limousin.

Poulet [poo-leh] Chicken.

— **de Bresse** [+ duh bres] Free-range, corn-fed chicken from Bresse; considered the finest in all of France.

— **de grain** [+ duh grI] A spring chicken 50–70 days old. Also called *poulet de marque* and *poulet de reine*.

— **de marque** [+ duh mahrk] See *Poulet de grain*.

— **quatre quarts** [+ kah-truh kahr] A young chicken approximately 45 days old.

— **de reine** [+ duh ren] See *Poulet de grain*.

— **au sang** [+ oh sA] Chicken simmered in red wine and seasoned stock and bound with the bird's blood.

Poulette, à la [poo-let] Describes various meat and fish dishes served with *sauce poulette*.

Poulette, sauce *Sauce allemande* enriched with whole butter and flavored with mushroom essence, lemon, and parsley.

Pouligny Saint-Pierre [pool-lee-nyee sA-pyer] A firm goat's-milk cheese from Berry.

Poulpe [poolp] Octopus; an eight-arm, soft-bodied octopod usually prepared by simmering or frying.

Pountari [poon-tah-ree] Pork forcemeat contained in cabbage or pig's caul and cooked in broth with vegetables. A specialty of Auvergne.

Pounti [poon-tee] A local dish from Auvergne composed mainly of pork and Swiss chard; baked *en casserole*.

Poupart [poo-pahr] A variety of giant crab, also known as *tourteau*.

Poupelin [poo-pe-lI] A *chou* pastry tart filled with cream Chantilly.

Poupeton [poo-pe-tO] A piece of meat or poultry that has been boned, flattened, stuffed, and rolled.

Pourriture noble [poor-ee-tür noh-bluh] Noble rot; a type of mold (*botrytis cinerea*) that appears on grapes left on the vine past the ordinary harvest time. This mold causes the grape to dehydrate, which concentrates their sugars, thus producing dessert wines (Sauterne, Barsac) of excellent quality.

Pourly [poor-lee] A soft goat's-milk cheese from the Yonne Valley in Burgundy.

Pourpier [poor-pyeh] Purslane; a plant having a thick stalk and yellow flowers. It is mainly used as a vegetable (stalk and leaves), as a salad green, or as an herb.

Pourrous negres [poor-roo neg-ruh] Dumplings made from corn and wheat flour; poached in the water in which black pudding has been cooked; a specialty of the French Basque Provinces.

Pousse-amour [poos-sah-moohr] *Pousse-café* in which an egg yolk is used as one of the layers. See *Pousse-café*.

Pousse-café [poos-kah-feh] (1) A cordial served at the end of the meal, often with coffee. (2) A fancy drink made by carefully pouring several liqueurs of various colors and densities in a special glass on top of each other without disturbing the previous layer; see *Pousse-amour*.

Pousse debout [poos duh-boo] A variety of potato.

Pousser [poos-seh] Literally "to grow"; refers to the action of yeast in bread dough.

Poussin [poo-sI] A chick.

Poutargue des martigues [poo-tahrg deh mahr-teeg] The roe from the gray mullet combined with olive oil and eaten like caviar; from Marseilles.

Poutine en nounat [poo-tee-nuh E noo-nah] A delicacy from Nice of freshly hatched fish.

Pouytrolle [pwee-trol] A local sausage-like Languedocian specialty composed of seasoned pork and greens stuffed in a casing.

Praire [prer] The name sometimes given to clams in parts of France.

Pralin [prah-lI] Praline; toasted almonds and hazelnuts combined with caramelized sugar. When the mixture is cooled, it becomes brittle and is crushed until the desired consistency is attained. Praline paste is the result of finely ground praline.

Praline [prah-leen] (1) A colored sugar coated almond. (2) A gâteau composed of génoise sponge iced with praline buttercream and garnished with hazelnuts.

Pratelle [prah-tel] A type of mushroom.

Premier cru [pruh-myeh krü] Refers to high-quality wine from specific vineyards in France. *Premier cru* wines are classified slightly lower than *Grand cru*.

Premonata [pruh-mo-nah-tuh] A local Corsican dish composed of braised beef and juniper berries.

Pré-salé [preh-sah-leh] Literally "salt-meadow," this term refers to lamb and sheep that graze in meadows close to the sea. The salty diet gives the lamb a special flavor that is much esteemed.

Presse [pres] The collective name for a variety of utensils used for puréeing or extracting juices from foods by means of a pressing action.

Presse purée [pres] Vegetable mill; a utensil used to purée cooked fruits and vegetables by forcing through small holes.

Prêtre [pret-ruh] A small, silvery sea fish.

Primeur [pree-mür] Term referring to early (young) fruits and vegetables.

Prince Albert [prIs ahl-ber] Describes beef stuffed with truffled foie gras, garnished with truffles, and served with *sauce au porto.*

Prince de Galle, garniture [+ duh gahl] (*For fish*) Oysters, mussels, rice, and crayfish tails; served with fish *velouté.*

Princesse, à la [prI-ses] Denotes that asparagus tips (and often sliced truffles) have been used in the preparation of a dish.

Princesse, sauce Béchamel sauce seasoned with chicken and mushroom essence.

Princière, sauce [prI-syer] *Sauce au vin blanc* garnished with crayfish tails and truffles.

Printanière, à la [prI-tah-nyer] Describes dishes prepared with fresh spring vegetables.

Printanière, beurre [buhr +] Puréed green vegetables incorporated into softened butter.

Printanier, sauce (1) *Sauce allemande* enriched with *printanière* butter (see *Printanière, beurre*). (2) *Sauce velouté* enriched with whole butter and garnished with fresh spring vegetables.

Prix fixe [pree feeks] See *Menu, table d'hôte.*

Prizzutu [pree-tsü-tü] A type of ham from Corsica having a slight resemblance to prosciutto.

Processor [pro-ses-suhr] A variety of snap bean (*mange-tout*).

Profiteroles [pro-fee-tuh-rol] Small hollow pastry balls made from *chou* paste stuffed with various sweet or savory fillings.

Progrès [pro-gre] A gâteau composed of almond meringue discs layered with buttercream and topped with roasted almonds.

Provençale, à la [pro-vE-sahl] "In the style of Provence"; indicates tomatoes, garlic, and olives and/ or olive oil are used in preparation of a dish.

Provençale, sauce Tomatoes, onions, and garlic sautéed in olive oil and simmered in white wine and veal stock.

Provence [pro-vEs] A coastal province bordering Italy in southeast France. One of the nations great culinary centers, Provence is the birthplace of several classic dishes, including ratatouille, *pistou*, bourride, bouillabaisse, aïoli, and *pan bagna*; see *Provençale, à la.*

Providence [pro-vee-dAs] A cow's-milk cheese made by Trappist monks near Cherbourg in Normandy.

Providence, garniture A rich garnish composed of foie gras, truffles, chicken quenelles, and olives; accompanies meat and poultry dishes.

Provins [pro-vI] A city in Champagne noted for the fine pears and Brie cheeses produced there.

Pruneau [prü-noh] Prune; a dried plum.

— *fleuri* [+ fluh-ree] A type of prune made from the Perdrigon plum. Also called *brignoles.*

Pruneaux fourrés [+ foor-reh] Refers to a variety of prune from Touraine.

Prune de la reine claude [prUn duh lah ren klohd] See *Reine Claude.*

Prunelle [prü-nel] Sloe plum; A very sour variety of plum used primarily to make jams and liqueurs.

Puant macéré [pwA mah-seh-reh] A soft cow's-milk cheese similar to Maroilles. This assertive cheese is produced mainly in Flanders.

Pudding/Pouding [poo-ding/poo-dI] A sweet or savory custard or soufflé-like dish. In former times pudding referred to boiled dishes.

Puits d'amour [pwee dah-moor] Small puff pastry rounds filled with sweet preparations such as pastry cream or jam and sprinkled with powdered sugar.

Purée [pü-reh] (1) Any food (usually cooked) that is finely mashed and sieved. The result is a thick, mushlike consistency. (2) A thick, creamy, strained soup.

Pyramide [pee-rah-meed] The collective name for certain goat cheeses shaped in the form of a pyramid, i.e., Valençay and Levroux.

Quadriller [kah-dree-yeh] Refers to foods (pastries, grilled meats, pâtés, etc.) marked with a crisscross pattern on its surface.

Quart [kahr] A version of Maroilles cheese.

Quasi [kah-zee] A rump steak of veal. Referred to a *cul-de-veau* in parts of France.

Quatre-épices [kah-truh-eh-pees] A combination of four spices including nutmeg, pepper, cloves, and cinnamon. See *Nigelle*.

Quatre-fruits rouges [+ frwee roozh] "Four red fruits"; refers to red currants, raspberries, strawberries, and cherries; used in jams and pastries.

Quatre-fruits jaune [+ frwee zhohn] "Four yellow fruits"; composed of oranges, lemons, citrons, and bitter oranges. Used in the same way as *quatre-fruits rouges*.

Quatre mendiants [+ mE-dyA] A combination of figs, nuts, raisins, and almonds. Used for a variety of sweet dishes.

Quatre-quarts [+ kahr] Term used in reference to a basic pound cake recipe made up of equal parts of flour, butter, eggs, and sugar.

Quenelle [kuh-nel] Light forcemeat dumplings made with meat or fish; formed into small ovals and poached in stock; used as a garnish or entrée.

Quercy [ker-see] A region in central France best known for its truffles.

Quetsche [kets-shuh] A variety of plum grown in Lorraine and Alsace used in tarts (*tarte aux quetsche*), jams, and liqueurs. They are also commonly dried to make prunes.

Queue [kü] Tail.

— **de bœuf** [+ duh buhf] Oxtail; the tail of an ox or steer; used in soups or braised and served as an entrée.

Quiche [keesh] A local specialty of Marseilles composed of bread slices topped with anchovies mixed with olive oil.

— A famous French dish originating in Lorraine featuring egg custard mixed with cheese, bacon, spinach, and so on; and baked in a pastry crust.

— **Lorraine** [+ lo-ren] This classic dish features a mixture of eggs, cream, bacon, and seasonings baked in a pastry shell; served as an appetizer or entrée.

Quignon [kee-nyO] See *Grignon*.

Quillet [kee-yeh] A sponge cake layered and iced with an orange-almond buttercream.

Quimperlé [kI-puhr-leh] A town in western Brittany famous for its *crêpes dentelles*.

Quinquina [kI-kee-nah] An aperitif flavored with cinchona bark or walnut leaves.

Quintal [kI-tahl] A variety of cabbage.

Rabiole [rah-byohl] A variety of turnip.

Râble [rah-bluh] Saddle; also called *selle*, this fine cut of meat (lamb, veal, venison, hare) consists of the unseparated loin extending from the last rib to the leg from both sides of the animal. The word *râble* usually refers to a saddle of hare.

Rabotte [rah-bot] (*Picardy*) Whole apples or pears wrapped in pastry and baked in the oven. Similar dishes include *douillon, bourdelot, boulaud,* and *talibur.*

Rachel, garniture [reh-chuhl] (*For grilled meats*) Artichoke hearts stuffed with poached marrow and served with *sauce bordelaise*. (*For fish*) Stuffed with a truffled fish forcemeat, asparagus tips, and cooked shrimp; served with *sauce au vin blanc*.

Rachel, sauce *Sauce normande* flavored with lobster and anchovies.

Racine [rah-seen] A French term referring to root vegetables; i.e., carrots, turnips, parsnips, beets, rutabaga, celeriac, and so forth.

Radis [rah-dee] Radish.

Rafraîchir [rah-freh-sheer] Refresh; cool. A French cooking term meaning to plunge blanched foods (typically vegetables) in ice water to stop cooking.

Ragoût [rah-goo] A thick, rich stew.

Raie [reh] Skate, ray; a large, flat winged fish commonly found in Mediterranean waters. The fins or wings are the only edible part of the fish.

— ***au beurre noir*** [+ oh buhr-nwahr] Poached skate with browned butter and capers.

Raifort [reh-for] Horseradish; an herb native to eastern Europe grown primarily for its pungent root, which is grated and used as a spice; very popular in Alsace.

—, ***sauce*** (1) Grated horseradish combined with moistened bread crumbs and heavy cream (2) *Sauce allemande* combined with grated horseradish and sour cream. (3) Demi-glace sauce flavored with grated horseradish, mustard, and vinegar.

Raiponce [reh-pOs] The word in parts of France for lamb's lettuce; see *Mâche.*

Raisin [reh-zI] Grape.

— ***sec*** [+ sek] Literally "dried grape"; raisin.

—, ***confiture de*** [kO-fee-tür duh +] Grape jam.

Raisiné [reh-zee-neh] A type of jam famous in Burgundy made from concentrated grape juice and fruit.

Raisins de malaga [+ duh mah-lah-gah] Raisins made from muscat grapes.

Raisins de table [+ duh tah-bluh] Refers to sweet grapes suitable for serving as a dessert.

Raite [reht] See *Rayte.*

Raïto [reh-toh] See *Rayte.*

Raiton [reh-tO] A small variety of skate. See *Raie.*

Râle [rahl] A type of game bird similar to the quail and considered a great delicacy in France.

Rambour(g) [rahm-boor(g)] A French variety of apple.

Ramequin [rah-muh-kI] Ramekin; a small, round earthenware baking dish used to serve soufflés, eggs, gratins, and so forth. In former times the word *ramekin* referred to a baked cheese dish or a small cheese-filled pastry.

Ramereau [rah-muh-roh] See *Ramier.*

Ramier [rah-myeh] Wood pigeon; a variety of pigeon highly regarded in France. Also called *ramereau* and *palombe.*

VOCABULARY

Râpe [rah-peh] Grater; a utensil of various shapes and sizes used to grate foods.

Raphael, garniture [rah-fah-el] (*For grilled meats*) Artichoke bottoms filled with diced carrots; shoestring potatoes; served with béarnaise sauce.

Rascasse [rahs-kahs] A spiny, ugly fish found in the Mediterranean; also known as *crapaud, truie de mer, diable de mer,* and *capone* (Corsica); essential to an authentic bouillabaisse.

Ratafia [rah-tah-fee-ah] An aperitif liqueur combining must and brandy; also a sweetened liqueur flavored with fruits or plants.

Ratatouia [rah-tah-too-yah] The name sometimes given to ratatouille in Nice; see *Ratatouille niçoise.*

Ratatouille [rah-tah-too-ee] A famous vegetable stew from Provence. Eggplant, summer squash, onions, and tomatoes seasoned with garlic and olive oil comprise a typical ratatouille.

— **niçoise** [+ nee-swahz] Ratatouille prepared with green peppers.

Raton [rah-tO] (1) Pastry dough combined with cream cheese (2) A small tart filled with sweetened cream cheese.

Rave [rahv] Refers to root vegetables such as turnips, radishes and rutabagas. See *Racine.*

Ravier [rah-vyeh] A dish used to serve hors d'œuvres.

Ravigote, beurre [buhr rah-vee-got] Parsley, tarragon, burnet, chervil, and chives blanched and incorporated with softened butter. It is also known as *beurre Chivry.*

Ravigote, sauce (1) (*Hot*) Sauce *velouté* flavored with a reduction of white wine and vinegar and enriched with *ravigote* butter. (2) (*Cold*) Oil and vinegar mixed with parsley, chervil, capers, tarragon, gherkins, onions, and chopped hard-cooked eggs.

Ravioli/Raviolle [rah-vyoh-lee/rah-vyohl] The French version of the Italian ravioli; small stuffed pasta dumplings. In Nice, it is stuffed with spinach; in Corsica, chopped herbs and Broccio cheese.

Rayte [reht] A type of relish made from tomatoes, garlic, walnuts, capers, and black olives simmered in red wine and seasoned with rosemary and fennel. Typically accompanies fish dishes. Also know as *raite* and *raïto.*

Reblochon [ruh-blo-shO] A soft, centuries old cow's-milk cheese produced in the moutains of Savoy.

Réchaud [reh-shoh] A small, portable, one- or two-burner heating unit used on a gueridon for tableside cooking.

Récollet (de gérardmer) [reh-kohl-leh duh zheh-rahrd-mehr] A French cow's-milk cheese from the Vosges in eastern France; first produced by the Récollet monks.

Recuite [ruh-kweet] The French version of the Italian ricotta; a fresh, cow's-milk cheese.

Réduire [reh-dweer] To reduce; refers to boiling down a stock or sauce until the desired flavor and consistency is attained.

Réforme, à la [reh-fohrm] Describes lamb or veal cutlets coated with bread crumbs and panfried; garnished with chopped ham and served with *sauce réforme.*

Réforme, sauce Sauce *poivrade* to which julienned truffles, hard-cooked egg whites, diced mushrooms, pickled ox-tongue, and chopped gherkins are added.

Régalade, à la [reh-gah-lahd] To drink a beverage without letting the bottle touch the lips.

Régence [reh-zhAs] The name given to several culinary preparations named after the regency period in France (1715–1723).

—, *garniture* [reh-zhAs] (*For fish*) Poached oysters, fish quenelles, truffles, roe, and *sauce normande*. (*For meat*) Chicken quenelles, mushroom caps, sliced truffle, foie gras, cockscombs, and *sauce allemande*.

—, *potage crème* [po-tahzh krem +] Cream of chicken soup combined with a purée of foie gras and garnished with sliced tongue and chopped chicken breast. A splash of kummel finishes the soup.

—, *sauce* (1) Demi-glace sauce flavored with truffle essence and white wine. (2) *Sauce normande* garnished with mushrooms and truffles and flavored with white wine. (3) Demi-glace sauce reduced with white wine and garnished with diced mushrooms and truffles.

Regina, garniture [ruh-zhee-nah] (*For meat dishes*) Mushroom caps, tomatoes stuffed with rice; green peppers.

Réglisse [reh-glees] Licorice; the dried root or extract taken from the licorice plant. Licorice grows wild throughout southern Europe and is used to flavor candies, medicines, liqueurs, and so forth.

Reguigneu [ruh-gwee-nyuh] (*Province*) (1) Sliced pork dipped in egg and panfried. (2) A bacon omelette.

Reims [rI] A city in Champagne noted for *nonnettes* (gingerbread cakes).

—, *biscuit de* [bees-kwee duh +] A small crisp vanilla-flavored cookie.

Reine [ren] A chicken weighing approimately four pounds.

—, *garniture à la* (*For poultry dishes*) Truffled chicken quenelles coated with suprême sauce.

—, *sauce à la* Suprême sauce combined with whipped cream and diced chicken.

Reine, à la (1) This term—named in honor of the daughter of Catherine de Médicis and Henry II—indicates that chicken is the featured ingredient in a dish. (2) A type of bread roll.

Reine Claude [+ klohd] A sweet, yellowish-green skinned plum; also referred to as *prune de la reine Claude*.

Réjane, garniture [reh-jahn] Duchess potato nests, blanched spinach, artichoke hearts, asparagus tips, and poached marrow; served with various entrées.

Relâcher [ruh-lah-heh] To thin out a sauce, purée, and so on, by adding liquid.

Relevé [ruh-lah-veh] (1) A French dining term, refers to the dish served just prior to the entrée. (2) Spicy.

Reliefs [ruh-leefs] The term used in France referring to the food leftover on the table after a meal.

Religieuse [ruh-lee-zhuhz] (1) A cake constructed of small round pastry (*chou*) balls filled with chocolate pastry cream and stacked upon each other in the form of a pyramid. (2) A tart filled with apple and apricot jam with currants; covered with strips of pastry arranged in a latticed pattern.

Religieuse, la The crust remaining on the bottom of a Swiss fondue.

Remonter [ruh-mO-teh] (1) Term meaning to add seasonings to a sauce, stew, and so on. (2) To fortify wine by adding alcohol.

Rémoulade, sauce [ruh-moo-lahd] Mayonnaise sauce combined with mustard, capers, gherkins, anchovies, and chopped hard-cooked eggs; seasoned with chervil and tarragon.

Renaissance, à la [reh-nuh-sAs] (*For meat and poultry*) Assorted vegetables and panfried potatoes; served with hollandaise or suprême sauce.

Rennes [ren] A town in Brittany famous for Maingaux cheese and *boudin blanc.*

Repère [ruh-pehr] A mixture of egg white and flour used to adhere decorations onto certain foods; see *Lut.*

Reposer [ruh-poh-seh] "To rest"; refers to certain foods that must be left alone for a short period of time to improve quality. Bread dough should be allowed to rest after mixing to relax the gluten; roasted meat should rest to allow the juices to settle.

Réserve [reh-serv] Term referring to wines of good quality.

Restes [rest] The French word for leftovers.

Restaurant [res-toh-rA] An establishment serving food to customers. In 1765, in Paris, Boulanger opened what is considered to be the first restaurant. In 1782, Antoine Beauvilliers opened La Grande Taverne de Londres in Paris, regarded as the first modern restaurant.

Réveillon [reh-veh-yO] The traditional Christmas or New Year's supper eaten in the early morning after Midnight Mass.

Revenir (faire) [ruh-vuh-neer (fehr)] To brown ingredients in butter.

Reverdir [ruh-vehr-deer] In former times this term referred to bringing back the color of green vegetables lost during blanching by placing the vegetables in a copper sulphate solution.

Revesset [ruh-ves-seh] A fish stew from Toulon (*Provence*) featuring sardines, anchovies, and other small coastal fish; green leafy vegetables are also characteristic of the dish.

Reynière [reh-nyer] A garnish for poultry dishes composed of glazed chestnuts, veal kidneys, and small sausages. Served with *sauce Madeira.*

Rhin, vins du [vIs dü rI] Rhine wines.

Rhône, côtes du [koht dü rOn] A 140-mile strip of wine-growing country situated between Lyon and Avignon in southern France producing several fine wines.

Rhubarbe [rü-bahrb] Rhubarb; a perennial plant native to Asia and having edible stalks that are used in making jams, pies, and compotes.

Rhum [rom] Rum; a spirit distilled from the fermented juice of cane syrup, molasses, or sugarcane.

Riceys Cendré [ree-see sE-dreh] A type of cheese ripened in vegetable ash. Also called *Champenois.*

Riche, à la [reesh] (1) A garnish for various meats comprised of sliced truffles, foie gras, quartered artichoke bottoms, and asparagus tips. (2) Describes fish garnished with sliced lobster tail and truffles and served with *sauce Victoria.*

Riche, sauce (1) *Sauce normande* with diced truffles and enriched with lobster butter. (2) Fish *velouté* cooked with mushrooms and oysters; enriched with egg yolks and cream.

Richebourg [reesh-boorg] A highly regarded *grand cru* red wine from Burgundy.

Richelieu [reesh-lyuh] A gâteau made of almond sponge layered with frangipane cream and apricot jam; covered with fondant and decorated with candied fruit.

Richelieu A fruit preparation consisting of semolina pudding (*see Flamri*) topped with sliced peaches and cream Chantilly; served with frangipane cream and apricot sauce.

Richelieu, à la A garnish for meat dishes made of stuffed tomatoes and mushrooms, braised lettuce, and château potatoes.

Richelieu, sauce *Sauce allemande* garnished with sautéed onions and seasoned with sugar, nutmeg, and pepper; finished with chervil butter.

Riesling [rees-ling] A white-wine grape usually associated with the great German whites; it is also used to produce the finest white wines of Alsace.

Rigadelle [ree-gah-del] The word for clam in parts of France along the Atlantic coast.

Rigodon [ree-gah-dO] (1) A type of crustless quiche usually containing ham or bacon; a specialty of Burgundy. (2) A type of bread pudding.

Rigotte [ree-got] The name for small, soft, round cheeses origionally made from goat's milk but now from a combination of goat's and cow's milk.

— **des Alpes** [+ deh ahlps] A type of cheese from Dauphiné similar to *rigotte de Condrieu*.

— **de Condrieu** [+ duh kO-dree-uh] A cheese from Lyon. See *Rigotte*.

— **de pelussin** [+ duh puh-lü-sI] A cheese from Auvergne. See *Rigotte*.

Rillauds [ree-yoh] A specialty from Anjou composed of cubed lean and fat pieces of pork slowly cooked in lard. Served hot or cold.

Rillettes [ree-yet] Tender, well-cooked pork shredded and mixed with pork fat until smooth. Used as a spread or condiment. *Rillettes* can also be made from poultry, rabbit, or goose; served cold.

— **d'Angers** [+ duh a-zhehr] a version of rillettes from angers (Anjou) made from pork belly and breast.

— **de Le Mans** [+ duh luh mAz] *Rillettes* from Le Mans made from pork shoulder cooked in goose fat.

— **de Tours** [+ duh toor] One of the most famous dishes from Touraine made from pork shoulder; noted throughout France for its quality.

Rillons [ree-yO] (Touraine) Pork pieces browned in lard with caramel. Very similar to *rillettes*.

Rimotte [ree-muht] A polenta-like dish from Périgord made with cornmeal. The cooked mixture is chilled and cut into squares; served as an entrée or side dish or sweetened for a dessert.

Rince-doigts [rIs-dwah] Finger bowl; a small bowl of warm water that is used by the guest to rinse his/her fingers at the table.

Rincette [rI-set] The French term for a shot of brandy poured into an empty coffee cup. The still warm cup helps release the brandy's bouquet.

Rioler [ree-yoh-leh] To arrange pastry strips in a lattice pattern on the top of a pie, tart, and so forth.

Ris [ree] Sweetbread; the thymus gland of lambs, pigs, and calves. Calf's sweetbreads (*ris de veau*) are considered the finest.

Rissole [ree-soh-leh] Small, deep-fried pastry turnovers containing various sweet or savory fillings.

— *de bugey* [+ duh bü-zhee] Small turkey and tripe pies traditionally served at Christmas.

Rissoler [ree-soh-leh] To brown.

Riz [ree] Rice.

Rob [rob] Fruit juice thickened by evaporation.

Robert, sauce [roh-ber] Sautéed onions, white wine, and vinegar reduced together and combined with demi-glace sauce; finished with prepared mustard and strained.

Robinson [roh-bI-sO] A garnish for various entrées made up of artichoke bottoms filled with chicken livers and topped with *sauce Madeira*.

Rocamadour [roh-kah-mah-door] A goat's- or ewe's-milk cheese from a town of the same name in Quercy. This small, round cheese is often wrapped in leaves.

Rocambole [roh-kahm-bohl] A variety of garlic grown in France.

Rochambeau [roh-shA-boh] A garnish composed of duchess potato nests with various fillings; Vichy carrots, braised lettuce, cauliflower *à la polonaise*, and anna potatoes.

Rocher [roh-sheh] A broad term for a pastry or candy having a coarse rocklike texture or appearance.

— *de glace* [+ duh glahs] A dessert concoction made up of chocolate, vanilla, pistachio, and strawberry ice creams layered in a mold and coated with sweetened whipped cream. The end product resembles a rock.

Rocquencourt [roh-kE-koor] A variety of *mange-tout* (snap beans).

Rognonnade [roh-nyO-nahd] A veal loin that still contains the attached kidney.

Rognons [ro-nyO] Kidneys.

Rognures [ro-nyür] Puff pastry trimmings; used to prepare *demi-feuilletée.*

Rohan, à la [ro-ahn] A rich garnish for poultry dishes composed of artichoke bottoms filled with foie gras and meat glaze; cockscombs and kidneys coated with *sauce allemande* in pastry cases.

Rollot [ro-yoh] A cylindrical or heart-shaped cheese from Picardy. This soft, full-flavored cheese is made from cow's milk.

Romaine, à la [ro-men] The name given to several dishes prepared in the style of Rome and the Lazio region.

Romaine, garniture (*For large roasts*) Chicken and spinach quenelles and gnocchi au gratin; served with tomato sauce.

Romaine, sauce Demi-glace sauce made with game stock combined with vinegar and slightly caramelized sugar; garnished with pine nuts, sultanas, and currants.

Romalour [ro-mah-loor] A type of cheese from the Loire region.

Romanée-conti [ro-mah-neh-kO-tee] An exceptional red AOC wine from the Vosne-Romanée in Burgundy.

Romanov [ro-mah-nahf] A garnish for large joints featuring cucumbers filled with duxelles, duchess potato nests filled with diced mushrooms, and celeriac bound with *sauce raifort.*

Romanov A preparation for strawberries in which the fruit is soaked in Curacao and topped with cream Chantilly.

Romarin [ro-mah-rI] Rosemary; an evergreen shrub whose aromatic leaves are used as an herb.

Rombu [rO-bü] A French nickname for turbot.

Romsteck [rO-stek] Rumpsteak; also spelled *rumsteck.*

Roncin [rO-sI] A type of bread pudding mixed with cherries; from Franche-Comté.

Rondeau [rO-doh] A wide, shallow, straight-sided pan with two handles.

Roquefort [rok-for] A blue-veined sheep's-milk cheese from Roquefort-sur-Soulzon in the Rouergue area of southern France. It is one of the world's oldest and greatest cheeses and is characterized by its sharp, salty taste and creamy texture.

Roquette [roh-ket] Rocket (*arugula*); a bitter, aromatic salad green from a Mediterranean shrub.

Roquevaire [roh-kuh-ver] A type of fortified wine from Roquevaire; in the Bôuches du Rhône.

Roquille [roh-kee-yuh] A French term for orange peel.

Rosbif [ros-beef] Roast beef.

Rosé [ro-seh] Pink.

Rose [rohs] A prickly-stemmed ornate flower. The petals can be candied or used as a flavoring in pastries and confections.

Roseberry [roz-behr-ree] A descriptive term for various meat dishes garnished with ravioli stuffed with duxelles; stuffed tomatoes, cucumbers, and French beans.

Rose chéri [+ cheh-ree] A dessert preparation featuring pineapple ice cream topped with sliced peaches and champagne-flavored custard; garnished with candied rose petals.

Roses nuées [+ nü-ehz] Sweetened whipped cream flavored with vanilla and strawberry purée; served as a dessert.

Rosette [ro-zet] A hard pork sausage from the Beaujolais region in southern Burgundy.

— *de Lyon* [+ duh lyO] A hard pork sausage of superior quality from Lyon.

Rosé, vin [vI +] Pink wine; produced from black grapes that are fermented on their skins for a certain period of time.

Rossini [ros-see-nee] Denotes that foie gras, truffles, and demi-glace sauce are main components of a dish; named after the great Italian composer Gioacchino Rossini.

—, *tournedos* [toor-ne-doh +] A famous dish featuring tournedos arranged on fried bread rounds and topped with foie gras and truffle slices; with demi-glace sauce.

Rostand [ros-tA] (*For tournedos and noisettes*) Quartered artichoke hearts, creamed mushrooms; served with *sauce Colbert*.

Rôt [roh] A term used in former times meaning roast.

Rothschild [roths-chah-yuhld] The name given to several culinary preparations after Baron de Rothschild.

—, *consommé* [kO-suh-meh] Pheasant consommé garnished with chestnut *royal*, sliced truffle, and a julienne of pheasant breast.

—, *huîtres à la* [wee-truh ah-lah +] Oysters wrapped in bacon and skewered; broiled.

—, *soufflé* [soof-fleh] A soufflé mixture (milk, flour, sugar, egg whites) flavored with candied fruit and Danziger Goldwasser; garnished with strawberries.

Rôti [ro-tee] Roast; (1) Meat cooked in the oven. (2) The actual piece of meat cooked in the oven.

Rôtie [ro-tee] Toast; a slice of grilled bread.

Rôtir [ro-teer] To roast.

Rôtisserie [ro-tees-sree] (1) A kitchen appliance that slowly rotates food (on a spit) over live flames or intense heat. (2) An area of the kitchen where roasted meats are cooked.

Rotisseur [ro-tee-suhr] In the classic kitchen brigade, the *rotisseur* is the cook in charge of roasting, frying, and grilling.

Rouelle [roo-el] A thick slice of veal cut across the leg.

Rouen [roo-E] A city in eastern Normandy having the reputation for excellent dining. Duck and foie gras from Rouen are exceptional.

Rouennaise, à la [roo-E-nez] A term indicating that duck or duck liver is featured in a dish; named for the city of Rouen, regarded as having the finest ducks in France.

Rouennaise, sauce Sauce *bordelaise* with the addition of red wine and duck liver purée; seasoned with cayenne pepper and lemon juice.

Rouergue [roo-uhrg] An area in southeast France in the department of Aveyron; famous for Roquefort cheese.

Rouge [roozh] Red.

—, *chou* [+ shoo] Red Cabbage.

Rougemont, sauce [roozh-mO] Mayonnaise sauce seasoned with tarragon.

Rouge de rivière [roozh duh ree-vyer] Shoveler duck; a wild duck of excellent eating quality. Also called *souchet.*

Rouget (de roche) [roozheh (duh rohsh)] Red mullet; a lean, firm-fleshed Mediterranean fish popular in France and the rest of Europe.

Rouille [roo-ee-yuh] A spicy condiment made from crushed garlic and red chili peppers combined with bread crumbs, fish stock, and olive oil. Traditionally served with bouillabaisse; from Provence.

Roulade [roo-lahd] Thin slices of pork or veal stuffed with various forcemeats and rolled.

Roumanille [roo-mah-nee-yuh] A

descriptive term for tournedos and noisettes garnished with anchovies fillets, pitted olives, sliced eggplant, and tomatoes; topped with *sauce Mornay.*

Roussette [roo-zet] (Périgord) A deep-fried corn fritter; (Beauce) A fritter flavored with orange and brandy.

Roussette, petite [puh-teet +] See *Saumonette.*

Roussillon [roo-see-yO] A region in Languedoc bordering Spain and the Mediterranean; represents the southernmost point in mainland France. Seafood and game make up a large part of this region's cuisine.

Roussir [roo-seer] To brown (usually meat) in butter.

Rouville [roo-vee-yuh] A variety of large, sweet pear; also known as *Martin-sire.*

Roux [roo] A mixture of equal parts of flour and butter or oil cooked slowly over low heat; used to thicken soups, stews, sauces, and so on.

— *blanc* [+ blA] White roux; roux cooked for a minimum amount of time in order to retain its white color.

— *blond* [+ blOd] Roux cooked to a golden brown color.

— *brun* [+ brU] Brown roux; roux cooked until a deep brown color is achieved.

Royale [roh-yahl] A custard made from consommé, eggs, and seasonings. It is typically cut into decorative shapes and used to garnish clear soups.

—, *à la* (1) Describes clear soups garnished with *royale.* (2) Describes dishes served with *sauce royale.* (3) A term applied to dishes prepared or garnished with fancy and/or expensive ingredients.

Royale, glace [glahs] "Royal icing"; pastry frosting made from confectioners sugar and egg whites.

Royale, sauce *Sauce velouté* enriched with cream and garnished with truffles.

Royans [roh-yA] A word used in the Charentes for sprats; a small sardinelike fish related to the herring. Sprats can be broiled or grilled and are available smoked, salted, or preserved.

Rubens, sauce [rü-bE] Hollandaise sauce made with fish stock and flavored with anchovy essence. Garnished with crayfish tails.

Rubis, sauce [rü-bee] (1) *Sauce velouté* flavored and colored with port wine and the juice of blood oranges. (2) Mayonnaise sauce combined with tomato purée.

Ruifard [rwee-fahr] A dessert tart from southeast France featuring apples, quinces, and pears; flavored with Chartreuse.

Rumsteck [rU-stek] See *Romsteck*.

Russe [rüs] A round lidded stew pan.

Russe, à la Describes a number of dishes prepared in the style of Russia; indicates that ingredients such as cucumbers, gherkins, herring, kasha, potatoes, and caviar are present in a dish.

Russe, salade [sah-lahd +] Diced carrots, turnips, mushrooms, French beans, and gherkins bound with mayonnaise sauce; garnished with truffle slices, lobster meat, caviar, tongue, and hard-cooked eggs.

Russe, sauce (1) *Sauce velouté* combined with sour cream and grated horseradish; seasoned with tarragon. (2) Lobster coral and caviar combined with mayonnaise sauce and seasoned with mustard. (3) Mayonnaise sauce combined with aspic jelly and vinegar. Used to bind macedoine vegetables.

Sabardin [sah-bahr-dI] A type of sausage made from pig's offal and ox intestines; a specialty from central France.

Sabayon [sah-bah-yO] The French version of the classic Italian dessert zabaglione; made by whisking egg yolks, wine, and sugar over simmering water or low heat until it becomes thick and frothy.

Sabayon, (sauces) This term refers to sauces made without roux and thickened with beaten egg yolks. Such sauces are light and frothy and are typically served with seafood.

Sablé [sah-bleh] A crunchy butter cookie often spread with jam and powered sugar.

Sabodet [sah-boh-deh] A type of sausage from central France (Dauphiné, Lyon) made from pig's head, tongue, and fatty meat.

Sacristain [sah-krees-tI] A twisted strip of sweetened puff pastry.

Safran [sah-frahn] Saffron; an expensive spice consisting of the dried, orange-yellow stigmas from a variety of crocus (*crocus sativus*); used to flavor and tint foods and is an essential ingredient in such dishes as bouillabaisse, risotto, and paella.

Sagan [sah-gahn] Describes various meats garnished with risotto, mushrooms stuffed with calf's brains, and sliced truffles; with *sauce Madeira*.

Sagou [sah-goo] Sago; the extracted starch from the sago palm. The granules are used as a thickener or in puddings and other desserts.

Sagourne [sah-goor-nuh] Fried pancreas; a specialty of Tours.

Sagranada [sah-grah-nah-dah] A hearty bean stew from western

VOCABULARY

Sagranada (cont.)
France made with garlic, potatoes, tomatoes, and salt pork; also spelled *saugrenée*.

Saignant [sA-nyahn] Literally "bloody," this term refers to steak cooked rare.

Saigneux [sA-nyuh] Term referring to the the neck of veal or mutton.

Saindoux [sA-doo] Lard; rendered pork fat used in cooking.

Saint Agathon [sI-tah-gah-thO] A type of cheese from Brittany.

Saint André [sI-tA-dreh] (1) A garnish for panfried fish consisting of sorrel purée, hard-cooked eggs, chopped parsley, and beurre noir. (2) A rich, creamy, French triple-cream cheese made from cow's milk.

Saint-Cloud [sI-kloo] A garnish for various meats composed of French peas, braised lettuce, and *sauce Madeira*.

—, sauce Tomato sauce infused with fresh tarragon.

Sainte-Alliance, à la [sEtah-lee-yAs] Refers to certain dishes garnished with truffles and foie gras. Also describes a dish of pheasant stuffed with woodcock purée.

Saint Florentin [sI floh-rE-tI] A soft, cow's-milk cheese from Burgundy often compared to Coulommiers.

—, garniture Describes dishes garnished with St. Florentin potatoes and morels in *sauce bordeaux;* with *sauce bonnefoy.*

—, pommes de terre [pom-duh ter +] Mashed potatoes seasoned with chopped ham; dipped in egg, coated with crushed noodles, and deep-fried.

Saint-Germain [sI-zhuhr-mI] This term denotes the use of green peas in a preparation.

Saint-Germain, consommé Beef consommé garnished with green peas, braised lettuce, and small chicken quenelles.

Saint-Germain, potage A famous green pea soup.

Saint-Henri [sI-tE-ree] The descriptive term for fried fish served with brown butter and garnished with *purée d'oursin.*

Saint-Honoré, gâteau [gah-toh sE-toh-noh-reh] A rich cake consisting of a thin round cake base bordered with glazed puff pastry balls (that form the walls of the cake); the center is filled with *crême Chiboust* and topped with caramelized sugar.

Saint-Hubert [sI-tü-ber] This term usually indicates that a dish has been prepared with a purée of game.

Saint Jacques [sI zhahk] Scallop; See *Coquilles.*

Saint-Lambert, garniture [sI lA-behr] (*For various meats*) Cauliflower florettes, glazed onions and carrots, green peas, and French beans.

Saint-Malo, sauce [sI-mah-loh] Fish *velouté* combined with white wine and shallots; finished with prepared mustard and anchovy purée.

Saint-Mandé [sI-mA-deh] A garnish for grilled meats composed of Macaire potatoes, green peas, and French beans.

Saint-Marc [sI-mahrk] Describes game garnished with chestnut quenelles and served with demi-glace sauce that has been flavored with juniper berries.

Saint-Marcellin [sI-mahr-sel-lI] A soft, goat's- and/or cow's-milk cheese from Dauphiné. At one time, St. Marcellin was one of the great goat cheeses of France.

Sainte-Maure [sI-mohr] A soft, creamy, goat's-milk cheese from Touraine.

Saint Menehould, sauce [sI muh-neh-hool] Béchamel sauce flavored with *glace de viande* and garnished with parsley and mushrooms.

Saint-Nazaire, garniture [sI-nah-zehr] A *salpicon* of oysters and lobster bound in white wine sauce and contained in puff pastry shells; accompanies various fish dishes.

Saint-Nectaire [sI-nek-tehr] A highly regarded semisoft cheese made from cow's milk from a town of the same name in Auvergne. French law strictly regulates its production.

Saint-Paulin [sI-poh-lI] A smooth, mild, pasteurized cheese produced in several areas of France.

Saint Pierre [sI pyer] John Dory; a firm-fleshed sea fish; a classic ingredient in bouillabaisse.

Saint Rémi [sI reh-mee] A soft cheese from the Franche-Comté and Savoy; similar to Pont l'Evêque.

Saint Saens [sI sah-en] A descriptive term for chicken *suprêmes* garnished with truffled foie gras croquettes, cockscombs and kidneys, and asparagus tips; served with suprême sauce that has been flavored with truffles.

Saintonge [sE-rtOzh] A coastal region in western France; together with Aunis and Angoumois, it makes up the Charente region; Saintonge is well known in France for the nectarines grown there as well as such dishes as *gigorit* and *farée*.

Saisir [seh-zeer] To quickly sear or brown foods.

Salade [sah-lahd] Salad.

Saladier Salad bowl.

Saladier lyonnais [sah-lah-dyer lyuhn-nez] A salad specialty of Lyon featuring poached sheep trotters, chicken livers, and pickled herring tossed with Dijon mustard, oil, and vinegar; garnished with hard-cooked eggs and fresh herbs.

Salaison [sah-leh-zO] To preserve foods by salting or soaking in brine.

Salamandre [sah-lah-mA-druh] "Salamander"; (1) A type of oven or grill that supplies intense overhead heat allowing foods to brown quickly. (2) An iron rod heated until red-hot. Held close to foods, the rod quickly browns the surface.

Salambô [sah-lA-boh] A small *chou* cake filled with *crème pâtissière* and glazed with fondant icing; garnished with chocolate sprinkles and/or pistachio nuts.

Salé [sah-leh] Salty

Salers [sah-leh] A strong, firm, cow's-milk cheese from Auvergne.

Salicoque [sah-lee-kohk] A local name for prawns in parts of the Charente region and Normandy.

Salière [sah-lyer] Salt shaker.

Salle à manger [sahl-la mA-zheh] Dining room.

Salmigondis [sahl-muh-gO-dee] (1) A ragoût of game, chicken and anchovy fillets in a spicy sauce. (2) A combination of leftover meats reheated in sauce.

Salmigondis (salade) [+ (sah-lahd)] A salad consisting of diced carrots, eggplant, potatoes, peas, beans, chicken, and fresh herbs tossed in olive oil and seasoned; bound with mayonnaise sauce and arranged on a bed of lettuce.

Salmis [sahl-mee] Any game stew, although typically it refers to a bird game stew.

—, *sauce* A heavily reduced game stock combined with demi-glace sauce and flavored with mushroom and truffle essence.

Salon de thé [sah-lO duh teh] Tea shop; a type of café offering coffee, tea, and pastries.

Salpicon [sahl-pee-kO] One or more ingredients finely chopped and bound with a sauce; commonly used as a stuffing, garnish, hors d'œuvre, and so on.

Salsifis [sahl-see-fee] Salsify; a root vegetable, also called oyster plant because of its slight oyster flavor.

Samaritaine, à la [sah-mah-ree-ten] Describes large roasts garnished with braised lettuce, dauphiné potatoes, and rice timbales; served with demi-glace sauce.

Sanciau [sA-syoh] A large, thick pancake or fritter typical of French country cooking. Common in several parts of France.

Sandre [sahn-druh] Pike perch; a large freshwater fish prepared similar to pike or perch; related to the perch.

Sang [sA] Blood.

Sangler [sA-gleh] To chill or temporarily preserve certain frozen preparations by packing in ice and salt.

Sanglier [sA-glyeh] Wild boar.

Sanguet [sA-gweh] Also *sanguette*; see *Sanguine*.

Sanguin [sA-ghI] A variety of wild mushroom brown in color and possessing a hearty, beefy flavor.

Sanguine [sA-gheen] Blood orange; a type of orange with deep red flesh.

Sanguine A French country dish composed of coagulated chicken blood sliced and fried like a pancake in goose fat. Various spellings include *sanguet* and *sanquette*.

Sanquin [sA-kI] Also *sanquine*; see *Sanguine*.

Sans-Gêne [sA-zhen] The nickname for the wife of M. Lefebre—an officer in Napoleon's army—and name for certain culinary preparations.

—, *consommé* [kO-suh-meh +] Chicken consommé garnished with cockscombs and kidneys and truffles.

—, *œufs* [uhf +] Poached eggs topped with sliced marrow and garnished with artichoke hearts; coated with *sauce bordelaise* flavored with tarragon.

Sansiot [sA-soh] Calf's head.

Sapinette [sah-pee-net] A homemade alcoholic beverage made in parts of France from the flower of certain fir trees.

Sarah Bernhardt [sah-rah bern-hahrt] (1845–1923) World-famous French actress and an inspiration for several culinary dishes.

—, *filets de sole* [fee-leh duh sol +] Rolled fillets of sole poached in seasoned broth and garnished with carrots and truffles; coated with *sauce vénitienne*.

—, *potage* [po-tahzh] Chicken consommé thickened with tapioca and garnished with sliced marrow, asparagus tips, chicken quenelles, and truffles.

Sarcelle [sahr-sel] Teal; a small wild duck found in France.

Sard [sahr] See *Lou sar*.

Sarde, à la [sahrd] Describes grilled meats garnished with rice croquettes seasoned with saffron, stuffed tomatoes, and braised cucumbers; with tomato demi-glace. Sautéed mushrooms and French beans replace the tomato and cucumber in a variation of this garnish.

Sardine [sahr-deen] A small, silvery, saltwater fish related to the herring that was once heavily fished in Sardinia. This versatile fish may be fried, grilled, or broiled and is sold fresh, salted, smoked, and canned.

Sargue [sahrg] A saltwater fish related to the sea bream and prepared in similar fashion.

Sarladaise, à la [sahr-lah-dahz] Describes meat dishes, particularly lamb and mutton, garnished with *pommes de terre à la sarladaise.*

Sarladaise, pommes de terre à la [pom-duh-ter +] Sliced raw potatoes and truffles panfried in butter.

Sarladaise, sauce A cold emulsion sauce made by incorporating oil into a mixture of (hard-cooked) egg yolk and cream. The mayonnaise-like sauce is flavored with chopped truffles and Armagnac.

Sarrasin [sah-rah-sI] Buckwheat.

Sarrasine, à la A garnish for large cuts of beef featuring small buckwheat (*sarrasin*) pancakes.

Sarriette [sah-ryet] Savory; an aromatic, menthaceous herb resembling a cross between mint and thyme, of which there are two species. Summer savory is used in soups, salads, meat, and bean dishes; winter savory is used mainly to flavor marinades and soft cheeses.

Sartadagnano [sahr-tah-dah-nyoh] Whitebait combined with olive oil and worked into a paste. The mixture is then panfried like a pancake and served with hot vinegar. A specialty of Nice.

Sartagnado/Sartagnano [sahr-tah-nyah-doh/sahr-tah-nyah-noh] See *Sartadagnano.*

Sassenage [sah-sen-nazh] A semihard, blue-veined cheese made in the Isère valley of Dauphiné.

Sasser [sah-seh] To clean thin-skinned vegetables by wrapping them in a towel with salt and rubbing. This method of cleaning vegetables is now rarely used.

Sauce [sohs] A seasoned liquid used to enhance the flavor of the dish it accompanies.

Sauciaux [soh-syoh] The name for *sanciau* in parts of central France. See *Sanciau.*

Saucier [soh-syeh] The chef in charge of preparing the sauces.

Saucière [soh-syer] Sauceboat.

Saucisses [soh-sees] Sausages; refers to small uncooked sausages. The origin of a specific sausage is typically included in its name; i.e., *saucisses d'Auvergne, saucisses de Lyon.*

Saucisson [soh-see-sO] Large cooked sausages served thinly sliced. Some of the finest French *saucissons* include those of Arles, Lyon, Mortagne, Strasbourg, and Luchon.

Sauge [sohzh] Sage; a perennial menthaceous herb native to the Mediterranean and widely used to season chicken, pork, cheese, beans, stuffings, and sausages.

—, sauce à la Demi-glace sauce fortified with a white wine reduction and seasoned with sage.

Saugrenée [soh-gruh-neh] (1) A hearty bean stew from western France made with tomatoes, potatoes, salt pork, and garlic. Also spelled *sagranada.* (2) A type of seasoned broth made with water, butter, herbs, and salt typically used to cook vegetables and/or fava beans.

Saumon [soh-mO] Salmon.

Saumonette [soh-mo-net] The French name for the lesser spotted dogfish. This sea fish—some-

Saumonette (cont.)
times called rock salmon or *petite roussette*—is best prepared fried or baked with tomatoes.

Saumure [soh-mür] Brine; a salt-and-water solution used for pickling or preserving foods.

Saupiquet [soh-pee-keh] This term, meaning "highly salted (or spiced)," refers to an ancient sauce made up of red wine, onions, bacon, vinegar, cinnamon, and ginger and thickened with toasted bread that has been soaked in stock; traditionally served with roasted meat or rabbit.

Saupiquet des amonges [+ deh ah-mOzh] (*Nivernais*) A dish of fried ham coated with a highly spiced cream sauce.

Saupiquet ariègeois [+ ahr-yezh-wah] A local specialty of Foix consisting of ham served over beans and topped with a spicy cream sauce.

Saur [sahr] Smoked, salted herring. See *Sauret, Soret*.

Sauret [soh-reh] A term now rarely used for smoked, salted herring. See *Saur, Soret*.

Sausage [soh-sazh] A variety of potato cultivated in France.

Sauté/Sauter [soh-teh] To cook foods in a sauté pan (*sautoir, sauteuse*) over high heat with a small amount of fat.

Sauté Refers to a dish that has been cooked by sautéeing; i.e., *sauté de poisson, sauté de poulet*.

Sauter See *Sauté/Sauter*.

Sauternes [soh-tehrn] A wine-growing region of Bordeaux famous for the sweet, golden wines produced there.

Sauteuse [soh-tuzh] A shallow pan with sloping sides used for sautéeing foods.

Sautoir [soh-twahr] A shallow, lidded, straight-sided pan used to sauté certain foods. *Sautoirs* are typically long-handled with heavy bottoms.

Sauvignon (blanc) [soh-vee-nyO (blA)] An important white wine grape used in Bordeaux and the Loire Valley to produce the wine known as Blanc Fumé.

Savarin [sah-vah-rI] A baba cake baked in a ring mold and then soaked in a rum or kirsch-flavored syrup. The cake is filled with patissière cream mixed with candied fruit. Named after chef/writer Brillat-Savarin.

Savary [sah-vah-ree] The name of a garnish for tournedos and *noisettes* composed of duchess potatoes filled with braised celery and topped with demi-glace sauce.

Savoie [sah-vwah] Savoy; a mountainous province in eastern France bordering Italy and Switzerland. Savoy is perhaps best known for its dairy products (cheese, cream, and butter) and freshwater fish (perch, *lavaret, féra*, eel, and so on).

—, biscuit de [bees-kwee duh +] A very light, airy sponge cake made with flour, sugar, egg yolks, and a large amount of beaten egg whites.

Savoyarde, à la [sah-voh-yahrd] Describes meat dishes served with potatoes *à la savoyarde* (see *Savoyarde, pommes de terre à la*). This term also refers to various egg dishes prepared with cheese and/or cream and garnished with potatoes.

Savoyarde, gratins [grah-tI +] Various sliced vegetables (eggplant, zucchini, sweet potatoes) layered in a buttered casserole dish and covered with milk, garlic, and Gruyère cheese; sprinkled with butter and baked in a slow oven until golden brown.

Savoyarde, pommes de terre à la [pom-duh ter +] Thinly sliced raw potatoes arranged in a casserole dish and covered with beaten egg mixed with stock. The top is covered with Gruyère cheese and baked in a slow oven.

Saxe, à la [sahks] Describes a garnish for certain chicken dishes consisting of crayfish tails, cauliflower florettes, and *sauce écrevisse*.

Saxonne, sauce [sahk-suhn] *Sauce beurre blanc* flavored with fish essence, mustard, and lemon.

Scarole [skah-rohl] Escarole; a pale-green, leafy vegetable similar to chicory.

Schenkela [shen-kuh-lah] An almond-butter cookie from Alsace; typically made at Christmas time. Also spelled *schenkele*.

Schifela [shee-fuh-lah] (*Alsace*) Smoked pork shoulder served with bitter turnips.

Schwarzwurst [shvahrz-vuhrst] A type of smoked blood sausage (*boudin noir*) from Alsace.

Sciacce [skyah-cheh] A mashed potato pie from Corsica; traditionally served with tomato sauce and shredded cheese.

Scribe [skreeb] Describes various meat entrées garnished with rice timbales filled with foie gras.

Scubac [sku-bahk] See *Escubac*.

Sébaste [seh-bahst] Redfish; a firm-fleshed sea fish best cooked by poaching or baking.

Sec [sek] Dry; often used in reference to dry, nonsparkling wines. When used to describe champagne or other sparkling wines, *sec* indicates a sweet wine.

Secca [sehk-kah] A local jerked beef

from Provence often compared to prosciutto.

Séchage [seh-shahzh] The drying of meats, fish, fruits, and so on.

Sèche [sesh] Dried.

Seelac [see-lahk] Smoked black pollack preserved in oil.

Seigle [seh-gluh] Rye.

Sel [sel] Salt.

Selle [sel] See *Râble*.

Selles-sur-cher [+ sü-shehr] A firm, strong-smelling goat's-milk cheese from the Sologne region (southern Orléanais/northern Berry).

Selon grosseur [se-lO groh-suhr] A menu term indicating a dish—such as lobster—that is priced by weight.

Seltz, (eau de) [(oh duh) seltz] Seltzer water.

Sémillon [seh-mee-yO] A white wine grape that along with the Sauvignon Blanc grape produces the majority of white Bordeaux wines; the main grape used in the production of Sauternes.

Semoule [se-mool] Semolina; coarsely ground durum wheat flour used mainly for making pasta, gnocchi, soup, puddings, and other desserts. Other coarsely ground grains (rice, corn, buckwheat) are often referred to as semolina.

Sénonaise, à la [seh-nO-nez] Describes various fish dishes coated with *sauce matelote* and glazed under the broiler.

Septmoncel [set-mO-sel] A soft, smooth, blue-veined cheese made in several communities in the Jura mountains (by law at an altitude of 2,500 feet) from cow's milk. This highly touted cheese is also known as *bleu de Gex* and *bleu de Haut-Jura*.

Serac [se-rahk] See *Céracée*.

Serge [serzh] Describes small slices of meats coated with bread crumbs mixed with diced truffles and mushrooms and fried. Garnished with artichoke hearts, julienne ham, sliced truffles, and *sauce Madeira*; sweetbreads can also be prepared in this fashion.

Serpolet [se-rop-leh] Wild thyme; a variety of thyme used mainly in various meat and fish dishes.

Serrée [ser-reh] A sauce that has reached the point of completion.

Service à la russe [ser-vees ah-lah rüs] A style of table service in which food is bought to the guest, sitting at the table, course by course.

Service compris [+ kO-pree] A term found on certain restaurant bills indicating that everything (tax, tip, and so on) is included in the total.

Service de table [+ duh tah-bluh] Table setting.

Service en sus [+ E süs] A term marked on a restaurant bill indicating that the waiter's tip is not included in the total.

Serviette, à la [ser-vyet] Describes certain foods that are served on or wrapped in a napkin. *Truffes sous les cendres* (truffles cooked under the ashes), poached truffles, baked potatoes, and boiled rice are foods popularly served *à la serviette*.

Serviette de table [+ duh tah-bluh] Table napkin.

Sète [set] An important port town in Languedoc and home to several local fish specialties. See *Sétoise, lotte à la*.

Séteau [seh-toh] A variety of small sole.

Sétoise, lotte à la [lot-ah-lah seh-twahz] Monkfish poached in stock with olive oil and vegetables and garnished with the cooked vegetables; topped with the cooking liquid thickened with mayonnaise sauce.

Sévigné [seh-vee-nyeh] (1) Describes a dish garnished with braised lettuce. (2) A garnish for tournedos and *noisettes* consisting of braised stuffed lettuce, château potatoes, sautéed mushroom caps, and *sauce Madeira*.

Sévillane, à la [seh-vee-yahn] A term indicating that red peppers and tomatoes are present in a dish.

Sévillane, sauce *Sauce velouté* flavored with tomato and red pepper purée.

Sicilienne, à la [see-see-lyen] A descriptive term for: (1) Various fried meats garnished with rice timbales, potato croquettes, and tomatoes *à la sicilienne*; (2) Breaded fried fish garnished with sliced lemon, chopped hard-cooked eggs, parsley, capers, anchovies, and brown butter; (3) Various dishes garnished with macaroni mixed with chicken liver purée and bound with *sauce Mornay* (made with Parmesan cheese).

Sicilienne, tomates à la [to-maht ah-lah +] Tomatoes stuffed with a mixture of chopped sautéed onions, ham, basil, thyme, and Madeira wine; bound with mayonnaise sauce; topped with bread crumbs and baked.

Sigurd [see-gür] A garnish for certain meat entrées composed of stuffed tomatoes, ham dumplings, and *sauce aux truffes*.

Sili mor [see-lee mor] The name for the conger eel in Brittany. See *Congre*.

Singapour [sI-gah-poor] A gâteau composed of a génoise sponge filled with cut fruit (that has been poached in syrup) and glazed with apricot jam; decorated with candied fruit.

Singer [sI-zheh] To sprinkle a stew or ragoût with flour in order to thicken it.

Singer A term now rarely used meaning to add caramel coloring to a sauce, stew, and so on. See *Jus de singe.*

Sirop [see-rop] Syrup; a sweet, thick, usually clear liquid.

Siroper [see-roh-peh] A term meaning to soak or moisten (typically pastries; babas, savarins, génoise sponge cakes, and so on) with syrup; also referred to as *siroter.*

Siroter [see-roh-teh] To sip.

Six-yeux [sees-yuh] See *Oreille de mer.*

Sobronade [soh-broh-nahd] A hearty Périgourdine soup made with pork, potatoes, turnips, white navy beans, and garlic.

Socca [soh-kah] (*Provence*) A type of croquette made from chickpea flour (which is also called *socca*) that is fried in oil and dipped in sugar.

Soissons [swah-sO] The name in France for small white navy beans.

Sole [sol] Sole; firm-fleshed, delicately flavored flatfish of the family *soleidae.* Dover or Channel sole is the most highly prized variety of the true sole. Other varieties include the sand or partridge sole (*sole pôle, sole pelouse*) and the thickback sole (*sole panachée*). Petrale sole, lemon sole, and butter sole are popular types of flounder wrongly referred to as sole.

Solilem(me) [soh-lee-lem(muh)] A rich bread loaf that after baking is cut in two layers and sprinkled with melted, salted butter; the two layers are put back together and the bread is served hot.

Sologne [soh-loh-nyuh] A region in southern Orléanais/northern Berry considered the most fertile hunting grounds in France. The Sologne region is also noted for asparagus and Selles-sur-Cher cheese.

Solognote, à la [soh-loh-nyot] A descriptive name for roasted duck that is stuffed with its own liver mixed with bread crumbs; *à la solognote* also describes roasted lamb that has been marinated in white wine and seasonings; the reduced marinade is served as a sauce with the lamb.

Sommelier [som-muh-lyeh] The wine waiter or steward of an eating establishment responsible for choosing or suggesting the appropriate wine for a particular dish.

Son [sO] Bran; the outer husk of cereal grains removed during the milling process; high in carbohydrates, fiber, calcium, phosphorus, and vitamin B.

Sorbais [sor-beh] A version of Maroilles cheese.

Sorbet [sor-beh] A type of fruit ice typically made from fruit juice or purée, sugar syrup, and a flavored liqueur. Beaten egg whites are often added for lightness and volume. Sorbets are traditionally served between courses of a meal.

Sorbetière [sor-buh-tyer] An ice cream maker.

Soret [sor-reh] A now obsolete term for smoked, salted herring. See *Saur, Sauret.*

Sot-l'y-laisse [soh-lee-les] An obsolete term referring to the small pieces of flesh located in the backbones of poultry; once considered a delicacy.

Sottises [sot-teez] A type of boiled-mint candy, similar to *bêtises*, made in Valenciennes (Flanders).

Soubise [soo-beez] Denotes the use of onions or *sauce Soubise* in a dish.

—, **sauce** Béchamel sauce flavored with onion purée.

Sou fassum [soo-fah-suhm] See *Lou fassum.*

Soufflé [soof-fleh] A light, airy, delicate dish that can be sweet or savory and is usually served hot. Soufflés are made by incorporating beaten egg whites into a sauce; e.g., béchamel sauce (for savory soufflés), crème pâtissière (for sweet soufflés). Flavorings such as melted chocolate, fruit purée, savory purées, cheese, foie gras, and so on are added and the mixture is baked. Because of its delicate structure, it must be served immediately.

— **glacé** [+ glah-seh] Frozen soufflé.

Soufflé, pommes de terre [pom-duh-ter +] Puffed potatoes made by frying sliced potatoes ($1/_8$ in. thick) in 300 degree oil until they rise to the surface. The potatoes are then removed from the oil, and just prior to serving, they are plunged into 375 degree oil, which will cause them to puff.

Soum(a)intrain [soo-mI-trA] A soft, pungent, cow's-milk cheese from the Yonne Valley in Burgundy; similar to Saint Florentin.

Soupe [soop] Soup. Although *potage* and *soupe* are used synonymously, *soupe* generally refers to a thick, hearty, soup containing chunks of meat, vegetables, fish, pasta, rice, and so forth and served with bread. The term *soupe* is also used to describe classic soups garnished with bread; i.e., *soupe à l'oignon, soupe de poisson, soupe de pistou.*

— **à l'eau de boudin** [+ ah-loh duh boo-dI] A specialty soup from Périgord featuring cabbage, onions, turnips, leeks, and celery browned in goose fat and simmered in a stock in which blood pudding was cooked (see *Boudin noir*); the soup is served in a bowl over sliced French bread. Also called *bougras.*

— **au farci** [+ oh fahr-see] Small sausage-stuffed cabbages simmered and served in stock. A specialty of Auvergne.

— **dorée** [+ do-reh] A type of French toast traditionally served at Easter in parts of western France; also called *soupe rousse.*

— **du berger** [+ dü ber-zheh] Onion soup with the addition of garlic, tomatoes, leeks, and cheese; a local Béarn specialty.

— **rousse** [+ roos] See *Soupe dorée.*

Souper [soo-peh] Supper.

Soupière [soo-pyer] Soup tureen.

Soupirs de nonne [soo-peer duh nuhn] Small round puff pastry fritters that are fried in oil and then rolled in sugar; also called *pets-de-nonne* and *beignets venteux.*

Soupress [soo-pres] Meaning "under press," this term at one time referred to pressed fish—fish placed under a heavy weight resulting in a somewhat unrefined pâté.

Sourire [soo-reer] To simmer very gently.

Souris [soo-ree] The small, round, very flavorful piece of meat found at the end of a leg of lamb; considered a delicacy.

Sous-chef [soo-shef] The chef's assistant; generally second in command in the kitchen.

Sous la cendre [soo lah sA-druh] See *Cendre, sous la.*

Sous-noix [soo-nwah] See *Noix.*

Souvarov [soo-vah-rof] *Sablés* spread with apricot jam and sprinkled with powered sugar; served as a petit four. See *Sable*.

Souvarov, à la Describes feathered game (and poultry) stuffed with truffles and foie gras; served with demi-glace sauce that has been flavored with truffles.

Souwaroff [soo-wah-rohf] See *Souvarov*.

Sparaillon [spah-re-yO] A small species of *sargue*. See *Sargue*.

Spatule [spah-tül] Spatula; any kitchen utensil having a flat, somewhat flexible blade used to ice cakes, flip grilled items, remove or transfer hot or delicate preparations, and so forth. The blade may be broad or thin. See *Palette*.

Spatzele [spayt-suh-leh] See *Spetzli*.

Spetzli [speht-slee] (*Alsace*) Tiny dumplings made from flour, eggs, milk, and butter. The batter can be firm and cut to shape with a knife, or it can be thin and forced through a sieve into boiling stock. Very similar and no doubt inspired by the German spaetzle.

Sprat [sprat] Sprat; a small sea fish related to the herring common in European waters. Because of their high fat content, fresh sprats are best cooked broiled or grilled; commonly sold smoked, salted, or marinated.

Spunchade [spoon-shahd] A frozen dessert made from sugar syrup, fruit purée, and beaten egg whites; similar to sorbet.

Squille [skeey] A large, brownish-gray crustacean fairly common in Mediterranean markets. The *squille*, which is similar in appearance to shrimp, is excellent in soups, steamed, or boiled.

Staël [stah-el] A garnish for various meats consisting of mushrooms stuffed with chicken and green pea purée, breaded ground chicken patties, and *sauce Madeira*.

Stanley [stan-lee] Descriptive term denoting the use of onions (purée, sauce, and so forth) and curry in a dish.

Sterlet [stehr-leh] A small sturgeon highly regarded for its tender, flavorful flesh and is prepared in the same way as the salmon and sturgeon. The roe of the *sterlet* makes premium-quality caviar.

Stocaficado [sto-kah-fee-kah-doh] See *Estocaficado*.

Stockfisch [stohk-feesh] Dried salt cod; see *Estocaficada*.

Stoficado [sto-fee-kah-doh] See *Estocaficada*.

Storzapreti [stor-zah-pre-tee] A Swiss chard and Broccio cheese dumpling; a local specialty of Bastia (northern Corsica).

Strasbourgeoise, à la [strahz-boor-zhwahz] Describes dishes prepared Strasbourg style, which includes ingredients such as cabbage, saurkraut, sausage, pork, and foie gras.

Stufatu [stoo-fah-too] A Corsican specialty of stewed meat (typically mutton), onions, and mushrooms slowly cooked and served over macaroni. Also spelled *Stuffato*.

Subric [sü-breek] A sweet or savory *salpicon* that is portioned into bite-sized morsels and fried in a pan with butter; served as an appetizer, garnish, petit four, and so on. See *Salpicon*.

Suc [sük] (1) Liquid derived from pressed meat, vegetables, fruit, and so on. (2) Highly reduced stock or consommé. (3) The pan juices from a roasted meat (*suc de viande*).

Sucarelle [sü-ka-rel] A regional dish from southeastern France composed of snails simmered in stock with onions, peppers, tomatoes, and garlic.

Succès [sük-se] A cake composed of two layers of almond meringue sandwiched together with praline buttercream; iced with butter cream and garnished with almonds and marzipan.

Suc de viande [sük duh vyAd] See *Suc.*

Sucées [sü-keh] A rich pastry flavored with candied fruit; cut into small squares, and served as a petit four.

Suchet [sü-sheh] A descriptive term for fish coated with *sauce au vin blanc* and garnished with a julienne of carrots, celery, leeks, and truffles.

Sucre [soo-kruh] Sugar.

Sucrier [soo-kree-yeh] Sugar bowl.

Suédoise [sweh-dwahz] A classic dessert featuring poached fruit set in a mold and covered with fruit gelatine. When the dish is set, it is turned out and served with cream Chantilly.

Suédoise, à la Describes various dishes and preparations using traditional Swedish ingredients; i.e., potatoes, cranberries, beets, pork, dairy products, salmon, herring, reindeer meat, dill, saffron, cardamon, and so forth.

Suédoise, sauce A cold sauce composed of mayonnaise combined with apple purée and grated horseradish.

Suer [sweh] To slowly fry foods in fat in a covered pan.

Suglhupf [sü-guhl-hopf] See *kugelhopf.*

Suisse [swees] Switzerland; a country bordering Savoy and Franche-Comté (eastern France). Cheese (Gruyère, Emmental, Sbrinz) and chocolate are undoubtedly Switzerland's most famous food products.

Suisse An orange-flavored brioche formed into the shape of a tiny man. A specialty of Valence (Dauphiné).

Sully [sü-lee] A garnish for grilled meats comprised of braised lettuce, cockscomb, potatoes *parisienne*, and truffles; with demi-glace sauce.

Sultane [suhl-tahn] A large pastry that is contained under a spun sugar cage.

Sultane, à la (1) Denotes the use of pistachios or pistachio butter in a (sweet or savory) preparation. (2) A garnish for large cuts of meats featuring duchess potatoes in the shape of an Islamic crescent; braised red cabbage.

Supion [sü-pyO] The name for squid in the south of France; see *Calamar.*

Suprême [sü-prehm] (1) A term used sometimes to describe a choice fillet of fish. (2) Refers to elaborate dishes featuring ingredients such as foie gras, truffles, cockscombs, and so on.

Suprêmes (de volaille) [+ (duh volah-yuh)] Boneless, skinless poultry breasts.

Suprême, sauce Chicken *velouté* flavored with mushrooms and finished with heavy cream.

Surprise [sü-preez] Describes (generally sweet) dishes having a surprise center.

—, *omelette* [om-let +] See *Norvégienne, omelette.*

—, *oranges en* [o-rAzh E +] Halved oranges scooped out and filled with orange ice and coated with meringue. Browned quickly in the oven and covered with remaining half of the orange.

—, **pommes de terre** [pom duh ter +] Baked potato cups filled with mashed potatoes and covered with a potato lid.

Sur le feu, meringue [muh-rIg sü luh fuh] A method of making meringue in which the egg whites and sugar are whisked together over low heat.

Sur le plat [sür luh plah] Shirred eggs; eggs sprinkled with butter or cream and sometimes bread crumbs and baked in the oven.

Suzanne [sü-zahn] A garnish for tournedos and noisettes composed of stuffed lettuce and artichokes; with tarragon-flavored demi-glace.

Suzeraine [sü-zren] A garnish for various meats consisting of stuffed tomatoes and cucumbers and served with *sauce Madeira*.

Suzette, crêpes [krep sü-zet] A classic dessert traditionally prepared tableside in the dining room for the guests to watch. It is made by melting butter and sugar in a pan to which Cointreau and/or Grand Marnier is added and ignited; the crêpes are then dipped in the hot mixture and folded and presented to the guests.

Sylvia, sauce [seel-vyah] Hollandaise sauce flavored with fresh tarragon; similar to béarnaise sauce.

Table d'hôte [tah-bluh-doht] See *Menu, table d'hôte*.

Tablier de sapeur [tah-blyeh duh sah-puhr] A dish composed of ox tripe dipped in egg and bread crumbs and grilled. A specialty of Lyon.

Tacaud [tah-koh] See *Monie Borgne*.

Tacon [tah-kO] A French name for a young salmon.

Taglierini [tah-lyeh-ree-nee] A type of long, flat pasta popular in Corsica; similar to fettucine but narrower.

Taillevent [tah-yuh-vA] (1310–1395) Born Guillaume Tisel; fourteenth century chef and author of *Le Viandier*, one of the first French cookbooks.

Taillons [tah-yO] A French term used sometimes to describe round slices.

Talibur [tah-lee-buhr] See *Rabotte*.

Talleyrand-Périgord, Charles Maurice de [shahrl moh-rees duh tah-lee-rA-peh-ree-gohr] (1734–1838) A Foreign Minister to Napoleon as well as a statesman and diplomat, Talleyrand was perhaps best remembered as a celebrated gastronome; his name lives on in several culinary preparations.

—, **consommé** [kO-suh-meh] Chicken consommé garnished with diced truffles that have been cooked in sherry.

—, **garniture** Macaroni mixed with goose liver and truffles and bound with butter and Parmesan cheese; with *sauce périgourdine*.

—, **sauce** Sauce velouté enriched with cream and garnished with diced vegetables, diced tongue, and chopped truffles; finished with a splash of Madeira.

Talmouse [tahl-moos] A small, square cheese turnover of which there are several versions; served as an hors d'œuvre.

Talmouse A sweet tartlet filled with pastry cream and frangipane cream; topped with chopped almonds and baked.

Tamié [tah-myeh] A cow's-milk cheese from Savoy. Similar to *Reblochon*.

Tamis [tah-mee] Tammy cloth; a piece of cloth used for straining stock and sauces; also called *étamine*.

Tamponner [tA-poh-neh] To cover the surface of a sauce or soup with a thin layer of butter or oil to prevent a crust from forming.

Tantouillée/Tantouillet [tA-too-yeh] See *Gigorit*.

Tant-pour-tant [tA-poor-tA] A blend of equal parts of sugar and ground almonds used in the preparation of various baked goods.

Tapenade [tah-pee-nah-duh] A common Provençal condiment consisting of anchovies, capers, and black olives ground together with olive oil and spices. Pieces of tuna and garlic are often added.

Tapeno [tah-pee-noh] The name for the caper in Provence.

Tapinette [tah-pee-net] A curdled milk tart (*tarte au caille*) from Orléanais made from curd cheese, milk, eggs, and flour baked in a pastry shell.

Tapioca [tah-pee-oh-kah] A starchy food derived from the roots of the cassava plant. It is used primarily to thicken soups, sauces, puddings, and so forth.

Tarascon [tahr-as-kO] A town in Provence renowned for producing fine chocolates.

Tartare [tahr-tahr] An herbed, triple-cream cheese made from cow's milk in Périgord.

Tartare, à la Describes preparations that have been breaded, broiled, and served with a spicy sauce.

Tartare, bifteck à la [bif-tek ah-lah +] Raw, seasoned ground beef served with several garnishes, including raw egg yolks, chopped onions, capers, anchovies, and parsley.

Tartare, sauce Mayonnaise sauce prepared with a cooked egg yolk replacing the raw egg yolk and seasoned with finely chopped onions and chives.

Tartarinades [tahr-tahr-een-ahd] A chocolate candy produced in Tarascon (Provence).

Tarte [tahrt] A shallow, self-supported pastry shell filled with various sweet or savory fillings.

— **alsacienne** [+ ahl-sah-syen] A specialty tart from Alsace featuring custard and local fruit (plums, cherries, and so on).

— **bourbonnais** [+ boor-buhn-neh] A famous cheese and fruit tart from Bourbonnais (Burgundy). Also called *gouéron*.

— **des demoiselles tatin, la** [+ deh duh-mwah-zel tah-tI] A classic "upside-down" apple tart; the bottom of a baking dish is layered with butter and sugar followed by a layer of apples that is sealed with a pastry crust. As the tart bakes, the sugar turns into caramel and becomes the topping when the tart is turned out.

Tartelette [tahr-tlet] A small, single serving tart.

Tartibas [tahr-tuh-bas] A type of dessert pancake from Bourbonnais prepared with grapes and pears.

Tartine [tahr-teen] A slice of bread topped with any of various spreads—butter, cream cheese, jelly, and so on.

Tartouffes [tahr-toof] The name for potato in parts of Berry.

Tartoufle [tahr-too-fluh] An early name for the potato in France.

Tartouillat [tahr-too-yaht] A traditional dessert from central France featuring thick crépe batter baked in cabbage leaves. Cherries or apples are usually mixed with the batter.

Tasse [tah-suh] Drinking cup. In Burgundy the word *tasse* also refers to a *taste-vin*. See *Taste-vin*.

Tassergal [tah-suhr-gahl] Bluefish;

an oily, firm-fleshed fish found (in Europe) in the Mediterranean. This pleasant-tasting fish is best grilled, poached, or broiled.

Taste-vin/Tâte-vin [tahst-vI/taht-vI] A small metal (usually silver) cup used to taste wines. Also known as *coupole* and *tasse*.

Tatin [tah-tI] See *Tarte des demoiselles Tatin*.

Taupinière [toh-pee-nyer] A type of commercial chèvre cheese produced in France.

Tavel [tah-vel] One of France's most famous rosé wines produced in the southern Rhône Valley primarily from the Grenache grape.

Tende-de-tranche [tE-duh-trAsh] A cut of beef from the upper thigh area.

Tendron [tE-drO] A cut of beef, veal, or lamb taken from the end of the ribs to the breast bone.

Terrine [teh-reen] A lidded, oven-proof dish used to cook various meats; also the term for pâté cooked in a terrine.

—, pâté en [pah-teh deh +] See *Pâté en terrine*.

Terrinée [teh-ree-neh] See *Torgoule*.

Terrine paysanne [+ peh-yee-zahn] A type of beef stew made from cubed beef baked in a casserole with red wine, brandy, and beef stock until tender.

Tête [tet] The head of an animal.

Tête d' aloyau [+ dah-loy-oh] Refers to the meat from the end of the rump of beef.

Tête de cuvée [+ duh kü-veh] High-quality wine made from grapes crushed before the use of a wine press.

Tête de mort [+ duh mohr] The name sometimes used in France for Edam cheese. See *Edam*.

Tête de nègre [+ duh ne-gruh] (1) Petit four made of meringue frosted with chocolate butter-cream and garnished with grated chocolate. (2) A sweetened rice cake topped with chocolate sauce and Chantilly cream. See *Baiser de nègre*.

Teurt-goule [tuhrt-gool] Also spelled *teurgoule*; see *Torgoule*.

Thé [teh] Tea.

Thermomètre [ter-mo-met-truh] Thermometer.

Thon [tO] Tuna; a large, firm-fleshed, sea fish of the mackerel family.

Thon blanc [+ blA] The name for the albacore tuna in France.

Thonine [toh-neen] A small variety of tuna found only in the Mediterranean.

Thonné [tO-neh] Describes veal that has been marinated and cooked in olive oil, garlic, bay leaves, and lemon.

Thouna [too-nah] The name for *thonine* in Nice.

Thounina [too-nee-nah] The name for *thonine* in Séte.

Thourin [toor-I] See *Tourin*.

Thym [teem] Thyme; an aromatic herb related to the mint family. See also *Serpolet, Farigoule*.

Tian [tyahn] (1) Any sort of gratin (potato, vegetable) that is cooked in a *tian*. (2) A type of tart from Nice featuring kidney beans, spinach, peas, artichokes, and seasonings. (3) A type of earthenware baking dish from southern France.

Tianu [tyah-nü] The name of a small pan used in Corsica to cook stews, ragoûts, rice, and so on.

Tiède [tyed] Tepid.

Tignard [tee-nyahr] A type of blue cheese made from goat's milk.

Timbale [teem-bahl] (1) Any type of savory or sweet preparation baked or served in a pastry case.

Timbale (cont.)
(2) Any type of preparation cooked or served in a timbale. (3) The name given to cooked rice, *salpicons*, or vegetables pressed into a mold and turned out on a plate as a garnish. (4) A small, metal (typically silver) drinking cup; nowadays these kinds of timbales are used generally for decorative purposes. (5) A high-sided, drum-shaped mold in which various dishes are baked.

Timbale à la parisienne [+ ah-lah pah-ree-zyen] A sweet preparation consisting of poached apples, pears, apricots, pineapples, and raisins bound with apricot purée and stuffed into a brioche shell; coated with apricot glaze.

Tioro [tyoh-roh] See *Ttoro*.

Tire-bouchon [teer-boo-shO] Corkscrew.

Tisane [tee-zahn] A kind of curative tea made from an infusion of herbs.

Tisane de champagne [+ duh shApah-nyuh] A term that refers to a champagne of poor quality; the word was previously used to describe a light, sweet champagne.

Tisane à Richelieu [+ ah reesh-lyuh] Nickname for Bordeaux wines now rarely used.

Tisanière [tee-zah-nyer] A receptacle used for steeping and drinking tisane.

Tivoli [tee-voh-lee] A classic garnish for various entrées featuring mushroom caps filled with a *salpicon* of cockscombs and kidneys; asparagus tips.

Tocane [toh-kahn] Refers to new champagne, which is made from the first pressing.

Tôle [tol] Baking pan; a metal tray used to bake a variety of pastries.

Tomate [to-maht] (1) Tomato. (2) An alcoholic drink from Corsica combining pastis and grenadine. The beverage resembles tomato juice, hence the name.

Tomber [tO-beh] To cook certain vegetables in their own juices. (Old french cookery term.)

Tomber à glace [+ ah glahs] To reduce a stock or liquid to a thick consistency

Tome [tohm] See *Tomme*.

Tomme A local name for cheese in and around Savoy; the collective name for several cheeses made in the mountains of Savoy, Dauphiné, and Franche-Comté.

Tom-pouce [tom-poos] A small square shortdough pastry frosted with coffee buttercream and hazelnuts.

Tonkinois [tO-kee-nwah] A classic almond sponge cake layered and iced with praline butter cream and garnished with almonds, coconut, and orange fondant. *Tonkinois* is also the name for a nougatine-praline petit four.

Topinambour [toh-pee-nA-boor] Jerusalem artichoke; an edible tuber related to the sunflower. Though not a true artichoke, its taste is similar and is best eaten raw in a salad or cooked and served as a vegetable.

Toque blanche [tohk blAsh] A tall white chef's hat.

Torchon, au [oh tohr-shO] Describes cooked preparations served wrapped in cloth; similar to *à la serviette*.

Torgoule [tohr-gool] (*Normandy*) A type of baked pudding made with rice, milk, sugar, and cinnamon; known by several other names; *terrinée, teurgoule, bourre-gueule,* and *teurt-goule*.

Torta [tohr-tah] In Corsica, *torta* is a flat almond or pine nut tart.

Torteil [tohr-tehl] See *Tortell*.

Tortell [tohr-tel] An anise-flavored brioche.

Tortillon [tor-tee-yO] A twisted strip of puff pastry made with candied fruit and nuts; served as a petit four. See *Brassadeau*.

Tortue [tor-tü] Turtle.

Tortue, sauce Demi-glace sauce flavored with tomato purée, white wine, "turtle herbs" (see *Herbes à Tortuee*), truffles, and cayenne pepper; finished with Madeira wine.

Toscane, à la [tohs-skahn] Denotes the use of Parmesan cheese and ham in a preparation. Also describes noodles tossed with foie gras and diced truffles.

Totelots [toh-tuh-loh] A salad of mixed greens garnished with cooked pasta squares and hard-cooked eggs; tossed in oil and vinegar; from Lorraine.

Tôt-fait [toh-feh] A rich lemon-flavored cake made with flour, sugar, eggs, lemon peel, and melted butter; baked in a manqué mold. See *Moule à manqué*.

Touffe [toof] Bundles of herbs tied together.

Touiller [too-yehr] To casually stir or mix a preparation or ingredients.

Toulia [tool-yah] The name in Bigorre (Gascony) for the Béarnaise onion soup *oulliat*. See *Oulliat*.

Toulon [too-lO] A coastal Provençal town famous for its seafood (crab, red mullet, mussels) and capers. See *Esquinado toulonais*.

Toulonaise, à la [too-lO-nez] A descriptive term for poached fish stuffed with fish mousse and topped with fish *velouté*; garnished with mussels.

Toulousaine, à la [too-loo-zen] (1) This term describes various preparations stuffed or garnished with small chicken quenelles, braised sweetbreads, cockscombs and kidneys, sliced truffles, and mushrooms bound with *sauce Toulouse*. (2) Describes dishes prepared in the style of Toulouse. See *Toulouse*.

Toulouse [too-looz] A city in southern France (Languedoc) famous for foods such as sausage, lamb, beans, goose fat, olive oil, asparagus, tomatoes, plums, ham, garlic, duck, and carp.

—, sauce Sauce *allemande* to which a reduction of mushrooms and truffles is added.

Toupin [too-pI] A earthenware dish used in parts of France (Béarn, Savoy) to make *garbures*, ragoûts, stews, and so on; called *caquelon* in some areas of France.

Tourain [too-rI] See Tourin.

Touraine [too-ren] An area in the Loire Valley known as the "Garden of France" because of the superb quality and wide variety of fruits and vegetables grown there.

Tourangelle, à la Denotes the use of flageolet beans in a preparation.

Tourangelle, potage à la [po-tahzh ah-lah toor-A-zhel] A thick soup combining a purée of green beans and flageolets with *sauce velouté*; garnished with whole flageolets.

Tour de feuilletage [toor duh fuh-yuh-tazh] A French cooking term meaning to turn the puff pastry dough in order to create the several layers of butter that allows for a flaky pastry. Also known as *tourer*.

Tourant [too-rA] Swing or relief cook; the person covering for an absent cook.

Tour de pâtisserie [toor duh pah-tees-ree] A marble slab used for rolling out pastry dough.

Tourer [too-reh] See *Tour de Feuilletage*.

Touri [too-ree] See *Tourin*.

Tourifas [too-ree-fah] Strips of bread topped with mushrooms, ham, and bacon. The whole is then breaded and fried; a specialty of Auvergne.

Touril [too-reel] See *Tourin*.

Tourin [too-rI] An onion soup similar to *oulliat* with the addition of garlic and tomatoes. There are several variations and spellings.

Tournedos [toor-ne-doh] A small steak from the center of the tenderloin.

Tournée [toor-neh] The former name for *sauce allemande*.

Tourner [toor-neh] (1) To "turn" or shape vegetables (oval or round) with a small knife. (2) To turn sour or rancid. (3) To turn, flip, toss, stir, and so forth.

Touron [too-rO] A ring-shaped cake from the Roussillon flavored with almonds and pistachios. *Tourin* is also a type of almond paste flavored with ground pistachios.

Tourrin [too-rI] See *Tourin*.

Tourte [toort] The collective name for covered sweet or savory pies or tarts.

— *à la lorraine* [+ ah-lah lo-ren] See *Tourte de porc et de veau*.

— *de porc et de veau* [+ duh pork eh duh voh] A specialty from Lorraine featuring marinated veal and pork mixed in custard and baked in a covered pastry crust. Also called *tourte à la lorraine*.

— *de courge à la grassoise* [+ duh koorzh ah-lah grahs-swahz] A squash pie from Grasse (Provence).

Tourteau [toor-toh] The French name for the common crab found in Mediterranean and Atlantic waters.

Tourteau See *Tortell*.

Tourteau fromagé [+ fro-mahzh] A local Poitevin cheesecake made with goat cheese.

Tourteaux [toor-toh] A cornmeal pancake from eastern France.

Tourtière [toor-tyehr] (1) A round pie dish having plain or fluted sides used for baking tortes, pies, tarts, and so on; typically made of earthenware or metal. (2) A flan ring. (3) A type of fruit tart from Landes. (4) A chicken and salsify pie from Périgord.

Tourton [toor-tO] A rustic pancake from Limousin made from buckwheat flour. Also spelled *tourtou*.

Tourvillaise, à la [toor-vee-yez] A garnish for fish consisting of sliced mushrooms and truffles, oysters, mussels, and *sauce Mornay*.

Tourtou [toor-too] See *Tourton*.

Toute-épice [toot-eh-pees] Allspice; an aromatic berry from tropical America (particularly Jamaica) having a scent and flavor of a mixture of cinnamon, cloves, and nutmeg. Also known in France as *piment de la Jamaïque*.

Tranche [trAsh] Slice.

— *au petit os* [+ oh-puh-teet oh] A cut of beef from the middle of the rump.

— *grasse* [+ grahs] Top rump of beef.

Tranchelard [trAsh-lahr] Carving knife.

Trancheur [trA-shuhr] In classic dining room service, the *trancheur* is the waiter in charge of carving meat.

Trappiste [trah-peest] Originally the name for (cow's-milk) cheeses made by Trappist monks at La Trappe, Normandy. This term now describes similar cheeses made throughout France.

Trappistine [trah-pee-steen] An

Armagnac and herb-based liqueur made by Trappistine nuns.

Travaillé [trah-vah-yeh] Beaten, as in a mixture.

Travailler [trah-vah-yeh] (1) To mix or beat until smooth or well blended. (2) Describes natural changes in foodstuffs, such as the fermentation of wine, the yeast action in raw dough, and so forth.

Trébèche [treh-besh] A Poitevin cheese made from cow's milk or (rarely) ewe's milk characterized by its triangle shape. Also called *Trois-cornes*.

Trébuc [treh-bük] In Béarn, this term refers to the meat (ham, bacon, sausage, preserved goose and pork) that is added to the *garbure*. See *Garbure*.

Trèfle de cheval [tre-fluh duh shuh-vahl] See *Lotier*.

Tremper [trE-peh] To soak food in water.

Tremper la soupe [+ lah soop] To garnish soup with croutons.

Tremper le vin [+ luh vI] To combine water and wine.

Trénels [treh-nel] A local specialty of Millau featuring poached sheep's or calf's tripe stuffed with garlic, pork, and cloves. Similar to *tripoux*.

Trescat [tres-kah] See *Galutres*.

Tressé [tre-seh] "Braid"; the design of certain food preparations, particularlly pastries.

Tresses [tres] See *Tripoux*.

Trévise [treh-veez] Radicchio; a red-leafed variety of chicory used mainly in salads.

Trévise, à la (For small cuts of meat) Fried dumplings made with puréed mushrooms and artichokes; noisette potatoes, and *sauce Choron*.

Trianon, sauce [tree-ah-nO] A cold sauce composed of mayonnaise sauce combined with tomato and onion purée, diced *cornichons*, and pimentoes.

Triboulet [tree-boo-leh] The French name for Atlantic turbot, a white-fleshed flatfish of excellent eating.

Triestoise, à la [tree-es-twahz] Describes fish served on a bed of braised lettuce and garnished with quartered hard-cooked eggs and *noisette* potatoes; served with beurre noir.

Triomphe de farcy [tree-Of duh fahr-see] A long, green variety of French bean.

Tripa [tree-puh] A Corsican dish of sheep's tripe stuffed with spinach, chard, and the animal's blood; the tripe is tied and simmered in seasoned water.

Tripe, à la [treep] Describes certain egg dishes prepared with onions and béchamel sauce.

Tripes [treep] Tripe; the stomach lining of beef, pork, or sheep. Tripe is tough and requires long cooking time. Also known in France as *gras-double*.

— *à la mode de caen* [+ ah-lah mod duh kahn] One of Normandy's most famous dishes prepared by cooking tripe *en casserole* with onions, carrots, salt pork, ox feet, and seasonings. Apple cider and Calvados are added; and the lid is traditionally sealed with a paste made from flour and water; served with boiled potatoes.

Triple crème [tree-pluh krem] Refers to various soft-ripened cow's-milk cheeses having a minimum of 72 percent butterfat.

Tripotcha [tree-po-chuh] A type of blood pudding from the Basque Provinces made from calf's lungs and intestines; highly spiced with nutmeg, red pepper, and parsley. Also spelled *tripotch* and *tripotchka*.

Tripous [tree-poo] See *Tripoux.*

Tripoux [tree-poo] A specialty of Rouergue and Quercy composed of tripe stuffed with minced pork, veal, and garlic and braised over low heat for hours. There are several variations appearing under different names.

Trognon [troh-nyO] The hearts of certain vegetables or fruit; i.e., lettuce, cabbage, celery, artichokes, and so on.

Trois-cornes [trwah-kohrn] See *Trébèche.*

Trois-frères [+ frer] A cake made with rice flour and flavored with maraschino; baked in a special mold and garnished with angelica and almonds. See *Trois-frères, moule à.*

—, *moule à* [mool ah +] A special ring-shaped mold used for baking *trois-frères.*

Trompette-de-la-mort [trO-pet-duh-lah-mor] See *Craterelle.*

Tronçon [trO-kO] "Chunk"; a piece of food, usually referring to fish.

Troô [troo] A highly regarded goat's-milk cheese from Troô (Orléanais).

Tropique [troh-peek] A French culinary term referring to the hottest area in the oven.

Troquet [troh-keh] A French word for bar or tavern.

Trou du milieu [troo dü mee-lyuh] See *Normand, le trou.*

Troucha de bléa [troo-shuh duh bleh] A vegetable tart from Nice typically made with peas, spinach, artichokes, chard, and beans (*fèves*).

Trousser [troo-seh] To truss a bird in order to keep its proper shape during cooking. This term also refers to shellfish that is decoratively arranged as a garnish.

Trouvillaise, à la [troo-vee-yez] (*For fish*) Shrimp, mussels, and mushrooms; with *sauce aux crevettes.*

Troyen [trwah-yeh] A cow's-milk cheese from Troyes (Champagne) similar to Camembert. Also known as Troyes, Ervy, and Barberey.

Troyes [trwah] A town in Champagne famous for its andouillettes. See *Troyen.*

Trucha [troo-shah] A spinach and chard omelette from Nice.

Truches [troosh] A local name for the potato in parts of Berry.

Truffade/Truffado [trü-fahd/trü-fah-doh] A potato and cheese pancake, made with mashed or shredded potato and Tomme cheese; a specialty of Auvergne.

Truffat [trü-fah] See *Truffiat.*

Truffe [trüf] Truffle; an underground fungus that grows near the roots of certain trees (oak, beech, hazel, chestnut). This highly prized and expensive food is generally used to flavor sauces, consommés, eggs, poultry, foie gras, forcemeats, and so on. Truffles may also be eaten raw in salads or used as a garnish. See *Périgord.*

Truffe A local name once given to the potato in parts of France.

Truffe en chocolat [+ E shoh-koh-lah] Chocolate truffle; a chocolate confection made with chocolate, butter, cream, and flavored liqueurs.

Truffer [trü-feh] To add bits of truffles to a dish.

Truffes, sauce aux Demi-glace sauce flavored with Maderia and truffle essence; garnished with chopped truffles.

Truffiat [trü-fyah] A type of potato casserole from Berry. Also spelled *truffat.*

Trufflage [trü-flahz] A method of flavoring dishes by adding small pieces of truffles.

Truie [trüee] Sow; an adult female pig.

Truie de mer [+ duh mer] See *Rascasse*.

Truite [trü-eet] Trout.

— *au bleu* [+ oh bluh] A classic dish of fresh trout plunged live into boiling court bouillon; traditionally served with hollandaise sauce or melted butter.

— *aux amandes* [+ oh ah-mahnd] A famous dish featuring panfried trout garnished with toasted almonds and flavored with a sauce of lemon, parsley, and butter.

— *de mer* [+ duh mer] See *Truite saumonée*.

— *saumonée* [+ soh-mo-neh] "Salmon trout"; also known as sea trout (*truite de mer*).

Trulle [trül] A local name in parts of France for blood sausage (*boudin noir*).

Tsar, du [zahr] A garnish for fish featuring sautéed *agoursi* (See *Agoursi*), mushroom caps, and *sauce Mornay*; the finished dish is briefly glazed under the broiler.

Tsarine, à la [zah-reen] Term indicating that a dish is garnished or prepared with ingredients reminiscent of Russian cookery; i.e., cucumbers cooked in butter, caviar, mushrooms, poached eggs, cream sauces, and so forth.

Ttoro [to-roh] A bouillabaise-like soup from the French Basque Provinces featuring a variety of Atlantic seafood. Also spelled *tioro*.

Ttouron [too-rO] An almond/hazelnut sponge cake garnished with crushed pistachios and crystallized fruit; a specialty of the French Basque Provinces.

Tue-chien [tü-shyen] A celebration in eastern France for the end of the grape harvest.

Tuile [tweel] An almond/cookie shell used as a base for petits fours. Typically, when the cookies are taken from the hot oven and are still pliable, they are draped over a rolling pin or cup and left to harden. See *Mignon, Tulipe*.

Tulipe [tü-leep] A cookie shell similar to *tuiles* made without the almonds; used in the same fashion.

Turban [tür-bahn] Term referring to several preparations arranged in a circle on a serving plate. Also describes pâtés, forcemeats, mousses, and so on, prepared in a ring mold.

Turbigo [tür-bee-goh] A garnish for beef and lamb dishes composed of grilled *chipolatas* and mushroom caps; served with tomato-flavored demi-glace.

Turbot [tür-boh] Turbot; a large white flatfish found in Atlantic and Mediterranean waters. Turbot is highly regarded and is best prepared grilled or poached. See *Turbotière*.

Turbotière [tür-boh-tyer] A special fish kettle used for poaching turbot and other flatfish.

Turinois [tür-ree-nyah] A large confection made with chestnut purée and chocolate and flavored with *kirsch*. Also the name of a chestnut-flavored petit four.

Turque, à la [tür-kuh] Describes various dishes garnished with rice pilaf and fried eggplant.

Tyrolienne, à la [tee-roh-lyen] A garnish for a variety of dishes featuring fried onion rings and tomato *concassée*; served with *sauce tyrolienne*.

Tyrolienne, sauce (1) Béarnaise sauce made with olive oil instead of butter, sometimes with the addition of tomato purée. (2) May-

Tyrolienne, sauce (cont.)
onnaise sauce combined with tomato purée.

Upsala, à la [oop-sah-luh] A descriptive term for poached fish
garnished with braised fennel and
coated with *sauce vin blanc.*

Urbain-dubois, garniture [oor-bI-
dü-bwah] (*For poached fish*)
Coated with *sauce aurora* and
topped with crayfish tails, sliced
truffles, and crayfish purée.

Uzés, sauce [üz] Hollandaise sauce
flavored with anchovy paste and
Madeira wine.

Vacherin [vah-shuh-rI] The collec-
tive name for various soft cow's-
milk cheeses from Savoy and
Franche-Comté; i.e., Vacherin
Mont-d'Or, Vacherin des Bauges,
Vacherin d'Abondance, and so on.

Vacherin A classic dessert made
from rings of meringue (*vacherin
de meringue*) or almond paste
(*vacherin en pâté d'amandes*) layered on top of each other forming a bowl or crown; filled with
ice cream or whipped cream.

— *à la chantilly* [+ ah-lah shA-tee-
yee] A *vacherin* shell filled with
whipped cream that is flavored
with kirsch.

— *aux marrons glacés* [+ mah-
rohn glah-seh] A *vacherin* shell
made with almond meringue filled
with chestnut-flavored ice cream.

Valencay [vah-lE-seh] A firm goat's-
milk cheese produced in several
regions in central France.

Valaisienne, à la [vah-leh-syen]
Describes fish dishes served with
sauce genevoise mixed with
chopped gherkins and capers.

Valencienne, à la [vah-lE-syen] "In
the style of Valencia (Spain)"; describes dishes garnished with rice,
sweet red peppers, tomatoes, and
smoked ham.

Valentine, sauce [vah-lE-teen] A
cold sauce combining mayonnaise sauce with chopped tarragon, grated horseradish, and mustard powder.

Valérianelle [vah-leh-ree-ah-nel]
The name for lamb's lettuce in
parts of France; see *Mâche.*

Valeria, sauce [vah-leh-ree-ah]
Sauce vin rouge seasoned with
grated horseradish, chervil, and
powdered mustard.

Valkyrie, à la [vahl-kee-ree] A garnish for various game featuring
sautéed mushrooms and potato
dumplings; topped with game
stock thickened with cream and
flavored with juniper berries.

Vallée d'auge [vah-leh dazh] The
name for various poultry dishes
from Normandy prepared with
apples and/or Calvados.

Vallée d'ossau, fromage de la [fro-
mahzh duh lah vah-leh dos-soh]
Another name for Oleron cheese.
See *Oleron.*

Valois, garniture à la [vah-wah]
(*For fish*) Potatoes *parisienne*, fish
roe, crayfish tails; *sauce Valois.* (*For
poultry*) Anna potatoes and
sautéed artichoke hearts; veal
demi-glace.

Valois, sauce Béarnaise sauce flavored with meat glaze. Also called
sauce foyot.

Vanille [vah-nee-yuh] Vanilla.

Vanneau [vah-noh] (1) A French
variety of scallop. (2) A bird related to the plover once popular
in France.

Vanner [vah-neh] To stir (sauces,
syrups, and so on) until cooled.

Vapeur [vah-puhr] Steam.

—, *cuisson à la* [+ ah-lah kwee-sO]
To cook by steaming.

Varié [vah-ree-yeh] Assorted.

Varsovienne, sauce [vahr-soh-vyen]
Béchamel sauce flavored with

horseradish and orange juice.

Vauclusienne, à la [voh-klü-zyen] Describes fish panfried in olive oil, seasoned with lemon and parsley, and topped with the pan juices mixed with butter.

V.D.Q.S. (*Vins délimités de qualité supérieure*) Refers to wines of superior quality, but not quite that of wines labeled A.O.C.

Veau [voh] Veal.

Velours [vuh-loor] "Velvet"; describes preparations that are of smooth consistency (sauces, soups, creams, and so on).

Velouté, sauce [vuh-loo-teh] One of the basic French sauces, it is made with white stock (poultry, veal, fish) thickened with roux; it is the basis for numerous sauces. Also refers to soups that are thickened with cream, egg yolks, and/or butter.

Venaco [vuh-nah-koh] A soft cheese from Venaco (Corsica) made from goat's or sheep's milk.

Venaison [vuh-neh-zO] Venison; any type of wild deer meat.

Venaison, sauce (1) *Sauce poivrade* thickened with cream and flavored with red currants; also known as *sauce grand veneur*. (2) Demi-glace sauce reduced with game stock and enriched with butter; seasoned with red pepper.

Vendée [vE-deh] An area covering the western coast of Poitou. Vendée is famous for its vegetables, particularly cabbage and white beans. *Fressure vendéenne*, a ragoût of pig's offal, is a popular regional dish.

Vendôme [vE-dom] A firm cow's-milk cheese from Orléanais often compared to Coulommiers.

Vénitienne, à la [veh-nee-syen] Describes fish and poultry dishes served with *sauce vénitienne*. Poul-

try dishes are garnished with poached calf's brains, cockscomb, and mushroom caps.

Vénitienne, sauce *Sauce vin blanc* to which a reduction of shallots, chervil, tarragon, and vinegar is added; enriched with herb butter.

Ventadour, garniture [vE-tah-door] (*For tournedos and noisettes*) Poached bone marrow, sliced truffles, artichoke purée, and fried potatoes.

Verdi [vehr-dee] A term referring to fish dishes that are garnished with a *salpicon* of macaroni, diced lobster, truffles, and Parmesan cheese; bound with *sauce Mornay*.

Verdi, sauce A cold sauce made up of mayonnaise combined with sour cream and garnished with chopped spinach, diced gherkins, and chives.

Verdure [vehr-dür] A term referring to green herbs.

Verdurette, sauce [vehr-dür-et] *Sauce vinaigrette* combined with hard-cooked eggs and assorted green herbs.

Vergeoise [vehr-zhwahz] A type of brown sugar popular in France and Belgium.

Verjus [veh-zhü] An acidy green juice derived from unripe grapes. *Verjus* is used like vinegar.

Vernet, sauce [vehr-neh] Béchamel sauce garnished with chopped egg whites, chopped truffles, and gherkins and enriched with cream and herb butter.

Verneuil [vehr-nuhl] Describes meat or poultry that is breaded, panfried, and served with puréed artichokes and *sauce Colbert*.

Vernon [vehr-nA] A garnish for entrées featuring asparagus tips stuffed inside artichoke bottoms, hollowed-out turnips filled with mashed potatoes, and potato nests filled with puréed peas.

Véron, sauce [veh-rO] A combination of *sauce tyrolienne* and *sauce normande*. The sauce is flavored with anchovies and finished with *glace de viande*.

Véronique, à la [veh-rO-eek] A term denoting the use of white seeddless grapes in a preparation.

Vert, au [vehr] Refers to dishes prepared with a variety of green herbs; green-tinted preparations.

Vert-cuit [+ kwee] Describes foods barely cooked; almost raw.

Verte, sauce [vert] A cold sauce combining mayonnaise with a purée of green herbs; parsley, tarragon, chervil, watercress, and spinach.

Vert-pré [vehr-preh] (1) Term for broiled meats garnished with shoestring potatoes and watercress. (2) A garnish composed of asparagus tips, green peas, and green beans; for various entrées.

Vert-pré, sauce A green herb sauce garnished with green peas and asparagus tips.

Verts [vehr] The name in France for a variety of oyster.

Viande [vyAd] Meat.

Vichy, à la [vee-shee] Describes dishes served with Vichy carrots and château potatoes.

Vichy, carottes à la [kah-ruht ah lah +] Sliced carrots simmered in water seasoned with salt, sugar, and butter and reduced to a syrupy consistency; garnished with chopped parsley.

Vichyssoise [vee-shee-swahz] A creamy potato and leek soup served cold.

Victoire [veek-twahr] A variety of French yellow bean (*mange-tout*).

Victoria, garniture [vick-tor-yuh] The name for numerous dishes in honor of Queen Victoria. Fish dishes are typically garnished with lobster and truffles; other entrées may include truffles, artichokes, mushrooms, tomatoes, demi-glace sauce flavored with port wine.

Victoria, sauce (1) *Sauce normande* seasoned with diced lobster meat and chopped truffles. (2) *Sauce espagnole* flavored with port wine, red currant jelly, cloves, cinnamon, and orange.

Videler [veed-leh] To crimp the edges of a pie or tart shell.

Vide-pommes [veed-pom] The French name for an apple corer.

Viennoise, à la [vyen-nwahz] Describes breaded and panfried meat, fish, or poultry garnished with capers, chopped hard-cooked eggs, pitted olives, and lemon slices; served with browned butter and demi-glace sauce.

Viennoiserie [vyen-nwah-zuh-ree] Refers to a catagory of bakery products made with yeast or leavened doughs (croissants, buns, danish, and so on). Ordinary breads and pastries are categorized separately.

Vierge [vyerzh] Whipped butter combined with salt, pepper, and lemon juice; served with asparagus and other vegetables.

Vieux puant [vyuh pwA] See *Maroilles/Marolles*.

Vigneronne, à la [vee-nyuh-rohn] Denotes the use of grapes or grape products (wine, vinegar, brandy) in a dish.

Villageoise, à la [vee-la-zhwahz] Served with *sauce villageoise*.

Villageoise, sauce *Sauce velouté* or béchamel sauce combined with onion purée and flavored with mushroom essence; finished with cream and egg yolks.

Villedieu [vee-yeh-dyuh] A type of

Neufchâtel cheese from Normandy.

Villeroi, à la [vee-luh-rwah] Describes meat, fish, or poultry that is dipped in *sauce Villeroi* then in bread crumbs; deep-fried.

Villeroi, sauce *Sauce allemande* flavored with mushroom and truffle essences. The sauce is cooled and made thick enough to dip foods prepared *à la villeroi*. Onion purée or tomato paste are sometimes added for a variation.

Vin [vI] Wine.

Vinaigre [vee-ne-gruh] Vinegar.

Vinaigrette [vee-ne-gret] A cold dressing composed of vinegar, oil, and seasonings; oil and vinegar salad dressing.

Vin blanc, sauce au [vI blA] (1) Fish fumet reduced with fish *velouté* and enriched with butter. (2) Hollandaise sauce made with a reduction of fish fumet. (3) Fish fumet heavily reduced and enriched with butter.

Vincent, sauce [vI-sA] A combination of equal parts of tartare sauce and *sauce verte*.

Vin de liqueur [+ duh lee-kür] A fortified wine; i.e., port, Madeira, marsala, and so forth.

Vin doux naturel [+ doo nah-tü-rel] A wine that has its alcoholic content increased by the addition of brandy.

Vin gris [+ gree] A pale rosé wine.

Vin rouge, sauce au [vI roosh] (1) A reduction of red wine and fish fumet seasoned with cayenne pepper and anchovy essence; enriched with butter. (2) Demi-glace sauce combined with a red wine reduction and enriched with butter.

Vins délimités de qualité supérieure [vI deh-lee-mee-teh duh kal-ee-teh sü-peh-ryühr] See *V.D.Q.S.*

Vins de pays [+ duh peh-yee] Re-

fers to good-quality regional wines.

Vins de table [+ duh tah-bluh] Refers to ordinary simple wines.

Violet [vyoh-leh] A variety of yellow bean (*mange-tout*) from the Loire region of France.

Vire [veer] A town in Normandy producing an excellent andouille sausage.

Virgouleuse [veer-goo-luhz] A winter pear grown in Virgoulée (Auvergne).

Viroflay [vee-ro-fleh] (1) A town in France where a high quality of spinach is cultivated. (2) The name given to dishes that are garnished with *épinards à la viroflay* and château potatoes.

—, *épinards à la* [eh-pee-nahrd ah-lah +] Spinach *subrics* wrapped in spinach leaves and coated with *sauce Mornay* and Parmesan cheese; browned in the oven.

Visitandine [vee-see-tA-deen] A rich almond-flavored cake made with a large amount of egg whites; iced with a kirsch-laced fondant.

Vitelots [vee-tuh-loh] A dessert from Lorraine featuring pasta rings cooked in sweetened milk. The same pasta rings may also be cooked in water and served with a savory sauce as an entrée.

Vivandière, à la [vee-vA-dyehr] Describes fish fillets stuffed with duxelles and topped with an herbed tomato sauce and Parmesan cheese; cooked *au gratin*.

Viveurs [vee-vuhr] A nearly obsolete term referring to dishes seasoned with cayenne pepper or hot paprika.

Vladimir, à la [vlah-dee-meer] With sautéed cucumbers and zucchini, grated horseradish, and sour cream.

VOCABULARY

Vogels zonder kop [foh-guhlz zohn-duhr kohpf] A dish from Flanders featuring sliced beef stuffed with sausage and simmered in seasoned stock; typically served with mashed potatoes.

Volaille [vo-lah-yuh] Poultry.

Vol-au-vent [vol-oh-vE] A round or square pastry case made from puff pastry; used to contain numerous preparations.

— **à la financière** [+ ah-lah fee-nA-syer] Pastry cases filled with a *salpicon* of cockscomb, truffles, mushrooms, and chicken quenelles.

— **à la marinière** [+ ah-lah mah-ree-nyer] Pastry cases filled with mussels (and often other shellfish) in *sauce Bercy*.

— **à la reine** [+ ah-lah ren] A vol-au-vent filled with chicken and mushrooms in cream sauce.

Vouvray [voo-vreh] White AOC wines of outstanding quality from Vouvray in the Loire Valley.

Walewska, à la [vahl-ef-skah] The name for poached fish garnished with lobster meat, sliced truffles, and *sauce Mornay*; enriched with lobster butter.

Washington [wah-sheeng-tohn] Describes dishes accompanied by corn bound with suprême sauce.

William bon-chrétien [wil-yuhm bO-kreh-tyen] A variety of pear used mostly in canning.

Williamine [vee-yah-meen] Pear brandy.

William, poire [pwahr wil-yuhm] A sweet variety of pear from France; also the name of a fine pear liqueur.

Windsor [win-zuhr] A garnish for fish comprised of soft roe, oysters, and *sauce aux huîtres*. Windsor is also the name of a garnish for beef made of veal quenelles, sliced ox tongue, and mushrooms.

Xérès [gzeh-ez] The French word for sherry.

Xérès, sauce aux Demi-glace sauce flavored with sherry.

Yaourt [yah-oor] Yogurt.

Yorkaise, à la [yor-kez] With York ham.

Yorkshire, sauce [york-shuhr] *Sauce au Porto* flavored with red currants and orange zest.

Yvette [ee-vet] (*Garnish for fish*) Baked tomatoes stuffed with sole mousseline and coated with *sauce aux herbes*.

Zarzuela [zahr-zweh-lah] A type of thick seafood stew from Catalonia, Spain, seasoned with ham, tomatoes, onions, and peppers.

Zeste [zest] Zest; the aromatic rind of citrus fruits.

Zewelewai [zü-vuhl-va-yee] An onion custard tart from Alsace.

Ziminu [zee-mee-nü] The Corsican version of bouillabaisse prepared with red peppers and pimentoes and served over stale bread.

Zingara [zI-gah-rah] A garnish for meat and poultry comprised of a *salpicon* of ham, tongue, mushrooms, and truffles bound with demi-glace sauce and seasoned with tomato purée and tarragon. This term also denotes the presence of tomato and paprika in a dish.

Zungerwurst [zuhn-guhr-vuhrst] A tongue sausage from Alsace.